CRAFTING PEACE IN KASHMIR

On the author's earlier work, *Society, State and Security*

'One of the "must read" volumes for anyone interested in India and South Asia .... This is now easily the best single volume available on India's complex security environment and the response of the Indian State to those threats.'

Stephen P. Cohen, Senior Fellow,
Foreign Policy Studies, The Brookings Institution, USA

'At long last, the strategic and security community intellectuals have a book, indeed a ready reckoner, on the concepts and practices of security in its most comprehensive form ever done in this country.'

The Hindustan Times

'A courageous and thought-provoking book which looks at the concept of security in a wholly new way .... Koithara's brilliance emerges from his succinct analysis of Indo-Pak relations .... Should find a place on every strategic planner's table.'

The Pioneer

'A courageous, powerful and in-depth analysis of a very complex subject. It is incisive and informative .... A must for every library and all those interested in South Asian affairs in general and India in particular.'

Frontline

'A searching critique of the weak areas of the country's security environment and how they can be improved. Politicians, bureaucrats and others involved in the process of policy-making are bound to benefit greatly.'

The Statesman

'This book is of abiding interest to politicians, academicians, policy makers, defence personnel and all those engaged in the management of the country's internal and external security .... It must come as an eye-opener for the ruling elite.'

The Tribune

'I strongly recommend this book to students of Indian defence issues and to many in the government, both civil and military, as well as to politicians.'

George K. Tanham, RAND Corporation, USA

CRAFTING PEACE IN KASHMIR
Through a Realist Lens

VERGHESE KOITHARA

SAGE Publications
New Delhi ◆ Thousand Oaks ◆ London

Copyright © Verghese Koithara, 2004

First published in 2004 by

Sage Publications India Pvt Ltd
B-42, Panchsheel Enclave
New Delhi 110 017

Sage Publications Inc
2455 Teller Road
Thousand Oaks, California 91320

Sage Publications Ltd
1 Oliver's Yard, 55 City Road
London EC1Y 1SP

Published by Tejeshwar Singh for Sage Publications India Pvt Ltd, typeset in 10 pt Calisto MT by Star Compugraphics Private Limited, New Delhi and printed at Chaman Enterprises, New Delhi.

Library of Congress Cataloging-in-Publication Data

Koithara Verghese, 1940–
    Crafting peace in Kashmir: through a realist lens/Verghese Koithara.
        p. cm.
    Includes bibliographical references and index.
    1. Jammu and Kashmir (India)—Politics and government. 2. India—Foreign relations—Pakistan. 3. Pakistan—Foreign relations—India. 4. Peace-building—South Asia. 5. Peaceful change (International relations) I. Title.

DS485.K27K63   954'.6053—dc22   2004   2004012965

ISBN: 0–7619–3294–1 (US–Hb)   81–7829–421–4 (India–Hb)
         0–7619–3262–3 (US–Pb)   81–7829–400–1 (India–Pb)

Sage Production Team: Sunaina Dalaya, Rajib Chatterjee and
                         Santosh Rawat

To the precious memory
of our beloved son,
Nikhil

CONTENTS

LIST OF ABBREVIATIONS

AEC	Atomic Energy Commission
AJK	Azad Jammu and Kashmir
AP	Alliance Party
APC	All Party Conference
APHC	All Party Hurriyat Conference
BJP	Bharatiya Janata Party
BMD	Ballistic Missile Defence
CBM	Confidence Building Measure
C&C	Command and Control
CEP	Circular Error Probable
CI	Counter Insurgency
CNC	Ceylon National Congress
CTBT	Comprehensive Test Ban Treaty
CWC	Ceylon Workers' Congress
DOP	Declaration of Principles
DRDO	Defence Research and Development Organisation
DUP	Democratic Unionist Party
EC	European Community
EEZ	Exclusive Economic Zone
EPRLF	Eelam People's Revolutionary Liberation Front

EROS	Eelam Revolutionary Organisation of Students
EU	European Union
FDI	Foreign Direct Investment
FMCT	Fissile Material Cut-off Treaty
FP	Federal Party
GDP	Gross Domestic Product
GFA	Good Friday Agreement
GHQ	General Headquarters
HM	Hizbul Mujahideen
IDF	Israeli Defence Force
IPKF	Indian Peace-Keeping Force
IR	International Relations
IRA	Irish Republican Army
ISGA	Interim Self-Governing Authority
ISI	Inter Services Intelligence
JI	Jamaat-e-Islami
JIJK	Jamaat-e-Islami Jammu and Kashmir
J&K	Jammu & Kashmir
JKLF	Jammu and Kashmir Liberation Front
JVP	Janatha Vimukthi Peramuna
KLM	Kashmir Liberation Movement
KRL	Khan Research Laboratories
LFO	Legal Framework Order
LoC	Line of Control
LTTE	Liberation Tigers of Tamil Eelam
MKA	Ministry of Kashmir Affairs
MMA	Muttahida Majlis-e-Amal
MUF	Muslim United Front
NC	(Jammu and Kashmir) National Conference
NCA	National Command Authority
NDC	National Development Complex
NICRA	Northern Ireland Civil Rights Association
NPT	Non Proliferation Treaty
NWFP	North West Frontier Province
NWS	Nuclear Weapons State
PA	Palestinian Authority or People's Alliance
PAEC	Pakistan Atomic Energy Commission
PAL	Permissive Action Link
PDP	People's Democratic Party
PLO	Palestine Liberation Organisation

PLOTE	People's Liberation Organisation of Tamil Eelam
PM	Prime Minister
PML (N)	Pakistan Muslim League (Nawaz)
PML (Q)	Pakistan Muslim League (Qaed-e-Azam)
POK	Pakistan Occupied Kashmir
POW	Prisoner of War
PRP	Personnel Reliability Programmes
PSNI	Police Service of Northern Ireland
PTA	Prevention of Terrorism Act
RUC	Royal Ulster Constabulary
SAARC	South Asian Association for Regional Cooperation
SDLP	Social Democratic and Labour Party
SLFP	Sri Lanka Freedom Party
SMS	Sinhala Mahajana Sabha
SOSNI	Secretary of State for Northern Ireland
TELO	Tamil Eelam Liberation Organisation
TNT	Tamil New Tigers
TUF	Tamil United Front
TULF	Tamil United Liberation Front
UNCIP	United Nations Commission for India and Pakistan
UNGA	United Nations General Assembly
UNF	United National Front
UNP	United National Party
UNRIP	United Nations Representative in India and Pakistan
UNSC	United Nations Security Council
UUP	Ulster Unionist Party
UVF	Ulster Volunteer Force
WTO	World Trade Organisation

PLOTE	People's Liberation Organisation of Tamil Eelam
PM	Prime Minister
PML(N)	Pakistan Muslim League (Nawaz)
PML(Q)	Pakistan Muslim League (Quaid-e-Azam)
POK	Pakistan Occupied Kashmir
POW	Prisoner of War
PRP	Prisoner Rehability Programme
PSNI	Police Service of Northern Ireland
PTA	Prevention of Terrorism Act
RUC	Royal Ulster Constabulary
SAARC	South Asian Association for Regional Cooperation
SDP	Social Democratic and Labour Party
SLFP	Sri Lanka Freedom Party
SMS	Sinhala Mahajana Sabha
SOSNI	Secretary of State for Northern Ireland
TELO	Tamil Eelam Liberation Organisation
TNT	Tamil New Tigers
TUF	Tamil United Front
TULF	Tamil United Liberation Front
UNCIP	United Nations Commission for India and Pakistan
UNGA	United Nations General Assembly
UNLF	United Nations Front
UNP	United National Party
UNRIP	United Nations Representative in India and Pakistan
UNSC	United Nations Security Council
UPF	Ulster Unionist Party
UVF	Ulster Volunteer Force
WTO	World Trade Organisation

PREFACE

T his book had its tentative beginnings in 1998 when the Good Friday Agreement was signed in Northern Ireland. A close study of that conflict, which included two visits to the area, convinced me that what was being achieved in Northern Ireland was quite remarkable and that, despite their very different contexts, there were useful insights to be gained with regard to the India–Pakistan conflict over Kashmir. Many Indians and Pakistanis with whom I discussed this with were, however, dubious and felt that the Northern Ireland problem was much easier to resolve than the Kashmir issue. Since this did not seem to be the case to me, I decided to explore the hypothesis that the parties to any conflict tend to believe that the peacemaking difficulties faced in their own conflict are far more severe than in other cases. This then led me to study the Sri Lankan and Israeli–Palestinian conflicts as well.

My discussions with people on the opposite sides of the four conflicts—India–Pakistan, Northern Ireland, Sri Lanka and Israel–Palestinian—showed me that this hypothesis was largely true. I also discovered that people tended to be notably more objective about the nature of other conflicts than of their own. They had a more even-handed approach towards the rights and wrongs in other conflicts and often felt that less adversarial and more rational approaches on the part of both parties could help in resolving contentious issues. But about their own conflict the general view was that the problem lay almost entirely with the opponent. This suggested to me that a perspective created out of the study of other conflicts would be useful in exploring the peace possibilities present in India–Pakistan relations today. While only the India–Pakistan conflict has been examined in depth in this book, overviews of the conflicts in Northern Ireland, Sri Lanka and Israel–Palestine have been presented to provide an analytical backdrop.

This book was written during 2002–03, though much of which period, tensions between the two countries were very high. The thaw towards the end of 2003, which has led not only to the resumption of India–Pakistan dialogue but also to unprecedented Delhi–Hurriyat talks, could easily turn out to be another false dawn. But it is also possible that progress might result because of the intense politico–military learning experience the two countries have gone through since 1998. If it does, it might provide support for the central thesis of this book— that the India–Pakistan conflict over Kashmir is, in terms of its structure, far easier to deal with than thought by most people.

I owe a considerable debt to many retired and serving officers as well as scholars from several countries who gave me the benefit of their views in developing the logic and arguments presented in this book. However, since many of them, mostly serving officials, wish to remain unnamed I have decided not to mention names here. My gratitude to each of them is deep.

I want to thank my wife, Indira, for tackling the masses of research and conversation notes accumulated over five years and organising them in an accessible manner. I am also grateful to Ms Omita Goyal and others at Sage Publications for handling the publication process so well.

10 February 2004
The Nilgiris

INTRODUCTION

There is an apocryphal papal comment that 'the Arab–Israeli conflict has two possible solutions—the realistic and the miraculous; the realistic would involve divine intervention and the miraculous would see a voluntary settlement among parties.' Much of South Asian as well as interested opinion outside—popular, governmental and scholarly—would consider this comment equally apt to the Kashmir-focused conflict between India and Pakistan. The dominant prevailing view is that the Kashmir conflict is essentially non-resolvable for reasons of history, emotions and the stakes involved. This book examines a contrary hypothesis—that such a view, though widely held, is unjustified. For, while the history is bitter and emotions high, the stakes—the most important determinant of the tractability of a conflict—are neither as significant nor as opposed as they are made out to be.

Both the India–Pakistan conflict and India's problems with the Kashmiri discontented have spawned a good deal of scholarly literature. Most such writings are anchored in history—whether it is of post-1947 political, military and diplomatic events, or of the different streams of nationalism that gathered strength from the late nineteenth century, or of Hindu–Muslim interaction that goes back twelve centuries. This historical, as opposed to forward-looking, orientation of conflict scholarship has resulted in few writers wanting to suggest paths out of the quagmire in which the parties are stuck. In the rare cases where suggestions have been made, the authors, possibly because of a conviction that the chasm separating positions is unbridgeable, have tended to side with the arguments of one or the other side.[1] Those supporting India advocate freezing the status quo. Those favouring Pakistan or the disaffected Kashmiris favour solutions that take into account the 'disputed' nature of Kashmir's accession to India. In operational terms this results in the former commending that India and Pakistan should put Kashmir aside and improve relations in other areas, and the latter suggesting that a Kashmir-centred political dialogue should have priority.

The current difficulty in resolving the conflict is the presence within it of two separate tussles with a large dysfunctional interface. One is the power–political, territorial and ideological competition between India and Pakistan. The other is the one of the relationship between Delhi and Jammu & Kashmir (J&K) centred on the extent of autonomy that the state should enjoy. India, by far the strongest party, has adopted a hard line in both disputes. This has led to the other two, despite their very different objectives,[2] to seek not only to form a common front but also to erode the separation between the two tussles. This in turn has made it even more difficult for India to show flexibility with regard to either.

The political and security clash of interests that gave rise to the conflict in 1947 has become heavily encrusted with ideological, legal and moral arguments. Through heavy repetition these largely self-serving justifications have gained a strong grip on the popular mind in both countries. The conflict, as a consequence, has become increasingly focused on unilaterally constructed rights and wrongs, and not on the rational self-interest of parties. This slippage of the conflict in

---

[1] To get an idea of the many suggestions that have been put forth to resolve the conflict—from the standpoints of India, Pakistan and the Kashmiri disaffected—see Raju G.C.Thomas, ed., *Perspectives on Kashmir: The Roots of Conflict in South Asia*, Boulder: Westview, 1992; Robert G. Wirsing, *India, Pakistan and the Kashmir Dispute: On Regional Conflict and its Resolution*, London: Macmillan, 1994; and Mushtaqur Rahman, *Divided Kashmir: Old Problems, New Opportunities for India, Pakistan and the Kashmiri People*, Boulder: Lynne Rienner, 1996.

[2] The Kashmiri discontented hold a variety of views, but very few of them want to join Pakistan.

the popular mind from the realm of reason to the realm of emotion has made it a good deal more difficult to deal with. Framing the conflict in terms of the true clash of interests of the three parties and painting out the clutter of legalistic and moralistic arguments is a necessary first step in the search for common ground for productive dialogue. For this, it is essential to look at the structure of the conflict in terms of political realism.

In the South Asian context political realism must take into account domestic politics as much as international relations (IR). A major assumption of IR realist theory, derived largely from a study of modern Western states, is that states are unitary actors that interact only along their boundaries.[3] This idea of billiard-ball type contact between states, and its derivative that inter-state interaction can be insulated from intra-state happenings, cannot apply to India and Pakistan which had formed a single country a mere half century ago. The conflict between them billows deep into the domestic sphere in both countries and therefore the dialectic between domestic politics and foreign policy is crucially important. It alone can explain why the pathological domestic politics in the case of Pakistan and the discontent in J&K in the case of India have made it so very difficult for the two governments to engage one another purposefully. And also why the mobilisation of societies on religious basis, initially confined to Pakistan but increasingly seen in India as well, has made matters still more difficult. Because of domestic politics, no Indian or Pakistani government can act entirely rationally (pursuing only national interest) or unitarily (ignoring domestic divisions) as IR realist theory might suggest.

Undoubtedly, the core idea of IR realist theory—that states, having to operate in an anarchical environment, are compelled to define their interests as power and pursue them—is applicable to India and Pakistan.[4] Power is certainly the most significant factor in political realism. But power, for it to be looked at on a realistic basis, must be related to circumstances. Power must be appropriate to the context. Contests between asymmetrically resourced power structures—such

---

[3] For exceptions to this analytical trend in the West, see Jack Snyder, *Myths of Empire: Domestic and International Ambition*, Ithaca: Cornell University Press, 1991 and Bruce Bruno de Mesquita and David Lalman, *War and Reason: Domestic and International Imperatives*, New Haven: Yale University Press, 1992.

[4] For the theoretical basis of the dilemmas faced by India and Pakistan in this regard, see Hedley Bull, *The Anarchical Society: A Study on the Order of World Politics*, London: Macmillan, 1977.

as India and Pakistan—could go on for a long time because rival sides often have different views on what appropriate power is in their situation. An objective appreciation of the relativity of relevant power is also hampered by the timeframes used to evaluate it. Governments mostly act on the basis of short-term calculations. This leads to a tactical as opposed to a strategic evaluation of power relativity in making policy.

At the most fundamental level, political realism is about what is achievable. It looks at clashes of material interest and examines how they can be advantageously resolved. In this it is a-legal, a-moral and a-ideological except to the extent that legal, moral and ideological concerns have a practical impact. Costs are always a prime consideration, as are the benefits that can accrue from bearing them. A realist understanding of conflict goes beyond coercion and resistance, and a zero-sum perspective of benefits from their resolution. The possibility of resolving a conflict by creating a positive-sum calculus is wholly compatible with political realism. Realism calls for hard-headed thinking and minimising the role of emotion. It is a commonly encountered paradox that self-damaging, belligerent attitudes that are rooted in emotion are purveyed as realism.

Any protracted conflict has three key dimensions—structure, attitude and behaviour.[5] Structure refers to the situation in which the parties find themselves—the circumstances that had created and are now sustaining the conflict. It is largely constituted by the clash of interest of parties, but it also includes factors such as domestic politics and third-party involvement. Attitude stands for the psychological stances that the state and society on each side have developed towards the conflict and the opponent. Behaviour connotes the actions of parties and is largely under the control of governments. Each act of negative behaviour by state parties makes societal attitudes more pessimistic. According to many peace research findings, confirming similar findings in behavioural sciences, it is the dimension of behaviour that needs to be addressed first in seeking to end a conflict. Changes in attitude and structure can only follow. This finding is at variance with the common view that it is the constraints created by the structure of a conflict that are the chief barrier to peace.

---

[5] This widely accepted insight into inter-state and intra-state conflict behaviour was originally transferred from the field of psychology. See J. Galtung, 'Conflict as a Way of Life', in H. Freeman, ed., *Progress in Mental Health*, London: Churchill, 1969.

The reason why behaviour is so important is that it can even alter the structure of a conflict. When behavioural patterns are bad they bring into play new causes of anger and new interests resulting from them. They make positions appear less bridgeable than earlier. It is often a modification of behaviour, which calls for acting contrary to predisposition, that can best initiate positive interaction. A change in behaviour in favour of peace can lead to the structure of conflict being seen in a better light. And the two together can pave the way for antagonistic attitudes to thaw. A change in attitude is crucial for it alters the mindset that shapes interpretation of situations and responses. When all three dimensions of a conflict—behaviour, attitude and structure—begin to move, they reinforce one another as gear wheels do.

India and Pakistan can benefit from looking at the structure as well as the attitudinal and behavioural patterns of their conflict against a backdrop of the same dimensions of other conflicts. The study of conflicts where one is not emotionally involved is useful to recognise how important a role behaviour and attitude play in worsening the structure of a conflict. It will show how outsiders can see compromise and creative possibilities in bringing a conflict to an end which the participants themselves are unable to see. It can also help understand how both parties, not just one, contribute to conflict-prolongation and how cooperative efforts are essential to pull out of a downward spiral.

Every conflict is one of its kind in its detail and it is important not to fall into the trap of inappropriate analogy. Yet, examining the future of one's conflict by looking only into its past is problematic. Arguments and perspectives developed in the past to justify positions get internalised and act as a barrier to grasping the actual situation the parties are currently in and the strategic choices that are available today. Moreover, conflicts that show common characteristics—such as recurring violence and deadlocked negotiating positions—are often not so different that there are no useful pointers to be sought. For example, it is a frequently seen reality that if a serious conflict is neglected it does not fade away. Instead, it often mutates into a struggle that is more difficult to manage. Such mutations took place in Northern Ireland in 1968, in Sri Lanka in 1983, in Palestine in 1987, and in Kashmir in 1989.

The conflicts of Northern Ireland, Sri Lanka and Israel–Palestine have been analysed primarily to understand why their peace efforts have fared as they have. Northern Ireland has a peace process which, despite grave obstacles, has made remarkable headway in the last decade. In Sri Lanka, the peace effort beginning in December 2001, though still very precarious, has nevertheless made more progress than most had hoped for, especially considering the disastrous experiences of 1985–87, 1990–91 and 1994–95. In the case of Israel and the Palestinians, the peace path charted in Oslo in 1993 has now petered out, although the 1975–79 peace effort between Israel and Egypt had succeeded. The basic structure of each conflict, its historical burden, general patterns of attitude and behaviour, and strategic decisions made by leaders have all played a part in the way these peace efforts have progressed or foundered. Studying them can provide useful insights into the peace possibilities present in the India–Pakistan context and the pragmatic approaches available to exploit them.

While this book does lead to the conclusion that peace between India and Pakistan is possible on the basis of political realism, it recognises that there are many obstacles in the path. Pakistan is aware that it is incurring huge economic, social and diplomatic costs because of its struggle with seven-times bigger India. But it believes that withdrawing from the contest would lead to a precipitate weakening of central authority and a possible break-up of the country. It considers that its nuclear capability has neutralised India's conventional superiority and therefore it can continue to confront without running undue risk. India feels that time and global trends are in its favour and that sooner rather than later not only will Pakistan be compelled to give in on Kashmir but that it would also be forced to accept India's natural predominance in South Asia. As for the discontented in Kashmir, India thinks it can deal with them without major political concessions once it is able to stop Pakistan interfering.

Fifteen years of Pakistan-supported militancy in Kashmir (partially overlapping nine years in Punjab) has created highly negative emotions and perceptions within the Indian elite. Its mindset in relation to Pakistan today is not very different from what Pakistan's was in relation to India after 1971. Levels of anger are very high which can be seen in the support for extreme actions such as reneging on the Indus Water Treaty and attacking Pakistan. This in turn has made the paranoia in Pakistan about the Indian threat even more acute. In both countries aroused, negative emotions have created zero-sum perspectives that have made positions appear less reconcilable and terms less negotiable than they actually are. The perception that the goals of the two sides are irreconcilable has made promotion of peace psychologically hard and politically unsafe.

Yet, there are chances of and hope for peace. A realist lens view would show that conflict settlement becomes truly difficult only when, as is largely the case with Israel and the Palestinians, it is hard for any combination of terms to ensure the minimum needs of security, economic well being and honour to both parties. This is not the case in Kashmir, as it is also not the case in Northern Ireland and Sri Lanka. There are terms possible that can safeguard the essential interests of both India and Pakistan in today's conditions. The perception that this is not so rises partly from the current mood of heightened anger and partly from being prisoners to conceptions that have become outdated. An example of the latter is the oft repeated idea that the bases of Indian and Pakistani nationalism pose fundamental threats to each other. In the initial years of independence this was no doubt true—India was menaced by Pakistan's interest in subcontinental Muslims outside its borders and Pakistan was threatened by the possibility of partition being undone. But today this is not remotely the case. Pakistan, home now to only a third of colonial India's Muslims, has long ceased to exert influence over the remaining two-thirds in India and Bangladesh. Nor does India have any wish to seek *akhand bharat* (undivided India) that would triple the number of Muslims in the country.

The second reason for hope is that the India–Pakistan conflict is essentially about one material issue—Kashmir. Others are minor. Siachen is part of Kashmir, and the Sir Creek and Wullar/Tulbul issues are not significant. This is unlike the case with some other protracted conflicts. An example is the conflict between Greece and Turkey. Though the two countries have been able to manage their conflict without violence in modern times, it is a fact that it contains an ensemble of major issues that makes it difficult for it to be wholly resolved. Cyprus is not the only issue. There are other major ones like the Aegean continental shelf, military presence in Greek islands close to Turkey, territorial waters and air space. Even if Cyprus were solved, others would remain. In the case of India and Pakistan, if Kashmir were put behind there would no longer be a contest of substance, although politicised histories would no doubt continue to cause animus within segments in both societies.

Even in the case of Kashmir the stakes are not so great or the settlement path so difficult as they are generally made out to be. Kashmir is no great economic prize to either country. The three major rivers that flow through the state into Pakistan could have created a serious water resource tussle, but that has been settled by the Indus Water Treaty of 1960. In security terms, if the entire state had gone to one party it could have posed a geo-military threat to the other. But the division of the state as it took place in 1947–48 has eliminated this. The portion of the state in Pakistan's possession has given valuable geographic cover to the otherwise vulnerable northern half of Pakistani Punjab and the North West Frontier Province (NWFP). The fact that 64 per cent of the population of the part of the state with India is Muslim matters little. Their number is only about 5 per cent of the number of Muslims in Pakistan and therefore does not detract from the country's Muslim identity. The reality is that India does not need the part of J&K that is with Pakistan and Pakistan the part that is with India for any reason that has to do with security, economic interest and internal political coherence. The contest is now almost entirely on behalf of politicised emotions.

A resolution path in Kashmir would have been difficult if the territorially dissatisfied party were the more powerful one. But this is not the case. India, which has always been the stronger party and whose margin of superiority is constantly growing, is satisfied with the existing division. When power advantage and satisfaction with the status quo rest with the same party, a settlement largely adhering to the existing position becomes possible. If attitudes and strategies can be made more positive such a possibility can be converted into reality. Resolution would also have been difficult if there were a fundamental clash of interest between the Kashmiris in India and Indians at large, as it would have happened if the former had wanted to join Pakistan or the latter were unwilling to address Kashmiri needs. This too is not the case. The vast majority of Kashmiri Indians, while wanting to have much greater control over their affairs, do not wish to join Pakistan. And the vast majority of non-Kashmiri Indians are prepared to increase the freedom of governance enjoyed by the Kashmiris provided it does not jeopardise the country's security.

The challenge facing India today is to use its considerable superiority over Pakistan (which is more consequential in the political and economic fields than in the military) to end a conflict that is slowing the country's rise through global ranks. That facing Pakistan is to use its asymmetric leverage to end the conflict in a manner that will enable its imperilled state, society and economy to stabilise and prosper. These challenges are not being taken up largely because of two basic fears. Pakistan fears that negotiations with India can only lead down a blind alley resulting in the erosion of its leverage. India fears that a peace dialogue could get out of control if Pakistan and the Kashmiri discontented join hands. A workable peace strategy must address both these concerns.

It is crucially important to develop a forward-looking approach. There has to be a better understanding that the circumstances enveloping the conflict have changed a great deal and that many perceptions derived from historical grievances have little contemporary relevance. Several of the mainstream assumptions, expressed both in diplomacy and the media, need to be re-examined. One needs to see whether long-held positions are logically linked to the changed realities and whether professed interests and objectives cannot be modified to reduce the gap between the parties. The determinedly held view of many experts that the minima of India and Pakistan are not reconcilable needs rigorous scrutiny. So does the application of the concepts of national interest and rational choice. While what constitutes national interest in a broad sense is easy to pronounce, it is not easy to relate it to specific problems like Kashmir. The idea of rational choice also presents difficulty. While rational choice is related to cost-benefit calculations, there can be very different views on the criteria to be used for judging costs and benefits.

It is not possible to effectively explore the possibilities of peace in the India–Pakistan context unless the issue gets debated more widely and more thoughtfully, and a broad consensus develops that peace-making is both desirable and feasible. Without such a consensus, the periodic thaws that take place are unlikely to lead to durable peace. The self-confident and optimistic sections of the public in both countries, in whose thinking economic progress and socio-political stability loom large, should get more closely involved. And they must look at issues through a wide-angle lens that sees more than security concerns. Only when the articulate public modifies its views will compromises become possible for governments without heavy domestic political price. Strategic solutions that safeguard the essential interests of both sides are available, as this book will show. But for such solutions to gain political traction they must get connected to popular thinking.

The resumption of India–Pakistan dialogue and the initiation of Delhi–APHC (All Party Hurriyat Conference) talks in early 2004 provide a good opportunity for the two countries and for the Kashmiri discontented to construct a two-lane, mutually supportive road to peace. But the opportunity can be easily blown if the parties believe, as they have done in the past, that the other side has come to the talks because of exhaustion and that one's own side need make only cosmetic concessions. The ability to break the long deadlock lies largely with India, which is the advantaged party in all respects—possession, current superiority and greater potential. It has the resources to craft a peace process leading to an end game that safeguards its own and Pakistan's essential interests. But to exploit those resources India must develop creative ideas capable of providing incentive to both Pakistan and the Kashmiri discontented. The Line of Control (LoC)-into-Border deal lies within India's reach but it calls for vision, strategy and flexibility to get to it.

This book has ten chapters. Chapter 1, 'The India–Pakistan Conflict' and Chapter 2, 'The Problem of Kashmir's Discontented' present brief, realist overviews of the way the two parts of the conflict have evolved in parallel. Chapter 3, 'Conflict Drivers' looks at the factors that fuel the conflict, Chapter 4, 'Nuclear Danger' examines the impact that the acquisition of nuclear weapons has had on it, and Chapter 5, 'Kashmir and the Outside World' considers the way outsiders have influenced its evolution and are likely to influence it in the future. Chapter 6, 'Insights from Northern Ireland', Chapter 7, 'Pointers from Sri Lanka' and Chapter 8, 'Reflections on the Israeli–Palestinian Conflict' look at these conflicts in order to gain a better understanding of the way peace processes can move forward or run aground. Chapter 9, 'Moving from Conflict to Peace' looks at some key issues involved in peace processes, thus breaking the ground for the arguments and suggestions made in the last chapter, 'Creating a Peace Path in Kashmir' which examines the peacemaking opportunities that are present today and the pragmatic ways they can be made use of.

THE INDIA–PAKISTAN CONFLICT

T he conflict between India and Pakistan centred on Kashmir has many narratives and what might be called the master narratives of the two countries differ a good deal.[1] Facts are rarely in dispute; the big differences are in interpretations and interrelationships of events, and of motives. At the level of nationalistic writings, whatever suits one side is stressed and what does not is omitted or downplayed. There is contestation not only of the causes and the course of development of the conflict, but also of the reasons why it is eluding settlement.[2] Scholarly writings pose problems of a different sort. By their very nature they go into great detail—whether of legal contestations, diplomatic jousting or military tussles. While this serves to understand

---

[1] Whether Kashmir provides only an arena as many Indians contend or is the mainspring as most Pakistanis consider, both sides agree that it is the focal point of the conflict.

[2] To get an idea of these differences even in scholarly works, see Sisir Gupta, *Kashmir: A Study in India–Pakistan Relations,* Bombay: Asia Publishing House, 1966 and Alastair Lamb, *Kashmir: A Disputed Legacy, 1846–1990,* Lahore: Oxford University Press, 1990. For a neutral analysis, see Lars Blinkenberg, *India–Pakistan: The History of Unsolved Conflicts,* Vol. II, Odense: Odense University Press, 1998.

minutiae (for disinterested scholarship or partisan argumentation), it does not often help to focus on the political logic of the conflict.

Like most conflicts the India–Pakistan one is driven to a great extent by contending, value-laden histories. These one-sided narratives have gained great power over thought, feeling and action. They influence perception and judgement and frame the vision of future possibilities. It is important therefore to look at the history of this conflict from a neutral, realist standpoint. This will help to understand the unreasonableness of the common perception that one's own side has been consistently good and rational and the opponent has been neither. If one can understand the opponent's perspective, which is inevitably very different from one's own, one can see what drives him to behave as he does and whether incentives are possible to make him change. It helps to recognise the possibilities present to structure compromises and innovate positive-sum solutions. This chapter makes an effort to highlight key events and linkages from a distanced viewpoint.

SEEDS OF CONFLICT

While aroused Hindu–Muslim animus is certainly a major factor in the India–Pakistan conflict today, it was not so in the beginning. No doubt seven centuries of foreign-origin Muslim rule in India's Hindu heartland, the steady deterioration of Muslim position during the two subsequent centuries of British rule, and British efforts to exploit Hindu–Muslim differences to sustain their rule were all important factors. But none of these had much salience at the mass level in the run up to partition. There is no truth in the view that ancient animosities suppressed till then were destined to burst open. There is wide scholarly agreement that partition came about not because Hindu and Muslim masses had difficulty living together but because the elites of the two communities could not agree on political power sharing. At that time the religious and cultural anxieties felt by Muslims at large were wholly secondary to the political fears of their leaders.

The political contest for power, which began in the early 1930s between the Congress party that led the national independence struggle and the revivified Muslim League under Jinnah's leadership that concentrated on Muslim interests, eventually led to the country being partitioned. Partition, when it came, disappointed both countries. Rending the geographic and cultural cohesion of the subcontinent was a deep affront to Indians and a cause of serious anger at its precipitator, the Muslim League and the state that it created, Pakistan. Pakistanis too were unhappy because the state they got was more modest—in terms of size, ideological success and geographic security—than what the Muslim League had led them to expect. It is noteworthy that excluding those who shifted within the provinces of Punjab and Bengal, only one in twelve Muslims from the rest of India chose to go to Pakistan.

At independence, what was earlier a party political contest between the Congress and Muslim League under British oversight, mutated into an international struggle. Aside from mutual disappointment with partition, two reasons helped to turn this struggle vicious. One was the bitterness created by the violence that followed partition, killing about a quarter-million people and uprooting over fourteen million from their homes. The other was the rushed and disorderly departure of the British that made the process open to tweaking by each party to its advantage. The date of British departure was announced just seventy-three days in advance—hardly the lead time needed to divide the assets and administrative infrastructure of a country of India's size. The precise boundary delineation between the new states was not made known till after the British relinquished power. As for the princely states, which made for a fifth of the country's population and a third of its land, Britain set them legally free on the one hand but on the other advised them to join either India or Pakistan. In such a fluid situation, where power on the ground was of greater consequence than legal niceties, both sides inevitably played catch as catch can.

JAMMU AND KASHMIR

At the time of partition, Jammu and Kashmir had appeared to be a considerable prize to both countries. For Pakistan, the state was a large contiguous zone of fellow Muslims. The population was not significant, a shade over 1 per cent of undivided India's. But the territory was considerable—one-and-a half times that of East Pakistan, now Bangladesh. The state would give Pakistan a border with China, and India one with Afghanistan. It also had considerable bilateral military significance. If India had Pakistan Occupied Kashmir (POK)[3] it could pose a considerable military threat to the northern part of Pakistani Punjab and NWFP. On the other hand, if it had the whole of J&K Pakistan could seriously threaten Indian Punjab. From the resource point of view, there was the matter of rivers. All rivers from India whose waters were later allocated to Pakistan (Indus, Jhelum and Chenab) flowed out of J&K.

At the time of partition J&K, including Aksai Chin, had an area of 222,236 square kilometres. Of this Kashmir occupied only 10 per cent,[4] Jammu 14.4 per cent and the frontier districts as much as 75.6 per cent. Of the 1941 population census of 4.02 million, 77 per cent were Muslim and 20 per cent Hindu. The ceasefire line of 1949 gave Pakistan 37.4 per cent of the territory and about 28 per cent of the population. Aksai Chin, with 16.9 per cent of the state's area and virtually no population, came under the control of China during the 1950s. In 1963 Pakistan ceded to China another 2.33 per cent of the land claimed by India. Today 45.62 per cent of the original state territory is with India, 35.15 per cent with Pakistan and 19.23 per cent with China. The LoC dividing J&K is 778 km long and there is an uncontested border of 198 km between the part of state with India and Pakistani Punjab. In the Siachen area there is an undefined line of about 150 km separating Indian and Pakistani positions.

Of the area with India, Kashmir constitutes 15.8 per cent, Jammu 25.9 per cent and Ladakh 58.3 per cent. The total population of the part of state with India in 2001 was 10.01 million. The population percentage shares are Kashmir 52.4, Jammu 45.4 and Ladakh 2.2. In terms of religion, the percentages for the state as a whole are Muslims 64.2, Hindus 32.2 and others 3.6.[5] The region-wise percentage shares of Muslim population are Kashmir 95, Jammu 30 and Ladakh 46. Of the area with Pakistan (78,114 square kilometres), 83 per cent is in

---

[3] The Indian designation for the part of J&K with Pakistan is Pakistan Occupied Kashmir (POK), which is the term used in this book. Pakistan has divided POK into two parts, calling them Azad Jammu and Kashmir (AJK) and Northern Areas. These terms have been used where the two areas have to be referred to separately.

[4] The Valley is still smaller—3.6 per cent of the state's area even when measured from the ridges.

[5] The break-up of religious figures are based on 1981 census data. The 2001 figures on this are not yet available. There was no census in J&K in 1991.

Northern Areas (the Gilgit Agency, Baltistan and some principalities), while 17 per cent is in AJK. Virtually all the people in POK are Muslims, of who about 15 per cent are non-Sunni.

The state of J&K began to take shape in 1846 when the British captured the Kashmir Valley and sold it to the Dogra Maharaja of Jammu. Prior to this, during 1830–40, the Maharaja had captured Ladakh and Baltistan. He captured Gilgit in 1860. In 1935 the British formally leased the Gilgit Agency (which had been in their de facto control from 1899) from the Maharaja for a period of sixty years. Poonch, which till then was a separate entity, became a part of J&K in 1936. It was only then that the state attained the boundaries it had at the time of partition. Given these circumstances of its evolution, it is not surprising that J&K is uncommonly heterogeneous in terms of ethnicity, religion, language and governing tradition. For example, in 1947 about 34 per cent of its people spoke Kashmiri, 30 per cent Punjabi, 15 per cent Dogri and the balance 21 per cent about two dozen other languages and dialects. The state is also hugely skewed in terms of population distribution. At partition, about 95 per cent of the people lived and worked in about 10 per cent of the state's area. The name J&K reflects this land/people disjunction—the combined areas of Kashmir and Jammu account for less than a quarter of the state's land but for more than 95 per cent of its population.

In the run up to partition the Congress and the Muslim League could influence developments in the state only peripherally. The political tussle of consequence was between the Maharaja with his core base among the Dogra Hindus in Jammu and Sheikh Abdullah with his base among the Muslims in the Valley. Dogra rule was deeply resented in the Valley from the time it began in 1846. With all the land considered the personal property of the Maharaja (as he had 'bought' it from the British), there was heavy taxation and exclusion of locals from power. A famine in 1878–79 killed more than half the Valley's population. In 1932 Sheikh Abdullah set up the All J&K Muslim Conference with the objectives of liberalising the Maharaja's rule and protecting the interests of the Muslims in the state. Seven years later Abdullah dissolved the Muslim Conference and set up the more inclusive Jammu and Kashmir National Conference (NC). When the Muslim League passed the Pakistan Resolution in Lahore the next year, 1940, some others resurrected the Muslim Conference. A contest for the allegiance of the state's Muslims now started between Abdullah's secular NC, allied with the Congress at the national level, and the Muslim Conference, allied with the Muslim League that was pushing Pakistan's cause. The NC was dominant in the Valley while the Muslim Conference was more influential in the other Muslim areas of the state.

India and Pakistan look at Kashmir through different interpretative lenses.[6] India's case for the state hinges on two broad arguments, one legal and the other political. The legal one is that the state of J&K, represented by the Maharaja, acceded to India legally and that the commitment that India had made to obtain the concurrence of the people to accession was met when the state constituent assembly, elected in 1951 on the basis of full adult franchise, approved accession. Further, the 1957 constitution of J&K, enacted by the state's own constituent assembly, has made it an integral part of India. The political argument is that while Pakistan may have a different view, India has never considered that the people of undivided India were made up of two different nations, Hindu and Muslim, and therefore Pakistan has no claim to any part of the country on the basis of it being a Muslim-majority area.

Pakistan's case is also predicated on two positions, one legal and the other political. The legal one is that the accession was invalid for several reasons: that it was a violation of the 'Standstill Agreement' the state had signed with Pakistan, that an 'Azad J&K' government had been declared before accession, that the instrument of accession was conditional, and that India's dealings with the state from the beginning of Mountbatten's viceroyalty had been characterised by fraud.[7] The political argument is that the Hindu Maharaja of J&K state, which was 77 per cent Muslim, with Muslim majorities in all areas—Jammu (61 per cent), Kashmir (95 per cent) and the rest of the state (88 per cent)—and also more contiguous to Pakistan, had no right to accede his state to India. There are the parallels of Hyderabad

---

[6] For the contrasting Indian and Pakistani perspectives on what happened with regard to J&K during 1947–49, see C. Dasgupta, *War and Diplomacy in Kashmir, 1947–48*, New Delhi: Sage, 2002 and Alastair Lamb, *Incomplete Partition: The Genesis of the Kashmir Dispute, 1947–48*, Karachi: Oxford University Press, 2001.

[7] The accusation of 'fraud' is based on two unsubstantiated claims. One is that undue pressure was brought to bear on Maharaja Hari Singh to accede to India. The other is that of the three *tehsils* of Gurdaspur district of Punjab that were given to India (Pathankot, Batala and Gurdaspur), two had substantial Muslim majorities, and that had they not been given, India would not have had a road link with J&K at that time.

and Junagadh states. Moreover, the opinion of the people of the state has not been determined in an internationally acceptable manner.

THE 1947–65 PERIOD

In February 1947, when it became clear that the Cabinet Mission Plan of May 1946 (the last effort to keep India united) was a non-starter, Britain announced that it would leave India by June 1948. Four months later, when matters began to spin out of control, the departure was advanced by ten months. On 3 June 1947 it was announced that power would be transferred by 15 August. The Indian Independence Act 1947 was passed on 17 July and a week later Mountbatten advised the rulers of all princely states to join either India or Pakistan. Almost all of them took that advice, but J&K and a few others decided to explore the possibility of independence. To gain time the Maharaja proposed on 14 August Standstill Agreements with both India and Pakistan. Pakistan accepted but India, appreciating that it held the upper hand, chose to temporise. On 15 August the British restored the Gilgit Agency to J&K and three days later the Radcliffe Award, which gave India a road link with J&K through Gurdaspur in Punjab, was announced.

Pakistan knew that the political cards were stacked against it. At the popular level, Abdullah's NC—the dominant political force in the state—was aligned with the Congress. At the governmental level, the Dogra Maharaja was bound to go with India if his first preference for independence was, as it was certain to be, thwarted. Pakistan's counter advantage lay in geography. There were two good all-weather roads (from Rawalpindi and Abbotabad) to Domel—the gateway to the Valley. In the south, towards Jammu, there was another good road as well as a rail line from Sialkot. India's only link with the state was the Pathankot–Samba–Jammu road with several fordings. Further on, from Jammu to the Valley, the road through the Banihal Pass was snowbound half the year.

Pakistan, therefore, decided on the military option. In August 1947 there was a Muslim revolt against the Maharaja in Poonch. The military muscle was provided by some 60,000 World War II demobil-ised Muslim soldiers from Jammu, Poonch and Mirpur. The same month, the Gilgit Agency—militarily controlled by British-led Gilgit Scouts—went over to Pakistan. During September there were several incursions into the state from Pakistan all along the border south of Domel. Pakistan had been preparing for an invasion from August. On 22 October it pushed 7,000 armed Pashtun tribesmen in 300 trucks through the Domel–Mahura–Baramula–Srinagar road. Two days later a provisional 'Azad Kashmir' government was announced in Pulandri.

This forced the Maharaja's hand and he signed the Instrument of Accession with India on 26 October. Mountbatten, who then wore the new hat of post-partition India's Governor General, accepted it the next day, making the accession legally complete. In the letter accompanying the accepted Instrument of Accession Mountbatten wrote that 'after the invader was cleared and law and order restored, the question of the State's accession should be settled by a reference to the people'.[8] On the same day, 27 October, Indian Army units landed in Srinagar and the first India–Pakistan war began. Circumstances forced it to be a limited war. Pakistan could not commit its regular troops in the initial months because of the pretence that it was not involved in the attack and also because the British had threatened to withdraw their officers if it did.[9]

While Pakistan did enjoy access advantage into the Valley, its population led by Abdullah was solidly against the Pashtun marauders it had sent. More important, the overall military balance was decisively in India's favour. If India had launched a counter attack against Pakistan outside J&K, Pakistan would have been in deep trouble. The Pakistan Army was less than half the size of India's and the ratio of holdings of equipment and stores much worse. It was also in greater post-partition organisational disarray. India had other potent levers too. It could, and did, withhold 550 million rupees in cash balance, in addition to a part of the sterling balance due to Pakistan on the reasonable ground that the money would be used to sustain military aggression against India. This logic applied even more to holding back the military equipment and stores that were to be transferred to

---

[8] Indians blame Mountbatten for this note, as well as for 'pushing' Nehru to take the case to the UN. Pakistanis blame Mountbatten for accepting accession. Nehru and Mountbatten had a good relationship and each had influence on the other.

[9] In late October Field Marshall Auchinleck, nominal supreme commander of both armies, had got Jinnah to reverse his order to send the Pakistan Army into J&K when the Maharaja had acceded to India.

Pakistan. India also could (and it did for a few days in May 1948 when Pakistan committed its regular troops to the fray) partially impede the flow of water into Pakistan.

After about six months of fighting, India's military superiority began to tell. This led Pakistan to commit three brigades of regular troops in April 1948. Pakistan was able to occupy the areas they call AJK partly because it had excellent logistical access from north Punjab and NWFP, and partly because the people there—mostly Punjabi-dialect speakers—were more under the influence of the Muslim Conference than Abdullah's NC. Similarly, Pakistan could occupy the Northern Areas (the Gilgit Agency and most of Baltistan) because the area had few roads and they could be accessed better from the Pakistani side. But what Pakistan wanted most—the Kashmir Valley—eluded it. India's superior military power and Sheikh Abdullah's grip on the population proved too much.[10]

Peace efforts paralleled the fighting. India–Pakistan meetings were held in Delhi and Lahore from 30 October to 8 December 1947 under the auspices of the Joint Defence Council of the two dominions, but no agreement could be reached. On 1 January 1948, India lodged a formal complaint with the UN under Article 35 of the UN Charter. The UN, then in just the third year of its life, was firmly under the control of the US and the UK. Of the other Security Council permanent members, Kuomintang China and pre-de Gaulle France were closely allied with them and the Soviet Union had yet to become a major international player. After an initial resolution seeking restraint by both sides, the United Nations Security Council (UNSC) passed a substantive resolution three days later, on 20 January 1948, setting up a three-member United Nations Commission for India and Pakistan (UNCIP). Both sides accepted these resolutions.

To India's chagrin the trend of opinion in the UN, beginning early February, began to veer towards Pakistan's side. The geo-political interests of the US and the UK in West Asia as well as the framing of the issue in Hindu–Muslim terms played their part in this. The UNSC passed its first resolution on the settlement of the Kashmir problem

---

[10] For good military accounts of the 1947–48 war from the Indian side, see Lt. Gen. (Rtd.) L.P. Sen, *Slender Was the Thread: Kashmir Confrontation, 1947–48,* New Delhi: Orient Longman, 1969 and Maj. Gen. S.K. Sinha, *Operation Rescue: Military Operations in Jammu and Kashmir, 1947–49,* New Delhi: Vision Books, 1977. A revealing account from Pakistan's side is Maj. Gen. Akbar Khan, *Raiders in Kashmir,* Karachi: Pak Publishers, 1970.

on 21 April. The resolution called for the withdrawal of all Pakistani forces, a minimum presence by India, the appointment of a plebiscite administrator, and finally, plebiscite. Both sides rejected the resolution. On 13 August 1948 the UNCIP adopted its first resolution. Besides calling for a ceasefire, it asked Pakistan to withdraw all its troops and nationals from J&K and India to withdraw the bulk of its forces. It asked both countries to reaffirm their agreement to decide the disposition of the state in accordance with the will of the people. India accepted this resolution in broad terms while Pakistan, in effect, rejected it. Pakistan logically acknowledged the fact that with Abdullah's strong hold over the majority of the state's Muslims and the presence of Indian troops in the state, a plebiscite verdict would go against it. In December, both sides agreed to accept the ceasefire part of the UNCIP resolution, and an agreement was signed on 1 January 1949. On 27 July 1949, military representatives of India and Pakistan signed the Karachi Agreement demarcating the ceasefire line up to Point NJ 9842 near the Siachen glacier. Troop withdrawals behind the ceasefire line were completed by 31 October.

The efforts of the UN to move beyond the ceasefire and arrive at a settlement did not progress. On 14 March 1950, the UNSC passed a resolution winding up the UNCIP and appointing a United Nations Representative in India and Pakistan (UNRIP). It appointed Owen Dixon, an Australian jurist as UNRIP and Fleet Admiral Chester Nimitz of the US as Plebiscite Administrator. Prime Ministers Nehru and Liaquat Ali Khan met in Delhi (2–8 April) and again in Karachi (26–27 April). Both met Dixon in Delhi on 20 July. Dixon made suggestions to conduct a region-wise, rather than a state-wide, plebiscite, but this did not find favour. A year later, in April 1951, Frank Graham, an American diplomat, took Dixon's place. On 23 December 1952, the UNSC passed another resolution that urged Pakistan to reduce its troops to 3,000 to 6,000 and India to 12,000 to 18,000. Pakistan, recognising that its position was steadily weakening, accepted this. India, appreciating the same trend, did not. The last serious UNRIP effort to find a solution was Graham's proposals of 14 February 1953 which were rejected by both sides.

Under international pressure, a bilateral track was now tried. Prime Ministers Nehru and Mohammed Ali Bogra met in Karachi from 25 to 27 July 1953. Before they met again in Delhi over 16 to 20 August, Sheikh Abdullah was arrested, creating a popularity problem for India. India–Pakistan relations took a serious adverse turn soon after, when

Pakistan and the US signed a Mutual Defence Agreement on 19 May 1954. An irate exchange of letters, with a closure-applying one from Nehru on 29 September, ended this short bilateral endeavour. With Pakistan getting allied to the US, India decided to improve relations with the post-Stalin Soviet Union. An exchange of visits in 1955 by Nehru and Soviet leaders Khrushchev and Bulganin swung Soviet support behind India. In December 1955 Khrushchev declared in Srinagar, 'The question of Kashmir as one of the Indian Union states has already been decided by the people of Kashmir.' With Western support, Pakistan had Kashmir raised in the UN again in early 1957. But the Soviet Union vetoed the US–UK sponsored draft resolution. Thereafter, the threat of a Soviet veto effectively countervailed the efforts of Pakistan and its Western supporters to pressure India through the UNSC. The last report to the UNSC on Kashmir by a UN representative (Frank Graham) was on 28 March 1958. Nehru and Pakistani Prime Minister Feroze Khan Noon met in Delhi (9–11 September 1958) but failed to make any progress.

On 27 October 1958 General Ayub Khan brought Pakistan under military rule. A year later, on 1 September 1959, Ayub and Nehru met briefly in Delhi where the general made his non-starter proposal for the joint defence of the subcontinent. While Kashmir stayed deadlocked, good progress was made on another vital issue—the division of the waters of the Indus and its tributaries. The Indus Water Treaty, dividing the rivers three to each side, was signed in Karachi during Nehru's 19–23 September 1960 visit. In mid-1962 Kashmir came up before the UNSC again, but a resolution seeking to breathe life into the earlier ones was vetoed by the Soviet Union. Later that year came the Sino–Indian War (20 October to 21 November). India's need for military assistance enabled the US and the UK to pressure India to resume dialogue with Pakistan. Delegations headed by Swaran Singh and Zulfiqar Ali Bhutto met six times in Pakistan and in India, between 27 December 1962 and 16 May 1963. During these talks India reportedly offered Pakistan some 3,500 square kilometres of territory in certain areas along the ceasefire line starting from near Zoji La in the north to near Jhangar in the south.[11] But Pakistan, overestimating its leverage, wanted nearly the whole state and the talks ended in a

---

[11] A good account of the talks and their background is contained in Y. D. Gundevia, *Outside the Archives*, Hyderabad: Sangam, 1984. See also Rajesh Kadian, *The Kashmir Tangle: Issues and Options*, Boulder, CO: Westview Press, 1993, p.157.

deadlock. In 1964 Kashmir was once again discussed by the UNSC but the hovering Soviet veto ensured that no resolution was put to vote. Riots in the Valley in 1963 following the disappearance of a holy relic in Srinagar made it seem that the post-Abdullah Kashmir was simmering. Pakistan looked at Nehru's death in April 1964 and India's economic difficulties at the time as promising. From 1960 Pakistan's economy had been doing much better than India's, growing at nearly twice the pace. The 1960 Indus Water Treaty gave Pakistan the confidence that India could not now use water as a lever. The post-1960 canals to bring the Chenab waters to the riverbeds of the Ravi and Sutlej (whose waters were given to India) now also served as formidable military obstacles protecting Pakistani Punjab. Pakistan also reasoned that the military edge, which its post-1954 military modernisation and expansion with American help had given it, might soon be lost as a result of India's post-1962 build up. Pakistan also misjudged India's response if it were to attack Kashmir. It had long been India's intention to strike across the Punjab boundary if Pakistan did that. Inexplicably, Pakistan discounted this danger.

In 1964 Pakistan set up a joint General Staff-Foreign Office 'Kashmir Cell' to find a means of de-freezing Kashmir. Pakistan decided to test India first in an area distant from Kashmir—in the disputed, low-lying Rann of Kutch along the Gujarat–Sind border. Geography favoured Pakistan there and it made a brigade-strength attack on 9 April 1965. A ceasefire was agreed upon on 1 July 1965 under British auspices.[12] Pakistan considered the Kutch operation a military success and felt emboldened by India's restrained response. It now decided to move in Kashmir. Beginning 5 August 1965, Pakistan sent about 3,000 infiltrators into the Valley hoping to provoke an uprising. The Valley stayed quiet and India captured some crucial infiltration routes in the Uri–Poonch bulge and Tithwal. Despite this failure, Pakistan committed its regular army and attacked on 1 September. India counter-attacked on 6 September and a high-intensity war ensued. The war ended on 23 September in response to UNSC resolutions.[13] The 1965 war had a huge impact on Indian thinking. It was a deliberately planned and unprovoked war by Pakistan, exploiting a

---

[12] On 19 February 1968, the Kutch Tribunal Award gave Pakistan 780 sq.km of the 9,100 sq.km it had claimed, delimiting 403 km of the boundary in the process.

[13] A good, balanced analysis of the 1965 war is contained in Russell Brines, *The Indo–Pak Conflict,* London: Pall Mall Press, 1968.

difficult phase that India was passing through. Also, there was a great deal of offensive rhetoric such as 'Crush India' and boasting of the alleged martial superiority of Muslims, 'the descendants of Moghul conquerors'.[14] This contributed to the many communal riots, with heavy fatalities, that occurred in India in the years following the war.

THE 1966–88 PERIOD

The settlement of the 1965 war was achieved at the Tashkent Conference (3–10 January 1966) where the two sides agreed to restore the pre-war international border and the ceasefire line. Exchange of prisoners of war and troop withdrawals were completed in February. Indian and Pakistani foreign ministers met in March but could make no headway. India was now determined not to open Kashmir for discussion. Despite this there was no serious tension till a military crackdown began in East Pakistan on 25 March 1971 to nullify the huge electoral victory of Mujibur Rahman's Awami League three months earlier. Prodded by the ambitious Bhutto, General Yahya Khan (who had taken over from Ayub Khan in 1969 when the latter began to lose control) failed to realise that such a crackdown, which eventually pushed nearly ten million refugees into its territory, would give India a legitimate opportunity to intervene. The fourteen-day India–Pakistan war of 1971 began on 3 December, when a desperate Pakistan, cornered in the east, attacked India from the west. The war ended with the surrender of Pakistan's forces in East Pakistan on 16 December and India's unilateral ceasefire the next day.[15] The new state of Bangladesh was born and India captured 93,000 Pakistani prisoners of war and civilian internees.

---

[14] This rhetoric in fact reflected strategic thinking. On 29 March 1965, Ayub wrote a secret note to his Army Chief, General Musa, which in part read, 'As a general rule Hindu morale would not stand more than a couple of hard blows delivered at the right time and place. Such opportunities should therefore be sought and exploited.' See Stanley Wolpert, *Zulfi Bhutto of Pakistan*, New York: Oxford University Press, 1993, p. 90.

[15] For a good, neutral account of the 1971 war and its lead up, see Leo Rose and Richard Sisson, *War and Secession: Pakistan, India and the Creation of Bangladesh*, Berkeley: University of California Press, 1990.

The war was the result of Pakistan's effort to retain control of Bangladesh, but now it had to pay a price in Kashmir as well. After diplomatic preparations over several months Indira Gandhi and Bhutto, who had succeeded Yahya Khan, held discussions over 28 June to 3 July 1972 and signed the Simla Agreement. On Kashmir, a major gain for India was that a Line of Control replaced the 1949 ceasefire line that had stood through the 1965 war. While both lines were war-determined, the 1972 line did not involve any outsider, such as the UN, as the 1949 one did. The territories captured by the two sides in J&K stayed with them, unlike the case in 1965. The new LoC gave India not only a net gain of 283 square miles but also several key strategic features including in the Kargil area. By 30 December 1972 withdrawal of troops behind the international border and the new LoC was completed. Repatriation of prisoners began in September 1973 but was completed only in April 1974, after Pakistan had recognised Bangladesh in February. Indian and Pakistani foreign secretaries met in May 1976 for normalisation talks, and ambassador-level relations were restored. But no effort was made during this period, or later, to build better relations based on the Simla Agreement.[16]

Bhutto was ousted by General Zia ul Haq in July 1977. In April 1978 a pro-Soviet coup in Afghanistan caused serious fear in Pakistan of a strategic encirclement. In September, Zia made himself President after holding a referendum, but retained the position of Army Chief till the very end, having learned from the fate of Ayub Khan who had given up that post when he became President. In April 1979 Bhutto was executed, and the same month the US suspended all aid to Pakistan on account of its nuclear weapons programme. But everything changed when the Soviet Union invaded Afghanistan in December 1979. This, together with the rise of Khomeini to power in Iran in February that year, led to a U-turn in US policy. In September 1981 the new Reagan administration announced an economic–military assistance package of $3.2 billion over 1981–87. Despite considerable concern about Pakistan's nuclear programme, especially in

---

[16] For an analysis of the failure to build on the Simla Agreement, see P.R.Chari and Pervaiz Iqbal Cheema, *The Simla Agreement of 1972: Its Wasted Promise*, Delhi: Manohar, 2000. For the 'power background' of the Simla Agreement, see Imtiaz Bokhari and Thomas Perry Thornton, *The 1972 Simla Agreement: An Asymmetrical Negotiation*, Washington, DC: Foreign Policy Institute, Johns Hopkins School of International Relations, 1988.

Congress, the US continued its military support on account of the Afghanistan imperative. In 1986, a fresh six-year aid programme of $4.04 billion was announced. But another U-turn in US policy began when the Afghanistan peace accord was signed in Geneva on 14 April 1988 and the Soviets withdrew their troops over the next ten months. The 1980–88 period, when Pakistan both served and used the US, was fraught with long-term problems. Using the three million Afghan refugee pool to create a *mujahideen* (holy warrior) force to fight the Soviets helped spread a gun culture and a related drug culture in Pakistan. Similarly, the inflow of Saudi money served to encourage Sunni extremism, giving a fillip to sectarian fighting. In Zia's time the number of madrassas (Muslim religious schools) benefiting from Saudi financial support went up to 7,000 and their student strength to nearly a million. Zia took to a higher plane the Islamisation programme Bhutto had begun in 1973 to shore up international Islamic support. In August 1988 Zia was killed in a sabotaged air crash. Benazir Bhutto became Prime Minister in December but was kept under firm control by the new, Army-aligned President, Ghulam Ishaq Khan.

India–Pakistan relations were often tense during the Zia years (1977–88), but both sides were careful to keep matters under restraint. The Congress, which had ruled without interruption in Delhi since independence, was ousted from power in 1977. Under the new Prime Minister, Morarji Desai, relations thawed a little. The Salal Dam Agreement was signed in April 1978. Relations continued on an even keel despite Zia's increasingly Islamised military rule and Indira Gandhi's return to power in 1980. In November 1982 Zia and Indira Gandhi met briefly in Delhi (the first time in ten years that the heads of governments had talked since Simla) and agreed to set up an India–Pakistan Joint Commission. But relations deteriorated soon after when the Khalistan movement in Indian Punjab (which was quietly supported by Pakistan) gathered pace in the early 1980s. In April 1984 India occupied the high points of the Saltoro Range overlooking the Siachen Glacier. This extended the line of physical control to the glacial north where the line is not legally demarcated. India gained control of some 2,500 square kilometres of icy land that Pakistan claims is on its side of a 'correctly' extended LoC.

Meanwhile, Sikh insurgency in Indian Punjab was worsening. In July 1984 a major operation had to be mounted to clear militants from the Golden Temple in Amritsar—the holiest Sikh shrine—and in an act of 'revenge' Indira Gandhi was assassinated three months later. In 1985 there was some success in initiating regional cooperation when the South Asian Association for Regional Cooperation (SAARC) was formed. Besides Sikh insurgency, Pakistan's accelerating nuclear weapons programme was also ratcheting up tension. During 1982–84 there were media reports, claiming to be based on US intelligence reports, that India had plans to strike Kahuta—Pakistan's principal nuclear complex—with Israel as a possible partner. Pakistan had cause to worry. India too was concerned because it had a large nuclear complex near Mumbai within easy, over-the-sea reach of Pakistan's newly acquired F-16s. This was the principal reason for Zia's 17 December 1985 Delhi visit during which six normalisation measures, including an agreement not to attack each other's nuclear facilities, were announced. Zia visited India six times without a single return visit from India. He obviously considered it vital to ensure that India–Pakistan relations did not sink too deep before Pakistan had acquired its nuclear capability.

The first serious crisis in India–Pakistan relations after the 1971 war began in late 1986. The trigger was the well known Brasstacks exercise—the biggest peacetime military exercise India had conducted till then. A definite objective of the exercise was to bring pressure on Pakistan to discontinue its support for Sikh terrorism. India wanted to demonstrate that it now had the armour–air capability to drive deep into Pakistan's narrow 'waist' in Sind and southern Punjab, something it did not have earlier. Mutual positioning of offensive forces brought the situation to a flashpoint in January 1987, which was however defused the following month.[17] Tensions gradually subsided, and the Siachen talks that had gone into limbo in June 1986 resumed in May 1988. When Benazir Bhutto became Prime Minister following the death of Zia there was a shortlived improvement in relations. Rajiv Gandhi and Benazir Bhutto met in Islamabad during the SAARC summit of 29–31 December 1988 when the agreement about not attacking each other's nuclear installations, announced three years earlier, was signed.

[17] For a good study of the Brasstacks crisis and the 1990 crisis that followed, see Kanti P. Bajpai et al., *Brasstacks and Beyond: Perception and Management of Crisis in South Asia*, ACDIS Research Paper, Urbana-Champaign, January 1995.

THE POST-1988 PERIOD

The year 1989 began on a deceptively hopeful note. Pakistan was free of military rule after eleven years and Rajiv Gandhi and Benazir Bhutto were popularly seen as young leaders unburdened by the bitterness of partition. Following his December 1988 visit for the SAARC summit, Rajiv Gandhi visited Pakistan again in July 1989—the first regular bilateral visit in twenty-nine years by an Indian Prime Minister. But relations soon soured when Pakistan started a serious attempt to destabilise the Valley. In March 1990, following large-scale demonstrations in Srinagar, Benazir Bhutto spoke in POK of Pakistan's determination to fight for the Kashmiris for 'a thousand years'. By May, tensions rose and there were serious fears of a conventional war, with the scope of escalating into a nuclear one, breaking out.[18]

The violent agitation that began in the Valley in 1989 had largely local roots, the proximate cause being the exceptionally flawed state elections of 1987. The same year the Jammu and Kashmir Liberation Front (JKLF) which spearheaded the movement had begun to receive substantial training and logistical help from Pakistan. However, the JKLF and the scores of tiny organisations allied with it had more zeal than skill and the Indian security forces soon began to get their measure. This and the fact that the JKLF's political objective was an independent Kashmir caused Pakistan to switch its support to the Hizbul Mujahideen (HM), the military wing of the fundamentalist Jamaat-e-Islami Jammu and Kashmir (JIJK) whose aim was to get the state to join Pakistan. The HM worked closely with Pakistan's Inter Service Intelligence (ISI). Its 'Kashmiri' fighters included a large number of ethnic Punjabis from POK. By 1993 it had become obvious, not just to Indians but even to outsiders, that militancy in Kashmir had become primarily a Pakistan-run operation. Soon it also began to take the form of terrorism with civilians getting targeted. In January

---

[18] The spring–summer 1990 crisis had a potential nuclear dimension, unlike the winter 1986–87 crisis in the wake of Brasstacks. For good accounts of the crisis, see Michael Krepon and Mishi Faruqee, eds., *Conflict Prevention and Confidence Building Measures in South Asia: The 1990 Crisis,* Stimson Centre Occasional Paper No.17, April 1994, and Stephen P. Cohen, P.R.Chari and Pervaiz Iqbal Cheema, *The Compound Crisis of 1990: Perceptions, Politics and Insecurity,* ACDIS Research Report: University of Illinois at Urbana-Champaign.

1994, the India–Pakistan talks that had been going on at the foreign-secretary level since December 1990 were called off after seven rounds. By 1994 India's counter insurgency effort had matured. The JKLF renounced armed struggle and the other groups including the HM found themselves hard-pressed. This led Pakistan to pump in greater numbers of Pashtuns and 'non-J&K' Punjabis. It also increased the geographic spread of the conflict by pushing militants into the Muslim-majority districts in Jammu. A systematic effort to vitiate communal relations began with the massacre of non-Muslim civilians. Indian security forces found themselves seriously stretched once again. A provoked India passed a parliamentary resolution in 1994 insisting that POK must be recovered. It was only in March 1997 that foreign-secretary level talks, broken off in January 1994, could be resumed.

In May 1998, India, followed by Pakistan, conducted a series of nuclear tests. In a curious way the tests helped improve bilateral relations in the short run. Both countries got clubbed together in the realm of international criticism and sanctions, and there was a common interest to show the outside world that the two were responsible nuclear powers. This and some useful diplomatic ground preparation in progress since early 1997 paved the way for Prime Minister Vajpayee's 21 February 1999 'bus trip' to Lahore. The Lahore peace effort proved abortive because even before it had taken place, Pakistan had begun a major operation in the Kargil area. During the winter of 1998–99 a Pakistani force of some 1,500 occupied about 130 points along a length of 160 kilometres on the Indian side of the LoC, coming in as deep as 15 kilometres at places. This led to the Kargil War from mid-May to late July 1999. Restrained but effective Indian military action, supplemented by strong US pressure in the later stages, forced Pakistan to pull back.[19]

The Kargil intrusion was a limited probe based on the military judgement that increased counter insurgency (CI) commitments had weakened India's operational capability along the LoC. It had several objectives, ranging from jump-starting a flagging insurgency, focusing international attention on Kashmir in a nuclear-risk milieu, disrupting movement along the Dras–Kargil road (as India was doing on the Neelam River road to the west), putting pressure on Siachen, and

[19] For a neutral analysis of the war, see Ashley J. Tellis, C. Christine Fair and Jamison Jo Medby, *Limited Conflicts Under the Nuclear Umbrella: Indian and Pakistani Lessons from the Kargil Crisis*, Santa Monica, CA: RAND, 2001.

bringing alive a hitherto dormant high altitude sector forcing India to incur high long-term costs. Pakistan could not achieve its objectives, except to a degree the last one. Worse, Kargil turned out to be a huge diplomatic debacle to its initiator. India won unqualified international support—something it had not been able to in all its previous wars with Pakistan.

On 11 October 1999, General Pervez Musharraf, widely considered the man responsible for the Kargil War, ousted Nawaz Sharif and became the 'Chief Executive' of the country. This was followed on 24 December by the hijacking of an Indian Airlines aircraft to Kabul and the forced release of three high-profile terrorists. Though Pakistan's international standing plummeted on account of Kargil—reckless behaviour for a nuclear power—and the military coup, Pakistan chose to escalate terrorism. Groups like Lashkar-e-Toiba and Jaish-e-Mohammed, both almost entirely non-Kashmiri and later to be branded as terrorist organisations by the US, began suicide missions in 1998.[20] Kargil and the spurt in suicide attacks made India feel that its defensive posture had emboldened Pakistan and that a new aggressive approach was needed. Talk of a 'limited war' began in India in early 2000. Tensions remained high through 2000 and 2001. Then suddenly in May 2001, largely to assuage international concern at the long face-off by two nuclear adversaries, India invited General Musharraf for talks. No one was surprised when the ill prepared talks, held in Agra from 14 to 16 July, ended not only in failure but in acrimony.

Within two months of Agra came the 9/11 terrorist attacks in the US that triggered the American war on terrorism. Pakistan, strong supporter of the Taliban that sheltered al-Qaeda, was in a serious bind. But Musharraf showed impressive footwork and turned the country's Afghanistan policy on its head in two days. Pakistan not only ditched the Taliban but also provided valuable help to the US in its campaign in Afghanistan. India, on its part, calculated that the US war against global Islamic terrorism could be exploited to put pressure on Pakistan. The terrorist attack on the Indian parliament on 13 December (three months after 9/11 and two months after an attack on J&K's legislative assembly) gave India a good opportunity to meet

---

[20] The terrorists did not strap themselves with explosives and set them off as in Israel and Sri Lanka, but they carried out attacks that were unconstrained by escape plans and therefore extremely difficult to prevent or handle.

Pakistan's decade-plus attrition strategy with a crisis-initiation counter-strategy.[21]

India took tough diplomatic measures within days—unprecedented since 1971. They included withdrawal of ambassadors, sharp reduction of embassy staff on both sides, stoppage of all transport links between the two countries, and the banning of over-flights by Pakistani aircraft. More ominously, India started a serious military confrontation along the border, suggesting that an attack was inevitable if Pakistan did not contain terrorism in a manner satisfactory to India. It was a full mobilisation of the country's military forces, with the Air Force and the three strike corps of the Army placed in position to go across at very short notice. Mines were laid, ammunition forward-dumped and substantial forces moved from the east. Pakistan mobilised in response, creating a dangerously unstable situation. India did not serve an ultimatum in the classical sense—there was neither a deadline nor spelt-out action in the case of failure to comply—but the threat of war was unmistakable.

Although many commented otherwise, in actual fact India did not want war. Its hope was that the confrontation, with its attendant nuclear war risk, would make the US lean on Pakistan. Operation Parakram (code name for the confrontation) lasted ten months.[22] Musharraf, who had spoken on 19 September, soon after the 11 September attacks, publicly pledging Pakistan's support for the US-led war against terrorism, now also spoke against terrorism in Kashmir, on 12 January and 27 May 2002, but in a hedged manner. With terrorist attacks continuing in J&K and elsewhere, this could not satisfy India. India eased the confrontation when the US issued a travel advisory against India and Pakistan on account of war risk on 30 May, but the threat of war did not seriously recede till India called off the operation on 15 October. It was another six months, when Prime Minister Vajpayee made his 'new beginning' speech in Srinagar on 18 April 2003, before normalisation of diplomatic relations could begin.

Military rule was meanwhile getting consolidated in Pakistan. In March 2000 the Supreme Court validated the military take over of

---

[21] The attack on the Indian parliament is unlikely to have been authorised by the Pakistani government, considering the tight corner it was already in. Yet, groups it had been nurturing had done it.

[22] See Lt. Gen. V.K. Sood (Rtd.) and Pravin Sawhney, *Operation Parakram: The War Unfinished*, New Delhi: Sage, 2003.

October 1999. In April 2002 Musharraf conducted a tainted referendum that made him President for five years from October 2002. In August 2002 he issued a Legal Framework Order (LFO) that substantially amended the 1973 constitution, making the military's role in the country even stronger than it was in Zia's time. General elections held in October 2002 produced an indecisive result. But through engineered defections and qualified support from the Muttahida Majlis-e-Amal (MMA) and some small parties, the King's Party PML (Q)[23] was able to form a government under Prime Minister Zafarullah Khan Jamali. Bhutto's Pakistan People's Party (PPP) and Sharif's PML (N) found themselves in ineffectual opposition. Because of the refusal of non-PML (Q) parties to accept many provisions of the LFO, particularly that of Musharraf continuing as Army Chief, the LFO could not be made part of the constitution till 1 January 2004. That day, following Musharraf's promise to relinquish the post of the Army Chief by end 2004 and some other concessions, both the national assembly and the four provincial assemblies incorporated most of the provisions of the LFO into the 1973 constitution. Musharraf had finally secured a 'democratic' mandate for his rule.

Terrorist violence in J&K began to show a declining trend in the second half of 2003. On 22 October Delhi proposed twelve significant non-military confidence building measures (CBMs) including cross-LoC road travel. Pakistan responded on 23 November by offering a unilateral ceasefire. India responded positively and a ceasefire covering the LoC and the Siachen control line came into force three days later. The much-postponed SAARC summit in Islamabad, 4–6 January 2004, was not only a success, but at meetings on the margin the two countries also agreed to revive the long-shelved composite dialogue.

PEACE EFFORTS

The initial peace effort in Kashmir was centred on the UNSC and its representatives dealing with the conflict—UNCIP followed by UNRIP. The path, broadly agreed to by India and Pakistan during 1948–53, was to ascertain the choice of the people of J&K about the country

---

[23] PML stands for Pakistan Muslim League. The suffix Q stands for Qaed-e-Azam and N for Nawaz Sharif.

they wanted to join and abide by it. This route, through the medium of a plebiscite, however, proved difficult. The relevant UN resolutions required Pakistan to withdraw its forces from the parts of the state it had captured before the proposed plebiscite could be conducted—under UN supervision and with an Indian-controlled administration in position. This was unacceptable to Pakistan, which knew that it would lose the vote if the charismatic Sheikh Abdullah, who was then pro-India, were allowed to exercise his influence. The situation changed in 1953 when Abdullah was arrested. Now it was India's turn to refuse to go along with the UN resolutions. In 1955 the UNSC lost its impact on the dispute when the Soviet Union started exercising its veto power in India's favour.

Despite the unravelling of the plebiscite plan, the substantial US military aid to Pakistan from 1954, and the coming to power of the military in Pakistan in 1958, relations between the countries stayed on a fairly even keel till 1965. Pakistan, as the lower riparian country, had considerable incentive to see that the Indus Water Treaty, which was eventually signed in 1960, was not jeopardised. The US and the UK got another chance at peacemaking when the Sino–Indian War of 1962 took place. India's need for Western diplomatic and military support, and the impact its provision had on Pakistan, gave the US and the UK influence over both countries. This led to the December 1962–May 1963 India–Pakistan talks.

By this time the international community had recognised that the prospect of the whole state going to one of the two countries via a plebiscite was unreal and that the only plausible solution was a partition of the state. This was reflected in the 'Elements of a Settlement' presented by the US and the UK in April 1963 while the India–Pakistan talks were going on.[24] The paper suggested that '(e)ach must have a substantial position in the Vale', that both must have 'assured access to and through the Vale for the defence of their positions to the north and the east' and that '(t)here must be free movement of the people of the Valley throughout the Vale, and their relatively free movement to other parts of the Kashmir, and to India and Pakistan.' It was a possibilities-laden paper. If it had been developed through negotiations, Pakistan might have secured a few extra thousand square kilometres of territory. But Pakistan, with Bhutto

---

[24] US State Department, 'Foreign Relations of the United States 1961–63', *South Asia*, Vol. XIX, 1996.

playing the lead role, squandered the chance. Two years later, by trying to wrest the Valley militarily and failing in the attempt, Pakistan made it impossible to consider a settlement through a readjustment of the ceasefire line. The Tashkent Agreement that terminated the war did not contain any idea beyond restoring the status quo ante.

After the Tashkent Agreement India decided not to talk Kashmir with Pakistan or anyone else. India's position in this regard was considerably strengthened following the 1971 war. Nearly 100,000 prisoners and a substantial advantage in captured territory gave India great leverage. This enabled India to extract major concessions from Pakistan at the Simla talks that followed. *Sub-paragraph 1(ii)* of the Simla Agreement stipulated 'That the two countries are resolved to settle their differences by peaceful means through bilateral negotiations or any other peaceful means mutually agreed upon between them.' This meant that India–Pakistan differences including on Kashmir could be discussed outside a bilateral context only if both countries agreed to do so. *Sub-paragraph 4(ii)* of the agreement stipulated that the new LoC 'shall be respected by both sides without prejudice to the recognised position of the other side. Neither side shall seek to alter it unilaterally irrespective of mutual differences and legal inter-pretations. Both sides further undertake to refrain from the threat or use of force in violation of this line.' This clearly forbade any cross-border activity by Pakistan.

The Simla Agreement contained other important provisions too. *Sub-paragraph 1(iv)* said 'That the basic issues and causes of conflict which have bedevilled the relations between the two countries for the last twenty-five years shall be resolved by peaceful means.' *Paragraph 6* said 'Both Governments agree that their respective heads will meet again at a mutually convenient date and that in the meanwhile, the representatives of the two sides will meet to discuss further the modal-ities and arrangements for the establishment of durable peace and normalisation of relations, including the repatriation of prisoners of war and civilian internees, a final settlement of Jammu and Kashmir, and the resumption of diplomatic relations.' These clauses clearly indicate that a substantial effort was intended to be made post-Simla to settle the differences between the two countries, including on the Kashmir issue.

This intent was never carried through. Both countries effectively turned their backs on each other after Simla. It took four years after Simla for ambassador-level diplomatic relations to resume and more than ten years for the two heads of government to meet. When the two (Indira Gandhi and Zia) finally met in November 1982, the relations were vitiated because of Pakistan's support for Sikh terrorism, its pursuit of nuclear weapons, as well as major arms acquisitions by both countries. But both sides were keen to prevent tensions boiling over. The ministerial-level Joint Commission that was set up at that meeting met thrice—in June 1983, in July 1985 and, after a delay caused by the Brasstacks confrontation, in July 1989. The Commission did not discuss disputes between the two countries, but under its umbrella there were exchanges in diverse fields such as agriculture, trade planning, tea, cotton, railways, telecom, tourism and sports.

Tensions mounted in 1984 because of the Siachen operation, the Golden Temple operation and Indira Gandhi's assassination. Both Zia and the new Indian Prime Minister, Rajiv Gandhi, recognised the need for more substantial discussions than those taking place under the aegis of the Joint Commission. Zia and Gandhi, after two meetings at the margins of conferences in New York and Dhaka, met in Delhi in December 1985. It was an important meeting where the two agreed on six normalisation measures. These included a non-attack agreement with regard to nuclear facilities and the decision to discuss the disputes about Siachen, Wullar/Tulbul and Sir Creek. Kashmir stayed excluded. The Brasstacks tension during the winter of 1986–87 retarded progress, but when Zia passed from the scene and Benazir Bhutto became Prime Minister in December 1988, matters appeared to look up again. But the two Gandhi–Bhutto meetings in Islamabad—December 1988 at the SAARC summit and July 1989 for a bilateral summit—could not achieve much, given the flare-up that had begun in the Valley. By early 1990 the two countries were sliding towards war.

The violent disorder in the Valley gave Pakistan, for the first time since 1962, a lever to press India into talks. The seven rounds of foreign-secretary level talks that went on from December 1990 to January 1994, and Narasimha Rao's letter of October 1993 to Benazir Bhutto offering to discuss all issues including Kashmir stemmed from this. But while India did have a serious problem in J&K, it was not acute enough for it to need to discuss the territorial position. In the absence of flexible mindsets, what India wanted out of the talks (cessation of Pakistan-sponsored violence) and what Pakistan wanted out of them (change in the territorial status quo) did not have any bridging potential. The two countries therefore reverted to the traditional pattern of non-engagement for the next three years, from 1994 through 1996.

Motivation to talk rose again when the battlefield situation continued to stay stalemated. A rare coincidence of non-hawkish governments in both countries also helped. In March 1997 the two foreign secretaries met and two months later the Prime Ministers (Gujral and Sharif) met at the SAARC summit in Male. This led to a breakthrough and when the foreign secretaries met again the following month in June 1997 it was decided to set up eight working groups for discussions including on the key subjects of 'Kashmir' and 'Peace and Security'. Indian Prime Minister Gujral played a crucial, hands-on role in making this unprecedented, composite-dialogue agreement possible. But even after this agreement in principle, hesitation continued, for Kashmir was to be brought up for serious discussion after three-and-a-half decades. It was only when the two PMs (Vajpayee and Sharif) met in New York in September 1998 that the June 1997 agreement was given the green light. This was helped by the fact that the two countries had carried out nuclear tests four months earlier and both had been subjected to heavy international sanctions. The two foreign secretaries discussed 'Kashmir' and 'Peace and Security' at a meeting in October 1998, and the following month other representatives discussed the remaining six subjects.

These meetings and some back-channel contacts paved the way for the Vajpayee–Sharif summit of February 1999 in Lahore. For Pakistan and Prime Minister Nawaz Sharif (who had appeared powerful then, having despatched a President, a Chief Justice and an Army Chief in short order), the primary concern was Pakistan's sinking economy. For India, the motivations were to contain violence in J&K and to be seen as reasonable and responsible in the context of South Asia's nuclearisation. But the Pakistan Army was not supportive of a thaw. It had already moved inside the LoC in the Kargil area. As a consequence, India's positive expectations from Lahore were not matched in Pakistan. The Kargil War of May–July 1999 led relations into the deep freeze again. A mixed-motive invitation by Vajpayee to Musharraf led to the disastrous Agra Summit of July 2001. In Agra the Indian side was clearly divided on what to offer and accept in terms of preliminaries. Just as in Lahore Pakistan did not have an internal consensus, in Agra India did not have one. Within two months of the Agra fiasco came 9/11, and in another three months India's

ten-month long (December 2001–October 2002) threat of war—
Operation Parakram.

It was only in April 2003 that India gave indications that it was
willing to consider a resumption of dialogue. On the margins of the
SAARC summit in Islamabad in January 2004, the two sides agreed
to resume the composite dialogue, the only round of which was held
in October–November 1998. A series of conciliatory gestures by the
two sides, substantial pressure by the US, and a drop in terrorist
violence in Kashmir had made this possible. Musharraf, who in the
previous month had narrowly escaped two assassination attempts by
jehadis with links to Pakistan's security agencies, had recognised the
need to rein in the Islamists. For that, a reduction in tension with
India was vital. Vajpayee, whose moderate thinking had begun to
resonate stronger in an economically vibrant India, wanted to use
Pakistan's predicament to thaw relations, and if possible shape a course
towards settlement.

CHAPTER

THE PROBLEM OF
KASHMIR'S DISCONTENTED

2

The contest in Kashmir is not just between India and Pakistan. There is an important third party—the large number of discontented people in that state. Both Pakistan and India downplay the concerns of Kashmiris. The former seeks to reduce them to just another group of Muslims and the latter to one of its many language groups. Their sufferings, as a consequence of the India–Pakistan conflict, are not seen as salient. The taking to arms by a large number of Kashmiri youth in the late 1980s is attributed in India almost entirely to Pakistani machinations. Most Indians do not stop to think that if it had been possible to do so, Pakistan would have promoted an uprising in Kashmir long before it did in 1989. It had tried in 1965 but did not succeed. It took two more decades before resentment within the state could make an externally supported insurgency a viable proposition.

The alienation of Kashmiris has multiple causes including misrule over five decades, the conviction that Delhi has steadily encroached upon the state's autonomy, and the sharpening of their Islamic identity. Many in India attribute the estrangement largely to the rise of Islamic fervour. While the latter has played a major role in militarising

disaffection, it would be incorrect to consider it to be the cause of disaffection. Sheikh Abdullah had to be dismissed and arrested as far
back as 1953 (long before secular, syncretic 'Kashmiriyat' came under
any kind of Islamic threat) and none of his pro-India successors could
replace him or the ideas he symbolised in the hearts of most Kashmiris.
The estrangement that began then has strengthened over the years,
with the trend turning worse from 1984. The increasingly terrorist involvement of Pakistan in the state from 1989 has intensified Kashmiri
suffering, but it has not led to a significant reduction in their alienation
from India.

Most Indians and Pakistanis have an inadequate and flawed
understanding of what has been happening in J&K during the past
fifty-six years. In Pakistan, there is an exaggerated idea of the Islamisation potential of J&K. In India, there is a marked belittling of the
political estrangement and a wishful belief that economic largesse
and administrative efficiency can fix the problem. It is important that
both non-Kashmiri Indians and Pakistanis try to gain a truer and less
distorted understanding of the happenings in the state and of the
feelings and thinking of its people.

THE PRE-1953 PERIOD

The Dogra Maharaja's rule in J&K was Jammu-centric, and in the
Valley there was always opposition to it. In June 1932, soon after a
dozen protesters were shot dead in Srinagar, the then 27-year-old
Sheikh Abdullah and a few others formed the All J&K Muslim Conference. In June 1939, at Abdullah's instance, the Muslim Conference
was dissolved and the National Conference founded in its stead.[1] The
NC worked closely with the Congress, and a notable personal bond
grew between Nehru and Abdullah. Abdullah was strongly socialistic
and anti-feudal, more than Nehru was, and the NC's 1944 manifesto,
the New Kashmir, called for radical land reforms. In 1940 the Muslim

---

[1] The preference shown by Sheikh Abdullah and his followers for a composite, as
opposed to an Islamic form of nationalism, was not unique to Kashmir in pre-
independence India. In the NWFP (the heart of Muslim fundamentalism in Pakistan
today) Abdul Ghaffar Khan's Congress-aligned and anti-Pakistan Khudai Khid-
matgars was the dominant political force till 1946.

Conference was resurrected by some, and it began to work with Jinnah. The Muslim Conference could make little headway against the NC in the Valley, but it had strong influence in Poonch and the areas around it. In May 1946, Abdullah launched the Quit Kashmir agitation against Dogra rule and was arrested. The NC boycotted the January 1947 elections called by the Maharaja and in its absence the Muslim Conference emerged as the largest party.

Under pressure from Nehru, the Maharaja released Abdullah from prison on 29 September 1947 and made him the head of the state's emergency administration. On 27 October the state acceded to India and the India–Pakistan war began. A few weeks later, the working committee of the NC passed a resolution recommending the accession of the state to India and the resolution was ratified by a special convention of the representatives of the people of the state. Throughout the war (October 1947–December 1948), Abdullah and the NC provided strong support to India—both within the state and abroad. In May 1949 the leaders of the central government and the NC met in Delhi. It was agreed that the provisions in the constitution of India with regard to government in states would not apply to J&K and that a constitution of J&K shall be framed by the state's constituent assembly.[2]

The constitution of India, which came into force on 26 January 1950, had included J&K in Article 1 and Schedule 1 (schedule of states), thereby making the state's accession to India final. But in line with the May 1949 agreement it also contained a special article (370) to define the relationship between Delhi and J&K. Article 370 restricted Indian Parliament's legislative power with regard to J&K to external affairs, defence and communications. Other provisions of the Indian constitution could be extended to the state only with the prior concurrence of the state government, and subject to ratification by the constituent assembly. The first Constitution (Application to Jammu and Kashmir) Order issued in 1950 limited the application of Indian constitutional provisions to those mentioned in Article 370.

The J&K constituent assembly was elected in October 1951. From June to August 1952, central government and NC leaders discussed the relationship between Delhi and Srinagar to be reflected in the J&K constitution. On 24 August, what came to be known as the Delhi

---

[2] J&K is the only state in India with a constitution of its own.

Agreement was announced. The Agreement's significant contents were:

1. All powers other than those specified in the Instrument of Accession to remain with the state.
2. The state government was empowered to regulate the rights of the state's permanent residents.
3. Fundamental rights of the Indian constitution to be made applicable to the state, but with some modifications so that land reforms could be carried out without paying compensation.
4. Hereditary rulership to be abolished.
5. Disputes mentioned in Article 131 of the Indian constitution (centre–state and between states) to be dealt with by the Indian Supreme Court.
6. The jurisdiction of the National Election Commission to be confined to parliamentary and presidential/vice presidential elections.
7. Article 352 (declaration of emergency) to apply to the state in the case of external aggression, but in the case of internal disturbances it could be applied only with the approval of the state government.
8. Articles 356 (President's rule) and 360 (financial emergency) shall not be applicable to the state.

During this period serious opposition to Abdullah and the NC was building up in Jammu. Praja Parishad, formed in 1947 as the King's Party, spearheaded it. The agitation was directed at both Article 370 and the Delhi Agreement. The radical land reforms enacted in J&K during 1950–52, which appropriated all lands exceeding 22.5 acres without recompense, was a big blow to the state's overwhelmingly Hindu landlords. By mid-1952 the anti-Abdullah movement had become quite strong in Jammu, and had begun to find support from parties outside the state like the Jan Sangh and Akali Dal. Matters took a serious turn when Shyama Prasad Mukerjee, the Jan Sangh leader, was arrested when he entered the state and died while in custody six weeks later in Srinagar on 23 June 1953.

The growing agitation against Article 370 made Abdullah suspicious of and hostile to India. Although he had supported accession, he and Delhi had very different ideas on where the road should lead

from accession.[3] For Delhi, Article 370 (which is a temporary provision in the constitution) was a halfway house on the way to J&K's
full integration. Abdullah looked at it as a permanent feature that left
the state with internal sovereignty and minimal links with India. As
early as 14 April 1949 he had told *The Scotsman* that 'Accession to
either side cannot bring peace. We want to live in friendship with
both Dominions. Perhaps a middle path between them, with economic
co-operation with each, will be the only way of doing it.' Such statements periodically made during 1949–53 (when India and Pakistan
were battling in the UN), cast serious doubts about Abdullah's commitment to accession. Nehru was coming under pressure from both
sides. The agitation in Jammu, which had taken a distinct religious
hue, was threatening to spread to India's heartland. The partition massacres had taken place only five years earlier and refugee anger against
Muslims was still running high. Nehru met Abdullah in Srinagar in
May 1953 but their differences could not be bridged.

Abdullah's main card was the fact that the state constituent assembly
had not yet ratified accession. This ratification was critical to India
for it was to become the basis of India's assertion that it had fulfilled
the pledge of its Governor General that 'the question of the state's
accession [shall] be settled by a reference to the people'. In this high-
stake struggle with Delhi, Abdullah had serious vulnerabilities. The
powers of the head of state (Karan Singh, a man with roots deep in
Jammu) were not clearly defined, and could be stretched. Abdullah's
deputy, Bakshi Ghulam Ahmed, was an ambitious politician. His influence among the working class in Srinagar (the only major population
centre in the Valley) made it possible for him to control any pro-
Abdullah rising.[4] Abdullah had also alienated many other senior
colleagues by his imperious conduct. During the night of 8–9 August
1953 Abdullah was arrested under Karan Singh's authority, and Bakshi
made Prime Minister. Since India had constitutional control over the

---

[3] Abdullah and Maharaja Hari Singh had both wanted J&K to become independent. But the landlocked nature of the state, the unwillingness of both India and
Pakistan to permit that course, and the bad relations between Abdullah and Hari
Singh made that an unattainable objective. Once J&K acceded to India, Abdullah's
options became limited. The plebiscite proposals of the UN did not offer independence. His only hope was to enact a J&K constitution that would keep Delhi at bay.

[4] The Kashmiris, as had been generally assumed till the start of militancy in the
late 1980s, were a docile people who did not resist authority. Nearly four centuries of
outsider rule by the Moghuls, Afghans, Sikhs and Dogras had shaped their conduct.

state only with respect to external affairs, defence and communications at that time, the Indian position was that the decision was taken in Srinagar and that Delhi was not involved. The arrest of Abdullah marked the point when India made up its mind to turn its back on plebiscite. While Bakshi could administer the state with Delhi's backing, he had little of Abdullah's charisma and vote-catching ability—crucial in a plebiscite.

THE 1953–87 PERIOD

Bakshi stayed in power for ten years till October 1963. During this period the state was substantially integrated with the rest of India. This was done using Article 370 which permitted more provisions of the Indian constitution (besides external affairs, defence and communications) to be extended to J&K with the concurrence of the state government and ratification by the state constituent assembly. When the state constituent assembly ceased to exist in 1957, Delhi took the view that ratification by it was no longer necessary. Six months after Abdullah's ouster, on 15 February 1954, the state constituent assembly confirmed accession. Two months later custom barriers with the state were lifted. In May 1954, through Constitution (Application to Jammu and Kashmir) Order, the jurisdiction of the centre was extended to cover all subjects in the Union list, not just the three as was the case till then. The state constitution, five years in the making, came into force on 26 January 1957.

Bakshi had succeeded in keeping the NC flock together under him. In the March 1957 state elections the NC won 68 out of 75 seats. In 1958 Delhi felt confident enough to release Abdullah but his speeches questioning accession landed him back in jail within three months. In 1958 the state was brought under the purview of the All India Services and it also ceased to be financially autonomous. The permit system that governed the entry of non-J&K Indian citizens to the state was removed in 1959. The same year the jurisdiction of the Supreme Court was brought in, and in 1961 that of the Election Commission. While Bakshi was piloting these measures, the state administration was mired in corruption. Like most princely states in India, J&K had been poorly and venally administered during the Maharaja era. The situation could not improve after independence because Delhi was forced to privilege loyalty over integrity in state leadership. Large sums of development money poured into the state but much of it went to line the pockets of 'loyal' politicians and bureaucrats. In the 1962 elections the NC won 70 out of 75 seats. On 26 October 1963 a severe agitation gripped the Valley when the sacred relic of Prophet's Hair went missing from the Hazaratbal shrine. (It came back unexplained nine weeks later.) It was during this agitation that the Awami Action Committee under Mirwaiz Mohammed Farooq and the Plebiscite Front, which Abdullah's trusted lieutenant Mirza Afzal Beg had set up in 1955, emerged as rallying points for the opposition. Khwaja Shamsuddin who had replaced Bakshi four months earlier was in turn replaced in February 1964 by G.M. Sadiq who stayed in power for the next eight years. In April, partly as a consequence of the unrest in the Valley, Abdullah was released after being discharged from the conspiracy trial underway since October 1958. He soon started to question again the finality of accession. In May 1964 he visited Pakistan and was in the capital of POK when Nehru died on 27 May. In May 1965, when India–Pakistan relations were tense as a result of the fighting in the Rann of Kutch, Abdullah met Chinese Prime Minister Chou Enlai in Algiers. He was arrested on his return.

During 1964–65 two major steps were taken to curtail the state's autonomy further. Article 356 of the Indian constitution that empowers Delhi to take over a state government was extended to J&K in December 1964, and a Delhi-appointed governor replaced the J&K legislative assembly appointed Sadar-i-Riyasat (head of state) in March 1965. The J&K governor has powers that no other governor in India has. Under Section 92 of the J&K constitution he can assume any or all functions of the government. These powers had been meant for a Sadar-i-Riyasat responsible to the state legislature. Their transfer to an agent of Delhi made the position of the J&K chief minister even weaker than that of other chief ministers. The year also saw another blow to the state's freedom of action—this time in the party political sphere. In January 1965 the NC converted itself effectively to a state unit of the Congress party.

Meanwhile, Pakistan was planning military action. In 1964 the Kashmir National Liberation Front that later became the JKLF was set up in Pakistan. In August 1965 Pakistan sent about 3,000 infiltrators into the Valley in the hope of provoking an insurrection. But the Valley stayed quiet. In fact the Valley population helped Indian security forces round up the intruders. The next month saw the second India–Pakistan war, started by the latter. It ended with Pakistan failing to achieve any of its war objectives.

In the 1967 elections the NC-turned Congress won 59 out of 75 seats. In January 1968 Abdullah was released from detention and he started reiterating his call for self-determination. But there was no noticeable effect in the Valley. In May 1969 Abdullah announced that the Plebiscite Front would contest elections. In January 1971 he was externed from Kashmir and the Plebiscite Front declared unlawful. Towards the end of 1970 there was some terrorist activity in the Valley. From 1965 to 1970 several underground cells financed by Pakistan (sporting names such as al-Fatah, al-Baro and al-Kashmir) had come up, but they evoked no support.

In the March 1972 state elections, the NC-turned Congress won 57 out of 72 seats. The JIJK, contesting for the first time, won five. Abdullah, whose bargaining power had been notably dented following India's December 1971 victory over Pakistan, was permitted to enter J&K in June. He continued to stress autonomy but no longer questioned the finality of accession. In January 1973 the ban on the Plebiscite Front was lifted. Later in the year efforts to stabilise conditions in J&K by bringing a weakened Abdullah into the picture began. These culminated in the six-point agreement arrived at by G. Parthasarathy and Mirza Afzal Beg on 13 November 1974 and made public as the Kashmir Accord on 24 February 1975. The Accord recognised accession as final. But it provided for a review of laws enacted with respect to Kashmir after Abdullah's dismissal, although any change would have to receive Delhi's assent. On 25 February 1975, twenty-two years after he was deposed, Sheikh Abdullah took over as Chief Minister with the support of the NC-turned Congress party. In July Abdullah revived the NC after winding up the Plebiscite Front.

As soon as Abdullah came to power in 1975, Delhi sought to weaken him by encouraging not just his Hindu opponents in Jammu but even the Awami Action Committee of Mirwaiz Farooq and the JIJK. In March 1977, when it lost its thirty-year hold on power in Delhi, the Congress withdrew support to Abdullah. In the resultant June/July state elections (the fairest held in the state at least till 2002), the NC won 48 out of 76 seats. It won 40 out of 42 Kashmir seats (thus reaffirming Abdullah's huge popularity there) but could win only 7 out of Jammu's 32 seats. Later in the year, there were riots in Jammu protesting against regional imbalances—Abdullah's return to power was a cause for concern there. In August 1981 Sheikh Abdullah's son, Farooq Abdullah—a doctor who had lived mostly in England—became, in the subcontinent's familiar familial tradition, the president of the NC. In March 1982 the NC introduced a Resettlement Bill that would have permitted those who had left the state, including to Pakistan, to return. This bill, which the NC knew the centre would never countenance, was primarily an effort to garner Muslim votes in Jammu.

Sheikh Abdullah died on 8 September 1982 and Farooq Abdullah became Chief Minister. Sheikh Abdullah's death made Delhi feel that whatever little internal threat there remained in Kashmir after 1971 had now disappeared. The Congress, ruling at the centre, immediately started to squeeze Farooq Abdullah. The party no doubt remembered its earlier success in bringing the NC into its fold in 1965 by pressing a hapless Sadiq. In October the Resettlement Bill that had been returned by the governor was once again passed by the state assembly. Relations between the Congress, now back in power in Delhi, and the NC continued to worsen. The June 1983 state elections turned into a bitter fight between the two. Farooq Abdullah asserted that Delhi had dishonoured many of the commitments of the 1975 Kashmir Accord. On its part, the Congress, targeting Jammu voters, conducted an aggressive campaign with a distinct pro-Hindu bias. Reflecting the growing polarisation in the state, the NC won 46 seats, sweeping the Valley, and the Congress 26 seats with a landslide in Jammu.

The Congress now decided to play hardball. In March 1984 Delhi appointed as Governor Jagmohan, who had earned his political spurs during the 1975–77 Emergency. Three months later, after G.M. Shah was enticed to defect with thirteen members, he dismissed Farooq Abdullah without giving him an opportunity to prove his support on the floor of the House. This dismissal, purely in the interests of the Congress party, had a big impact in the Valley which had been relatively free of Delhi's control during the previous nine years. To many Kashmiris it appeared that dark days were returning. In 1985 the residuary powers under the constitution were transferred from the state to the centre—another big step in whittling down autonomy. February 1986 saw the first ever anti-Hindu riot in the Valley (in Anantnag) following a riot against Muslims in Jammu a month earlier. Jagmohan's 'tough line' that had made him reviled in the Valley and admired elsewhere had more than a little to do with this.

Central rule was imposed in March 1986 when the Congress withdrew support to G.M. Shah on the grounds of communal violence. The Valley now began to experience widespread popular demonstrations against Delhi. In November 1986 central rule was lifted and a chastened Farooq Abdullah came back as Chief Minister, heading an NC–Congress coalition. Two-and-a-half-years in the wilderness had taught him that Delhi's approval was more important for his survival than popularity in the state. The NC and the Congress jointly fought the March 1987 elections—widely regarded as the most unfree held in J&K. The NC won 38 seats, concentrated in the Valley, and the Congress 24, largely in Jammu. The Muslim United Front (MUF), an eleven-party alliance including the JIJK that came together to fight the elections, won only 4 seats despite credible expectations of doing far better.

THE POST-1987 PERIOD

The deeply flawed 1987 elections sharpened resentment against Delhi. There were widespread protests and violence in the Valley throughout 1988. On 31 July 1988 three bombs exploded in Srinagar. Matters took a serious turn the following year when a large number of young men, who had gone to Pakistan for training, returned. The year also saw MUF members quitting the assembly and the creation of the HM. In December a daughter of Union Home Minister Mufti Mohammed Sayeed was kidnapped, and five JKLF leaders were released in exchange for her release. Jagmohan, who had been replaced six months earlier, was brought back as Governor. He again dismissed Farooq Abdullah and instituted Governor's rule.[5] Protest demonstrations, large-scale arrests and police firings ensued. Huge popular demonstrations continued into the summer. In February the state assembly was dissolved. In May Mirwaiz Moulvi Farooq, Chairman of Awami Action Committee was killed—almost certainly by the HM. With his tough approach not appearing to work, Jagmohan was replaced within two months of his return.

---

[5] Governor's rule can be imposed only in J&K, unlike President's rule that can be imposed in any state including J&K.

The year 1990 saw considerable violence in the Valley and even some bombings in Delhi. There were over a hundred loosely organised militant groups in the Valley then. Tourist arrivals plummeted from over 700,000 in 1988 to 10,000 in 1990. During 1989–90 two army divisions and thirty-four para-military battalions were inducted into the Valley. The Army was tasked with a CI role for the first time in Kashmir. The physical presence of security forces in the Valley became overwhelming. The Armed Forces Special Powers Act and the Disturbed Area Act were extended to the Valley in 1990. Together, they gave enormous powers to security forces. These Acts were in addition to the J&K Public Safety Act in force since 1978 and the Terrorist and Disruptive Activities (Prevention) Act since 1987. In August 1990 a large number of JKLF and other opposition groups leaders were arrested, but the insurgency continued to gather steam with the HM now playing the dominant role. The importance that the HM gained at the JKLF's expense helped Pakistan to turn the Kashmiri nationalist movement into a partly pro-Pakistan Muslim movement.

During 1990–91 militancy extended from Srinagar to the countryside. Meanwhile, communal feelings were being aroused across India by an agitation to build a Ram Temple where the demolished Babri Masjid stood. Advani's *Rath Yatra* (chariot procession) of 1990 was a major marker. That year also saw the start of violence against Kashmiri Pandits and their exodus from the Valley. The demolition of Babri Masjid in December 1992 and the serious communal disturbances that followed, especially in Mumbai, increased local support for the militants in Kashmir. The insurgency steadily worsened during 1990–93, with Pakistan pumping in better-trained militants and in larger numbers. Harkat-ul-Ansar, directly associated with Afghan mujahideen, entered the state in late 1992. By 1993 the number of militants in the Valley had risen to about 10,000 from under 1,000 in 1990. In 1993 the concept of unified security headquarters was in place, and security forces began to dominate every habitation through a 'grid system'. In 1994 the J&K government created a 3,000-strong Special Operations Group that soon attained notoriety as an above-the-law force. In May that year the JKLF, which had been severely mauled in the preceding four years, declared an unconditional cease-fire. Although the total number of militants had been steadily coming down from 1994, the proportion of foreigners (mostly from POK, Pakistan and Afghanistan) had been going up. These militants were better trained than those who were in action earlier, and the operational ascendancy the security forces had gained got eroded.

Between 1989 and 1992 about thirty parties and organisations opposed to the NC and the central government got together on a minimum platform. In March 1992 they formed the APHC, also referred to as the Hurriyat. The prominent groups in the Hurriyat are People's Conference, Awami Action Committee, Muslim Conference, JIJK, JKLF and People's League. The Hurriyat evolved much like the MUF had during 1986–87. But the Hurriyat refused to take part in elections for reasons that included the electoral thwarting of the MUF in 1987 through malpractice. Many Hurriyat constituents, like MUF constituents earlier, have links with Pakistan's ISI and get its funding support. They thus function in a semi-legal political zone. Their leaders are periodically arrested under various special acts and kept in custody, sometimes for years, without trial.

Parliamentary elections were held in the state in May 1996, and state assembly elections in September–October. In the state elections the NC won 57 of 87 seats. The state-wide turnout was 48 per cent, but there were complaints of malpractice and coercion by security forces, especially in rural areas. In the 1998 and 1999 parliamentary elections, voting percentages were only in the vicinity of 20. The formation of the Farooq Abdullah ministry in October brought nearly seven years of Governor's rule to an end. The Bharatiya Janata Party (BJP), which is staunchly opposed to any special status for J&K, came to power at the centre in 1998 at the head of a coalition. Farooq Abdullah, who had learned in 1984 the importance of being in Delhi's good books, promptly aligned the NC with the BJP. As a consequence, his political position within the state became even weaker.

Terrorism, featuring large-scale suicide attacks, intensified in 1998. The upper hand the security forces had been gaining since 1996 was weakened. Support for violence was no longer confined to Valley Muslims. In 1995 violence had spread to the Doda district in Jammu where the population is ethnically linked to Kashmiris. Later it spread to two other Muslim majority districts in Jammu. Punjabi-speaking Muslims largely inhabit these districts, as is the case in neighbouring AJK. The Armed Forces Special Powers Act and the Disturbed Area Act were extended to these Jammu districts. On 24 July 2000 the HM declared a unilateral ceasefire. This led to a meeting with an Indian delegation on 3 August. The ceasefire was called off on 8 August on account of the HM's insistence that Pakistan should be made a party to the talks. On 19 December Delhi announced a qualified ceasefire which it called off on 23 May 2001, shortly before inviting General Musharraf for the Agra Summit in July.

Violence continued unabated throughout 2001 and 2002, but began to show a slight decline in 2003. Outsiders sent in by Pakistan have been playing a steadily increasing role in the violence, but it is not a wholly cross-border enterprise as has been portrayed in the Indian media. According to government sources, 14,356 militants were killed in the 1990s, of which only 2,538 were foreigners. The proportion of foreign militants killed has been going up. But even in 2001, of the 2,020 militants killed, only 625 were foreigners.[6]

In June 2000, a year after the Kargil War, the J&K assembly adopted (with only sixteen out of eighty-seven members voting against it) an Autonomy Resolution calling for a greater measure of autonomy for the state. Delhi rejected it the following month without any discussion. This resolution had its beginnings in 1994, when the out-of-power NC began preparing for the next elections. Greater autonomy under Article 370 became the NC's main plank in the 1996 elections. Soon after coming to power in October the NC government initiated two autonomy studies—one with regard to autonomy for J&K as a whole and another with regard to autonomy for regions within J&K. The NC was not serious about the Autonomy Bill. It was merely going through the motions in order to redeem its 1996 electoral pledge in preparation for the 2002 elections.

The report of the second committee—on autonomy for regions within J&K—also got nowhere. The committee had suggested an eight-unit division of the state. Kashmir is to be divided into three units, all almost entirely Muslim. Jammu is to be broken into three— a Hindu dominant Jammu unit (by far the biggest of the eight units) made up of Jammu, Kathua and Udhampur districts, a Muslim majority Chenab unit made up of Doda district and the Mahore *tehsil* detached from Udhampur; and a Muslim majority Pir Panjal unit comprising Poonch and Rajouri districts. Ladakh is to be divided along the present district boundaries—Buddhist majority Leh and Muslim (Shia) majority Kargil.

State elections were held in October 2002 when Operation Parakram was still in progress and violence was raging in the state.[7] In the state

---

[6] Gautam Navlakha, *Economic and Political Weekly*, 16 February 2002, p. 608.

[7] Unlike the rest of India where five years is the norm, state elections in J&K, under its own constitution, are held every six years.

as a whole the turnout was 46.2 per cent, although in the Valley it was only 29.6 per cent. These elections were more fair than the 1996 elections, not to speak of the hugely flawed 1987 one. Delhi was keen to ensure a good turnout, but it was disinterested in the results. For the first time the NC faced a serious challenger in the Valley in the form of the People's Democratic Party (PDP). The PDP was formed in 1999 and comprised opposition groups that did not subscribe to the Hurriyat policy of electoral boycott. Out of 87 seats the NC won 28, Congress 20 and the PDP 16. In Kashmir (46 seats), the NC's seats were down to 18 from 44 in 1996. In Jammu (39 seats) it was down to 9 from 14. A Congress–PDP coalition government, with the PDP leader Mufti Mohammed Sayeed as Chief Minister for the first three years, assumed power.

The Hurriyat, within which there was always considerable difference of opinion on how to deal with Delhi, split in September 2003 into a moderate group led by Moulvi Abbas Ansari and a pro-Pakistan group headed by Syed Ali Shah Geelani of JIJK. In October Delhi announced that it was willing to talk to the Ansari group at the level of the Deputy Prime Minister. The first round of talks took place in January 2004.

THE AREA WITH PAKISTAN

From the beginning Pakistan took the convenient but legally doubtful view that Gilgit, Baltistan and the small principalities within them were tribal areas and that in those parts the Dogra Maharaja had been only suzerain and not sovereign. It chose not to consider these areas part of J&K or of AJK. From 1949 they have been administered from the national capital. In August 1972 these areas (83 per cent of the POK territory) were formally separated from AJK. The territory is subdivided into the districts of Gilgit, Ghizer, Diamer, Skardu and Gauche. Because of the sparse population (1.2 million people making for a population density one-twelfth AJK's) and the tribal nature of the society, there is little political consciousness in the area. Universal adult franchise reached there only in April 1994 when the Benazir Bhutto government established a twenty-four member council. But even this has changed matters little on the ground. Northern Areas continue to be controlled by Force Commander Northern Areas, assisted by a divisional commissioner.

AJK is made up of large parts of Poonch and Mirpur districts and slivers of western Jammu and north-west Kashmir. Much of its territory lies along the south-western slopes of the Pir Panjal Range. There are about 2.7 million people in AJK that makes for 17 per cent of POK's territory. Most people of AJK speak dialects of Punjabi and are culturally close to the people of the Potohar plateau—the Pakistan Army's recruiting heartland. Initially Ghulam Abbas, who had led the Muslim Conference from its resurrection in 1940, was prominent in AJK, but his independent thinking was not to Pakistan's liking and he was soon sidelined. Sardar Abdul Qayyum, the leader of the 1947 Poonch revolt, replaced him and since then has been the area's most prominent leader. The political system in AJK largely conforms to the traditional *biradari* (kinship group) social system of the land.

Technically, Pakistan has not absorbed AJK, which has its own President and Prime Minister. But in reality it is controlled by the Ministry of Kashmir Affairs (MKA). The 1955 Kashmir Act provided for party-based elections to a small state council. The 1970 Kashmir Act created a presidential system. The first true elections with universal franchise were held in 1970. The 1973 Pakistan Constitution (still in force) does not make any reference to AJK. In 1974 Zulfiqar Bhutto replaced the presidential system in AJK with a parliamentary system. The area, Mirpur particularly, has a large diaspora in the West that not only sends considerable remittances but is also politically active. The Kashmir Liberation Army in Britain that murdered an Indian diplomat in 1984 was a largely Mirpuri organisation. Gulf money during the Zia decade fuelled a spate of construction of mosques and madrassas.

The bond of religion is what has enabled Pakistan to maintain control over POK with far greater ease than India has been able to in J&K. A degree of ethnic and cultural commonality between POK and North Punjab/NWFP has also helped. Yet, there have been problems. In public, AJK politicians always maintain their allegiance to Pakistan, but in private they are quite vocal about the need for greater autonomy. The Kashmir Liberation Movement (KLM) was formed in 1958, largely because sections of the Muslim Conference became suspicious of Pakistani intentions. The JKLF, founded in Pakistan in 1964 by Amanullah Khan and Maqbool Butt, had a vision of an independent J&K. It maintained links with the MC and the KLM in POK, and the Plebiscite Front in J&K.

It is true that the JKLF does not enjoy much support in AJK, but it is also true that the majority of people in AJK would prefer weaker rather than stronger links with Pakistan. The AJK Constitution Act of 1974 does not allow questioning the accession of the state to Pakistan. Clearly, Islamabad has some worry about the independence option. In June 1990 JKLF Chairman Amanullah Khan created a stir by announcing the establishment of a provisional government of J&K that would be separate from both Pakistan and India. AJK politicians have consistently argued since 1950 that Northern Areas should be a part of AJK. There have been occasional demonstrations against Islamabad, especially in Mirpur.

From Discontent to Militancy

The animus that has developed in Kashmiri society against India is of a more recent vintage than its India–Pakistan counterpart. It took four decades for what were only feelings of separateness, which the Valley Kashmiris had always felt towards mainstream India in common with other remote people like the Nagas and the Mizos, to mutate first into alienation, then discontent and finally militancy. While there is little doubt that the violence in Kashmir is mostly Pakistan-promoted, the origin of anger that vast sections of the Kashmiri society feel against India preceded the outbreak of violence, and had its roots in Kashmir itself. Social conflicts move in an exponential way with barely noticeable growth for many years and then a rapid increase in the rate of change—as occurred in the Valley in the 1980s. What went largely unnoticed earlier, became abruptly dramatic.

The roots of disaffection that turned to militancy in 1988 go back to 1953 when Sheikh Abdullah, whose hold on the Valley was of a truly exceptional order, was cast aside. Bakshi, Sadiq and Syed Mir Qasim are seen—not so much at the time but in retrospect—as puppets of Delhi who sold the state's autonomy in return for being propped up in venal office. During their rule, twenty-eight Constitution (Application to Jammu and Kashmir) Orders were issued. Out of 395 Articles of the Indian constitution, 260 became applicable to the state. Out of ninety-seven entries in the Union List, as many as ninety-four and out of forty-seven entries in the Concurrent List, as many as twenty-six became operable in J&K.[8] This was a far cry from the situation in mid-1953 when only two Articles and one Schedule of the Indian constitution (Articles 1 and 370, and Schedule 1) were applicable to the state, and the state government dealt with all subjects except external affairs, defence and communications.

The erosion of state autonomy may have been less unacceptable if democratic accountability in governance and good administration had been ensured. But this could not be, given the mutual connivance that developed between Delhi and the NC at the expense of the people. As a result, the state could never pull out of the corrupt, petty despotic mode of administration prevalent in most Indian princely states before independence. Despite the ritual of elections, democratic space remained stifled in J&K, in sharp contrast to mainstream India. The NC could never govern when it had problems with the centre. As years went by, it began to depend increasingly on Delhi's, and not the people's, support. The Congress had been involved in J&K politics from 1953, and during 1965–75 it actually took over the NC. After the 1975–82 interlude of relative freedom of action during Sheikh Abdullah's rule, the NC reverted to toeing the line of the party that ruled in Delhi.

Young, educated Kashmiris hold Delhi and the NC jointly responsible for subverting democracy in J&K. The dismissal of Farooq Abdullah in July 1984, the forced resignation of G.M. Shah in March 1986, the forced marriage of the NC and the Congress in November 1986, and finally the March 1987 elections that were blatantly rigged against the eleven-party MUF all contributed to alienation turning to violence. The leader of the HM, Syed Yusuf Shah, now in Pakistan, was one of the thwarted MUF candidates of 1987. The tough response to the popular, largely non-violent agitations during 1986–88 and the somewhat indiscriminate offensive against the homegrown militants of JKLF during 1989–92 did not help matters. The decade of 1987–96, when there were no elections and where three years of manipulated NC–Congress rule was followed by nearly seven from Delhi, served to harden anger and animus. A new generation that had reached voting age in the 1980s felt that, while the democratic rights of the

[8] See Riaz Punjabi, 'Autonomy and Participatory Federalism', *World Focus*, Vol. 23, Nos 10, 11, 12, October–December 2002, pp. 21–23.

Kashmiris had been undermined even during 1953–75, they were truly trampled upon from the beginning of 1984.

Other negative perceptions paralleled the feeling of political helplessness. Despite huge developmental subsidies, living standards have not risen much, and remain well below that of comparable Himachal Pradesh. During the 1980s, when things began to go seriously wrong, J&K's growth rate was a third of the country's average. There is no industry to speak of. Colleges turn out large numbers of graduates, the majority of whom find no work. Government jobs are sought after, partly because of the opportunity for corruption. Because higher-level central and quasi-central government jobs are filled on all India basis, non-Muslim outsiders occupy the bulk of such jobs in the state. This issue has created a huge groundswell of resentment. Development in education and communications, carried out with heavy central funding, has paradoxically contributed to alienation by raising awareness levels and opening mobilisation channels.

The feelings of hostility generated by what was perceived as subversion of democracy and discrimination in employment got augmented when general life in the Valley got dislocated beginning 1989 as a result of CI measures. A common objective of terrorists everywhere is to provoke repression. Cordon and search operations caused not just inconvenience but humiliation as well, especially to women. Rural and border areas where most Kashmiris live have no media presence to act as a check on security forces. Great anger is caused when provoked soldiers fire at bystanders and innocents are killed by security personnel who carry out delayed retaliatory strikes following militant ambushes. The fine line separating tough military conduct and excessive brutality is difficult to find in the murky conditions of CI operations. It is hard to respond in discriminate or proportionate manner when coping with highly leveraged asymmetrical threats that terrorism present. Tensions running high and troops getting edgy are built into the paradigm, as are human rights violations and the killing of innocents. These, in turn, provide a steady flow of recruits into the ranks of the militants.

Official figures put the Kashmiri civilian death toll under 30,000 but there are many responsible estimates that put it much higher.[9] There is the highly emotional issue of custodial and faked encounter

---

[9] Omar Abdullah, Minister of State for External Affairs, stated on 18 December 2001 that 61,000 lives had been lost in J&K since violence began.

deaths, which have been unofficially put at over 3,000 during
1984–94 and over 6,000 during 1994–2000.[10] There are large numbers
of widows and orphans, parents who have lost their children, and
those who have been subjected to torture. There are detainees under
special legislation. In 2003, in addition to those behind bars there
were over 36,000 who were free on parole but with cases hanging indefinitely over their heads. Because of slanted media coverage, Indians
in general have little idea of the levels to which the security and self-
respect of the Kashmiris have been degraded since 1989.[11]

The situation is given an added edge by the fact that, because they
are recruited on an all India basis, about 95 per cent of the military
and para-military personnel operating in J&K are non-Muslim and
99 per cent non-Kashmiri. Their numbers too are huge—in the Valley
there is one security man for every four working-age males. The all-
too-obvious antagonism of the Muslims in the Valley and elsewhere
in the state has inevitably resulted in reciprocatory bitterness towards
them among security personnel. There is resentment against the locals
for their uncooperative attitude, for the help many of them give the
militants, and for allowing militants to rise from their ranks. The anger
and animus felt by both sides feed on each other, a dynamic inherent
in any CI situation.

The Kashmiri identity has always had an Islamic strand. But it has
other strands as well, such as language and the feeling of belonging
to a remote, nature-favoured valley. Sheikh Abdullah had played on
all the different strings of Kashmiri identity to make it rally behind
the NC. But when the secular vision he had raised began to fade, the
Islamists who had been sidelined in 1939 (when Abdullah converted
the Muslim Conference to the National Conference) re-entered the
stage. The slow growth of the JIJK through the 1960s went unnoticed
till it captured five seats in the 1972 elections. Gradually it became
possible in Kashmir to discredit secular politics on the grounds of
suffocation of democracy and sleaze. The world-wide Islamic resur-
gence, beginning in the late-1970s, inevitably had its impact in the
state. Madrassa promotion and mosque-building accelerated.

[10] Vernon Hewitt, *Towards the Future? Jammu and Kashmir in the 21st Century*, Cambridge: Granta Editions, 2001, p. 179
[11] See T. Joseph, 'Kashmir, Human Rights and the Indian Press', *Contemporary
South Asia*, Vol. 9, No. 1, March 2000, pp. 41–45 for a revealing juxtaposition of the
coverage of violence in the Valley by the Indian media and the situation depicted by
alternate media sources.

Promotion of Islam in the state also got a boost from the spurt of communal riots that occurred in the rest of India in the 1980s. There were major riots in Moradabad (1980), Bihar Sharif (1981), Moradabad–Meerut and Baroda (1982), Nelli (1983), Bombay–Bhiwandi (1984), Ahmedabad (1985–86), Meerut (1987) and Bhagalpur (1989) where Muslims were the principal sufferers. In 1992–93 there were post-Babri Masjid destruction riots in Mumbai, Surat, Ahmedabad, Kanpur, Bhopal, Delhi and other places. While the communal riots in the rest of India in the 1960s and 1970s had little impact in the Valley, those in the 1980s and 1990s did. This has had to do not only with the sense of Islamic identity becoming more prominent in J&K but also with improved mass communications.

A young generation in its twenties—more educated, more politically conscious, more self-assertive—provided the backbone for militancy when it began in the 1980s. Pakistan's planning, training and logistic support was a big factor but not the only one. There was considerable public support for the 'boys' of JKLF and other groups of local fighters. Kashmiris are now disenchanted with the course militancy has taken. In the ruthless cycle of terror and counter-terror it is they, not the foreign militants or the security forces, who have been the principal victims. Yet, despite fatigue and distress, the link between militancy and popular feelings continues to be fairly strong. In 1990 and 2002 terrorists gunned down two of the most popular leaders in the Valley—Mirwaiz Moulvi Farooq and Abdul Ghani Lone. Yet, their sons who have succeeded to their leadership positions continue in the militant-friendly Hurriyat. A part of the explanation is that the public still sees the local militants as pursuing a genuine cause. For all its terrorist violence, Kashmir militancy has never degenerated to the self-seeking criminality seen in Punjab in the 1980s.

Resolution Efforts

From the very beginning, the resolution of differences between India and the discontented in J&K has been hampered by the persistence of two opposing streams of thought in India. One stream called for the recognition of the special circumstances under which J&K joined India, and for giving the Kashmiris as much freedom of governance as possible without endangering the state's ties with India. This approach sought to enlist the Kashmiris as willing supporters in India's tussle with Pakistan. The counterpoised view has been to ignore the special circumstances of accession and to make the Kashmiris accept that they are no different from any other group of Indian citizens. This way of thinking inevitably meant that it was not the voluntary cooperation of the Kashmiris, but their forced acquiescence that was to be sought. Delhi's strategy to deal with the Kashmiris has always been burdened by these contrary impulses.

During the past fifty-six years there have been only two attempts on India's part to pursue a proactive approach to settle the internal dimension of the Kashmir problem. The first peace attempt began in early 1949 after the India–Pakistan ceasefire became effective and the UNCIP became active on behalf of the UNSC. With Gopalaswamy Ayyangar (Prime Minister of J&K, 1937–43) playing the lead negotiating role for Delhi and Mirza Afzal Beg playing the counterpart role, talks began on how J&K's then conditional accession should be reflected in the Indian constitution. This issue was settled in the middle of 1949. The inclusion of J&K in Article 1 and Schedule 1 of the Indian constitution finalised later in the year made it impossible for the state to leave the Indian Union without a constitutional amendment. Article 370 gave considerable autonomy to the state at that point, but it contained a crucial provision: that the J&K constituent assembly could approve additional Articles of the Indian constitution being made applicable to the state. This made the nature of the yet-to-be framed J&K constitution a matter of utmost significance.

The Delhi Agreement negotiated by the two sides and publicised in July 1952 was an effort to ensure that the conflicting desires of the two parties—Delhi's for control and Srinagar's for freedom of action—were reconciled. The relations between the two parties, already problematic by then, deteriorated rapidly thereafter. This proved disastrous in an environment where the risk of the US and the UK, acting through the UNSC imposing a course of action that had the potential to take a part of the state away from India, was seen as fairly high. The only safe course for Delhi was to have a dependable head of government in Srinagar who would ensure that the state constituent assembly confirmed accession quickly and thereafter drafted a state constitution that met India's security needs. Abdullah, reneging even on accession in some of his speeches, was certainly not dependable. That effectively brought the first attempt at peacemaking to an end.

After getting Sheikh Abdullah out of the way in 1953, Delhi's objective became limited to achieving law and order in the state, not winning the allegiance of the people, especially of the Valley. The threat posed by Pakistan was the reason for this. The whole focus centred on getting a Delhi-dependent government in J&K to whittle down the autonomy of the state by passing the needed legislation. In this Delhi was amply successful. During the twenty-two years of Bakshi-Sadiq-Mir Qasim rule (1953–75) the autonomy of the state was progressively and comprehensively destroyed.

The second attempt at finding an internal settlement took place during 1972–75. After India's resounding victory in the 1971 war and the Simla Agreement that followed, Pakistan went out of the Kashmir picture. Both Indira Gandhi and Sheikh Abdullah recognised this. The former gauged that she could now force Abdullah into an agreement that ensured the continuance of the status quo, and the latter accepted that he had no choice but to go along. The Kashmir Accord of November 1974 did contain a provision to review post-1953 legal changes, but since any change required Delhi's approval the provision became a non-starter. The 70-year-old Lion of Kashmir, now a lion in winter, recognised this. Abdullah's efforts became limited to ensuring that he was not deposed again, that his friends had a chance to enjoy the pickings of office denied them so long, and that his son succeeded him. During the seven years he had before his death, he achieved all three objectives, but failed in aligning with Delhi to work out a long-term settlement that would take care of the imperatives of Indian nationalism and Kashmiri aspirations. Delhi, on its part, mistakenly thought that the taming of Abdullah and his prospective passing from the scene had defused all opposition. It did nothing but try to further the Congress party's political fortunes in the state.

Seven years after Sheikh Abdullah's death, the JKLF-led insurgency exploded in the state in 1989. By 1991 the violence became largely Pakistan-directed, and by 1995 almost entirely Pakistan-sponsored. The state was ruled directly from Delhi for nearly seven years— January 1990 to October 1996. To find a negotiated settlement, Delhi had no one to talk to in the state. The NC and its leader Farooq Abdullah were unpopular and ineffective. Delhi chose to maintain a façade of flexibility with regard to autonomy. In 1993 Prime Minister Narasimha Rao offered to discuss everything except secession. But Delhi knew that unless it brought violence under control it would be negotiating from a position of weakness. India's basic peace strategy in Kashmir since 1989 has been to turn public opinion against Pakistan and the militants. This is sought to be done by making the Kashmiris accept that Indian security forces are going to stay in strength in their midst for as long as it takes and that the Pakistani lifeline that sustains militancy will be severed soon.

The only incentive being offered is economic help. India has not been able to offer any political carrot in the form of partial restoration of eroded autonomy. From the late 1980s the political climate in India has become more disapproving of making any concession on autonomy. The always murky demarcating line between Pakistan and the Kashmiri dissidents in Indian minds has got largely rubbed out. India is convinced that if it waits it out for a few more years the Kashmiris will stop supporting the militants, and militancy will die. The series of interlocutors that the V.P. Singh, Narasimha Rao and Vajpayee governments appointed—Fernandes (1990), Pilot (1991), Pant (2001), Jethmalani (2002) and Vohra (2003)—were meant to play nothing but a cosmetic role. The Hurriyat steadfastly refused to talk to any of them. The ice is now broken with the Ansari faction's January 2004 talks with the Deputy Prime Minister.

CHAPTER

CONFLICT DRIVERS   3

T he India–Pakistan conflict with its focus on Kashmir has several drivers, the nature and relative importance of which have changed over the years. While a contest for territory and people provided the initial thrust, ideological differences about the role of religion, the democratic content of governance, and a competition for power soon became comparably important. A contest for power between two countries, one of which is seven times bigger than the other, may appear implausible, but not if the weaker country has convinced itself—as Pakistan has irrationally done—that unless it persists with the fight, it will be done in. The contest over Kashmir is now less a pursuit of well-defined strategic goals than one where emotions, internal political dynamics and international opportunism have come to play major roles.

This chapter explores the key factors that drive the tussle today. It makes a brief survey of the biased understandings of the conflict widely prevalent in both countries and among the discontented in J&K, which not only diverge considerably from one another but also from objective reality. It then looks at the deep feelings of insecurity—primarily in Pakistan but also in India—and the matter of political exploitation of religious feelings in both countries. This is followed by an examination of two factors that are specific to Pakistan—the country's deeply problematic political system and the Pakistan Army. The latter is regarded by many, even in Pakistan, as the primary current barrier to the resolution of the conflict. The indifference shown by the people of both countries to the costs incurred on account of the conflict and the reasons for it are examined next, followed by a look at the way attitudes have hardened over the years on both sides, thus making it very difficult to look for mutually advantageous solutions. The belief that 'for one to win, the other must lose' has become a major problem.

SLANTED COMPREHENSION

Thinking at both the state and popular levels is affected by competing constructions of reality that set the context for perceptions and expecta-tions. Direct learning from experienced hostility and vicarious learning from historical and current writings condition people and institutions. Collective internalisation of contrasting maps of the same ground is not unusual. During the Cold War there were very different under-standings on the two sides of events like the Berlin Blockade, the U-2 shoot-down and the placement of missiles in Cuba. In South Asia, the problem is aggravated by the rhetorical exaggeration that charac-terises speeches and commentaries in the region. This leads to cognitive rigidities that make people think, as in an old cartoon in *The New Yorker*, 'What do you mean, "my country, right or wrong"? Since when has our country ever been wrong?'

There are black and white images of enemy and self on both sides, with a high degree of complementarity.[1] This leads to opposite answers to the usual question concerning any event—who started it? All acts are judged by the question, who did it, rather than on facts. One's

---

[1] For very similar adverse images of one another during the Cold War, see R. Stagner, *Psychological Aspects of International Conflict*, Belmont, CA: Brooks, 1967. For their long-standing presence in South Asia, see A. Haque, 'Mirror Image Hypothesis in the Context of Indo-Pakistan Conflict', *Pakistan Journal of Psychology*, Vol. 8, 1973, pp. 13–22. See also Sam Keen, *Faces of the Enemy: Reflections on the Hostile Imagination*, New York: Harper and Row, 1986.

own belligerent actions are seen as compelled responses, while those of the opponent as deliberately malicious. Psychological double standards of a high order are in play, and picking facts to suit prejudices is common. Balanced, scholarly writings on Kashmir are little read, and end up as academics writing for other academics. Problems of selective highlighting of news and biased commentary have become serious. Some key areas where the understanding of the conflict has been seriously hampered because of pre-existing beliefs and cognitive bias are considered in this chapter. These are Hindu–Muslim history, the freedom struggle and partition, the Kashmir issue, the causes of India–Pakistan hostility, the wars between them, the Simla Agreement, the role of outsiders, the causes of Kashmiri discontentment, the post-1989 violence, and the ground realities.

In both countries there are Muslims and Hindus who hold stereotypical views of each other, hugely divergent from reality. In Pakistan there are images of devious, wily, sanctimonious Hindus, and in India of fanatical, vengeful, medieval Muslims. Such opinions are rarely expressed in public, but they do litter many private conversations and underpin the thinking of some in the policy-influencing strata in both countries. In Pakistan, the textbooks for compulsory 'Pakistan Studies' actually contain some of these stereotypes.[2] In India such ideas are propagated much less blatantly, although they have recently begun to creep into Indian textbooks as well.[3] Popular books, from the beginning in Pakistan and more recently in India, portray Hindus and Muslims as having waged an unremitting struggle against each other in undivided India from the twelfth century, if not from the eighth. This is a huge caricature of the truth of the two communities living essentially in peace, separately but proximately, throughout India for close to a millennium—despite occasional communal fighting, and in the distant past some forced conversions and destruction of temples. Sadly, for reasons of national justification in Pakistan and political contestation in India, a historically untruthful picture of communal enmity and warfare has been marketed.

[2] See Khursheed Kamal Aziz, *The Murder of History: A Critique of History Textbooks in Pakistan*, Lahore: Vanguard, 1993.
[3] See Ifran Habib, Suvira Jaiswal and Aditya Mukherjee, *History in the New NCERT Textbooks: A Report and an Index of Errors*, Kolkata: Indian History Congress, 2003.

In the case of the freedom struggle against the British, there are differing views in both countries about its logic and course.[4] In India it is believed that the Muslims had stayed out of the struggle and came in to vivisect the motherland when the essentially Hindu effort was about to bear fruit. The Pakistanis believe that Muslims could not join the freedom struggle under the leadership of the Congress because that party always had a strong anti-Muslim, Hindu-Mahasabhaite faction. On partition too there are differing views in Pakistan. One view is that the Muslims had to go their separate way because the Congress was not willing to accept a loosely-structured India—suggested by Cripps and Cabinet Missions—that would have safeguarded Muslim interests. The other view, peddled to create a historical rationale for Pakistan, is that from the late nineteenth century the Muslims had a vision of a separate state.

The fact is that at the level of the elite, the bulk of Muslims had shown only a lukewarm interest in the freedom struggle. While they were all for freedom—for the Muslim elite had suffered disproportionately under the British—their principal concern during the struggle was to see that they did not suffer in what they feared would be a Hindu-dominated, free India. The Muslim masses, unlike the Muslim elite, had never shown any interest in Pakistan. The Muslim League had lost badly to the Congress in reserved Muslim seats in the 1937 elections. The1945–46 elections that made Pakistan possible were held in a surcharged, polarised communal atmosphere. But even then, the League could win only 60 per cent of the Muslim votes. It is noteworthy that only 10 per cent of Muslims—like other Indians—had enjoyed franchise in that election. When one also considers that only 8 per cent of Muslims (excluding those who shifted within the divided provinces of Bengal and Punjab) went from India to Pakistan, it is clear that the Muslim masses had shown very little interest in the creation of Pakistan.

On Kashmir, there are widely differing perceptions. Indians are convinced that accession to India by the Maharaja in October 1947 and its ratification by the state constituent assembly in May 1954 does not leave any room for doubt about either the legality or the fairness of accession. They accept that a Maharaja should not be allowed to

[4] See Krishna Kumar, *Prejudice and Pride: School Histories of the Freedom Struggle in India and Pakistan*, New Delhi: Viking, 2001.

go against the will of the people. But the people, represented by the Kashmir constituent assembly, had approved the Maharaja's decision. Kashmir's case cannot therefore be compared with those of Hyderabad and Junagadh. Indians believe that the UN should have made Pakistan withdraw from Kashmir in 1948 without a plebiscite, since Pakistan had attacked the state without cause. Indians feel that their 1948 commitment to hold a plebiscite was overtaken by Pakistan's refusal to withdraw troops from the state.

Pakistanis on the other hand believe that Mountbatten did them a grievous injustice in accepting accession, and major powers in failing to enforce the UNSC resolutions on plebiscite. Pakistan's view is that it could not withdraw its forces from the state, as called for in the UN resolutions, because voting would not have been fair in a plebiscite conducted with the state under an Indian administration. Pakistanis are convinced that there was collusion between Delhi and Maharaja Hari Singh, and that Mountbatten under Nehru's influence had turned a Nelson's eye to it. They also believe that the wishes of the Kashmiri people had not been satisfactorily ascertained, and that India achieved the ratification of the accession by the constituent assembly of the state in May 1954 only by incarcerating Sheikh Abdullah the previous August.

Most Indians believe that it was the founding of Pakistan on the basis of religion—implying thereby that Hindus and Muslims cannot live peacefully together—that has led to all the subsequent problems between the two countries, including on account of Kashmir. They believe that Pakistan has no choice but to persist with an anti-Indian stance to justify the rationale for its creation. With Islamic extremism having steadily gained strength in Pakistan, it is seen as inevitable that a democratic secular state like India and a military-controlled denominational state like Pakistan would have difficulty living side by side. Pakistanis see the issue differently. They consider that the two-nation theory was a political argument advanced to ensure that subcontinental Muslims lived in a state where they were not mar-ginalised, just as the one-nation argument of the Congress was meant to achieve a Hindu-dominated India. They hold that India's secular rhetoric, while once convincing, now sounds thin with large gaps developing between rhetoric and policy, and between policy and praxis. They believe that India flaunts secularism abroad while undermining it within India, calling it pseudo-secularism.

There are opposite views about the causes of India–Pakistan hostility. A strongly promoted position in India is that Kashmir is not the cause of the hostility. Indians believe that Pakistan looks at the subcontinent in terms of two religious 'nations', rather than two modern states. It is also believed that Pakistan has no historical or cultural lineage and is, therefore, compelled to define itself against India, from which it was carved out. In support of their contrary view that Kashmir is the only serious dispute between the two countries, Pakistanis point out that other disputes have been settled peacefully. Kutch was settled through arbitration. The land/EEZ boundary dispute pertaining to Sir Creek has not been a cause of serious tension. Even a very high-stake issue like the division of the Indus River System was settled amicably. Siachen is part of the J&K problem. Pakistanis even claim that, except in the case of Kashmir, India and Pakistan share a largely common worldview. The voting records of India and Pakistan in UN forums have been very similar, especially after the end of the Cold War. The positions of the two countries in economic forums like the WTO have also been very close. Pakistanis argue that it is only the Kashmir dispute that is preventing India and Pakistan from cooperating, both regionally and globally.

Indians and Pakistanis carry different understandings of the wars they have fought. Indians regard the 1947–48, 1965 and 1999 wars as the result of deliberate and unjustified aggression on Pakistan's part. Pakistanis regard the 1947–48 war as the consequence of India sending its troops into J&K on the basis of an invalid accession. Few Pakistanis deny that they deliberately started the 1965 war, although some claim that they were left with no choice because of India's refusal to discuss Kashmir. About the 1971 war, both sides accept that it came about because of Pakistan's internal problems. But beyond that they differ. Indians hold they had no choice but to get involved when ten million refugees were pushed into India. Pakistanis insist that India took malicious advantage of its internal difficulties. Few Pakistanis deny that the 1999 Kargil War was the result of a deliberate plan of encroachment, although some argue that it was an operation, like the war of 1965, that was forced upon them by India's stonewalling on Kashmir.

The Simla Agreement of 1972 has also become contentious. India insists that the agreement has superseded the UN resolutions of 1948–53. The essence of the Simla Agreement, as far as Indians are concerned, is the commitment to not violate the LoC and to resolve the Kashmir issue through bilateral discussions. Pakistan accepts the bilateral focus, but argues that if the bilateral track did not work (and it has not worked for over thirty years) then 'other peaceful means', as provided for in the agreement, should be tried. They say that there is no repudiation of the UN resolutions on plebiscite in the agreement. The agreement says that India and Pakistan shall meet to discuss 'a final settlement of Jammu and Kashmir'. Pakistan argues that this proves that India could not contest the existence of the dispute even in Simla. The Simla Agreement is a short document, yet selective quoting has led to very different popular understandings of it.

Pakistan is certainly on the defensive, with no ground to stand on at all about the clause in the Simla Agreement that forbids any inter-ference across the LoC. That is why Pakistan insists on claiming—in the face of total disbelief by everyone including the people of Pakistan themselves—that it extends only moral and diplomatic support to the 'freedom fighters' of that state. During arguments some claim that Pakistan's breach on this count should be set against India's breach in not accepting that there is a dispute and in not discussing the issue purposefully for three decades. Some argue, in a similarly dubious way, that Pakistan's pretence of not being responsible for cross-border terrorism falls into the same category as the Indian claim that the arrest of Sheikh Abdullah in 1953 was a decision taken in J&K. But for that arrest, they say, India would not have got the J&K constituent assembly to ratify accession.

With hindsight, the view articulated in India is that it could have, and should have, driven a harder bargain in Simla, insisting on con-verting the ceasefire line not into a line of control but into an agreed border. This is considered a fanciful notion in Pakistan. Against India's card of the territory it had captured, Pakistanis feel they had the card of non-recognition by the US, China and other rich Islamic countries for Bangladesh's desperate need for aid. They discount the 93,000 prisoners India was holding, arguing that India could not have held on to them given the global norms on POW repatriation. They contend that if Bhutto had conceded more in Simla he would have been re-placed by a general—an unwelcome outcome for India

In both countries there are feelings that third parties have worked to the advantage of the opponent. Indians believe that before 1947 Britain had tried to weaken the Congress-led freedom struggle using the Muslim League as a favoured counterweight. Pakistanis believe that the British were biased against Muslims after the 1857 uprising. They point out that, in contrast to the many regiments in the British Indian Army which consisted of only Hindus, there was never one that was constituted of only Muslims. Indians believe that it was the huge partisanship shown in the UNSC by the US and the UK in favour of Pakistan that helped to keep the Kashmir issue alive after the 1947–48 war. Pakistanis believe that the US and the UK never exerted the pressure they should have on India to abide by its initial commitment to plebiscite.

Just as there is a wide divergence between the perspectives of India and Pakistan, there is also one between those of India and the Kashmiri discontented. Indians believe that, far from exploiting the Kashmiris, India has bent over backward trying to help them. An example is the fact that in 2001–02 the state of J&K, with 1 per cent of India's population, got from the Union Government Rs 45.77 billion as financial assistance, which was as much as 10 per cent of the total assistance provided to states by the centre. And, 90 per cent of the assistance provided to J&K has been in the form of grants. The discontented in Kashmir see the matter differently. They argue that little of the money has reached the masses in the state who remain very poor even by Indian standards. Moreover, in their view, the basic issue is not economic but political. They claim that Delhi 'used' Abdullah when it was under pressure during 1947–53 and then jailed him to avoid fulfilling its obligations under the 1952 Delhi Agreement.

The disaffected regard as illegitimate all decisions taken by the state constituent assembly to whittle down autonomy after Abdullah's arrest, on the ground that they were achieved by corrupting men like Bakshi and Sadiq. The 1975 agreement that brought Abdullah back to power had provided for a review of post-1953 changes, but it was never done. The 1975 agreement, in their view, was evaded the way the 1952 one was. Indians see the political issue differently. They feel that with Pakistan posing a serious security threat autonomy is not a realistic aim to pursue. The Kashmiris have been alienated because 'administration' has been neglected, and if improved, the situation could be turned round.

There is wide difference of opinion about the violence that started in 1989 and has been going on since then. Indians feel that there was no justification for violence since democratic remedies are available in India to deal with grievances and dissatisfaction. More to the point, there would have been no militancy in the state had Pakistan not

trained and armed JKLF and HM fighters during 1988–92, and thereafter sent in large numbers of non-Kashmiri militants into the state.
The madrassa and mosque building boom that started in the state in
the late 1970s has played a large part in fostering disaffection. Most
importantly, the kind of violence that Pakistan is carrying out in the
state—targeting civilians more than security forces—is pure terrorism.
Pakistanis see the issue differently. They argue that there was severe
pre-existing disaffection in the state and that it was their duty to help
subjugated fellow Muslims who, moreover, according to their reading
are also their countrymen. The Kashmiris feel that 1989 was essentially
an internal development in the state brought about by gross misrule
and political chicanery, although few of them would deny that it was
the involvement of Pakistan that has kept the contest going.

India and Pakistan read the ground realities differently. Indians
generally believe that once Pakistan's terrorist effort is defeated India
should be able to win the goodwill of the Kashmiris through improved
governance and stepped-up economic assistance. Many Pakistanis
believe that with the arousal of Islamic consciousness in the state
since the mid-1970s, the majority of Kashmiris would prefer to join
Pakistan. In reality, this is nothing but wishful thinking. An A.C.
Nielsen opinion poll in September 2002 showed that only 1 per cent
of Kashmiris wanted to join Pakistan. Earlier that year, in May, a
MORI International survey put the figure at 6 per cent. Clearly there
is virtually no support, even today, for taking up the Pakistan option.
There is little support for the independence option either, seen as
politically and economically impractical. Most Kashmiris want to stay
with India, but with much greater control over their affairs and a sharp
reduction in the presence of security forces.

FEELINGS OF INSECURITY

Of all the conflict feeders that operate in the India–Pakistan context,
the one that plays the most direct role is the feeling of insecurity experienced by both sides. Arguably, it is internal insecurity more than
external insecurity that poses the greater problem. Pakistan was born
extraordinarily insecure. Being a seceding state it did not inherit a
colonial infrastructure of state management at the macro level. There

was also its dysfunctional geography—two halves of culturally divided people, separated by 1,600 kilometres of hostile territory. The latter fact led to Pakistan being seen as a candidate for break-up from the beginning, and that actually came to pass within a quarter century. Viewed objectively, the separation of East Pakistan ought to have made Pakistan more cohesive and therefore more confident. But this did not happen, largely for psychological reasons. The puncturing of the idea on which Pakistan was created—unity in Islam—was frightening. The belief that it was Indian machinations that led to the break-up stoked fears that India might try to do it again.

The current Pakistan, in its ethnic and linguistic make up, is no more diverse than India is. But the political and societal consolidation that India has achieved through the integrative powers of democracy and social development has eluded Pakistan. Military domination and social backwardness have been largely responsible for this. Domination by Punjabis—till 1972 as a minority of 28 per cent and later as a majority of 58 per cent—through the control of military and bureaucratic levers has not helped. The injection of a large number of Urdu and Gujarati speaking Mohajirs (refugees), constituting as they do nearly a tenth of the population, has also been a destabilising factor. In Karachi, the economic hub of Pakistan, Mohajirs make up over half the population while native Sindhis account for less than a tenth. The drugs and guns culture brought in by the Afghan involvement has created more stress. All these have combined to create a very adverse internal security situation, and the spectre of fragmentation continues to haunt the country.[5]

The internal security situation, at the fundamental level, is far better in India. Democracy and development have knit the country together politically and economically, and a supra-regional sense of, and pride in, being an Indian has become very strong. Yet, old fears linger. The shock of the country being partitioned has left deep scars, and the ghost of Muslim separatism is far from exorcised from many minds. As a consequence, Kashmir is seen largely as a Muslim problem. This and the persistence of minor insurgencies in some other parts of the country—tribal ones in the northeast and Maoist ones elsewhere—have ensured that internal threats are treated very seriously and the

[5] See Christophe Jaffrelot, ed., *Pakistan: Nationalism without a Nation*, New York: Zed Books, 2001.

suggestions for their non-coercive solution very warily. This mindset has had a deep impact on the country's approach to J&K.

Pakistan is also very anxious about external security. It is deeply insecure about India and only a little less so about Afghanistan. The non-recognition of the Durand Line border by Afghanistan, the relative inaccessibility of the border region, and the difficult-to-control Pashtun tribes living on both sides of the border have all contributed to Pakistani fears about its western border. The fear of India to the east is very strong and has grown considerably after 1971. Pakistan feels that India is determined to dominate the smaller countries in the subcontinent and wants to claim the lost political and security hegemony of the British Raj. A noted observer of the South Asian region has commented that 'Pakistanis see themselves overpowered and overwhelmed by a militant India, increasingly Hindu and extremist, a state dominated by religious considerations and a sense of missionary zeal to extend Indian influence to the furthest reaches of South Asia and neighbouring areas'.[6]

Pakistan has deep military apprehensions. India has always had a conventional military advantage, except during 1956–63 when there was a degree of parity because of US military aid. India's accelerated build-up from 1973 has continuously widened its margin of superiority, despite the substantial aid Pakistan got from the US during 1981–88. The acquisition of nuclear weapons has given Pakistan a degree of comfort from 1990. But Pakistan knows that India can develop a range of conventional options against it without Pakistan being able to threaten plausible nuclear retaliation. This deep fear of India has led Pakistan—dominated as its security imagination is almost entirely by military logic—to the high-risk strategy of keeping India militarily preoccupied. The clandestine support provided to the Sikh insurgency in Indian Punjab during 1979–93, and the more overt involvement in J&K from 1988 have stemmed from this frame of mind. So has the less conspicuous aid provided to insurgent groups in the northeast through Bangladesh and Nepal. Looking as it always does through a military prism, Pakistan tends to highlight its military successes (such as tying down a third of India's infantry and para-military forces in J&K) and make light of the huge economic and diplomatic penalties

---

[6] Stephen P. Cohen, 'Causes of Conflict and Conditions of Peace in South Asia', in Roger E. Kanet, ed., *Resolving Regional Conflict*, Urbana: University of Illinois Press, 1998, p. 110.

it has had to pay. Such a blinkered approach also leads it to politico-military bungles like the Kargil War.

The kind of offensive-defence logic that underpins Pakistan's security strategy against India has led it—and India—to confront the difficult dynamics of 'Security Dilemma'. The core idea of Security Dilemma is that the effort of one side to increase its security would inevitably invite a response, and this would pave the way to a spiralling competition that is unlikely to improve the security of either side and may also lead to war.[7] Security Dilemma essentially springs from a perception of threat and the need to respond. Threat is generally perceived as a composite of power, offensive capability, aggressiveness and nearness.[8] From Pakistan's point of view, all four components are present in the threat posed by India. From the Indian point of view, all except (superior) power are present in that projected by Pakistan.

Some of the characteristics of security dilemma, notably present in the India–Pakistan situation, include mutual distrust, action-response progression, unreined military competition and military domination of security thinking. The drive to establish effective deterrence has always been a part of addressing the security dilemma. Deterrence in turn hinges on capability as well as resolve. Pakistan, lagging in capability, has always tried to show that its resolve is higher. But on Kashmir, Indian motivation is no less as the violent struggle in J&K for the past fifteen years—with Indian military and para-military strength in the state tripling in the process—shows. As the logic of security dilemma predicts, Pakistan's raising the ante—deadlier attacks, widening of the operations zone and enlargement of the scope of operations as in Kargil—has only lead to counter-escalation by India. The ten-month-long Operation Parakram was a vivid example.

Asymmetry in power configuration has aggravated the security dilemma. While India enjoys substantial superiority in overall military

---

[7] The concept of Security Dilemma was first developed by John H. Herz in 'Idealist Internationalism and the Security Dilemma', *World Politics*, Vol. 2, No. 2, January 1950, pp. 157–80. For the further development of the idea see Robert Jervis, 'Co-operation Under the Security Dilemma', *World Politics*, Vol. 30, No. 2, January 1978, pp. 167–214, and Charles L. Glaser, 'The Security Dilemma Revisited', *World Politics*, Vol. 50, No. 2, October 1997, pp. 171–201.

[8] Stephen M. Walt, *The Origins of Alliances*, Ithaca, NY: Cornell University Press, 1987, pp. 21–34, 262–85.

power, in the specific context of J&K Pakistan enjoys some advantages such as a section of the population in the state being discontented, a border that is difficult to seal, short supply lines, terrain and climate that are advantageous to insurgents, and highly motivated jihadis. When military capabilities are structured differently in this manner, it becomes difficult to evaluate how they would play out in the long term. The nuclear capability of the two sides has worsened matters by adding to uncertainty. Since neither side has a clear idea of the capability of the other side's nuclear forces and the doctrine governing it, there is large scope for misjudgement and the adoption of dangerous strategies based on the extremes of wishful thinking and worst-case assumption.

Exploitation of Religion

Both India–Pakistan hostility and the discontent in J&K have been fuelled by the political use of religion. With vast reservoirs of people prone to religious appeal present in both countries, it is not difficult to make use of religion instrumentally. During Zulfiqar Bhutto's rule in the mid-1970s, Pakistan declared Ahmediyas heretical, banned alcohol and made Friday the weekly holiday. The pace of Islamisation increased when Zia took over and the involvement in Afghanistan began. Hudud, the Islamic criminal law, was introduced in 1979. The promotion of militant Islam through madrassas and training camps was a corner-stone of the US–Saudi–Pakistani campaign plan in Afghanistan. As a result, while the nine-year campaign cleared the Soviets, it left behind a damaging fundamentalist legacy in Pakistan. Matters did not improve even after the Soviets left, because active Pakistani involvement in Afghanistan continued till September 2001. While the Islamists created huge problems within Pakistan—by erecting barriers of dogma against modernity and fuelling intra-Islam sectarian fighting—they also provided Pakistan with a potent weapon against India in Kashmir. From about 1993 Islamic militants became the main cadres fighting in J&K.

The nurturing of Islamists for military purpose in Afghanistan and Kashmir inevitably had a big domestic impact. The political parties that were in power in Pakistan during 1988–99 (Nawaz Sharif's PML[N] and Benazir Bhutto's PPP) had little choice but to enlist Islamist support. The Islamic parties—Jamaat-e-Islami (JI), Jamiat Ulema-e-Islami, and Jamiat Ulema-e-Pakistan being the major ones—had little electoral appeal themselves. They never won more than 5 per cent of the votes in any national election till they all combined to form the MMA for the 2002 elections. Even then, and despite the strong anti-US and Islamist feelings generated by the war in Afghanistan, they could win only 8 per cent of the national vote, much of it in backward NWFP and Baluchistan. While their electoral power is limited, the Islamists have significant other leverage. They have committed cadres with considerable disruptive potential; they have good support among the lower-middle classes; and most important, they have a strong link with the army, which needs them for its semi-war in Kashmir and for possible resumed action in Afghanistan.

In India, the use of religion for political purpose started to gain ground in the 1980s when the BJP began to be seen as a good alternative to the declining Congress. The rise of the BJP inevitably strengthened its Hindutwa (Hindu ethos) ideology at the expense of composite nationalism that had defined India for many decades. The promotion of Hindutwa as a means to unite Hindus, heterogeneous in terms of caste and language, had a natural nationalist appeal to many of the elite and the middle class. There is wide agreement on the need for the cultural, though not necessarily religious, primacy of Hinduism.

There are important features that distinguish Islamism in Pakistan from Hindutwa in India. Islamism has a strong religious content that leads to doctrinal differences and sectarianism. Hindutwa, because of Hinduism's lack of dogma, is a big tent under which many ways of thinking can gather. As a result, Hindutwa proponents are broadly unified, unlike their Islamist counterparts in Pakistan. While this is a plus point for India, there is another that is negative. Islamism in Pakistan is directed primarily against outsiders. Hindus make for only about 3 per cent of the Pakistani population and are not seen to pose any internal threat. To Pakistanis, the Hindu threat is wholly external. It is not so in India, where many Hindus see Muslims as a potential internal threat. The latter not only form a widely distributed 14 per cent of the total population but also constitute a majority in the disaffected J&K.

Pakistan's Political System

If Pakistan had been a stable democracy, it is likely that the aspirations of the Pakistani masses for peace and development would have been better reflected in the country's dealings with India. In turn, India would have approached the problem more positively than it has been doing. There are many reasons, historical and social, for the failure of democracy to take root in Pakistan. It is an unhelpful oversimplification to think, as many Indians do, that the failure is entirely attributable to the political ambition of the country's army. The fact that the masses in Pakistan, and not the small English-speaking class, are as much disillusioned with the country's politicians as with the army is worth thinking about.

Pakistan came into existence in circumstances unpropitious for democratic rule. Since the Muslim League had no mass base in Pakistan (its base was in areas that remained with India), Jinnah decided to become Governor General exercising the viceregal powers of the Government of India Act 1935, rather than Prime Minister accountable to parliament. The 1935 Act governed Pakistan till March 1956. Jinnah's death in September 1948 and Liaquat Ali Khan's in October 1951 robbed the League of even the little effectiveness it had. Bureaucrats now slotted in at the top. Ghulam Mohammad became Governor General in October 1951 and was succeeded by Iskander Mirza in August 1955. The first Constituent Assembly was dismissed in October 1954 to prevent a strong Prime Minister emerging, which in its wake would have enhanced the political clout of East Pakistan. The second Constituent Assembly also produced a Parliamentary Constitution. To forestall the general election scheduled under it, Iskander Mirza abrogated it in October 1958 and took power, only to find it snatched from him by General Ayub Khan. To prevent universal franchise weakening the army-bureaucratic power system, Ayub Khan created a manageable electoral college of basic democrats in October 1959, and followed it up with a Presidential Constitution in June 1962.

This constitution lasted seven years, till General Yahya Khan suspended it in 1969. The third constitution, drafted under Bhutto's direction, came into force in August 1973 creating a parliamentary government. Zia suspended it in July 1977, and when he resurrected it in December 1985 it had been stripped of its defining feature of parliamentary supremacy. The 1973 constitution is now thirty years old and counting, but perverting amendments have made it a parody. The democratic content of Pakistan's governance can be gauged from the fact that in the fifty-six years of its existence, extra-parliamentary power to dismiss the Prime Minister and dissolve parliament has been absent for only six years—during 1973–77 and 1997–99.

The areas that constitute Pakistan have traditionally been border areas of India, and governed by the British in a more authoritarian style than other parts. The freedom struggle did not arouse popular consciousness here. The political party of consequence in Punjab was the landlord-dominated Unionist Party in league with the British. Things changed little after independence. Land reform programmes initiated by Ayub Khan in 1959 and Bhutto in 1972 were gimmicks designed to buy support for their regimes. Feudal landlords continued to dominate the countryside, especially the agricultural heartlands of southern Punjab and Sindh. A narrow elite of landlords, industrialists, traders, bureaucrats and the military, aided by an environment of feudal relationships and bureaucratic dominance, controlled politics and the economy.

The first eleven years of the country's life (1947–58) saw not only seven Prime Ministers but also the fragmentation of the Muslim League. No new serious political party rose in West Pakistan till Bhutto formed the PPP in 1967. Bhutto's 1972–77 rule was a disaster for democracy. It was his complete intolerance for democratic opposition that led to the military takeover of 1977. It was eleven years before political parties could come to power again. By then there were two relatively balanced parties—the PPP under Benazir Bhutto and the PML (N) under Nawaz Sharif. Sharif had largely been built up by the army as a counterweight to the PPP. Article 58-2B of the 1973 constitution brought in by Zia made the Prime Minister directly beholden to the President and indirectly to the Army Chief. When Sharif was elected in 1997 with a huge majority, he had the article repealed. This saved him from being dismissed constitutionally. Instead, he was ousted by a military coup in October 1999, giving validity to the cynical view that Article 58-2B was a necessary safety valve against military intervention.

Democratic leaders of Pakistan have consistently failed to project legitimacy. Not once during the four times that the Army seized power (Ayub in 1958, Yahya in 1969, Zia in 1977 and Musharraf in 1999) or the four times that Prime Ministers were dismissed by the President (Junejo in 1988, Benazir Bhutto in 1990, Sharif in 1993 and Bhutto again in 1996), was there serious popular protest. Political leaders are not considered worth standing up for. Every political leader since 1972 has tried to establish the dominant party model and fortify personal position by unfair means. None of them sought to create a fair, workable government–opposition relationship or to stabilise the processes and norms of parliamentary democracy.

Low legitimacy of political parties is accompanied by low effectiveness. If economic growth is taken as an indicator, it was 3.4 per cent during the pre-military rule years (1947–58), 5.9 per cent during the Ayub period (1958–69), 4.3 per cent during the Bhutto period (1972–77), 6.5 per cent during the Zia period (1977–88), 3.4 per cent during the Benazir–Nawaz alternations (1989–99) and 3.6 per cent during the first four Musharraf years (2000–2003). There were extraneous reasons for the better economic performance during military rule (exploitation of East Pakistan by Ayub, and the Gulf Boom and the Afghan War helping Zia), but these do not matter to the masses. The bottom line is that political leaders in Pakistan have consistently lacked both legitimacy and effectiveness, and have been unable to generate popular support to keep the Army at bay.

THE PAKISTAN ARMY

The Pakistan Army constitutes the most serious obstacle today in the way of India and Pakistan settling their differences.[9] Pakistan's mainstream political parties have become much less anti-India than they once were because of the dual realisation that fighting India was futile and that it helped the army domestically. But the army's anti-Indian focus has remained unaltered—to the detriment of the country's as well as its own long-term corporate interests.

What is one to make of the Army's political future? Can a popular leader tame it? Can external pressure weaken it? Neither history nor a reading of the current situation can offer confident answers. But

---

[9] For a very biased view of India presented to its officers by the Pakistan Army establishment, see Lieutenant Colonel Javed Hassan, *India: A Study in Profile*, Rawalpindi: Army Press, 1990.

some conclusions that tangentially address these questions can be reasonably drawn. One, there is considerable fear and distrust of India among the masses that buttresses the army's political position. The Pakistani masses believe that Pakistan cannot survive if the Army is weakened. Two, while the broad masses do not believe that the Army is capable of governing Pakistan well, they do not think that political parties can do it better. Three, the Army, if it continues to wield direct political power, will become unpopular because it is no more capable of putting the country on a satisfactory economic growth path than are political parties. The Army knows this and therefore prefers to operate from the wings to the extent possible.

The organisational superiority of the Army, relative to other elite groups, is its big strength. Zulfiqar Bhutto and Nawaz Sharif both tried the dual tracks of cultivating and splitting the Army without success.[10] Zia and Musharraf, carefully picked by Bhutto and Sharif, did neither master any good. During the Zia years, corps commanders and a few other top officers became a key collective political decision-making body and continue to be so.[11] The Army is not a narrowly-based Punjabi organisation. Punjabis, with a population share of 58 per cent, provide about 65 per cent of officers and about 70 per cent of men. Pathans, with a share of 16 per cent, provide 22 per cent of officers and 25 per cent of men. Mohajirs are present close to their population share at the level of officers. The Salt Range and Potwar regions of Northern Punjab and the adjoining districts of NWFP still provide a disproportionate share of soldiers, but at the officer level the regional and language make up is more diverse.[12]

When the military first took power in Pakistan, it was more secular than the political and bureaucratic classes. American influence from 1954 furthered earlier secular traditions inherited from the British. It was only in Ayub Khan's 1962 constitution that the word 'Islamic'

---

[10] Bhutto tried to use Tikka Khan whom he appointed chief after failing with a three-month experiment with Gul Hassan Khan. Sharif tried it with his failed attempt to appoint Khwaja Ziauddin the chief and his earlier effort to wean away officers like Quetta corps commander Tariq Pervez.

[11] For the army's involvement in running the civil administration, see Hasan-Askari Rizvi, *Military, State and Society in Pakistan,* London: Macmillan, 2000, and General K.M. Arif, *Khaki Shadows: Pakistan Army 1947–97,* Karachi: Oxford University Press, 2001.

[12] For good books on the Pakistan Army, see Stephen Philip Cohen, *The Pakistan Army,* revised edn., Karachi: Oxford University Press, 1998 and Brian Cloughley, *A History of the Pakistan Army,* Karachi: Oxford University Press, 1998.

was dropped from the country's name. (It had to be reinstated the following year under political pressure.) When links with the US military frayed and those with the Gulf countries enlarged, the emphasis on Islam grew. Islamic influence rose sharply during the Zia years, as he openly encouraged the pietistic, yet fundamentalist, Tablighi Jamaat. Though not encouraged, more dangerous types of Islamic organisations also made inroads into the forces. The Jamaat-e-Islami was involved in the September 1995 coup attempt—the so-called 'Zia generation' of Islamist officers is indeed a fact.[13]

During the Ayub years the military largely kept away from civil administration. This changed during the Yahya period, and even more so during the Zia years. This pattern has continued under Musharraf. The involvement of the military in civil affairs has hurt its professional competence.[14] The problem has worsened over time. Recognising that the true seat of power is the Army Chief's office in Rawalpindi and not the President's in Islamabad, all military presidents after Ayub—Yahya, Zia and Musharraf—have hung on to the Army Chief's post. Their efforts to separate military and civil responsibilities at the centre, usually by having a Vice or Deputy Chief run the Army and a Principal Staff Officer to the President coordinate civil affairs, has not worked satisfactorily. Nor has the provincial level effort to separate functions between governors and corps commanders.

Ruling the country has never been easy for the Army. Ayub in 1969 and Yahya in 1971 had to relinquish power ignominiously. Even Zia's position was becoming untenable when death intervened in 1988. The army has also led the country to three disastrous wars. The 1965 war was partly the result of the Army's effort to consolidate its political hold through military success, the 1971 war the result of making an utter mess of national politics, and the 1999 Kargil war the result of poor politico-military judgement. Yet, the Army as an institution has not come under popular attack. Even in 1971 it was the 'drunken

---

[13] The casualties of the post 9/11 Islamist cleansing fall into this category—General Muhammad Aziz Khan, now moved to the decorative job of Chairman Joint Chiefs of Staff, Lieutenant General Muzaffar Usman, Deputy Chief of Army Staff till then, and Lieutenant General Mahmood Ahmed, Chief of ISI till then, among others.

[14] The penalty the military has paid for this is well captured by Lt. Gen. Gul Hassan Khan, who was Director of Military Operations during the 1965 war, Chief of General Staff during the 1971 war and briefly Army Chief in 1972. See Gul Hassan Khan, *Memoirs of Lieutenant General Gul Hassan Khan*, Karachi: Oxford University Press, 1993.

Yahya and his incompetent cronies' who were pilloried, not the Army as a whole.

INDIFFERENCE TO COSTS

A big driver of the conflict is the indifference shown in both countries to the costs being incurred. The fighting that has gone on so far has not directly affected most people in either country. The 1947–48 and 1999 wars, and the low-intensity fighting going on since 1989, have all been confined to the state of J&K, well away from centres of population and economic activity. Even the general wars of 1965 and 1971 did not cause much suffering, lasting as they did three and two weeks respectively, with fighting confined to combat and combat support areas. In Pakistan, which has suffered precipitous economic decline since 1990 on top of serious social problems beginning in 1980, there is a growing realisation—at least within the middle class—that the conflict with India is not cost-free.[15] India doesn't see it this way because, relative to Pakistan, it has done quite well in the areas of economic and human development during the last two decades.

In both countries no serious causal relationship is recognised, at both the policy and media levels, between economic performance and the Kashmir problem, or for that matter between external and internal turbulence. The discourse on political economy is confined to purely economic issues and not related to those of national security, socio-political stability and human development. The politico-social context of economic development is acknowledged perfunctorily, but never analysed or discussed seriously. There is no recognition that hostility and violence, constantly in the headlines, have served to distract influential public opinion and distort policy thinking.

Pakistan has been by far the greater sufferer. Pragmatic economic policies, the exploitation of East Pakistan till 1971, and the spillover of Muslim West Asia's affluence from 1974 had all helped Pakistan to maintain an economic growth rate averaging 2 percentage points above India's during 1960–80. This lead shrank in the 1980s, and from

---

[15] See Major General Mahmud Ali Durrani, *India and Pakistan: The Costs of Conflict and the Benefits of Peace*, Karachi: Oxford University Press, 2001.

1992 India's growth rate has been consistently higher. This, plus Pakistan's higher population growth rate, led to India's per capita GDP overtaking Pakistan's in 2002—for the first time since the early 1950s. In purchasing power parity terms, India's per capita GDP had overtaken Pakistan's three years earlier. The basics of Pakistan's economy have never been solid, with growth inconsistent and socially skewed. The best years of the economy—the 1960s—were characterised by the exploitation of the peasantry within a feudal framework. Savings and investment rates have remained consistently low—averaging about three-fifths of India's. Poverty percentages have steadily worsened, skidding from 18 in 1988 to 32 in 1999.[16] Pakistan has been left at the post in today's knowledge-dominated world. The information technology boom in software and IT enabled services that has taken India by storm and changed its global image has caused barely a ripple in Pakistan.

Pakistan is badly hit by high defence expenditure. Defence spending, as a percentage of GDP, was 6.4 in the 1950s, 6.5 in the 1960s, 6.2 in the 1970s, 6.6 in the 1980s, and 5.5 per cent in the 1990s, with a peak of 7.5 in 1971–72 and a nadir of 4.7 in 1962–63. These figures, calculated from Pakistan's annual Economic Surveys, substantially understate the real expenditure. (To a lesser extent, this is so in India too.) The actual defence burden borne by the Pakistan economy, averaged through the past half century, has been nearly 10 per cent of GDP. Yet, despite bearing a GDP-share defence burden two-and-a half times India's, Pakistan has fallen consistently behind in terms of combat capability. This is not surprising considering that India's economy is now more than seven times that of Pakistan's, and the size advantage is continuously growing. A qualitative military edge now magnifies the quantitative one that India has always had over Pakistan.

The conflict has taken its economic toll on India too. But since this has largely been in terms of opportunity costs, there is less recognition of the fact. There is little understanding that the country is not doing as well as it could, and even less of the link between conflict pursuit

---

[16] For good presentations of the travails of Pakistan's economy in recent decades, see Ishrat Hussain, *Pakistan: The Economy of an Elitist State*, Karachi: Oxford University Press, 1999; Pervez Hasan: *Pakistan's Economy at the Crossroads*, Karachi: Oxford University Press, 1998; Omar Noman, *Economic and Social Progress in Pakistan: Why Pakistan did not become a Tiger*, Karachi: Oxford University Press, 1997; and Sharukh Rafi Khan, *Fifty Years of Pakistan's Economy: Traditional Issues and New Concerns*, Karachi: Oxford University Press, 1997.

and economic penalty. The fact that 1992–2004 has been India's best economic period ever (and Pakistan's worst ever), the continuous growth of food stocks and foreign exchange reserves, and the great IT boom have all contributed to a buoyant popular mood. The darker side of the economy has gone largely unnoticed. The high 1992–96 growth rate of 6.9 per cent has been followed by a less impressive 4.9 per cent during 1996–2002, although there was a strong upward trend in 2003. Much of the growth has come from a few high-productivity segments in the services sector. Agricultural, infrastructural and manufacturing sectors, with some exceptions, have not shown much dynamism. Employment generation has been poor and fiscal deficit has stayed high. More worryingly, rural–urban and inter-regional fissures have widened, and there has been a growing gap between the expectations raised and the results achieved.

Pakistan has suffered in the human development field too. At independence, the percentages of literate in both countries were about the same. In 2001, it was 47 in Pakistan and 65 in India. The gap in female literacy is even wider. Pakistan has a major problem with its population growth rate. It is 1.4 times India's and 1.2 times Bangladesh's. Pakistan's expenditure on defence has been nearly 150 per cent of its combined spending on health and education, compared to 60 per cent in India and 15 per cent in Western Europe. Pakistan's growing handicap relative to India in basic education, and still worse in higher education is now playing out in terms of technical and managerial inferiority, impacting on its economy and even on its military capability. Pakistan had a historic advantage over India in health indicators. These too have now turned adverse.

Both Pakistan and India have borne heavy costs in terms of social instability. In Pakistan, the constant stress on Islamic identity (partly to keep alive its claim for 'Islamic' Kashmir) has made the ground fertile for extremist Islam. The emphasis on Islam has inevitably led to the exposure of its many sectarian divides. The fanatic Sunni group, Sipah-e-Sahiba, killed over 3,600 Shias during the 1990s and continues to kill. The lethal mix of small arms and drug money has boosted crime throughout the country. Pakistan's economy has been hurt more than India's by internal violence because most of it is taking place in urban areas with the epicentre in Karachi, the business capital of the country. Pakistan cannot deal effectively with floating guns and sectarian fighting so long as it wants Sunni radicals to fight in Kashmir.

India too has paid a big social price—the rise of militant communalism. The animus stemming from partition massacres had barely begun to die down when the wars of 1965 and 1971 came, seriously vitiating the communal atmosphere. Communal flare-ups began to mount, climbing higher in the 1980s and 1990s. Indian Muslims have remained remarkably loyal to the country because of India's secular character. But if communalism continues to gather steam and Muslim feelings of being targeted as a community increase, India runs the risk of individuals within the community falling prey to roused emotions and outside machinations. Spurred by India–Pakistan hostility, India is frittering away the invaluable social capital it had accumulated over half a century. The shielding of internal Hindu–Muslim relations from the poison of India–Pakistan enmity that India had managed in the past is threatening to get undone.

Both Pakistan and India have paid a big price in the external field. Pakistan is widely seen as fanatical, conflict-ridden and aggressive, and out of step with global trends and concerns. Its effort to quarantine its activities in Kashmir from international revulsion against terrorism has failed. It was one thing for Pakistan to embrace Islamic radicalism in the 1980s with US support and quite another to persist with it today. India too is paying a cost. Its tolerant, pluralist image acquired during the first half century of freedom is getting eroded. After what happened in Gujarat in early 2002, Hindu violence is no longer being seen abroad as uncharacteristic aberrations. India should ponder over a senior US official's statement that 'It is simply a fact of life that India will not realise its immense potential on the global stage until its relationship with Pakistan is normalised .... The festering conflict with Pakistan distracts India from its larger ambitions, helps create an environment that scares off capital and absorbs valuable resources.'[17]

The hostility between India and Pakistan is the rock on which all efforts to promote cooperation in South Asia have foundered. Economic cooperation within ASEAN could only begin when Indonesia, Malaysia, Singapore and the Philippines put away their political differences. In Western Europe it was the security cooperation provided by NATO that made possible the remarkable economic cooperation that led to the European Union and the Euro. Geographically and culturally, few regions are better suited for close economic

---

[17] Richard N. Hass, Director of Policy Planning Staff, US State Department, in Hyderabad on 7 January 2003.

interaction than South Asia. India–Pakistan hostility has not only prevented this becoming possible but has also given smaller countries opportunities to take advantage. India's Foreign Secretary, Kanwal Sibal, said at the French Institute of International Relations on 17 December 2002: 'India is a country wounded by terrorism. Virtually all our neighbours, by choice or default, by acts of commission or omission, compulsions of geography and terrain, have been or are involved in receiving, sheltering, overlooking or tolerating terrorist activities from their soil directed against India.'

Pakistanis and Indians watch happenings in China, but in a detached manner. The outstanding economic progress China has made from 1979, using the foundation of human and social development achieved in the three preceding decades, is talked about but rarely analysed with seriousness. The following figures give an indication of the huge gap that has developed between China and the two countries:[18]

Human Development Indicators	India	Pakistan	China
Life Expectancy 2001	63	63	70
Under-5 Mortality Rate 2001	93	109	39
Youth Literacy Rate Male (15–24)	80	72	99
Youth Literacy Rate Female (15–24)	66	43	97
Population Growth Rate (1980–2001)	1.9	2.6	1.2
Population Growth Projected Rate (2001–15)	1.2	2.2	0.6

Economic Development Indicators	India	Pakistan	China
Per Capita GNP 2001 in $	460	420	890
Per Capita GNP (PPP) 2001 in $	2,820	1,860	3,950
GDP Growth Rate 1990–2001	5.9	3.7	10.0
FDI 2001 in $ bn	3.4	0.4	44.2
Defence Exp/GDP percentage (2001)	2.5	4.5	2.3

Both sets of indicators, human development and economic development, ought to be of deep concern to India, and even more to Pakistan. In the realm of human development, India and Pakistan were at par with China in 1950, but by 1975 the latter had gone vastly ahead. In the economic field China was marginally behind India and well behind Pakistan as late as 1978. Now it is notably ahead of India and far ahead of Pakistan. During the two decades from 1981 to 2001, while

[18] From World Bank, *World Development Indicators 2003*.

India had averaged a growth rate of 5.6 per cent and Pakistan 5 per cent, China had averaged 9.8 per cent. If present trends continue (and also taking into account China's faster-falling population growth rate), China's per capita income could become about three times India's and four times Pakistan's by 2015. It is more than a coincidence that after its border war with Vietnam in 1979—the year China's economy took off—China has remained uninvolved in any fighting inside or outside the country.

HARDENED PERSPECTIVES

The long conflict has hardened (and fossilised) views on both sides. In India, the general assessment is that since the fundamentals of power are in India's favour, the important thing is to hang tough and wait for the inevitable acknowledgement by Pakistan of India's unassailable superiority. In Pakistan, the dominant strategic belief is that making peace on India's terms will fatally weaken the country, and that regardless of India's growing superiority it is possible to manage the conflict. This expectation of indefinite conflict has strengthened the position of hawks on both sides, enabling them to control the respective frameworks of conflict discourse. Within their frameworks, where debatable assumptions have been reified into certainties, it has become impossible for peace preferences and peace perspectives to emerge, and for alternate voices to become audible.

The strength of the hardline perspectives in both countries is that people of many persuasions have contributed to its creation and sustenance. The stimulus comes from varied sources such as nationalism, religion and militarism. Many hawks are not realists. Emotions, prejudices and perceptual distortions colour their thinking. Very often there is more attitude than ideas in the views they propagate. Yet, because they are influential within national security establishments, their views resonate well. They have established frameworks of analysis, pertinence of facts and causal relationships for the rest of the elite. By exaggerating the opponent's bottom line, they have been able to preempt efforts to find compromise or creative solutions. They have sold the idea that the enemy will respond only to force and coercion, and not to reason. They overplay the opponent's aggressiveness and underplay his capability, thereby exaggerating threat and discounting risk.

In both countries the hawks paint unrealistic scenarios and push for fanciful objectives. In Pakistan, the line is peddled that the asymmetric advantage it enjoys in Kashmir is very significant and that it can keep the state in the grip of militant and counter-militant violence indefinitely. Even after 9/11 and the arousal of global anger against Islamic terrorism, many Pakistani hawks continue to wax optimistic. They think that so long as they can prevent attacks against it, the West would not be too concerned with what happens in Kashmir. They ignore the difficulty of keeping extremists under control and pointed in the right direction, particularly in view of the strong anti-US feelings in Pakistan. They hope that by generating anti-Muslim repression across India they can make India lose social cohesion and international support. Although there is no longer any cultural discounting of Indian military capability, there is a lingering belief that India is socially brittle. Finally, there is the idea that the threat of first use of nuclear weapons will keep India restrained.

Indian hawks, on their part, entertain the idea of converting Pakistan into a pliable state by isolating its Army. During Operation Parakram some of them felt that through a re-enactment of the Falklands War, Musharraf could be turned into a Galtieri. It is believed that if the ante is raised high enough, Pakistan can be made to concede in the face of economic stagnation and global pressure against terrorism. The international community they believe is likely to be slowly convinced that Kashmir is a problem created entirely by Islamists. Some Indian hawks entertain visions of a US–India–Israel alliance against Pakistan, and a few even see India destroying the Pakistan military under cover of yet-to-be developed ballistic missile defence (BMD). At another level, some think that in order to accelerate India's rise through the global power hierarchy it is essential to show 'strength', particularly towards Pakistan. Some believe that the conflict provides good political cover for large defence budgets.

A major problem in both countries is the phenomenon of 'false optimism', prevalent among hawks the world over.[19] The focus is always on one's strengths and the enemy's weaknesses. Each side thinks that the other's long-term costs are greater. In both countries there are some who regard the opponent as a fundamentally weak entity that can be made to unravel. Seductive visions of the opponent's resolve

---

[19] Stephen Van Evera, *Causes of War: Power and Roots of Conflict*, Ithaca: Cornell University Press, 1999.

crumbling hover before them. This false optimism with regard to victory is unsurprisingly accompanied by false pessimism with regard to peace prospects. There is insistence that the two countries are structurally conflicted and that no experiment in policy can change that. It is asserted that the opponent is both unwilling and incapable of compromising—a position that helps to avoid examining one's own willingness to compromise. Hurdles on the peace path are emphasised, creative possibilities deprecated, and suggestions of common ground termed illusory.

Nuclear Danger

T he acquisition of nuclear weapons by India and Pakistan has reduced the risk of a major war breaking out on account of Kashmir, but it has greatly increased the level of destruction that such a war could wreak. In neither country is there much popular awareness of the latter fact. Public consciousness is repressed about the possibility of matters getting to the nuclear level, as well as about the consequences that would stem if that came to pass. In India the public image of nuclear weapons, till recently, has been that of a great-power attribute and not of a military resource. In Pakistan the perception has always been that of a military equaliser. But even there the risks have failed to register because of the faith in the solidity of nuclear deterrence. Because of the mutual confidence (even at leadership levels), that nuclear warheads shall not rain upon them, their acquisition has not done much to moderate risk-taking behaviour.[1]

The fact that no nuclear weapons were used during the half century that the US and the Soviet Union confronted each other has implanted

---

[1] This chapter has drawn on the author's paper 'Coercive Risk-Taking in Nuclear South Asia', published by Centre for International Security and Co-operation, Stanford University, 2003.

a somewhat simplistic faith in nuclear deterrence in subcontinental minds. There is little recognition of the very different manner in which the South Asian nuclear arsenals are structured, managed and operated compared to those of the accepted nuclear powers. The opacity of the two arsenals, their relatively low safety and security cover, and the absence of nuclear CBMs have all made nuclear risks in South Asia—inadvertent and deliberate—higher than in the case of Cold War adversaries. This, and a penchant for coercive risk-taking, have added significantly to the dangers posed by the Kashmir conflict. In this chapter the structure of the two arsenals, the way they are managed, the implications of their opacity, the asymmetric nuclear strategies of the two sides, the risks that are being run, and the possible consequences of coercive risk-taking in J&K are examined.

NUCLEAR ARSENALS

Pakistan started its nuclear weapons effort in earnest in 1972. Through a well-structured espionage programme in Western Europe and help from China, it succeeded in producing deliverable nuclear weapons, without testing, by 1990. India had a broad-based programme going back to 1948. It could have exploded a bomb by the late 1960s, but concern for international reaction delayed an explosive test till 1974. Even that test was not followed up with a focused bomb effort. The weapons programme accelerated in the late 1980s, but India acquired operational nuclear capability only after Pakistan had attained it. India's nuclear search has always had multiple objectives, and deterring Pakistan is only one of them. In 1974, India's objective was to demonstrate technological capability and latent great-power potential. This later evolved to a search for strategic autonomy and achievement of strategic parity with China. India's decision to test in 1998 was largely driven by the latter two objectives. Pakistan's nuclear effort in contrast has had a unifocal, sustained purpose—to deter India from using its superior conventional capability.

Pakistan went from aircraft to missiles much faster than India. It was lucky to have a proliferation-indifferent friend in China and a barter-seeking one in North Korea. The recently confirmed nuclear enrichment technology transfer from Khan Research Laboratories (KRL) in Pakistan to the latter country was a quid pro quo for the supply of

medium-range missiles, later produced in KRL as Ghauri. Pakistan
knew that improving Indian air defence—such as is now being achieved
with the Phalcon airborne early warning system and large numbers
of sophisticated interceptors—would make it difficult for Pakistan's
ageing F-16-As to penetrate it. India is more confident of the penetration capability of its aircraft and therefore has been less anxious to
shift to missiles.

India's US-directed effort to stop Pakistan's bomb programme failed
because of the decade-long (1979–88) strategic window open to the
latter on account of the Soviet presence in Afghanistan. An Indian
preventive air strike on Pakistan's nuclear facilities during this period
was not possible for both political and military reasons.[2] Some have
argued that if India were keen that Pakistan should not become a
nuclear power, it should not have tested in 1998 as that enabled Pakistan to test too. This view does not take into account the fact that, in
military terms, the testing did not add much to the nuclear weapons
capability that Pakistan had had for nearly a decade, although in
political terms it no doubt did. Besides, notwithstanding the gain the
chain of events would confer on Pakistan, India had to test to ensure
that the Comprehensive Test Ban Treaty (CTBT), underpinned by the
Non Proliferation Treaty (NPT), did not freeze its strategic inferiority
relative to the great powers, especially China.

Publicly available estimates of warhead potential during 1999–2001
range from 50 to 100 for India and 30 to 50 for Pakistan. These estimates are based on fissile material availability, which in turn is derived
largely from reprocessing and enrichment rate calculations. There is
no publicly accessible data about how many bombs might actually
have been made with the available fissile material. In addition to its
primary fissile material route of uranium enrichment, Pakistan now
has a small plutonium reprocessing capability. Going the other way,
India has now acquired some enrichment capability. With reprocessing
and enrichment as well as conversion of fissile material into weapons
now going on at maximum speed in both countries, it is quite possible
that within a few years Pakistan will have warheads in high two-digit
figures and India in low three-digit figures. While new testing is

[2] Till it acquired nuclear weapons, Pakistan had been protecting its highly vulnerable
nuclear facilities in Kahuta and elsewhere through conventional deterrence, not
defence. Its high card had been the vulnerability of a big concentration of Indian
nuclear assets, close to the economically central city of Mumbai, to Pakistani F-16s
coming over the sea.

unlikely unless a recognised Nuclear Weapons State (NWS) carries out a test, the data gathered by the two countries from their May 1998 tests should enable them to improve warheads. Both are pursuing boosted fission designs. Weapon yields, a few years from now, could climb past the 100-kiloton mark. Whether India will have the confidence to go in for thermonuclear weapons as well, without further testing, is not clear.

Pakistan is manufacturing liquid fuel, 1,500-km range, North Korea-derived Ghauri II missiles at KRL and solid fuel, 700-km range, China-derived Shaheen I missiles at the National Development Complex (NDC) in Fateh Jang. Solid fuel, 300-km range Hatf-III (Chinese M-11) missiles are also being manufactured at the NDC. Pakistan is developing longer-range versions of both Ghauri and Shaheen. It is likely that Pakistan will eventually concentrate on the Shaheen series for bulk production. In India both Agni and Prithvi are being manufactured at Bharat Dynamics near Hyderabad. Agni is now available in a single-stage version of 750-km and a two-stage version of 1,500-km, both using solid fuel. Extended range Agnis with ranges going up to 3,000 km are on the production horizon. India's initial concentration for bulk production is likely to be on the Pakistan-specific, single-stage 750-km version of Agni, first tested in January 2002.

Ghauri, Shaheen, Agni and Prithvi are all mobile missiles. India would ideally want ranges up to 5,000-km to be able to hit all parts of China from a wide range of launch positions. Pakistan would similarly want ranges up to 3,000-km to bring the entire Indian mainland within range from safe launch positions in Baluchistan and NWFP. Testing of missiles is unlikely to be constrained. The US, Russia and China are going to keep testing missiles, especially because of the US's need to develop BMD and the Russian and Chinese need to penetrate it. This and its need to target China effectively will keep missile tests going in India. This in turn will provide testing space for Pakistan. One can expect to see improvements in South Asian missiles in the areas of range, circular error probable (CEP), reaction time, reliability, operational ease and ground mobility. The CEP-yield curve up will be pushed further up, addressing it from both missile and warhead ends.

A big factor of uncertainty is the future course of Chinese help to Pakistan. China has been diluting its public support to Pakistan on the latter's political differences with India. There are also stronger indications that China wants to be seen as adhering to the global norms on nuclear and missile proliferation. But given China's long-standing support for Pakistan's missile programme, it is difficult to predict confidently China's future behaviour. It is with Chinese help that Pakistan has been able to move from Hatf-III (based on M-11) to Shaheen I (probably based on M-9) to Shaheen II (probably based on M-18).

ARSENAL MANAGEMENT

As their arsenals expand and the employment dimension gets more strongly factored in, demands relating to safety, security, survivability and readiness (with many of these demands working at cross purposes) will pose major problems to both countries. Safety concerns with regard to nuclear weapons are basically in the areas of accidental explosion and radiation leakage. Virtually no design detail of the weapons of the two countries are publicly available, but considering the techno- · logical limitations under which both work it is unlikely that either would have been able to incorporate features such as those found in the Enhanced Nuclear Detonation Safety (ENDS) system employed in the US. It is not known how well one-point-principle[3] issues involving fire-resistant pits, conventional explosive sensitivity to heat and shock, strong–weak link circuitry, etc. have been tackled. The requirement to keep warheads and delivery systems (and perhaps even the fissile and non-fissile sections of the warhead) separate for reasons of security and survival could add to design and maintenance problems relating to safety. The relatively small number (six at best) of explosive tests carried out by each country, and that too in a time-compressed manner, raises worries about design safety as well.

Security concerns about nuclear weapons relate primarily to unauthorised use on the one hand and seizure and theft on the other. Both countries have chosen to rely on mobility and dispersal to enhance the survivability of their weapons. The number of locations to be made secure goes up as weapons are moved about. Transportation security also becomes a harder problem to tackle. This has fallout with respect to both unauthorised use and seizure/theft risks. To prevent unauthorised use of nuclear weapons, reliance on 'authorisation' control (such

---

[3] Intended to ensure that non-programmed conventional explosion does not trigger nuclear fission.

as secure codes) is not enough. There must be 'enablement' control through systems such as Permissive Action Links (PALs). The control technology for PALs is not very difficult to develop. But the parallel need for secure, wide-band communications capability to transmit enablement programmes confidently is not easy to create when launch control nodes are both distant and mobile. Neither country possesses PALs at present.[4]

Risks of seizure and theft are also serious. There are both outsider and insider risks. The outsider risk is more in Pakistan than in India because of the much higher presence of terrorist groups in that country and the fact that some of them enjoy links with a few in positions of authority. The insider risk is also higher in Pakistan because of the greater spread of radical ideologies in that country. The quality of personnel reliability programmes (PRP) in the two countries is not known. Pakistan has one advantage over India in that the entire structure controlling its nuclear weapons and delivery systems is with the military, while in India it is divided among the military, the Atomic Energy Commission (AEC) and the Defence Research and Development Organisation (DRDO)—all with differing ethos and systems. The overall responsibility for system effectiveness, in practical terms, is not clear.

Survivability concerns regarding nuclear weapons are much more serious in Pakistan than in India. India has (or will eventually have) much greater numbers of weapons and delivery systems. It also has a bigger land mass over which to distribute them. More important, India has to worry only about Pakistan as a source of threat to its systems. Because of the risk of weapons falling into the hands of radical Islamists, Pakistan cannot discount threats from Israel and the United States as well.[5] India and Pakistan have chosen to make their systems difficult

---

[4] Even if the US were to offer PAL technology it would be difficult for either country to accept it because of the fear that surreptitious tracking technology might be incorporated in it.

[5] It is reported that Pakistan moved its nuclear weapons to six new secret locations in early November 2001 or earlier—at least a month before the terrorist attack on Indian Parliament and the resultant Indian mobilisation. ('Pakistan Moves Nuclear Weapons', *The Washington Post*, 11 November 2001.) The only threat to Pakistan's weapons at that time was from the US on account of Taliban/al-Qaeda fears. There were reports of US and Israeli Special Forces training together for this purpose. See Seymour M. Hersh, 'Watching the Warheads: The Risks of Pakistan's Nuclear arsenal', *New Yorker*, 5 November 2001.

to locate rather than difficult to destroy after location. The locating difficulty is being built up through a series of interlocking steps involving dispersal, mobility and deception. By distributing delivery systems and warheads separately in a large number of locations, the number of targets to be destroyed can be vastly increased. This problem can be made more acute by having a larger number of hide-outs than there are hardware sections to be hidden, and by moving hardware among them. It can be taken a step further through measures such as camouflage, use of dummies and disinformation. Agni, Prithvi, Ghauri, Shaheen and M-11 are all road-mobile. They can be made rail-mobile as well since many military bases in India and Pakistan have rail links. For air delivery, both countries have several airfields from which the needed types of aircraft can operate.

The measures being adopted to enhance survivability have a broadly adverse relationship with those being pursued to promote safety and security. Theoretically viewed, the more locations there are where assets can be hidden and the more frequently they are moved, the better should be their survivability.[6] But the larger the number of locations and the greater the frequency of moves, the greater too the security risks and (to a lesser degree) the safety risks. To strike a compromise between survivability risks on the one side and security and safety risks on the other, the general approach being adopted is to keep assets concentrated in a small number of secret locations during peacetime and to disperse them widely when tensions rise. This is based on the assumption that a bolt-from-the-blue attack can be ruled out.

The term 'readiness', when applied to a nuclear arsenal, connotes the ability to deliver one or more nuclear strikes effectively against a planned target array in a chosen timeframe. Such readiness can have different implications depending on the nuclear doctrine adopted. India's readiness level ought to be related to two facets of its doctrine— no first use and massive retaliation. These call for the ability to absorb a strike and then retaliate with a large salvo within a few hours. Pakistan's readiness level has to be related to different requirements—the need to initiate nuclear weapon use in response to conventional military setbacks and the need to make graduated use thereafter. Relative to India's, Pakistan's doctrine calls for not only a more robust command

---

[6] This is a theoretical conclusion. In practice it is quite possible that if assets are moved frequently the chances of their hiding places getting known may actually go up and lead to a decrease in survivability.

and control (C&C) system, but also an arsenal that can respond flexibly in the context of a wider variety of demands.

The C&C challenges (command chain integrity and connectivity) posed by dispersal and movements are considerable. Any National Command Authority (NCA) has to continuously maintain both negative control (weapons never launched unless ordered) and positive control (weapons always launched when ordered). In India's case where the doctrine calls for executing only two strikes (a massive retaliatory strike with the provision for a reserve strike), and that too in a not very time-sensitive manner, there is adequate time to shift emphasis from negative to positive control. In Paskistan's case, where a greater number of strikes have to be planned for, and that too in a flexible manner related to battlefield developments, both negative and positive controls have to work with a high level of effectiveness all the time. This, when combined with connectivity problems stemming from infrastructural limitations, will make Pakistan's C&C system more decentralised than India's, making pre-delegation quite likely.

Nuclear Opacity

The May 1998 tests and the developments since then have not reduced the opacity of the two arsenals in any way except that it is now established that both sides have nuclear weapons with effective means of delivery. Beyond that there is no public knowledge regarding even elemental issues such as the number of bombs/warheads and their yield, the types and numbers of nuclear-capable aircraft, and the types and numbers of nuclear-capable missiles and their accuracies. There is no information about how nuclear operations are being conducted during peacetime and are planned to be conducted during war. There is no knowledge of how issues relating to safety, security, survivability and readiness are being tackled. Nor about field-level operational structures and the kind of personnel who man them. Nor is anything known about communications and intelligence structures.

The opacity is partly the result of pressures exerted by the external environment and partly the result of internal needs. The two countries are not violating any international regime by possessing nuclear weapons, as they are not parties to the NPT or any other control regime. Yet neither would an NWS under the NPT and many countries, particularly the US, like to constrain their capabilities. Prudence therefore demands that they keep their vulnerabilities, political and military, low by revealing as little information as possible. This is particularly so since both countries have decades of intense technical and organisational development ahead of them. In Pakistan's case there is the additional vulnerability posed by the need for illegal external assistance for some of its nuclear and missile programmes.

The most important reason for the two countries to seek opacity for their arsenals has to do with ensuring deterrence. Both their first use and retaliatory strike capabilities are predicated on the secrecy of the locations of warheads and delivery systems. Equally important, their systems have many technical and organisational vulnerabilities which, if made known to the adversary, can seriously degrade survivability. The concealment of the size, characteristics and locations of their arsenals is critical to both countries and therefore the transparency needed for nuclear CBMs is seen as highly dangerous.

The limited technical intelligence capabilities of the two countries also contribute to opacity. Signal intelligence capabilities are not significant on either side, especially Pakistan's. Electronic intelligence capabilities are also weak especially further away from the borders. In the reconnaissance field India has a slight edge with its satellites and reconnaissance aircraft. But as far as continuous real-time monitoring of the opponent's nuclear delivery systems is concerned, both sides are effectively blind. This places a heavy premium on strategic warning.[7] Relying on strategic warning without corroboration from nuclear-specific technical intelligence can lead to miscalculations. Uncertainty about the capabilities and intentions of the adversary in a crisis situation can create 'first strike instability' and lead to major mistakes in estimating the risks and benefits from striking first.

BMD is not feasible for either country for a long time to come. Ballistic missile flight times, allowing for boost and re-entry phases are about ten minutes over 1,200 km and thirteen minutes over 2,000 km.[8] The latter distance will take care of most vital targets in the two countries. Even if India is able to acquire the Israeli Arrow system (coupled with the Green Pine radar system it is acquiring), the kind of readiness

---

[7] Strategic warning depends on an overall assessment of political and military intelligence.

[8] M.V. Ramana, R. Rajaraman and Zia Mian, 'Nuclear Early Warning in South Asia: Problems and Issues', *Economic and Political Weekly*, 17 January 2004, pp. 279–84.

levels needed to deal with the time problem involved is unlikely to be achieved for a long time.

Most security commentators know little about the 'operational' nuclear capabilities of their own country, and still less about how it interacts with the adversary's. As a consequence public perceptions about what is possible during crisis bargaining can get unreal. To a much less but nevertheless significant degree, this applies even to those involved in nuclear decision-making. This seemingly difficult-to-conceive problem grows from two sources. One, for reasons of security and survivability, the knowledge of one's own nuclear capabilities is tightly rationed and compartmentalised. Two, the knowledge that is disseminated is based on 'proprietary' inputs from different organisations with little system-level oversight. This can lead to over or under confidence on the part of the NCA about the capabilities at its command, which in turn can pose serious danger in crisis situations.

The dominant view in both South Asia and outside is that the prevailing condition of opacity is a good thing. India and Pakistan consider non-transparency essential for the survivability and security of their current arsenals, as well as for their future development. The outside world thinks that opacity is good to ensure that the South Asian arsenals are not legitimated, thereby weakening the non-proliferation regime even more. Before the 1998 tests the effort was to make the vague concept of non-weaponised deterrence prevail, and after the tests for the equally vague concept of non-deployed deterrence to take its place. In conditions of opacity no markers could be established earlier for non-weaponisation and none can now be established for non-deployment.

In discussions the Israeli parallel is sometimes invoked to advance the merits of keeping the South Asian arsenals shrouded. This ignores a fundamental difference between the Middle Eastern and South Asian situations. In the former region, where a one-sided nuclear capability is reinforced by conventional superiority, there is no danger of a conflict escalating into a nuclear one. In South Asia, where both adversaries have nuclear weapons and where one side has the sub-conventional advantage and the other the conventional one, there is a danger of it occurring. This is now gradually being better understood. There are calls for striking a better balance between ambiguity and transparency. Deterrence stability during the Cold War got established, largely in the wake of the 1963 Cuban missile crisis, through increased transparency of each other's arsenals as well as their central C&C systems. Such levels of transparency are clearly impossible in South Asia, given the fears about survivability and the lack of legitimacy surrounding the arsenals. Yet, innovative ways have to be explored to find a path through the competing needs of opacity and transparency so that the risks of escalation are reduced.

NUCLEAR STRATEGIES

The nuclear strategies of both countries emphasise deterrence, but there is a fundamental difference between the two in that Pakistan's strategy is aimed at deterring a conventional threat from India, while India's is aimed at deterring a nuclear one from Pakistan. Since a conventional confrontation is easier to develop and must almost invariably precede a nuclear one, Pakistan's deterrence has to function much more actively than India's. This has an impact on force structure, force posture, and the relationship between conventional and nuclear strategies. As the conventional military balance continues to shift in India's favour, Pakistan's reliance on its nuclear capability will increase and so will its effort to lower the nuclear threshold. Thus Pakistan's strategy is likely to emphasise not just 'first use' but 'early first use' in the coming years. The big problem for Pakistan is that not only is the conventional military balance in India's favour, but so is the nuclear one. Pakistan was able to maintain conventional operational parity with India for many decades, but is now losing ground rapidly. Much the same is going to happen in the nuclear field.

Nuclear deterrence works in the minds of not only those who are connected with the two NCAs but also of the articulate public in the two countries. The contest to influence them in strategically favourable ways has now begun. India wants to impress Pakistan with the logic of rational deterrence theory and make it understand the significance of escalation dominance and net payoff at each level. It wants to make Pakistan do rational utility calculations by absorbing the reality that in the case of a full nuclear exchange it is likely to lose at least ten times the percentage of population compared to India's.[9] Pakistan on

---

[9] This is based on the fact that Pakistan's population is only one-seventh India's, and the weight of a full-scale Indian strike is likely to be at least one-and-a-half times that of Pakistan's.

the other hand wants to impress India that it is absolute damage and not relative damage that matters. It wants to establish that if Mumbai, Delhi and a few other cities get hit, it will set the country back by generations and that mere survival will not do it any good. It also wants to have accepted that under conditions of strategic stress its NCA might resort to first use even though it would amount to a Samson act.

Pakistan's effort would be to maximise nuclear uncertainty in times of crisis while India's would be to minimise it. If one were to use the analogies developed by Thomas Schelling and Paul Nitze, Pakistan would like to establish that nuclear risk-taking and its consequences in South Asia would resemble Russian roulette with the outcome relying on chance, while India would want to prove that it would resemble a game of chess with the outcome determined by rational logic and relative superiority.[10] Each country would want to make its respective mix of logic and scenario-visualisation prevail, not only in the mind of the rival but also in the mind of the global community.

Finally there is the employment component of the two nuclear strategies. Both countries have publicly ruled out preventive and pre-emptive strikes. Going by its declared position India will use its nuclear capability only to retaliate after one or more nuclear weapons have been launched against it.[11] But it has also stated that its response strike would be a large-scale, society-destroying one. India wants Pakistan to understand that there is no scope for nuclear bargaining through limited strikes. India has therefore taken the position that it will respond with a massive nuclear strike should Pakistan use even a low-yield nuclear weapon against an Indian target, even inside Pakistani territory.

Pakistan has chosen an employment strategy very different from India's, both with regard to the sequencing of strikes and the weight of strikes. It has taken the position that it will use nuclear weapons in first use against India if certain vaguely defined redlines involving territorial loss, military loss, economic strangulation and internal stability are crossed.[12] Pakistan has also let it be known that it will use

---

[10] See Richard K. Betts, *Nuclear Blackmail and Nuclear Balance*, Washington, DC: Brookings, 1987.

[11] The Prime Minister has said so in parliament. The Draft Nuclear Doctrine's position is that 'no first use' will only apply to non-nuclear powers and that too to those not aligned with nuclear powers.

[12] Lt. Gen. Khalid Kidwai, Director General of Pakistan's Strategic Plans Division has been quoted on this. See Paola Cotta-Ramusino and Maurizio Martellini, *Nuclear*

nuclear weapons in a graduated manner, starting with counter-military targets. Pakistan's hope is that it can limit India's retaliatory strike by the logic that even a full-weight Indian strike will not be able to prevent Pakistan initiating a retaliatory strike of its own, which will do India far greater damage than would have been done by Pakistan's initial strike.

If one looks at the emerging India–Pakistan nuclear balance through the deterrence theory lens, one could find reasons to support the stances of both deterrence optimists and deterrence pessimists.[13] The optimists would argue that nuclear deterrence has worked in South Asia for over a decade despite great political hostility, regular border clashes and cross-border terrorism, and that when a war did break out (in Kargil) it stayed restrained. The pessimists would counter that the Kargil War did not spin out of control only because of US intervention and, what was more, the two sides would appear to have drawn dangerously divergent lessons from it. India seems to have concluded that it was possible to fight a limited conventional war under the nuclear threshold. Pakistan believes that while Kargil-size operations could pose problems, it was possible to persist with smaller-scale, transborder operations.[14] If Kargil was a Pakistani effort to test India's nuclear fear, Operation Parakram was, in part, an Indian effort to test Pakistan's fear of India's superior nuclear capability.

NUCLEAR RISKS

The nuclear risks present in the subcontinent can be broadly categorised as 'arsenal risks' and 'employment risks'. The former stems from the very existence of nuclear arsenals and is largely related to the areas of safety and security. The latter is concerned with the employment of nuclear weapons, deliberate or inadvertent. The 'arsenal risks'

Safety, Nuclear Stability and Nuclear Strategy in Pakistan (available at http://www.mi.infn.it/~landnet).

[13] For an educative optimist–pessimist argument on deterrence with a special chapter on South Asia see Scott D. Sagan and Kenneth N. Waltz, *The Spread of Nuclear Weapons: A Debate Renewed*, New York: W.W. Norton, 2002.

[14] Pakistan-sponsored terrorist attacks in Kashmir registered a notable rise after the Kargil War.

present in South Asia with regard to safety and security are difficult
to evaluate. It is hard to estimate how the 1998 shift from a 'non-
weaponised' to 'non-deployed' posture has impacted on safety and
security issues. It is clear that warhead and missile numbers are now
increasing, limited more by production capacity than by international
restraints. The speed of constituting weapons systems, in terms of
both fissile core insertion in warheads and mating warheads with missiles, is being enhanced. This increase in numbers and readiness levels
would place greater demands on safety and security. Pakistan's difficulties in this area are likely to stem from its first use posture and
technological and financial constraints. India's are likely to emanate
more from its divided forms of control and custody, and an extreme
form of need-to-know that could impact on training and drills.

Virtually nothing is known of the field organisations of the two
countries that are responsible for operating nuclear weapons and delivery systems. This is a major cause for concern since the conduct of
nuclear operations, both during peace and war, is an extremely complex and demanding business.[15] In both countries field operations at
the military level are being carried out essentially on single-service
basis—with the respective Armies responsible for missile delivery and
the Air Forces for air delivery. A significant field-operations role is
also being played by technical organisations in both countries—the
AEC and the DRDO in India, and the PAEC/NDC and the KRL in
Pakistan. This applies to bombs/warheads as well as delivery missiles.
Inadequate bug proofing of systems and insufficient technical know-
how of military operators are the major reasons.

The 'employment risks' in South Asia, as elsewhere, can be broadly
categorised as preventive, pre-emptive, inadvertent and escalatory. A
bolt-from-the-blue preventive strike is very difficult. While such a strike
might catch many delivery systems in their peacetime concentrations
it would not catch them all. In the case of bombs and warheads, which
are much easier to hide, the numbers destroyed are unlikely to be significant. The pre-emptive war risk is even less. Destroying the bulk of
each other's arsenals after the systems have been dispersed on crisis-
warning is operationally impossible for both countries. Seemingly
definitive intelligence about the opponent's decision to launch a nuclear strike can thus pose an excruciating dilemma. On the one hand

[15] See Ashton B. Carter, John D. Steinbruner and Charles A. Zracket, *Managing Nuclear Operations*, Washington, DC: Brookings, 1987.

a pre-emptive strike will make a 'probable' strike 'assured'. On the other hand, the level of destruction suffered is likely to be less after a pre-emptive strike.

An inadvertent strike from either side, stemming from deficiencies in intelligence, C&C and decision-making, cannot be ruled out.[16] Since India and Pakistan have not gone in for a launch-on-warning posture (for reasons of readiness and surveillance inadequacies), defective intelligence should not pose a serious hazard. But scrambled C&C is a major potential danger especially when missiles and warheads are 'projected' in a crisis. This danger will steadily rise as missile and warhead numbers increase. It will also shoot up periodically when crises occur. Poor decision-making can also spell danger, particularly in Pakistan where narrow military considerations have tended to dominate strategic decision-making dysfunctionally.

The other type of inadvertent war risk—decisions rolling out of control down an escalatory slope—can also arise in the India–Pakistan context. There is deep mistrust, poor communications and, most dangerously, a mutual discounting of one another's resolve and capability. Two attendant conditions exacerbate this danger. One is the opacity of arsenals that makes it difficult to monitor changes in threat perception by observing changes in readiness level. Warning statements tend to be taken as bluffs, which often they indeed are. The other problem is that both countries tend to take risks in the expectation that third countries, especially the US, will intervene. This belief in the international community's willingness and ability to act as a safety net can lead to more dangerous acts being executed on the high wire than would be the case otherwise.

The last among employment risks arises when a leadership considers escalatory nuclear initiation. This risk takes form mostly when one party begins to feel that the outcome of a war will be less severe, in terms of ratios of politico–military losses between the two countries, after a nuclear exchange than without one. In a conventional war with India, Pakistan could well find itself facing national humiliation (occupation of parts of the country), permanent territorial loss (parts of POK), break-up of the country, or a permanent weakening of the

---

[16] For inadvertent war risks see Barry P. Posen, *Inadvertent Escalation: Conventional War and Nuclear Risks*, Ithaca, NY: Cornell University Press, 1999; and Robert Jervis, *The Meaning of Nuclear Revolution: Statecraft and the Prospect of Nuclear Armageddon*, Ithaca, NY: Cornell University Press, 1989.

influence of the Army or Punjab in the affairs of the country. In such a situation a Pakistani leadership, especially an Army one, might well decide on a nuclear strike. The thinking, under extreme strategic stress, could be that ruining India would salvage some pride even though Pakistan would be devastated in the process.

If one looked at the spectrum of nuclear risks in South Asia through the organisation theory lens, one will find considerable cause for concern.[17] The organisations controlling and operating nuclear weapons in both countries are ad hoc, compartmentalised and heavily reliant on relations between key individuals. What is more, they have been grafted on existing systems not known for high standards of reliability. The two countries, especially Pakistan, also have serious technical and financial constraints. The fact that political and operational constraints come in the way of adequate training of personnel and testing of systems should also cause disquiet. So should the fact that these organisations, for reasons of secrecy, are structured very differently from the experience-based systems of recognised NWS. More worrying, when weapons are deployed in a crisis in the two countries, operating personnel and systems shall suddenly be brought under vastly increased stress. This does not occur in the case of NWS as their weapons are always deployed.

COERCIVE RISK-TAKING

The dominant characteristic of India–Pakistan relations since the late 1980s has been the attempt by both sides to coerce one another. This has had a good deal to do with nuclear weapons. India's Brasstacks exercise in the winter of 1986–87 is seen by some as partly an attempt to provoke a war before Pakistan acquired nuclear weapons. Similarly, Pakistan's takeover of the Kashmir insurgency in 1990 had a strong link to nuclear weapons, for it was the ability it had acquired by then to deliver nuclear weapons using F-16 aircraft that emboldened it to embark on such a highly provocative course. The well-known

[17] See Sagan in Scott D. Sagan and Kenneth N. Waltz, *The Spread of Nuclear Weapons: A Debate Renewed*, New York: W.W. Norton, 2002

Stability–Instability Paradox has become relevant in South Asia.[18] The paradox is that nuclear weapons create stability and instability simultaneously. While nuclear weapons serve to deter high-end war, the huge constraints on their use make it possible for certain types of provocations and operations to be carried out with less risk. The scope for such activities between Pakistan and India are dynamic and are determined not only by relatively static features such as the military balance, the nature of stakes and the shapes of military vulnerability curves, but also by more transient factors such as domestic contexts, leadership inclinations and international conditions.

The violence that exploded in the Kashmir Valley in 1989 led to fears in the following spring of a conventional war with the scope of escalating into a nuclear one. Although Pakistan steadily escalated its involvement in J&K through the 1990s, India exercised considerable control. To many it was a matter of surprise that India did not begin substantial strikes across the LoC when, by 1993, the fighting had become almost wholly Pakistan-directed. (During the period 1980 to 1988, Soviet and Afghan aircraft had carried out frequent attacks on camps inside Pakistan that supported mujahideen in Afghanistan.) Pakistan attributed India's restraint to the deterrence effect of its nuclear capability, and this led to its decision to escalate threat and risk by occupying the Kargil heights. India fought the Kargil War in a restrained manner—without striking inside Pakistan or opening new fronts—taking into account nuclear risk and international pressure.

In initiating the Kargil War Pakistan had carried out a quantum escalation of risk. The only historical parallel for two nuclear powers fighting one another is the Sino–Soviet border skirmishes of 1969. But the total fatalities in those clashes were less than a hundred, and there had been no fighting between the two countries before or since. In Kashmir, between 30,000 and 60,000 have been killed in thirteen years of continuous warfare since nuclear weapons arrived in the subcontinent.[19] It has been coercive risk-taking of a high order by Pakistan.

---

[18] The concept was first articulated by Glenn Snyder in 'The Balance of Power and the Balance of Terror', in Paul Seabury, ed., *The Balance of Power*, San Francisco: Chandler, 1965. For its application in South Asia, see Michael Krepon and Chris Gagne, eds., *The Stability–Instability Paradox: Nuclear Weapons and Brinkmanship in South Asia*, Report 38, Washington, DC: Stimson Center, June 2001.

[19] See footnote 9 in Chapter 2.

India therefore decided that coercion must be met with counter-coercion. The Indian security community sought to develop the concept of a 'limited war' that would stay within control. The concept however had little specificity. The general thinking was that a war could be kept limited by restricting the goals sought and the means employed. There was little exploration of vital issues like Pakistan's nuclear thresholds, the ways in which international pressures could build up, and how an initiated limited war was to be concluded.

The global war on terrorism gave an opportunity to test the coercive value of the concept of 'limited war'. Operation Parakram, which began in mid-December 2001, was intended to compel the Pakistani military government to cut its ties with terrorist groups. Pakistan, discredited internationally during the previous two years for its Kargil recklessness, military coup and Taliban connection, was put under huge pressure by India's crisis-initiation strategy. The jihadis now became a major problem. Viewed in principal–agent terms, the ideologically driven agent now wanted to coerce the tactically cautious principal. Pakistan's attempt to counter Indian pressure through nuclear threats created a new dilemma. Saddled with the image of Islamic fanaticism, Pakistan could ill afford to acquire one of nuclear irresponsibility. Manoeuvring as Pakistan had been doing, making simultaneous use of nuclear deterrence against conventional attack and sub-conventional coercion to achieve political objectives, is something no other country has tried to do. The serious risks the strategy carried, bilateral and international, now came to the fore. But Pakistan held tight, helped by the US's need for its help in tracking down al-Qaeda.

It is unlikely that India will repeat this kind of confrontation-by-mobilisation. Learning from experience, India is now more likely to go for low-key but hurting responses. Through appropriate acquisitions India could generate the option of punishing long-range shelling or rocketing, something that Pakistan cannot match. Or it could opt for sharp, limited air attacks on terrorist targets using precision guided munitions (PGMs). Or even for a naval blockade of Karachi and Port Qasim. Through such limited actions India could dare Pakistan to counter-escalate. Because of India's decisive superiority on every rung of the conventional escalation ladder, it will have no problem with whatever Pakistan might do as long as matters remain conventional. The problem will arise if Pakistan finds itself compelled to go nuclear. How quickly it might get to such a situation would depend on the way a conventional war unfolds. Given the huge frontage over which such a war will be fought and the fact that there would be deep air strikes, it would be difficult for Pakistan to judge the point at which the war had begun to impose unacceptable costs—political or military. In today's India–Pakistan war-fighting context there are no clear 'saliencies', the crossing of which can mark a clear escalation. There are in fact no firebreaks between sub-conventional and conventional wars, and between conventional and nuclear wars. A variety of weapons and operational practices link the first pair, and the tactical use of nuclear weapons and conventional strikes on nuclear reactors link the second pair.

A big problem in Pakistan is the General Headquarters (GHQ) of the Army that has a major role in every facet of the country's security policy—foreign, military and nuclear—regardless of whether the country has a military or an elected head of government. The GHQ is both overloaded and narrowly advised. In the foreign policy field it is incapable of factoring in adequate expert advice. But it is at the nuclear level that its dominance is most dangerous. On the one hand its conventional and nuclear strategies are closely integrated, while on the other the nuclear strategy is inadequately tied with foreign policy considerations and overall national objectives. As a consequence military considerations, more than any other, are likely to drive its nuclear policy. Under high stress Pakistan is capable of crossing the nuclear barrier without examining adequately the consequences of such action or the alternative courses of action that are available.

Despite what its publicised 1999 doctrine (still a 'draft') might say, India is unlikely to respond massively to a symbolic strike by Pakistan. Pakistan's surviving reserve capability will not make a massive strike logical at that stage. It could only lead to strategically purposeless mutual ruination. But it is entirely possible that India's response strike would not be marginally-plus but substantially-plus because India would want to bring the nuclear exchange to an immediate end. But a heavy Indian strike may well force Pakistan to respond with a similar strike. At this point weaknesses in damage assessment, alerting intelligence and C&C could all come into play in an extremely dangerous manner. The ability of the international community, including the US, to influence decisions in Delhi and Islamabad would be insignificant once the first nuclear weapon of whatever yield is exploded.

The international community is important to the two countries in their efforts to choreograph the nuclear war risk in different ways.

Both are aware that for a host of reasons, ranging from the possibility of a global economic depression to environmental contamination, the world cannot lean back and watch the two fight a private nuclear war. Yet, Pakistan wants to establish that if India launches a conventional war it may have no choice but to reach for the nuclear trigger. In holding out the nuclear war risk Pakistan would be trying more to get the international community to pressure India to stay its hand than to impress India directly. Similarly, in threatening Pakistan with a conventional war that could escalate to a nuclear one India would be trying more to get the world to squeeze Pakistan and make it adhere to the new anti-terrorist global norms than to fight it to a finish. Neither country wants a conventional war any more than it wants a nuclear war. But the logic of escalation that parallels the logic of coercion could see matters slipping out of control despite neither country wanting them to.

KASHMIR AND
THE OUTSIDE WORLD

T he role the outside world has played in shaping the course of the India–Pakistan conflict is seen differently in the two countries. In India the general view is that, but for the involvement of outsiders that gave Pakistan false hopes, the conflict would have petered out long ago. The dominant Pakistani view is that, had the outside world not stayed aloof after 1953, the problem would have been settled by now. Outsiders themselves tend to think that, given the extreme positions consistently taken by the two sides, the tussle has been basically unresolvable and that the little outside involvement there has been has not made any difference one way or the other. The end of the Cold War competition and the rise of the United States as the power hub of the world have modified these perceptions slightly. Many in the two countries and a few elsewhere now think that the US can, if it wishes to, play a more effective peacemaking role than was possible earlier. There is also a feeling that the acquisition of nuclear weapons by the two countries has made their battling more dangerous than earlier—not just for themselves but also for the larger international community.

A few key issues are discussed here. We first examine the current unipolar context and its impact on the conflict. While the Soviet Union before its dissolution and China have played important roles in determining the way the conflict has progressed, the key external player all along has been the US. It is therefore important to have a balanced understanding of the historical interaction between India and Pakistan on the one side and the US and the West in general on the other, and even more about how it is likely to play out in the future. A brief look at the historical record and the evolving contours of India's and Pakistan's relationships with China, Russia and the Muslim World is also rewarding. The three areas where the international community takes a keen interest in South Asia—nuclear weapons, terrorism and democracy—have become important. How the parties to the conflict look at the unfolding international context and are trying to take advantage of it also needs to be understood, as does the kind of interest that outsiders are likely to take in South Asia in the future and the influence that they are likely to bring to bear.

The Unipolar Context

The collapse of the Eastern Bloc and the Soviet Union during 1987–90 brought the world back to the conditions of the first few years following World War II—a period of unchallenged military and political supremacy of the US. The 1990s saw the US military machine in a position to exercise punitive power almost everywhere. At the political level no country including Russia and China could oppose it. The US economy, which had been losing ground earlier, shrinking from one-half the size of the global economy in 1950 to one-third the size in 1990, showed a spurt. During 1995–2001 the US's share of the world's economic growth was nearly double its share of the world's economy. However, this improved position, built on huge internal and external debt, was not unassailable. The US's strongest suit was its military superiority and it concentrated on making that invincible. Its military lead over all others—including other NATO countries, Russia and China—became so great that military resistance to the US became inconceivable. This new situation, unsurprisingly, led to an American vision that the world order should now rest on power and not on international law or multilateral institutions.[1]

While the new reality of American military dominance and the impossibility of resisting it—at least actively—are clear to everyone, there is little clarity about its implications for inter-state and intrastate conflicts that do not impact on the US directly. American unilateralism, which climbed a peak during the Iraq war in the spring of 2003, seems to have become more nuanced in its aftermath: witness the willingness to seek French and German help in dealing with the nuclear ambition of Iran, and Chinese and Russian help in dealing with North Korea's. There is less talk of a virtual empire, and greater effort at figuring out what the US can and cannot do. In any case, the new America is an over-engaged power that has to shift attention constantly from trouble spot to trouble spot. Its strategic plate is spilling over and it is unable to structure allegiances and obligations. This has given rise to the necessity-forced idea of situation-determined, kaleidoscopic coalitions.

With too many problem areas to deal with and no stable strategic context to link them, the US feels it best to have flexible tie-ups governed by the convergence of interests on each particular issue. The US is no longer able to nor particularly wants to maintain a steady relationship even with other NATO countries. High manoeuvrability among all states as well as issues is seen as a new strategic imperative. Philosophical consistency in defining its position on different issues is seen as both undesirable and unnecessary. The need to pursue national interest single-mindedly makes it undesirable and the ability to control narrative through information dominance makes it unnecessary. American relations with the rest of the world are therefore not getting restructured. Rather, they are moving from a condition of structure to one of deliberate flux. This is the new reality that both India and Pakistan have to reckon with.

---

[1] For a good exposition of the frequently heard argument that the US must act as the world's policeman, see Philip Bobbitt, *The Shield of Achilles: War, Peace and the Course of History*, London: Allen Lane, 2002. For a more restrained view of what the US can do, see Joseph S. Nye, *The Paradox of American Power: Why the World's Only Superpower Can't Go it Alone*, Oxford: Oxford University Press, 2002.

SOUTH ASIA AND THE WEST

America's relationships with India and Pakistan have been charac-terised by a good deal of balancing from the beginning. The notion of Pakistan as a staunch ally of the US during the Cold War, and a Cold War-orphan later, is as oversimple as that of India as pro-Soviet during the Cold War, and with an affinity to the US thereafter. In reality, US–Pakistan relations during the Cold War period were never as close as Pakistan had wishfully and India had suspiciously thought they were. India was by far the more desirable subcontinental partner for the US in 1947, although the UK had a different view. But India's search for strategic autonomy through non-alignment and the way the US dealt with Kashmir in the UNSC drew the countries apart. Pakistan took advantage of this and offered the US nearly everything it wanted in return for military help. During 1954–55 Pakistan not only signed a mutual defence agreement with the US, but also became a founding member of two new anti-communist military alliances—the Baghdad Pact and South East Asian Treaty Organisation (SEATO). Pakistan's utility to the US in the 1950s was two-fold—to help gather intelligence of Soviet nuclear and missile capabilities, and as a possible support base in case of a Soviet move into to the Gulf region. This usefulness reduced after 1960 with the arrival of intelligence-gathering satellites and Shah's Iran becoming a seemingly stalwart US ally.

The 1962 Sino–Indian War caused major damage to Pakistan's relations with the US. For the US, Red China was then anathema and it had little hesitation in coming to India's aid. Pakistan on the other hand had been getting close to China from 1959 when India's relations with that country began to go downhill. The US military help to India —although insubstantial—upset Pakistan which had conceived its relationship with the US differently from the way the latter had. For the US the alliance had a purely anti-communist focus and India was out of its scope. This came to the fore during the 1965 India–Pakistan War when the US cut off military aid to Pakistan. The military aid re-lationship between the two countries was not to blossom again for fif-teen years, till 1980. It is noteworthy that even during 1955–65—the closest the US and Pakistan have ever been—Pakistan had received only $2.5 billion in aid from the US while India got as much as $10.5 billion.[2] Of course, unlike Pakistan, India got no military aid and had to buy equipment at much higher prices from Britain and France. After 1962 the US and India increased their strategic cooperation quietly. Beginning 1965, US devices to monitor Chinese nuclear and missile tests were implanted on Nanda Devi and later in Arunachal Pradesh.[3] The 1970s saw US relations worsening with both countries. For India, the US's tacit acceptance of Islamabad's heavy-handed repression in East Pakistan in 1971 was as unacceptable as was to the US the signing of the Indo–Soviet Friendship Treaty that year. The public coming together of the US and China in 1972 did not help. Pakistan on its part felt deeply let down by the US during the 1971 war. It failed to understand that Nixon could not have tilted any more in Pakistan's favour than he did, given the strong public and congressional sentiments against such a course. Public disapproval in Pakistan of the US, growing from 1963 with Zulfiqar Bhutto playing a major role in its promotion, registered a quantum jump after the 1971 war. The lifting in 1975 of the US arms embargo against Pakistan—in place since 1965 and partially eased in 1970 and 1973—helped little because it did not lead to any worthwhile arms flow.

Zia's military coup in 1977 alienated US public opinion. But what caused the greatest damage to US–Pakistan relations at this time was Pakistan's single-minded pursuit of nuclear weapons. In September 1979, two days after Bhutto was executed, the US invoked the Symington sanctions against uranium enrichment and cut off all military and economic aid. In November an enraged crowd burned the US embassy in Islamabad. But things changed dramatically the next month when the Soviet Union invaded Afghanistan. Nine days after the invasion, President Carter lifted the Symington sanctions and a month later the US offered $400 million in military aid. Zia, who understood the new context, turned it down as 'peanuts'. The Reagan administration that came to power in January 1981 was less concerned about Pakistan's nuclear programme than about the need for its help in Afghanistan.

[2] Shirin Tahir-Kheli, *The United States and Pakistan, The Evolution of an Influence Relationship*, New York: Praeger, 1982, p.155.

[3] M.S. Kohli and Kenneth Conboy, *Spies in the Himalayas: Secret Missions and Perilous Climbs*, New Delhi: HarperCollins, 2002.

The 1981–87 US aid programme of $3.2 billion, with a substantial military content including the potent F-16A/B fighters, brought the two countries very close. But the Reagan administration, like the Eisenhower administration in the 1950s, was careful not to be seen as too pro-Pakistan and maintained good relations with India. This was despite strong disagreements with regard to Afghanistan, Cambodia and the US's stepped-up naval presence in the Indian Ocean.

American policy towards Pakistan did another U-turn when the Soviet Union withdrew from Afghanistan. Non-proliferation concerns, masked during the Afghan War, reappeared. The US Congress had always been very concerned about Pakistan's nuclear programme. In 1985 it had passed the Pressler Amendment aimed specifically at Pakistan. That amendment required that no aid was to be given to Pakistan unless the US administration certified each year that Pakistan was not pursuing a nuclear weapons programme. The administration, for reasons of fighting the Soviets in Afghanistan, so certified the next five years. But this Nelson's eye policy came to an end in October 1990 and all US assistance—military and economic—was abruptly stopped. With the $4.02 billion 1987–93 military aid programme shut midway, even some F-16 aircraft already paid for were not delivered. This led to a massive resurgence of anti-US feelings in Pakistan. This time, unlike in 1963 and 1972, the anger had a strong Islamic cast. The World Trade Centre in New York was bombed in 1993 which contributed to the US's threat to declare Pakistan a terrorist state. American concern with Pakistan's nuclear weapons was also rising. There was a spate of intelligence leaks during 1992–93 about Sino–Pakistan collusion in nuclear and missile fields.

Meanwhile, US relations with India were improving. With the demise of the Soviet Union and India's economic liberalisation, India began to be seen in the US as a friendly, growing power. The dominant perception in the West regarding the violence in Kashmir began to change. From about 1995 the violence came to be seen more as a Pakistan-promoted activity than an indigenous phenomenon. Consequently, international concern began to shift from human rights violations by Indian security forces to terrorism by Pakistan-supported jihadis. Pakistan's support to the Taliban in Afghanistan also hurt its image. Its clandestine occupation of Indian territory in the Kargil area and the summer war of 1999 that it led to did further damage. The image suffered another body blow when Pakistan came under military rule later that year. President Clinton's effusive praise for India during his media-shaking visit in 2000 (and his finger-wagging admonition of Pakistan's military government during a quick six-hour trip to that country) showed the new India–Pakistan balance in US calculations. American commitment to India got a further boost when the China-wary Bush administration took office in January 2001. The new administration's indifference to the CTBT also made India's (and Pakistan's) May 1998 nuclear tests a less serious issue than before.

The disappointment in India was therefore tremendous when the 9/11 attacks later that year turned Pakistan from a near-pariah to a valuable ally in official US eyes. Although India showed great keenness to help, the fact was that it had little to offer in Afghanistan. Pakistan on the other hand could deliver a great deal once Musharraf made the crucial decision to ditch the Taliban. The long, difficult-to-access Afghan–Pakistan border with Pashtun tribes living on both sides as well as the ISI's close links with the Taliban and the Pashtuns in general made that possible. The bases that Pakistan provided to the US— Jacobabad, Pasni, Dalbandin and Shamsi—also mattered. As a result, during India's ten-month long Operation Parakram the US put much less pressure on Pakistan to stop terrorist attacks in Kashmir than India had hoped for. What made a big impact on the US was Pakistan's capture and delivery of over 500 al-Qaeda operatives by June 2003, a far greater number than the US forces operating in Afghanistan had achieved. The US reciprocated with the lifting of 'democracy' sanctions, debt write-off, debt-rescheduling, soft loans from multilateral institutions, and a promise of $3 billion in economic and military assistance over the period 2005 to 2010. A till then shunned Musharraf found himself treated as an honoured statesman by Bush—the same way Ayub Khan was once by Eisenhower, Yahya Khan by Nixon and Zia by Reagan. But Musharraf should have known that the US's bonhomie with all three military predecessors had soured later.

India–US relations have been growing since the late 1980s on strong fundamentals. Once the Soviet factor was out of the way, popular and congressional approbation in the US for India's democracy and the tolerant nature of its society and state became more manifest. In parallel, India's economic growth, which has averaged 6 per cent during 1992–2003, has not only made its markets and investment opportunities attractive but also made it a potential counterweight to China in Asia, supplementing Japan. India's impressive performance in the field of information technology and the growing influence of the well-to-do Indian diaspora have also made perceptions of India more positive.[4] India on its part, with huge elite and middle class support, is now determined to forge the closest possible ties with the US. It sees the US as its biggest export market, fount of technology and source of investment. At the political level, the US is seen as capable of giving it a considerable leg up in its effort to move up the global hierarchy.

Pakistan's relations with the US have been, and are likely to be, much more problematic. The periodic overthrow of democracy by the military has always been a problem. Pakistan's nuclear technology, much less securely and responsibly controlled than India's, is another serious issue. Then there is the high level of Islamic radicalism and anti-West feelings that have taken root in the country. Pakistan's poor economic performance and rising poverty levels since 1990 and the worsening lag in crucial social indicators like literacy, technical education and gender balance have also sullied its image. The result is that the popular image of Pakistan in the US has been going steadily downhill, even though for reasons of military necessity US administrations have frequently found it useful not to reflect it in their actions. Pakistan desperately needs long-term US support to help its economy grow, but it has no means today of establishing a sound basis for the needed relationship.

The US has never had any serious interest in Kashmir going to Pakistan or becoming independent, as some in India felt it had because of its earlier support for the plebiscite route to settlement. The primary interest of the US in the 1950s was to see that India and Pakistan settled their differences so that no opening was provided for communist penetration. After the failure of the India–Pakistan talks of 1962–63 promoted by it and the UK, the US realised that there was little it could do. With India and Pakistan strengthening their respective ties with the Soviet Union and China during the 1960s, the US decided it best to maintain a neutral, passive attitude on Kashmir. After the 1965 war the US also realised that being the dissatisfied party Pakistan was more likely to resort to aggression, and therefore military superiority on India's part rather than military parity was more conducive to peace.

---

[4] The number of Indian Americans more than tripled to 1.2 million during 1987–97. Their number now is ten times that of Pakistani Americans. An India caucus was formed in US Congress in 1992 which now has over a quarter of House of Representatives members in it.

This accounted for the US not providing any serious military assistance to Pakistan after 1965, till Afghanistan made it inescapable in 1980. For the same reason, the US was quite pleased when the 1972 Simla Agreement took the Kashmir dispute out of the UNSC and made it a matter for bilateral negotiations. When violence erupted in J&K in 1989 and Kashmir once again began to cause international concern, the US administration took the position that while it was no longer urging a plebiscite in J&K, it considered the state a disputed territory. Secretary of State Colin Powell stated on 15 October 2001 that the US viewed the Kashmir issue central to and at the heart of the India–Pakistan dispute and that it should be resolved in accordance with the aspirations of the Kashmiri people. At the same time, the US has repeatedly made its opposition clear to any Pakistani attempt to resolve the dispute through the use of force. The net result of these carefully balanced US stances is that, while Pakistan and the Kashmiri discontented can derive some comfort from it in conceptual terms (acceptance that the territory is disputed and that Kashmiri aspirations are important), they can derive little in operational terms because of the US position that use of force is unacceptable and that the problem must be resolved through bilateral discussions.

The positions of other Western countries have largely paralleled that of the US. Britain had played an important role in shaping international perceptions on Kashmir in the initial years. But after helping to achieve a settlement of the Kutch border conflict of 1965 its role has steadily declined. It has continued to sell military equipment to both sides although in declining quantities because of lack of demand. France has sought to maintain an equidistant position, while trying to sell as much military equipment as possible to both sides. To the West in general, India is now a very important trading partner and investment opportunity and, therefore, far more important in their foreign policy framework than Pakistan is.

SOUTH ASIA AND OTHERS

Outside the West, the countries that have had an impact on the India–Pakistan conflict are China, Russia/Soviet Union and the West Asian Muslim countries. China had taken no position on the conflict till the 1962 Sino–Indian war. But after that, and more so after the signing of the 1963 Sino–Pakistan border agreement that demarcated the border between Xinjiang and what Pakistan calls the Northern Areas, China began to take a stance strongly supportive of Pakistan. During the 1965 and 1971 wars it not only provided strong diplomatic support to Pakistan but also attempted to create military tension along its border with India. The worsening Sino–Soviet tensions and the improving Indo–Soviet ties from the early 1960s also contributed to bringing China and Pakistan together. In 1973, China made the big decision to help Pakistan with its nuclear weapons programme. It also stepped up its supply of conventional military equipment. But the poor quality of Chinese equipment made it of little use in balancing what India was getting from the Soviet Union.

In 1972 not only did China and the US come together strategically against the Soviet Union, but China also became a permanent member of the UNSC, replacing Taiwan (Nationalist China). China was already a member of the five-country nuclear club. Membership of the UNSC and NWS clubs, the end of China's radical phase and the dramatic opening of its economy all contributed to China adopting a more responsible international stance from the end of the 1970s. By 1979 China's support to the rebels in India's northeast had ceased. By the early 1980s China had moved away from its earlier diplomatic stance of total support to Pakistan on Kashmir, and there was a measured improvement in Sino–Indian relations. Then came the ice-breaking visit of Prime Minister Rajiv Gandhi to China in 1988 which was followed by Prime Minister Li Peng's visit in 1991, Prime Minister Narasimha Rao's visit in 1993 (during which the important Agreement to Maintain Peace and Tranquillity along the Line of Actual Control was signed), and President Jiang Zemin's visit in 1996. Although relations were briefly strained in 1998 because of the ill-conceived Indian effort to link its nuclear tests to a threat from China, they got quickly back on track. China did not support Pakistan during the 1999 Kargil War and kept silent during Operation Parakram. Since 1990 India has been able to move sizeable forces from positions against China to positions against Pakistan. The June 2003 visit of Prime Minister Vajpayee saw the initiation of a special emissaries dialogue on the border dispute.

However, improvement in Sino–Indian relations has not been accompanied by a weakening of Sino–Pakistan ties. Apart from conventional military supplies, China has continued its clandestine support to Pakistan's nuclear and missile programmes. This support has serious implications, for it is the deterrence provided by Pakistan's nuclear weapons that has enabled it to promote violence and terrorism in Kashmir. China has yet to apportion any blame to Pakistan for what has been going on in Kashmir. Clearly, China sees propping up Pakistan against India as a course of action that continues to reward. It is a low-cost approach to hobble India geo-politically and economically.

China's economy is continuing to grow at nearly three times the global average, and it is now in the process of overtaking the US as the dominant trade partner across much of East Asia. Moreover, Chinese and US economies are getting substantially interlinked through US investment in China, China's purchase of US treasury bills, and US consumer demand for cheap Chinese goods. These economic facts and China's willingness for the present to go along with America's politico-military dominance across the world make it unlikely that US and China would jeopardise their relationship in the short-to-medium term. While China-bashing is a recurring election-year activity in the US, no US administration has seriously clashed with China since the two countries normalised their relationship three decades ago.

Moscow's influence in India–Pakistan affairs ceased from the time of the Soviet Union's demise. The Soviet Union's UNSC veto was very important to India from 1955 to the Simla Agreement of 1972. India's need for Soviet diplomatic support lessened after that but the Soviet Union continued to be, and now Russia continues to be, a very useful source of relatively low-cost, high-technology equipment. Today, the military supply connection is almost all there is in the Indo–Russian relationship. Indian (and Chinese) purchases play a big part in keeping Russia's arms industry alive. Soviet–Pakistan relations were at their lowest ebb during the 1979–88 Afghan war. Relations did not improve much even after its conclusion since Pakistan sought to promote Islamic radicalism in Central Asia. Today Russian interest in the subcontinent is far less than Soviet interest earlier. Central Asian republics, steadily slipping out of the Russian grip, now form a huge geographic inter-position between Russia and South Asia. The country's run-down navy is now out of the Indian Ocean, and India's need for Moscow's diplomatic support has evaporated. Non-military trade is in the doldrums: in 2002, it amounted to just $1.6 billion—a minuscule figure even in comparison to the unimpressive Sino–Russian figure of $7 billion and the Sino–Indian figure of $6 billion.

Muslim countries too have seen a depletion of their influence in South Asia. During the 1965 and 1971 wars, the West-leaning Muslim countries supported Pakistan diplomatically (some even offered military equipment), while the non-aligned ones (with the exception of Indonesia in 1965) generally adopted a neutral position. Till 1972, despite its founding basis, Pakistan was not seriously involved in international Muslim politics, including in the emotive matter of Palestine. But its perceived abandonment by the West in 1971 and the post-1973 oil wealth of the Gulf monarchies drew Pakistan into the arms of the latter. When the Iranian revolution of 1979 deepened the Sunni–Shia divide along the Gulf in 1979, Pakistan went along with the Sunni–Arab countries to the West. The Saudi money that gushed into Pakistan for the Afghan war from 1980 boosted radical Islam further, with considerable repercussions in Kashmir later.

India has always been sensitive to the need to ensure that Islamic countries do not look at Kashmir in Muslim–Hindu terms, as they do at Palestine in Muslim–Jew terms. Uninterrupted supply of oil has been important. So has been the need to ensure that earnings from the Gulf region continued to flow. Even today, remittances from Muslim countries not only far exceed India's remittances from the rest of the world, but also exceed India's software export earnings. In its endeavour to safeguard its position in the Muslim world, India is helped by two factors: India is seen by the global Muslim society as a country where Muslims, including Kashmiris, are well treated despite the rise of Hindutwa. Second, the Muslim world has always been a fragmented one. Fractures along conservative–radical, ethnic, and Sunni–Shia faultlines have made a unified Islamic position impossible on most issues. India has had success in taking advantage of these, including Afghan–Pakistan and Iran–Pakistan divisions.

The 1979–88 decade was the heyday for Pakistan in the Muslim world. It was seen as a plucky Muslim country taking on an atheistic superpower on behalf of the Islamic *umma*. During those years Pakistan got about $25 billion in remittances and it had military missions in eighteen countries comprising some 20,000 personnel. The end of the Afghan war and the collapse of the Soviet Union brought this Islam-based golden period to an abrupt close. The ideological fissure between the West and Islam, papered over till then, got exposed. It began to widen and became a chasm in 2001, trapping Pakistan. The care Pakistan had been taking to stay clear of radical Muslim countries and row along the US-leaning, conservative ones was of little use now, with even Saudi Arabia facing US ire. Pakistan is now in the very unenviable position of having to constantly tune its external and internal policies to manage the US on the one side and the Islamists on the other. This is going to be arduous work with the US and the Islamic World seemingly set for a long period of conflict.

Pakistan is in no position to contain India in the Islamic world, which has rarely been as strategically weak or internally shaken as it is today. Its governments have their hands full steering a safe course between societal anger and US wrath. They have little inclination to take sides in the India–Pakistan conflict. The Middle East is therefore unlikely to cause any concern to India for some time. In the short-to-medium term, a more serious problem might emerge closer home—from Bangladesh. The rhetoric against illegal Bangladeshi migrants and the perceived ill-treatment of Muslims in India is playing a more important role in the deteriorating India–Bangladesh relations than many recognise. The passage of three decades has largely erased the 'colonial' rule of Pakistan from Bangladeshi memory. A 'big brother-cum-anti-Muslim' image of India has been gaining ground. A country of 130 million Muslims sharing a 4,350-kilometre border can cause a good deal of problems for India if there is support for Pakistan among sections of its society and the state. The anarchical situation developing in neighbouring Nepal adds to the danger.

GLOBAL CONCERNS

The public introduction of nuclear weapons into the military arsenals of India and Pakistan in 1998 has generated international anxiety about the violence in Kashmir that was not there earlier. Kashmir is now seen by many as a nuclear danger point. This was visible in the unprecedented, unified great-power pressure applied on Pakistan in 1999 to withdraw from the Kargil area, and the continuous high-level diplomacy that the US and others resorted to during the 2001–02 Operation Parakram. Great-power efforts to roll back or even cap the nuclear weapon capabilities of the two countries were effectively given up by 2000, when virtually all economic sanctions imposed on the two countries following the 1998 tests were lifted. The changed US approach towards the spread of nuclear weapons—shifting emphasis from international law-based non-proliferation, to force-based counter-proliferation—has also helped to make the two countries' nuclear capability more acceptable. The world is now finding itself pushed to address the risk of nuclear war in the subcontinent more from the demand side (cause of war) than from the supply side (means of war). The fear of nuclear war has also made the merits of each side's position on the Kashmir dispute even less a matter of interest than earlier. Instead, the objective of finding a workable solution to the conflict has become the main focus.

India and Pakistan are aware that while the level of global acceptance of their nuclear weapons did register a quantum increase with their 1998 tests, they still have a long way to traverse before they can hope to become NWSs and secure the freedoms and benefits that this status brings. To a degree the two are on probation right now where they are expected to demonstrate responsible conduct in three major areas: material and technology security, adherence to the provisions of strategic regimes, and keeping war risks under control. India has no serious problem with the first two, but the third will pose a challenge as long as Kashmir remains militarily contested. For Pakistan all three areas pose difficulty. Leakage will remain a concern as long as radical groups have influence in the ruling circles. Strategic regimes could continue to be violated so long as Pakistan needs outside help to improve its nuclear missile arsenal. As for war risk, being the revisionist party in Kashmir, Pakistan will find itself more tempted than India to manipulate threats and risks.

Recent revelations that have forced Pakistan to accept that it had provided nuclear technology to North Korea, Iran and Libya and to publicly indict the country's nuclear icon, A.Q. Khan, are bound to have repercussions. Pakistan will no longer be able to barter strategic technologies with North Korea, or provide them to other countries for financial and material gain. Help from China is also likely to get restricted. The low-key US reaction to these revelations is primarily the result of Pakistan's current usefulness in Afghanistan. But there is another reason as well. Now that the nuclear weapon infrastructures of Iraq and Libya have been eliminated and that of Iran brought under a degree of control, the US is less worried about any new Islamic state acquiring nuclear weapons. Therefore, it finds it more advantageous to co-opt rather than confront Pakistan, the only Islamic country with nuclear weapons.

Terrorist attacks against US interests occurring through the 1980s and 1990s, and culminating in the 9/11 attacks of 2001, have placed terrorism at the top of the global concerns list. Terrorism has also become firmly twinned with Islamic fanaticism. With the inconsequential exception of Basque separatists there is no non-Muslim group that poses a terrorist danger to any Western country today. Pakistan-nurtured terrorism in Kashmir is increasingly seen as an Islamic project connected to the threat faced by the West. But there are differing views on how best to deal with that connection. There are two broad streams of thinking in this regard. The ideological one, represented by the neo-conservatives in the US, is based on three interconnected premises: Islam is a unified adversary, it is organically hostile to the West, and it is not possible to compromise with it. Under this line of thinking, terrorism in Kashmir is a serious indirect danger to the West and must be uprooted. The pragmatic stream looks at the issue differently. It feels that Islamic society, globally and even within individual countries, is diverse and it is in the interests of the West to take advantage of that diversity to isolate the fanatics. It also feels that the West must concentrate on the threats that confront it directly, and should not enlarge the danger by taking on threats faced by other countries.

Both these divergent lines of thinking are likely to have their impact on Western policy. The unprecedented fissure that occurred among NATO countries in the run up to the 2003 Iraq invasion had much less to do with the morality of the US's action than with the question whether the conquest of Iraq would make the West more safe. Most Europeans do not think that the US can safeguard them today from the danger of diffused Islamic anger, with its many and resilient roots, the way it could protect them from the Soviet military threat during the Cold War. The realpolitik issue coming to the fore in the West is not whether terrorist violence can be justified or not under any circumstances, but rather what is the best way of dealing with it. The reality that the struggle against terrorism is going to be long, inchoate and messy, with varying objectives and stakes among countries, makes a clear, consensual view on this very difficult.

The issue of addressing what is often termed the 'root causes' of a conflict is part of this problem. From a realist perspective, the matter of dealing with root causes calls for it to be looked at, not from the moral angle, but from its practical usefulness in each case. The US, with a plethora of problems to be handled world-wide and also possessing huge reserve power to deal with problems as they arise, has generally not been inclined to look at root causes. But most Europeans are not certain that a pure fire-fighting approach, as opposed to one that also incorporates fire prevention, is the best way to tackle Islamic anger. As a result there is unlikely to be a global, unified approach towards terrorism. Even in the US, the policy will shift and mutate. The neo-conservatives are not going to be permanently ensconced in the driving seat.

The new focus on terrorism has pushed the 1990s concern for democracy temporarily into the background. Pakistan's first spell of military rule, 1958–71, was not a serious embarrassment as authoritarian dispensations (colonial, monarchical, communist and military) were then common across the globe. But global perceptions of acceptable forms of governance had begun to change by the time Zia took over power in 1977, and had transformed radically by the time Musharraf did a replay in 1999. It was the recognition of this that kept Musharraf from imposing martial law and made him choose the curious title of Chief Executive to start with. Zia was lucky, and Musharraf luckier that external happenings baled them out within two years each of mounting their coups—Zia by the Soviet invasion of Afghanistan and Musharraf by 9/11. Still, Musharraf is far more exposed to the 'threat' from democracy than Zia was. Ruling as he did before the Soviet collapse, and when military rule was still the norm in Latin America and Africa, Zia did not have to face the same level of global revulsion for authoritarianism that Musharraf has had to. Nor does Musharraf have the benefit of martial law that Zia had to keep internal critics at bay.

While 9/11 has made Musharraf's military-led rule temporarily acceptable, its longer-term impact could be less helpful. The growing perception that one of the main causes of Islamic radicalism is the lack of democracy in Muslim countries is not going to help the military in Pakistan. At the same time, the US is aware of the need to distinguish the long-term desirability of promoting democracy and the shorter-term problems such promotion could create. Elections during 2002 brought to the fore undesirable Islamic parties—from the US point of view—in Turkey and Pakistan. In both countries, and in others like Algeria and Indonesia, the power of the military is seen as providing a useful restraint. The reluctance of the US to introduce one-person, one-vote democracy in both Iraq and Afghanistan also points to this.

THINKING OF PARTIES

The outside world influences the India–Pakistan conflict not only by the interest and positions it takes on the Kashmir issue, but also through the general setting it creates. The impact of the external world on Indian and Pakistani thinking is less through direct interventions than through the way it shapes environment and discourse. Since 1990 three major developments in the world—American dominance of global politics, nuclear weapons with India and Pakistan, and a marked international sensitisation to the perils of terrorism—have become very relevant to the way the conflict is being seen.

India and Pakistan are conscious that the way America perceives the conflict has become crucial. Each is trying hard to get the international community, led by the US, to accept not only its view of what the conflict is about, but also its prescription for dealing with it. An intense competition for outside approval was not necessary during the Cold War days when international relationships had more structure and durability, and outside intervention was considered less likely and less consequential because of the bipolar constraint operating on it.

Both countries have factored in this new reality. India is seeking to broaden and deepen its relationship with the US. The alacrity with which it embraced the US plan for missile defence in May 2001 had as its objective not only the development of military-technology cooperation, but also the strengthening of diplomatic closeness. India's falling in line with the US in its opposition to the International Criminal Court, and its edging towards the US's position on the Kyoto Protocol on climate change showed the new Indian desire to prove itself a weighty and reliable ally of the US in the class of Britain, Israel, Japan and Australia.[5] India is hoping that in the long term the US will find it necessary to break the power of Islamic countries and also balance China within Asia, and that in both endeavours India would have much to offer. Pakistan is aware that it cannot compete with India—with its advantages of a much bigger economy, democracy,

---

[5] Although India did not send troops to Iraq in the summer of 2003, the Indian elite was largely in favour of doing so. There were many mainstream editorials and opinion pieces urging their despatch.

and stronger civil society links—in forging a broad-based relationship with the US. Its strong suit continues to be in the narrow field of military usefulness—once it was against the Soviet Union, now it is against al-Qaeda and other anti-US Islamists spread across Pakistan and Afghanistan. Pakistan believes that there is going to be no easy or early end to the Afghan problem.

Divergent perceptions characterise the strategic thinking of India and Pakistan with regard to nuclear weapons. India believes that its lack of aggressive intent and the democratic restraints on its NCA makes its nuclear weapons safe, and that the world sees it as so. It also thinks that the world can never feel comfortable with the nuclear weapons of Pakistan. The decision-making risks emanating from the narrow, military-dominated structure of Pakistan's NCA as well as the security risks inherent in an Islamist environment are seen as too high for comfort. The Pakistani reading of the situation is different. It recognises that its non-proliferation claims have received a body blow as a result of recent disclosures regarding North Korea, Iran and Libya. Yet it thinks that the US is unlikely to get hurting tough with it. For one, Pakistan considers that the point where its weapons could be taken out without causing massive destruction is now past, and that the US knows it. Also, that the best bet the US has to keep nuclear weapons and material safe in Pakistan is the country's Army. Pakistan believes that the US has no choice but to come to terms with its nuclear arsenal and that it would not be in the latter's interest to let India back Pakistan into a corner.

On the terrorism front, India is hoping that sooner or later Pakistan will be squeezed between the rock of the US and the hard place of Islamic radicals. The balancing act that Pakistan is currently playing is seen as unsustainable, and that sooner or later it will have to tilt to one side. If it tilts in favour of Islamists, US sanctions would make its economy implode, and if it tilts against them internal strife would make the country ungovernable. Both paths are seen as taking Pakistan to a precipice. Pakistan reads the situation differently. It thinks that the US would be forced to pursue parallel courses—extirpating Islamic terrorists along one and cultivating moderate Muslim states along the other. To do this persuasively, attacks on Muslims in some places will have to be balanced by favours done to Muslims elsewhere. Pakistan thinks that while the US would not be able to do the latter in Palestine, it can be led to do that in Kashmir if Pakistan plays its cards adroitly.

A part of the Kashmiri discontented think in parallel with Pakistan on the issues of terrorism and nuclear weapons. They believe that it is not in the US's interest to accept the Indian portrayal of Kashmiri violence as a case of pure terrorism. They think that Kashmir—like Bosnia, Kosovo and Chechnya—is a good place for the US to show its concern for Muslims. In the case of nuclear weapons, they believe that the Pakistani capability is providing a useful source of pressure on their behalf.

OUTSIDERS AND THE FUTURE

With outside concerns about Kashmir much higher now than it was a decade ago, what are the prospects of it generating genuine peace-making potential? Has the US got the inclination, political will and leverage to embark on a serious peace effort? Is the perception that the US is now in a unique position to forge peace well founded? A detached look at the situation is likely to provide some cheer, but not much. The leverage that the US has with the two countries has increased, but its will to get involved has not. For one, the US is seriously and uneasily stretched in its global role. For another, it is wary of burning its fingers in a seemingly doomed endeavour. The recent optimism, shown by many in India and Pakistan in this regard, arises largely from the unrealistic belief that the US can and is willing to pressure the other side to make deep concessions (which that side has steadfastly refused to make for half a century), while seeking nothing significant from one's own side.

India has always been against outside involvement in Kashmir. This stems partly from the perception that material concessions can be sought only from India because it is the in-possession party. But an important second consideration is that any form of outside involvement in South Asia, regardless of its outcome, could weaken India's regional dominance. Moreover, India is aware that international perceptions of the Kashmir problem vary from its own. Even though few hold today that Kashmir should go rightfully to Pakistan on the basis of religion, many outsiders consider the territory disputed. Similarly, while there is little support for the right of self-determination of groups like the Kashmiris, there is a feeling that the autonomy they once enjoyed should be restored, at least partly. Also, though the violence currently taking place in J&K is seen as largely Pakistan-promoted, there is a parallel perception that India was responsible for creating the conditions that made it possible. Finally, there is the reading that the nuclear risk in the subcontinent is real and requires addressing. Such perceptions are seen to be making it difficult to arrive at an outsider-involved settlement acceptable to India.

Till recently India's security community had shared these fears uniformly. But now there is a growing segment within it that thinks that while these perceptions may have relevance at popular levels abroad, at policy-making levels they no longer have an impact adverse to India. This stems from two calculations. One is that by now the world has accepted that under no circumstances can India be persuaded to let go even a small part of the territory that is with India—except in the context of minor adjustments to the LoC to make it better manageable. The other is that India's new relationship with America is based on a durable congruence of strategic interests and the US will not do anything to damage it. Pressuring India unduly on the Kashmir issue is certain to do that.

Being the weaker as well as the change-seeking party, Pakistan has always sought international intervention in Kashmir. Initially, this was based on the perception that the US, and the larger West, were supportive of its stance and that the UNSC resolutions on plebiscite would help it. Even after this position changed, with the Simla Agreement making the UNSC resolutions ineffective, Pakistan has continued to be keen on an international (read US) role. This stems from the calculation that the US, if it plays a role in the negotiations, is likely to see that Pakistan is at least somewhat satisfied so that the conflict is brought to an end. The twin factors of discontent among the Kashmiris and the nuclear war risk, Pakistan believes, would make it difficult for the US to push for a settlement that wholly endorses the Indian position.

The US, on its part, knows that for all the impact of unipolarity, it is in no position to press India and Pakistan to accept a settlement that one of the sides is unable to live with. The US has never had any serious political leverage with India. Even in India's very constrained post-1962 war position, it could not be pressed to make any serious concession on Kashmir during its six rounds of negotiations with Pakistan. And in other security matters—most notably in acceding to the NPT and CTBT—India has shown that it is immune to pressure. Much the same is true of Pakistan. The US could not coax it to abandon its very vulnerable nuclear programme during 1973–79, when the US was in a position to apply heavy pressure and Pakistan had no means of exerting counter-pressure. Today, with Pakistan's nuclear assets beyond surgical divestment and it being in a position to manipulate the Islamist danger, the US's ability to press it is even less.

If the US is unable to exert results-producing pressure, can it offer inducements that can make a difference? What would work best with India are political rewards. A seat in the UNSC can be a big lure, but the US would require considerable international cooperation to expand the Security Council in a manner that strengthens rather than weakens its control over it. Amending the NPT to legalise India's nuclear arsenal can also be a big incentive, but it would pose problems as such a step would bring in Israel and Pakistan as well. What the US can probably do best in the short term is to offer economic carrots. Aid, bilateral as well as multilateral, and debt-restructuring can be very attractive to Pakistan. Preferential market access can make a difference to India too. Steps like US–India and US–Pakistan free trade zones, though difficult to negotiate, are also possible.

D espite the continuing difficulties experienced in making the power sharing government work, the conflict in Northern Ireland is on a winding-down path and its petering out in the not so distant future appears a reasonable prospect. In India and Pakistan there is little understanding of how bitter the relations once were, not just between Dublin and Belfast, but also between Dublin and London. And how deeply antipathy and rancour had seeped into their societies, much more than they have in the subcontinent. Also, how embedded were the roots of the conflict, and how irreconcilable were positions and objectives. It must be recognised that it was not just the changed socio-political landscape of Europe that has led to the abatement of the conflict. If it were so, the Basque problem in Spain—less difficult in many ways—should also have been on a settlement path by now. Progress in Northern Ireland has come about for reasons that have to do with changes in people's thinking. These include recognition of costs, rethinking of positions, and a more sophisticated understanding of conflict structures and conflict subsidence. It is worth trying to understand how this conflict, which had gathered strength over three centuries, was put on a resolution path.

The Northern Ireland and Kashmir scenarios have many differences. The most obvious one is that, while the former is mainly an internal conflict the latter is largely an international one. Moreover, while the Irish Republic has been helping Britain to set the conflict on a subsiding path in recent decades, Pakistan has been doing its best to fuel the internal component of the Kashmir conflict. At a broader level, there is the reality that nationalist and religious passions are less potent in today's Europe than they are in South Asia. Also, while in Northern Ireland there are two fairly clear-cut contesting communities, in J&K the religious and cultural mix is more complex. While these points of dissimilarity are important, they do not detract from the fact that Northern Ireland has been a significant success story of conflict abatement in a world where such stories are few and can therefore offer insights—not lessons or templates—on how opposed visions of the future can be made to slowly converge.

EVOLUTION OF THE CONFLICT

People from Britain first came to Ireland in substantial numbers in the twelfth and thirteenth centuries. This did not create a problem and the Anglo–Norman culture of the newcomers blended fairly easily with the Irish–Gaelic culture of the local people. There was no religious divide then as both societies were Catholic. The position changed when new waves of British settlers came in the sixteenth and seventeenth centuries. The new arrivals considered themselves distinct from and superior to the native Irish, and this led to a colonial ethos that visiated their relationship. The newcomers, English and Scots, dispossessed the native Irish of much of their agricultural land using force. A religious divide also surfaced when England and Scotland became largely Protestant at the beginning of the mid-sixteenth century. Political domination, economic exploitation, and cultural denigration marked the British colonial period.

There were two major Irish military campaigns to dislodge the British, in the 1640s and from 1689 to 1691. Both ended in decisive victories for the British. In 1720 British parliament declared its right to legislate directly for Ireland, and the Irish executive became British appointed. Thereafter, the Irish lay largely subdued till a major revolt led by Wolf Tone, an Irish Protestant, took place in 1798. That too was crushed, as were later ones in the nineteenth century. Trade restrictions were imposed on Ireland, as Britain did in the case of its colonies. The industrial revolution bypassed the island, and its plantation economy was used to generate profits for Britain. In the nineteenth century, the economic gap between Britain and Ireland widened dramatically and famines became frequent in Ireland. The huge Irish emigration to America from the mid-nineteenth century was prompted by economic distress.

In the late nineteenth century, Irish resistance to British colonial rule began to gather momentum. London was forced to consider changes and three Home Rule bills were introduced one after the other, the last in 1912. The idea of Home Rule, which would make Irish–Catholics, over three-quarters of the population, politically dominant was unsettling to Protestants who were largely concentrated in the province of Ulster in the north-east of the island. They strongly opposed Home Rule, and insisted that if it were to come, Ulster should be separated from the rest of the island. The Protestants raised the Ulster Volunteer Force as a militia, and the Nationalists (Catholics) raised the Irish Volunteers. Meanwhile, there was the Easter Rising of Catholics in Dublin in 1916. In the 1918 elections, the militant Sinn Fein won a spectacular victory, and in 1919 they made a symbolic proclamation of the Irish Republic.

In 1920 Britain passed the Government of Ireland Act, partitioning the thirty-two county island into southern Ireland with twenty-six counties (83 per cent of the area) and northern Ireland with six counties—out of the nine in the province of Ulster. Two of these six counties had Catholic majorities but overall, Protestants outnumbered Catholics two to one. The Nationalists protested against the partition, and during 1919–22 there was considerable fighting. An Anglo–Irish Treaty was signed in 1921, whereby the majority of Nationalists accepted the partition, and two new political entities—Irish Free State and Northern Ireland—came into existence.

The 1920 Act had provided for a Council of Ireland leading to the eventual establishment of a Parliament of Ireland. The Anglo–Irish Treaty of 1921 had provided for boundary adjustments based on local preference. Both were worrying to the Protestants of Ulster. The Council of Ireland threatened the durability of partition, and the Boundary

Commission the territory's borders. The Irish Republican Army (IRA), closely connected to the Republican political party Sinn Fein, was active on both sides of the border. The Unionists soon got the better of the IRA militarily. This weakened the bargaining strength of the Irish Free State, and the British interest in seeking a compromise evaporated. The Council of Ireland never met, and the Boundary Commission gradually collapsed. In December 1925, both parties accepted the 1921 boundary, and the functions of the Council of Ireland were transferred to Dublin and Belfast parliaments.

Opposition to the partition continued strongly in the Irish Free State. When the legendary Eamon de Valera became Prime Minister in 1932, he sought to sever the state's links with Britain thereby deepening the divide with Northern Ireland. A new constitution, enacted in July 1937, asserted Dublin's de jure authority over Northern Ireland. Although the Irish Free State was deeply opposed to the partition, it could do little. Northern Ireland's Protestants were militarily well organised, and supported by Britain. Moreover, the Irish Free State was dependent on Britain for its exports and imports. Sinn Fein and the IRA were an embarrassment, for not only did they provoke Britain and Northern Ireland, but also created internal disturbances in the south. The IRA never received any official support from the south after the early 1920s.

The Unionists had a siege mentality from the time Northern Ireland was created. The Catholics in the territory, a third of the total, wanted partition undone. So did the Catholics of the Irish Free State, who outnumbered Northern Ireland Protestants nearly three to one. To add to this, the state that they had carved out was a deeply unequal one, squarely based on Protestant supremacy. Its ideology did not permit the Catholic–Irish to be incorporated into an egalitarian, pluralist society. Through franchise control and gerrymandering of constituencies, the Unionists kept control over local councils even in Catholic-majority areas. In the territory's parliament, Stormont, majoritarian domination became the order. Land sales to Catholics were blocked, and Catholics were deliberately discriminated against in the areas of public housing and public employment. So also in private employment. The Catholic unemployment rate was never less than twice that of the Protestants. Public facilities in Catholic areas steadily declined.

Government-supported sectarian marches were resorted to to intimidate Catholics. Discrimination and browbeating were used not only to subdue Catholics but also to induce them to emigrate. From the mid-1920s the rate of Catholic emigration from Northern Ireland, relative to population, was about four times that of Protestants. The armed Royal Ulster Constabulary (RUC) was formed in 1922. There was also the Protestant Special Constabulary, whose part-time 'B' specials were allowed to keep their arms at home. Coercive laws were passed which had no parallel in Britain or in the Irish Free State. Internment without trial was regular.

The Irish Free State stayed neutral during World War II, deeply angering the British. Ireland's ports and airfields could have been very useful in combating the German submarines then strangling Britain. Northern Ireland was strongly supportive of the war effort, and this strengthened the Unionists' position with the British. The Irish Republic (or Eire) was established in 1949, and it chose to leave the British Commonwealth. The Republic decided to stay out of NATO too. These decisions were prompted by the determination to not get politically involved with Britain in any manner. In 1949 London passed the Ireland Act, affirming that any change in the constitutional status of Northern Ireland could only occur with the consent of its assembly, thereby giving the Unionists an effective veto over any decision that London and Dublin might take concerning them.

The IRA carried out some attacks in Northern Ireland during 1956–62, but they could not be sustained. The IRA was as strongly policed against in the south as it was in the north. Most Catholics in the north did not support the IRA as they knew that it was no match for the security forces, and that IRA violence only led to greater repression of the Catholic community. The community was sullen but stayed subdued. The two decades after World War II were a golden age for the Unionists. The economy was doing well, the Nationalists were under control, London was happy with the state of affairs, and internationally there was little concern expressed against the discrimination and intimidation the Catholics were subjected to. The Unionists ignored the discontent steadily building up among the Catholics.

By the mid-1960s, the Catholic community of Northern Ireland had become quite different from what it had been at the time of partition four decades earlier. It had grown apart from its co-religionists in the south, realising that it could not look south for any tangible support. Though their disadvantage in terms of education and employment continued in relative terms, they had made substantial progress in absolute terms. The welfare system introduced in the UK after World

War II helped them greatly. They were no longer the backward Irish peasants they used to be derided as. Their self-confidence and self-help capacity had grown. The focus of their struggle had also altered. Undoing the partition was no longer a priority. It was seen as an impractical aim to pursue in the short- to medium-term. What concerned them most were the conditions of their existence, as individuals and as a community. Ending institutionalised discrimination became the core objective.

In 1963 the twenty-year premiership of Basil Brooke came to an end in Northern Ireland. Terrence O'Neill who had a slightly more modern vision succeeded him. Labour under Harold Wilson came to power in the UK the following year. Unlike Conservatives, Labour was not interlocked with the Unionists. The period saw civil rights catching global attention, as a result of the Black civil rights movement in the US. O'Neill knew that some steps were necessary to bring Northern Ireland into the modern world. In 1965 he met Nationalist leader Sean Leman, breaking a Unionist taboo in place since 1937 of not talking to the Nationalists. The year also saw the rise of Ian Paisley, an unabashed Protestant supremacist who in 2004 continues to lead Protestant opposition to compromising with the Catholics.

O'Neill's effort to ease tensions came too late. The year 1966 saw the formation of the Northern Ireland Civil Rights Association (NICRA) by Catholics and the revival by Protestants of the Ulster Volunteer Force (UVF) that had spearheaded the fight against Catholics at the time of partition. The UVF killed two Catholics in the summer of 1966, inaugurating the violence that was to engulf the territory. The NICRA and the student-led People's Democracy began a series of civil rights marches in October 1968 that led to serious violence. There was rioting and violence on a continual basis, and very soon the IRA entered the fray. In August 1969 the British Army was deployed for peacekeeping. In January 1970 the IRA's inability to protect the Catholics during the ongoing fighting led to both the Sinn Fein and the IRA getting split—into moderate 'official' and extremist 'provisional' groups. The 'official' groups soon faded and the 'provisionals' came to be known as Sinn Fein and the IRA.

Meanwhile, London tried to contain violence. Beginning August 1969, a series of steps were taken to reform the police. In April 1970 moderate Unionists formed the Alliance Party (AP), and extremists led by Ian Paisley the Protestant Unionists, which in October 1971 became the Democratic Unionist Party (DUP). The Ulster Unionist

Party (UUP), which had been in unbroken power since 1922, was now challenged from both ends of the Unionist spectrum. In June 1970 Conservatives returned to power in London under Edward Heath, who was not supportive of hardline Protestant politics. The Social Democratic and Labour Party (SDLP), which was to immediately become the main nationalist party, was formed in August. In 1971, the IRA militant campaign began to take a serious toll. Protestant para-military groups (Paras) also became active. That year saw 147 people, including fifty-nine security personnel killed.

Matters got worse the next year, during which 467 people including 146 security personnel were killed—the highest annual toll of the campaign. On 22 February the army shot dead fourteen unarmed demonstrators. This was to have a tremendous impact. On 30 March London prorogued the Northern Ireland Assembly and imposed direct rule. The structure that had underpinned Northern Ireland governance for fifty years was gone. A Northern Ireland office was created, and William Whitelaw was made Secretary of State for Northern Ireland (SOSNI). Whitelaw gave special category status to IRA prisoners and the IRA responded with a ceasefire on 26 June. In early July secret negotiations with the IRA were held in London and included Gerry Adams and Martin McGuinness, both of whom were to become prominent public negotiators for the Sinn Fein later. But negotiations soon broke down and the IRA ended its brief ceasefire on 13 July. A week later came Bloody Friday when twenty bombs exploded in Belfast. London now decided, for the first time, to seek the help of Dublin. In May 1973, a path-breaking white paper, which not only visualised a devolved government requiring support from both communities, but also cooperation between Dublin and Belfast, was issued.

A new assembly for Northern Ireland was elected on 28 June 1973. It saw those opposing the white paper in majority among the Unionists. On 21 November Whitelaw announced agreement on the new executive. It was to have one AP, six Unionist and four SDLP ministers. The UUP leader was to be Chief Executive and the SDLP leader his deputy. On 6 December 1973 a conference took place in Sunningdale, England, in which, besides delegations led by British and Irish Prime Ministers, leaders of the Unionists, SDLP and AP also took part. The Sunningdale conference agreed on a Council of Ireland, drawn equally from the Irish government and the Executive. The council, which was to act by unanimity, was to have 'executive action' in eight areas including natural resources, electricity and transport. Sinn Fein was kept out of all this, and the IRA reacted by exploding bombs, for the first time, in Britain.

The power sharing executive began to function in January 1974, but ineffectively because of determined Unionist opposition to the idea. In February London saw a change of government from Heath's Conservatives to Harold Wilson's Labour. In May a Unionist-instigated general strike crippled Northern Ireland, and the First Minister and his executive resigned. In July London published a white paper proposing the election of a constitutional convention. In the elections for the convention held in May 1975, the big winner was the United Ulster Unionist Coalition which was 'united' only against the Sunningdale Agreement. In November the convention proposed a return to an essentially Stormont structure. That was not acceptable to London and the convention was dissolved in March 1976.

Both Northern Ireland and Eire saw huge peace marches in 1976. Its cross-community organisers, Mairead Corrigan and Betty Williams, shared a Nobel Peace Prize for their efforts but the marches soon faded from memory. In May 1977 the Unionists, trying to repeat their May 1974 success, tried another general strike with the idea of installing a majoritarian executive, but it did not succeed. That year also saw the Nationalists getting their first bit of encouragement from the US, when President Carter expressed his support for a peaceful solution in Northern Ireland. Meanwhile, Ireland was moving closer to Europe. It joined the European Monetary System in 1979 while Britain stayed out. General elections in Britain in May 1979 brought to power Margaret Thatcher who was more sympathetic to the Unionist cause than her predecessors Wilson and Heath.

Thatcher toughened British policy against the Nationalists, and 1980 saw IRA prisoners launching a hunger strike against the ending of their special category status accorded in 1976. The 1980 hunger strike was followed by another in 1981, which saw ten prisoners dying over May–October, beginning with Bobby Sands on 5 May. The hunger strikes provided the biggest boost to the Nationalist cause after the 1968–69 civil rights marches. A hundred thousand people attended Sands' funeral. The strikes transformed the image of Sinn Fein, and to an extent that of the IRA, among Catholics in both parts of Ireland. In the October 1982 assembly elections, the Sinn Fein, till then marginalised in electoral politics, got as much as 54 per cent of the votes that the SDLP polled. The growing strength of the Sinn Fein worried both London and Dublin. This led to the two coming together, after two years of arrested relations because of Thatcher's tougher policy against the Nationalists.

The two Prime Ministers met in November 1983 and the inter-governmental council began to operate. Between November 1983 and March 1985, the council met thirty times, paving the way for the 1985 Anglo–Irish Agreement. The talks did not derail despite an IRA bomb attack on 12 October 1984 at the Conservative Party conference in Brighton shortly to be addressed by Thatcher. The Agreement was an international treaty, signed under considerable media glare at Hillsborough, Northern Ireland, and deposited with the United Nations. It provided for Dublin to be consulted on Northern Ireland issues through an inter-governmental conference to be serviced by a permanent secretariat at Maryfield, outside Belfast. Despite Margaret Thatcher's iron-lady image, the agreement was greeted with cries of 'treachery' and 'rewarding terrorism'. The 'marching season' of sum-mer 1986 saw huge confrontations. There was also escalated violence by the Paras and the IRA.

In January 1987 the leaders of the SDLP and Sinn Fein—Hume and Adams—began a series of meetings to explore the substantive issues that separated the two parties. These centred on Sinn Fein's positions, contrary to the SLDP's, that the Unionists should not be allowed a veto over the right of Irish people to self-determination and that Britain was still not agnostic towards Irish unity. In 1989 London outlawed the still widespread discrimination against Catholics. This was partly a response to European Community (EC) pressure, and also to a 1984 campaign in the US to link investment to fair employ-ment practices. Violence continued meanwhile, but at a reduced level than in the 1970s. Against the 1,982 killed during the1970s, only 778 were killed during the 1980s. The figures for the security forces were 555 and 312.

In 1990 London once again opened secret channels of communi-cation with Sinn Fein. It was during this dialogue that the Sinn Fein conveyed its agreement in principle to the critical idea that, till a major-ity within Northern Ireland decided otherwise, the territory would stay a part of the UK. This was a huge change in its position, in which the Hume–Adams dialogue of 1988–89 had played a big role. But London was still not prepared to deal with Sinn Fein publicly. In No-vember that year, Peter Brooke, SOSNI, stated that Britain had 'no selfish or strategic or economic interest in Northern Ireland'. In other words, Northern Ireland's future was entirely up to the people of the territory. A month later John Major replaced Thatcher as Prime Minister. In March 1992 Brooke was able to say that London expected negotiations to take place soon on the basis of three interlocking relationships—Strand One concerned with the devolved administration in Northern Ireland, Strand Two focusing on North–South structures, and Strand Three dealing with the relationship between the UK and the Republic of Ireland.

By 1993 dialogues were active at three different levels. Besides the publicised talks between the SDLP (Hume) and the Sinn Fein (Adams) as well as London and Dublin, there were secret talks between London and the Sinn Fein. The climax of these efforts came in the form of the Downing Street Declaration of 15 December 1993 by the British and Irish Prime Ministers. Unlike in 1985, this time the UUP was on board. The heart of the declaration was the formal acceptance by the British government that it was for the people of 'the island of Ireland alone, by agreement between the two parts respectively, to exercise their right of self-determination on the basis of consent, freely and concurrently given, North and South, to bring about a united Ireland, if that is their wish.' The declaration made it clear that London had no interest of its own with regard to how the future of Northern Ireland unfolded. It is noteworthy that this significant declaration came about despite 1992–93 witnessing some of the most damaging IRA bomb attacks in England. The Sinn Fein accepted the declaration in December 1993 and the Ulster Defence Association, the umbrella group of Paras, accepted it in August 1994.

On 31 August 1994 the IRA announced its 'complete cessation of military operations'. This had been helped by the secret negotiations between London and the Sinn Fein, the Hume–Adams dialogue, and the greater interest the US had been taking since President Clinton took office at the beginning of 1993. Gerry Adams was allowed to visit the US in the summer of 1994 and he made two further visists later that year. On 13 October the Combined Loyalist Military Command announced its own ceasefire. On 22 February 1995 the British and Irish Prime Ministers set out their 'Frameworks for the Future'. The first framework showed a possible governmental structure with provisions for cross-community agreement on contentious issues. The second framework suggested North–South institutions that would have 'executive, harmonising and consultative functions'. These major steps—the Downing Street Declaration of December 1993 and the Frameworks for the Future of February 1995—caused major disquiet in Unionist ranks. They responded by intensifying their summer 'marches'. Compared to 2,120 marches in 1985, there were 3,500 in 1995.

Meanwhile, decommissioning of arms by the IRA became a major issue. London and the Unionists had made decommissioning a precondition for all-party talks involving the Sinn Fein. On 28 November 1995, the British and Irish Prime Ministers agreed to establish a body under former US senator George Mitchell to report on decommissioning. Two days later, President Clinton visited Belfast to give a boost to the peace process. The Mitchell Group, in its report of 24 January 1996, suggested that decommissioning of arms and political negotiations should move forward in tandem. The continuing exclusion of the Sinn Fein from the formal peace talks and the increasing pressure on decommissioning IRA arms led to the IRA breaking its seventeen-month ceasefire through a major bomb attack in London on 9 February. Meanwhile, London wanted to elect a new political forum to provide the participating parties with a democratic mandate. But the forum, elected on 30 May, never got going because the Sinn Fein was excluded for want of IRA ceasefire and the SDLP stopped attending it in September. The summer of 1996 saw serious rioting, triggered by marches.

On 1 May 1997, Labour under Tony Blair won a decisive victory. Unlike Major, Blair was not dependent on Unionist support in Westminster. The 1997 marches, after a good deal of brinkmanship by both sides, went off relatively peacefully. On 22 July, the IRA announced a new ceasefire, and this led to the Sinn Fein being brought into formal discussions for the first time. Negotiations began under Mitchell in September. The DUP and the United Kingdom Unionists (UKU), representing as much as 40 per cent of the Protestant electorate, refused to take part, but all others including the Sinn Fein did. The negotiations were difficult, but with the substantial personal involvement of Prime Ministers Blair and Ahern, and support from President Clinton, the agreement was signed on Good Friday, 10 April 1998. The agreement reiterated that any future union of North and South would depend on the consent of the two electorates, given separately. The agreement called for the repeal by the UK of the 1920 Government of Ireland Act, and by Ireland of Articles 2 and 3 in its 1937 constitution which claimed Northern Ireland as its own.

A 108-member assembly was to be elected by proportional representation and key decisions were to have cross-party support. The

Executive was to have a First Minister and a Deputy First Minister, elected on a cross-community basis. Membership of the Executive was to be allocated to parties on the basis of the number of seats. The whole arrangement, particularly on decision-making, was quite complex and was designed to assure the Nationalists that there would be no return to pre-1972 majoritarianism. A North–South Ministerial Council, drawn from the Assembly and the government in Dublin, was to take decisions 'by agreement' on a range of subjects including education, agriculture, transport and tourism. There was also to be a British–Irish Council, representing London and Dublin, the Northern Ireland Assembly, and the devolved parliaments in Scotland and Wales. This would deal with issues such as transport links, the environment and culture. The section on decommissioning of arms required parties 'to use any influence they have, to achieve decommissioning of all paramilitary arms within two years'. This hope has not been recognised even after six years. A schedule was set to release prisoners belonging to ceasefire-observing paramilitary organisations within two years. There was also provision to set up a commission to look into policing—a priority issue for the Catholics—as well as commissions for human rights and equality.

In parallel referendums held on 2 May 1998, 71 per cent in Northern Ireland and 94 per cent in the Republic endorsed the agreement. Within Northern Ireland, the Unionists backed the agreement by only a narrow majority. In the assembly elections held on 25 June, the parties that supported the agreement won 80 seats and those opposed to it 28. David Trimble of the UUP became First Minister and Seamus Mallon of the SDLP his deputy. Trimble and Hume (leader of SDLP) were jointly awarded the Nobel Peace Prize for their efforts. But this, like the one awarded to Corrigan and Williams two decades earlier, was more to encourage them to keep the peace process going rather than in recognition of clear success. The Unionists who were against the agreement instigated serious violence during the summer marching season, and there were some deaths. Much worse was a bomb set off by dissident Republicans (calling themselves the Real IRA) in Omagh that killed twenty-nine. But such was the scale of popular reaction to this that the group suspended its operations.

There was a long delay before the power sharing Executive could take office because of Unionist insistence that the IRA should start decommissioning its arms. First Minister David Trimble faced pressure on this not only from the opposition Unionists but also from within his own party. Finally, on 2 December, the Executive took office. But seventy-two days later, on 11 February 2000, London suspended the Assembly. On 6 May the IRA agreed to have a South African political leader, Cyril Ramaphosa and a former Finnish President, Martti Ahtisaari periodically inspect selected arms caches to confirm that they were not being used. The Assembly was restored on 1 June. The Unionists saw arms decommissioning as the critical part of the Good Friday Agreement. For the Sinn Fein and the IRA, arms decommissioning was only a part of a package that included other vital matters such as police and judicial reforms.

The deadlock not only paralysed the Assembly but also resulted in moderates on both sides losing ground. In the 7 June 2001 British parliamentary elections, Ian Paisley's hardline DUP got 22.6 per cent of the votes, very close to the UUP's 26.8 per cent. On the Catholic side, Sinn Fein overtook the SDLP—21.7 per cent to 21 per cent. To put pressure on the IRA to decommission arms, Trimble resigned from the First Minister's post in July, but returned soon. On 2 August, the dissident Real IRA exploded a bomb in London. On 16 August the IRA, whose terrorist image had already seen a mild revival earlier in the year when some of its men were found with an insurgent group in Colombia, agreed to a scheme of actual decommissioning. What the IRA had agreed to earlier on 6 May 2000 was that observers would ensure that some IRA arms caches were not being used. The term then used was 'deactivation'. Both deactivation and decommissioning applied to only a small part of the IRA's large quantity of weapons, much of it acquired from Libya during 1986–87. No outsider knows how much there is altogether, and the locations where they are stored.

Within a month of this came the al-Qaeda attacks in the US. The war against terrorism made the IRA, and by association the Sinn Fein, vulnerable to charges of terrorism. To step up pressure, David Trimble resigned his post as First Minister again. On 23 October 2001 the IRA announced that some of their weapons had been put permanently beyond use, and the head of the arms decommissioning body, General John de Chastelaine of Canada confirmed this. The British government responded by dismantling some watchtowers and listening posts. And the British parliament decided to permit its four Sinn Fein MPs to draw allowances and use office space, although they still could not take their place in parliament because of the refusal to swear allegiance to the British Crown. David Trimble returned as First Minister. But the pressures on him were highlighted when he lost a vote of confirmation in his attempt to get back to the post of First Minister as two of his own party members voted against him. In Northern Ireland, such a vote requires separate majorities from both Protestant and Catholic parties. It required the stratagem of a Protestant member of the neutralist Alliance Party shifting allegiance temporarily to the UUP for Trimble to get confirmed in the second attempt.

In April 2002 General de Chastelaine announced that the IRA had decommissioned another set of weapons. But this kind of piecemeal decommissioning, and that too in secrecy, was unacceptable to the Unionists, and increasingly to London in the new counter-terrorist mood of the times. Blair said that 'crunch time' had come and that the IRA could not postpone total decommissioning any longer. In early October there was a report of an IRA spy ring in Stormont. With Trimble about to resign again, London suspended the assembly on 14 October. In response, the IRA announced on 31October that it was ceasing cooperation with de Chastelaine's Decommissioning Commission. In early 2003 the British and Irish governments started working on a 'road map' to chart the future of the peace path. This was to be announced on 10 April, the fifth anniversary of the GFA. It was called off because the Sinn Fein's acceptance of the provisions of the road map was not clear enough. New elections to the assembly scheduled for May were also postponed.

When elections were finally held on 26 November 2003, Paisley's hardline DUP won 30 seats against the 27 won by Trimble's UUP. On the Catholic side, the Sinn Fein won 24 seats against 18 won by the SDLP. The moderate AP won 6 seats and others 3. Compared to the June 1998 elections, both the UUP and the SDLP lost ground. Yet, those opposed to the GFA had only won 31 seats (against 28 in 1998) in an assembly of 108. The rules call for the largest parties on the two sides (in this instance the DUP and Sinn Fein) to nominate the First Minister and the Deputy First Minister. With Paisley refusing to talk to the Sinn Fein and wanting the Good Friday Agreement re-negotiated, the power sharing Executive stayed in limbo.

THE CONFLICT IN PERSPECTIVE

Although Britain and Ireland are also involved, the fundamental conflict in Northern Ireland is between the Protestants and Catholics of

Northern Ireland. The differences between them go beyond religious sectarianism. The Protestants have a mixed cultural background with Irish, English and Scottish strands in their make up, while the Catholics have their roots entirely in Ireland, and have a strong Irish–Gaelic sense of identity. The Catholics tend to consider themselves the true natives and regard the Protestants as part-settlers. The Catholic approach to the conflict is dominated by two issues. The first, and the more salient one at present, is the need to end the political and economic discrimination the community has always been subjected to. The second is the need to assert their Irish-ness, which they feel requires bringing the divided people of the island together. On the first point, there is little difference in thinking among Catholics, but on the second there is. Till the mid-1990s, the SDLP and Sinn Fein symbolised that difference. The SDLP represented those Catholics who were inclined to let the partition erode gradually, while the Sinn Fein, till recently, represented those less patient about its undoing.

In both communities there are people who may be broadly grouped as constitutionalists and militants. On the Protestant side, the constitutionalists represented by the UUP had been in a strong position soon after the partition. Through gerrymandering and voter list manipulation, they ensured that they were unchallenged not only at Stormont but also at the local level. Marches were organised not just to celebrate Protestant military victories, but also to intimidate Catholics by capturing public space with the support of the state. During the half century 1921–72, Stormont enjoyed considerable legislative and executive autonomy, and had near-total control over domestic spending and social policy. Special legislation such as the Special Powers Act (1922) and Public Order Act (1951) were used to subdue Catholics. To back this unethical legal framework, there was an armed constabulary staffed exclusively by Protestants. With London closing its eyes, the Protestants were comfortable with their 'constitutional' path. They felt no need for any militant action till the civil rights movement began in the mid-1960s and Stormont could not handle it.

On the Catholic side, neither the militants nor the constitutionalists mattered till the mid-1960s. The IRA had carried out some attacks in the 1930s and during 1956–62, but they had been ineffectual. The Catholics who had tried the constitutional path were also blocked— through gerrymandering of constituencies, intimidation and brute majoritarianism. It was the civil rights upsurge in the late1960s that energised both the constitutionalists and the militants. Support for a more combative constitutional path represented by the SDLP, formed in 1970, snowballed. The Sinn Fein too found support from younger, more radical Catholics. The Protestant administration now found itself opposed strongly, both at the constitutional and militant levels.

London's position on the conflict has changed considerably over the years. Till the civil rights movement gathered strength in the late1960s, London had found little quarrel with Stormont. There were large sections of British society, particularly in the ranks of Conservative Party supporters, who did not want to run the risk of the United Kingdom getting reduced to Britain, even at a distant date. When direct rule from London was imposed in 1972, the idea was to restore law and order, ensure a modicum of civil rights for Catholics, and then go back to Stormont governance. Most people in Britain saw the Sunningdale agreement of 1973 as little more than window-dressing to placate the Catholics. It was only in 1985 when the Anglo–Irish Treaty was signed in Hillsborough, and that too by Margaret Thatcher, that the people of Britain began to adjust themselves psychologically to the possibility of Northern Ireland merging with Eire some time in the distant future.

From the early 1920s to the mid-1960s, the Irish Free State and its successor Eire took little interest in Northern Ireland affairs. For the record, Dublin had always maintained its intent of achieving eventual unification, but because of the huge power disparity between it and Britain, it had been careful not to extend anything more than moral support to Northern Ireland's Nationalists. It was tough with the IRA. The people of Eire also supported the non-interfering policy. The Sinn Fein, after the initial years, attracted little popular support in the south. The position changed in the late 1960s when Northern Ireland turned volatile and Dublin could see the possibility of promoting eventual unification without clashing with London. From the early 1970s, London and Dublin have trodden a largely cooperative path, although they have disagreed on many occasions, especially during the Thatcher years.

The big stake in the conflict today for both Protestants and Catholics is not the issue of the north–south merger, but that of political power and economic advantage. Despite the fact that the territory has been governed from London since 1972, the dominatory structures instituted by Stormont during the previous half-century are still largely in place. The concept of power sharing, even if it begins to be effectively implemented, will take a long time before it can work changes on the ground. The unemployment rate among Catholics is still nearly double that among Protestants. The Catholic share in public housing is proportionately much less. The public infrastructure in Catholic neighbourhoods lags behind. Catholics have a big stake in overcoming these imbalances quickly, and Protestants an equally big one in slowing things down.

The issue of identity is of much less consequence now, although both sides whip up concern about it. The Protestants feel that to maintain their identity it is essential not to get subsumed within the Irish–Gaelic Eire, where they would be a minority of about a quarter of the total population. They point at the special position given to both the Catholic Church and the Gaelic language in the Irish constitution. But this is not a serious issue. Just as the Irish constitution was amended in 1998 to remove its irredentist clauses, the clauses with regard to religion and language could also be amended should the island become united. Moreover, union is a distant prospect. Even if the current higher birth rate among Catholics is maintained, a Catholic electoral majority is improbable before 2020. Most Catholics would like as early a merger as possible with Eire, but nearly all are prepared to wait till demographic change makes it possible.

For London, there is little at stake in the conflict today, except that of ensuring peaceful conditions in Northern Ireland. In economic terms, Northern Ireland had long become a burden on and not an asset to Britain. In the late 1960s, the subvention from London for public expenditure in Northern Ireland was under 10 per cent. By the early 1990s it had reached about one-third of the total, or nearly $5 billion a year. This huge drain on the British exchequer was partly on account of security spending and partly because of the high welfare payments brought upon by the stagnant Northern Ireland economy. From the mid-1960s to the mid-1990s, the unemployment rate in Northern Ireland was about twice that in Britain.

Eire's rapid economic growth beginning in the 1960s, which saw it becoming one of the fastest-growing European economies since the 1980s, has also had an effect. Thinking in Ulster, which many in Britain shared, of Eire as socio-economically backward began to change, and the economic argument for keeping Northern Ireland separate crumbled. It began to be seen by increasing numbers that Northern Ireland's economic downturn could not be reversed without ending discontent in the territory, and also perhaps without closer relations with Eire. Dublin has a stake in seeing that the political unity of the island is restored as early as possible, but it also has a stake in ensuring that if and when the merger does come about it would not be left with a discontented Protestant community. It needs to see that the merger does not come through a fiercely contested vote. It has to work to change the perception of Ulster's Protestants regarding the fall-out from a possible union.

There has been, and there continues to be, a great deal of antagonism between the two communities. This needs to be looked at separately at the level of extremists and moderates. Among extremists, there has been little reduction of animus on either side. Enemy images are still very strong and there has been a determined effort to keep grudges alive and fan distrust. At the level of moderates on both sides, there has been a definite reduction in animosity. They have seen progress being made towards peace in a manner where the interests of both sides are taken care of fairly. While moderates outnumber extremists on both sides, the percentage of moderates is higher on the Catholic side. This is because the changes that are occurring have 'redressal' as a major component, and therefore they are inevitably of greater benefit to the Catholics.

Britain brought to bear substantial capabilities on the conflict. Military capabilities were used primarily against the IRA, and only marginally against the Paras. In fact recent investigations have shown that both British military intelligence and RUC Special Branch had used Paras in their battle against the IRA.[1] Britain also introduced tough anti-terrorist laws beginning 1971, allowing suspects to be interned without trial and normal rules of evidence suspended at their trials. Recently, several suspects convicted under these rules have turned out to be innocent and released. But despite harsh laws and the employment of over 17,000 regular troops and substantial local para-military forces, as well as highly advanced intelligence capabilities, Britain could not break the IRA (whose core strength never exceeded 250) during the three decades the two fought actively. This was primarily because the IRA enjoyed substantial popular support among Catholics. Britain had little leverage with the Catholics, though it tried to gain some through Dublin. It had a fair amount with the Unionists because

---

[1] See London metropolitan Police Commissioner Sir John Stevens' report released on 19 April 2003. The report not only states that RUC special branch and military intelligence colluded with loyalist murder gangs, but that they also continuously obstructed his enquiry for years.

of the huge subvention from London that was needed to keep the Belfast administration going. But the Unionists had counter-leverage upon London through British public opinion, and occasionally by helping the Conservative Party get a parliamentary majority.

Northern Ireland has paid a big price for the fighting that went on for three decades from 1968. When the island was partitioned in 1920, Ulster had been its industrial heart, and Northern Ireland's per capita income was far higher than that of the Irish Free State. That lead continued till the early 1960s when social malaise in the territory brought economic malaise in its wake. Today the per capita income of Eire is above Northern Ireland's. The territory has paid high non-economic costs too. Nearly 4,000 persons have been killed in Northern Ireland since 1967, which is a significant number for a territory whose total population is only 1.7 million. Besides the loss of lives, the killings have also created a massive legacy of inter-community animus.

Why was this conflict that erupted in 1968, and which Britain has been trying to resolve since 1973 with the help of Eire, not brought under control till 1998? The basic reason is that 1968 had only marked a new stage in the Irish–British conflict that had seen serious fighting from as far back as the 1640s. Anger and distrust go back a long way on both sides. The Unionists had internalised a feeling of superiority as well as a belief in the efficacy of intimidation. This made it difficult for them to come to terms with the substantially changed post-WW II standards, especially in Europe, with regard to civil rights and minority rights. The Sunningdale agreement of 1973 and the power sharing Executive that it produced showed that London had begun to make a major strategic shift. But the Unionists continued to believe that they could resist both power sharing and intra-island contacts. They persisted with their stonewalling even when Margaret Thatcher, whose instincts were more pro-Unionist than that of most British MPs, signed the Hillsborough Treaty in 1985. Unionist obduracy delayed the next step, the Downing Street Declaration, to 1993. The next two steps, the Frameworks agreement of 1995 and the historic GFA of 1998, were also delayed because of the Unionists' refusal to accept that the terms of battle had changed fundamentally.

Violence by the IRA also helped to prolong the conflict. What had brought the end of Stormont in 1972 was not the terror wreaked by the IRA, but the moral challenge that the civil rights movement had posed to Britain. In the satellite TV era, the visuals of civil rights demonstrators being set upon by Unionist thugs with the support of the state would have diminished Britain in the eyes of the international community. Fortunately for the Unionists, the violence of the IRA helped shift attention from people's rights to terrorism. IRA terrorism began just when the Palestinians had, by their actions against Israel, sensitised the West against it. Violence by the IRA and counter-violence by the Paras also vitiated the general atmosphere, making negotiated peacemaking difficult. The viciousness of the Paras had been no less than that of the IRA. But the IRA attracted greater condemnation because the Paras were popularly seen as 'responding' to IRA violence. Also, unlike the Paras, the IRA regularly carried out attacks in Britain in the belief that 'one bomb in London is worth ten in Belfast'—the same dubious logic that has prompted Pakistan-based terrorists to carry out attacks in Delhi and Mumbai.

THE PEACE PROCESS

It took twenty-five years to traverse from Sunningdale to GFA. What lies ahead? There are pessimists who look at the reluctance of the IRA to decommission arms and the inability of hardline Unionists to psychologically accept the terms of the GFA and fear that the peace process will get bogged down, even if it does not unravel. But such pessimism appears unwarranted. Today the vast majority of Northern Ireland's people are in favour of peace, on the terms set out in the GFA. Catholics are almost wholly behind it. The IRA, despite its slowness in destroying arms, has had to give up for good the option of restarting violence. And there is not even fringe support for groups like Real IRA and Continuity IRA which want to persist with violence. In Britain and Eire, there is near unanimous support for the agreement that is being implemented. The only disturbing factor is the lukewarm support among the Protestants.

In getting this far with the peace effort, the willingness of London from the early 1970s not only to adopt a more neutral stance towards the Protestant–Catholic conflict but also to overcome its own possessive feelings towards the territory has played a big part. From 1972 all British Prime Ministers have been supportive of a negotiated peace. Edward Heath and Harold Wilson were personally committed to a peace that accommodated Nationalist interests. Margaret Thatcher, during her long premiership from 1979 to 1990, was less sympathetic to the Nationalists, and the peace process did slow down during her time, particularly in the years before 1985. John Major was more pro-peace, but his narrow majority and dependence on Unionist MPs limited his initiatives. Tony Blair came to power in 1997 with a decisive majority, and the strong personal interest he took helped to make the historic GFA possible.

The farsighted and moderate leadership of David Trimble of the UUP on the Protestant side, and that of John Hume of the SDLP and Gerry Adams of the Sinn Fein on the Catholic side—all key players through the 1980s and 1990s—has contributed a great deal. Trimble and Hume worked in parallel to make their respective constituencies less hostile to the other. It was not an easy task at all. Both were running huge political risks. Trimble was and continues to be very exposed to being branded weak-kneed by Paisley. Hume had to guard his flanks from the Sinn Fein, which he did by gradually bringing the latter to a more moderate path. Hume's persuasive powers and Adam's clear thinking had much to do with the Sinn Fein's crucial acceptance of a majority veto within Northern Ireland. Trimble could not bring round Paisley. So he has tried to limit the support Paisley could attract by straddling the line separating cooperation and confrontation with the Nationalists.

The SDLP's success in the early 1970s in getting British support for its moderate line convinced many Catholics that an 'inside the system' approach could get them gains. The Catholic vote that used to be ineffectually dissipated began to concentrate on the SDLP, and with the help of electoral reforms introduced by London they captured local power in a number of areas where the Catholics are in a majority. This convinced moderate elements within Sinn Fein–IRA that not only was the electoral approach worth trying, but that if they did not adopt it the Sinn Fein was likely to lose popular support. Although the IRA did not finally give up violence till 1997 (IRA's earlier ceasefires could always be counted in months), it had become clear by 1993 that the Sinn Fein (and IRA) were genuinely looking for peace. The Sinn Fein's commitment to the electoral path got a boost when its share of Catholic votes began to grow when the IRA abjured violence.

In moving this far, Britain has had to conduct long and patient rounds of negotiations with several groups—the UUP, harder-line Unionist parties like the DUP, the moderate SDLP, the IRA-linked Sinn Fein, and the Irish government. The fact that there has been since 1972 a cabinet minister responsible solely for Northern Ireland has been a big help. The bipartisanship that Conservatives and Labour developed over Northern Ireland policy also contributed. This played a major role in swinging public opinion, both in Britain and in Northern Ireland, behind the peace process. Civil society meetings involving people with links to all parties have been regularly held. These have included a wide range of people—politicians, academics, members of think tanks, members of developmental and human rights NGOs, among others.

Soon after the 'Troubles' began in 1968, Britain found it prudent to act more like an external party to the conflict than as a participant in it. This difficult detachment enabled it to put pressure on the Unionists and make them understand that the maintenance of the status quo was no longer possible. Britain's willingness to seek the help of the Republic was also a significant factor. When Eire recognised that Britain had made a strategic decision in favour of securing peace by accommodating Catholic concerns, it began to cooperate closely with it.

It was during the Carter administration that the US first showed an interest in the conflict. Since then the US has had to manoeuvre between its stance on terrorism which worked against the Nationalists, and its position on human and civil rights which worked in their favour. During the Reagan–Bush years of 1981–92, America largely stayed out, partly on account of the Thatcher government's sensitivity and partly on account of its own strong stand against terrorist violence. When Clinton got to the White House in 1993, with a less ideological John Major in Downing Street, the US began to take an interest in the underlying causes of the conflict. This US interest played a role in the February 1995 Frameworks Agreement, and even more in the historic GFA. The role played by former US Senator George Mitchell in bringing the two sides together, especially during the three years between the Frameworks Agreement and the GFA, was significant.

The European Union has played a less direct, yet significant, role. At one level, EC/EU concern for human rights pushed London to take a stronger position against security force excesses in Northern Ireland. At another, the dilution of nationalistic thinking that the EC/EU has been gradually bringing about in Europe has helped to make the concept of sovereignty more malleable, thereby making it easier to accommodate divergent allegiances. If the Euro begins to circulate on both sides of the Irish border (it is already in use in the south) and

Britain (and thereby Northern Ireland) reduces their opt-out positions on EU rules, there will be increasing harmony of economic and social structures between Eire and Northern Ireland. If that happens, a possible majority decision in Northern Ireland a decade-and-a-half from now to join Eire will have little impact on personal lives.

Peace is being built on the basis of a compact between Protestants and Catholics which, till the early 1990s, was not acceptable to either side. The new bargain is that in return for the Catholics accepting the partition of the island effected in 1920, they would immediately be offered a share in ruling power in Northern Ireland, and also the prospect of the eventual merger with Ireland. The Catholics had to give up their non-acceptance of partition which they had maintained for seventy-eight years, and the Protestants had to accept a new governing arrangement where the majority would not enjoy the kind of power normally prevalent in democracies. The Unionists, as long as they are in a majority, will have a veto right over changing the territory's affiliation from London to Dublin, but the tilted politico-economic field they had built to their unfair gain during the Stormont years would have to be levelled fairly soon.

The concept of power sharing has played a major creative role in making peace possible. Under the power sharing concept, the minority Nationalist parties in the territory have not only been given a share in governance, but also an effective veto in areas of important legislation. This is a huge departure not only from the way Northern Ireland had been governed in the past, but also from the pattern of a general parliamentary form of governance, especially that of Britain where majority power is unchecked even by a constitution. Another major creative endeavour has been the acceptance of the idea that the Republic of Ireland has a legitimate interest in the affairs of Northern Ireland, and that in certain areas it will have a voice and role. This agreement has been formalised through the 1985 treaty between the two governments.

How much has the Northern Ireland reality changed in the years that have passed since the GFA was signed and the power sharing Executive first installed? On the ground, it is a mixed picture. Housing continues to be very segregated. Segregation had worsened in the 1970s and 1980s and there is no sign of a reversal of this trend. Barricades put up by both communities litter the streets, and police cars are routinely stoned. Community policing by both the IRA and the Paras continue, and there is considerable tolerance of illicit para-military activity. The crippling psychological wedges driven by decades of violence and tension are still in place. In the wake of the GFA, Northern Ireland's economy has seen a mild upswing based on expectations of stability and some politically guided investment. But there has been no boom and the territory's economy continues to do less well than Eire's.

There has been a big decline in violence. The release of large numbers of prisoners after 1998 has helped, although the issue of giving amnesty to fugitives has yet to be addressed. Recent violence has been directed more against Catholics than the other way round. In 2001 twelve Catholics were killed as against two Protestants. There have been mob attacks against Catholics, including against school children. This has not evoked a violent response from the Catholic side, mainly because they feel that they are gaining under the new system. Belfast now has a Sinn Fein Lord Mayor and four of the five city councils in the province have Catholic majorities. But this has not translated into effective administrative power, since nearly 80 per cent of civil officials and 90 per cent of the police continue to be Protestants.

The Catholics as a community recognise that they have benefited from the 1998 agreement. But they feel that the pace of progress has been much slower than promised. The most important issue for the Catholics is the creation of a more equitable police and judicial system. The RUC (hated by the Catholics) was restructured in November 2001 and given a new name—the Police Service of Northern Ireland (PSNI). Since then, a recruitment ratio of 50:50 is in force with a view to increasing the Catholic share in police. A police board to oversee the PSNI has also been created. While the SLDP has taken its place on the board, the Sinn Fein has not on the grounds that police reforms so far have been largely cosmetic. It wants to transfer policing and justice functions to the assembly where both could be brought under more open scrutiny. The Sinn Fein also wants an immediate reduction of British Army presence in the region. In the Catholic perception, the British Army has always worked hand-in-glove with the RUC, now PSNI. They also want a judicially enforceable bill of rights and equality legislation as they consider the existing commissions for equality and human rights inadequate.

Protestant perception of power sharing is much less positive. They feel the GFA has benefited Catholics disproportionately. This perception is a true reflection of the reality, but so is the Catholic perception that they continue to be significantly disadvantaged. Among

Protestants there is frustration that the Sinn Fein is gaining electorally among Catholics at the expense of the moderate SDLP. There is concern that if Catholics mass behind an IRA-aligned Sinn Fein, power sharing arrangements would become more difficult. Protestants want the IRA's militant influence to be removed from the political functioning of the Sinn Fein. There is unease that the IRA's refusal to disarm even after five years of the GFA might at some point lead to violence breaking out again. The continuing intelligence-gathering operations and punishment beatings within the Catholic community by the IRA give some legitimacy to this fear. This is the strategic reason behind the Protestant insistence that, unless the IRA declares the war over, decommissions all its weapons in a verifiable manner, and ends all paramilitary activity, they will not permit power sharing to operate.

Protestants recognise that the choice now available to them is between power sharing and Whitehall rule. Even hardliners like Paisley accept that there can be no going back to unrestrained majority rule. But they believe that Whitehall rule is preferable to a power sharing scenario in which the IRA is permitted to keep its arms. They feel that the Catholics have a greater stake than the Protestants in seeing that the power sharing system works. The power sharing assembly and executive created on 2 December 1999 has already been suspended four times—four months from February 2000, two short suspensions in 2001, and the ongoing 16-month-long suspension from October 2002. The Protestants calculate that the IRA will have to eventually come round on the decommissioning issue to ensure that the Sinn Fein is able to influence governance.

The GFA has achieved a great deal but it has now begun to lose momentum and needs a fresh boost. The Blueprint for Peace that the British and Irish Prime Ministers were planning to release on 10 April 2003 was intended to provide this. It could not be released essentially because terms, linkages and timelines could not be agreed upon with regard to the IRA's disarmament on the one side, and effective police and other reforms on the other. London wants the IRA to commit itself to a clear schedule of visible disarmament. In return, the blueprint offers the Catholics new criminal justice legislation and modifications to police supervision arrangements, including a police ombudsman. A special judicial commission is to be set up to deal with 'on-the-run' cases. There is also a promise to reduce British troops from the current 14,000 to 5,000 by the end of 2005. During 1994–2003, troop strength has only come down from 17,000 to 14,000. A new International

Monitoring Body is to be created to ensure that all parties comply with the commitments they make with regard to the blueprint.

The matter of IRA disarmament faces two hurdles. At one level, there is the understandable difference in perspective between the politicians of the Sinn Fein and the soldiers of the IRA. At another level, even some politicians of the Sinn Fein are not convinced that the time is appropriate to give in to disarmament. They know that with the Catholic community now wholly committed to the peace path and the world determinedly set against threats of violence, the leverage they have by maintaining the option of returning to violence (which is what holding on to the IRA arsenal seeks to achieve) will slowly crumble. Yet they want to ensure that before they agree to comprehensive disarmament they should use the leverage their arms give them to get the best possible deal they can on the issues of concern to Catholics. They know that while they have veto power against harmful new legislation in the power sharing assembly, they have no power to pass legislation to rectify the many lacunae in the existing framework of laws. They therefore want adequate Westminster legislation to address their concerns before they concede to disarmament.

This big tussle with serious stakes is reflected in the inability of the Assembly, the Executive and the cross-border bodies to function effectively so far. Yet there is little doubt that trust levels have grown on all sides. London is much more confident than before that the IRA will not return to the path of violence. The Unionists have greater confidence that the Nationalists will not at a future date press for the merger of north and south unless a majority in Northern Ireland is in favour. The Nationalists are now more assured that their disadvantaged position in terms of economic opportunity and civil rights are likely to be rectified with some speed.

At some point in the not too distant future the Sinn Fein is likely to force disarmament upon the IRA. The leverage that the Sinn Fein has with London and the Unionists comes decreasingly from the IRA's arsenal, and increasingly from the fact that once the IRA ceases to be a para-military organisation, there will be global pressure—especially from the US and the EU—on London to overcome the community-based inequalities present in Northern Ireland. But even when the IRA disarms and the power sharing assembly/executive and the cross-border bodies begin to work uninterruptedly, there will still be problems. With Protestants trying to slow-down and Catholics trying to hasten change, there will be deadlocks in the assembly that will have to be broken by London using Westminster's continuing right to legislate for Northern Ireland. This will not be easy for London to do without facing criticism either for being partisan towards the Protestants, or for 'caving in to Nationalist agitators'.

The matter of cross-border bodies will also pose problems. The Unionists are determined to ensure that these bodies remain on paper because they can see danger ahead if the Republic and the Nationalists in Northern Ireland begin to cooperate. This is particularly so in the context of the threat of the Catholics becoming a majority in the territory, paving the way for the undoing of the partition. The threat is distant, but real. The 2001 census of Northern Ireland declared that there were 53 per cent Protestants and 44 per cent Catholics in the territory. The declared results have probably under-counted Catholics, for the raw census data had 46 per cent stating that they were Protestants, 40 per cent said they were Catholics and 14 per cent said 'no religion'. Even the declared 9-percentage-point majority that the Protestants had in 2001 has shown a marked decline from the 16-percentage-points in 1991. Forty years ago, in 1961, the difference was as much as 26 points. With the age profile of the Catholics still younger than that of the Protestants, the prediction that Catholics will gain a population majority around 2012, and a voting majority before 2020, has a realistic ring to it.

INSIGHTS FOR KASHMIR

The Northern Ireland peace process has exceptionally good documentation, reportage and analysis. While the Arab–Israeli peace efforts are also well covered, the coverage does not have the same range of standpoints as Northern Ireland has. A close study of the Northern Ireland peace process can offer a range of illuminating insights regarding approaches, styles, structures and processes that have achieved results, and more often have failed to. It can teach one—in the context of Kashmir—a great deal about how important the roles of key individuals are, how difficult it is to change institutional mindsets, how hard it is to achieve internal consensus and coherence, and much more. But such an effort is beyond the scope of this short section. All that can be attempted here is to develop some insights on a few broad aspects that have relevance for Kashmir.

Pakistan is the party that can benefit the most from an objective macro look at the Northern Ireland problem. The positions of the Irish Free State in 1921 and that of Pakistan in 1947 had a good deal in common, especially with respect to the perception of having received a raw deal. The strong desire of the Catholics of Northern Ireland to join the Irish Free State (and later Eire)—in sharp contrast to the lack of interest on the part of Indian Muslims to join Pakistan—should have logically added to the Irish determination to undo the partition. But what did the Irish Free State actually do? Beyond laying a symbolic claim for Northern Ireland in its 1937 constitution, it did nothing. Instead of getting sucked into a draining irredentist effort, the Republic decided to concentrate on its economy. In 1955, the per capita GDP of Eire was about half of Britain's. By 2001 it had shot up to $22,850 against Britain's $25,120. In terms of purchasing power parity, Eire's per capita income is now higher than Britain's—$27,170 against $24,340.[2] During the 1990s when Pakistan's growth rate lagged nearly 3-percentage-points behind India's and its per capita income fell behind India's for the first time in forty-five years, Ireland's economy was growing at the rate of 7.7 per cent against Britain's 2.7. Pakistanis certainly need to ponder on where they might have reached had they opted for the positive path that Ireland took, instead of the self damaging one they have persisted with for over half a century.

India too can find many points that bear pondering upon. These are, however, more with regard to India's actions within Kashmir than those towards Pakistan. The militancy that exploded in the Kashmir Valley in 1989 bears a close parallel to the outbreak of 'Troubles' in the towns and cities of Northern Ireland in 1968. Both were manifestations of the unhappiness, resentment and anger that had been building over a long time. Some have attributed the problem that began in Kashmir in 1989 to a combination of poor ability to deliver development and an increase in the mobilisation capability of the people.[3] This is a perceptive view and much the same combination had worked to create violence in Northern Ireland two decades earlier. The Welfare State that the UK created after World War II had played a big role—through education and social security—in developing the mobilisation capacity of the territory's Catholics. At the same time, just as successive

---

[2] World Bank, *World Development Indicators 2003*.
[3] This view has been expressed forcefully in Sumit Ganguly, *The Crisis in Kashmir: Portents of War, Hopes of Peace,* Cambridge: Cambridge University Press, 1997.

J&K administrations have failed to do, Stormont refused to address the serious grievances the Catholics had. The combination of awareness development and mounting grievance has been a potent cause of trouble in both Northern Ireland and Kashmir.

A related parallel linking both conflicts shows how an aroused environment of popular anger provides space for promoters of violence. The IRA's attempt to spark violence in the 1930s and the 1950s had failed utterly for want of popular support. But when the IRA entered the fray in 1968 it met with success because of the changed popular mood. This has a close parallel to the failure of Pakistani efforts in 1965 and 1970–71 to inflame the Valley, and the success they met with in 1989. It is also worth noting that, despite the huge problems IRA violence had created for them (stringent policing by the government and reprisals by the Paras), large sections of Catholics continued to support the IRA—passively or surreptitiously. Much the same has happened in J&K.

In Northern Ireland the British Army's counter-IRA effort, despite the great support provided by para-military and police organisations of the province, soon got bogged down. The British learned an early lesson about the danger of employing the Army against one's own people when British para-troopers shot dead fourteen unarmed demonstrators on the Bloody Sunday of 30 January 1972. The impact this made contributed a great deal to the end of Stormont majoritarian rule later that year. The British Army changed its tactics thereafter and became much less heavy-handed. But with the RUC persisting with its unchanged ways, there was no noticeable change in the perceptions of the Catholics towards the British Army—they continue to hate them. This has a close parallel to the problems encountered by the Indian Army in J&K.

After London did away with Stormont and brought the territory under direct rule, attention was focused on addressing the grievances and meeting the aspirations of the Catholics. Well-intentioned efforts were made, both legislative and administrative, to overcome the political and economic discrimination that the Catholics were suffering from. But given the structural nature of the inequalities in the territory, the efforts could not make much headway. An area where definite success was achieved was that of elections. By the 1980s, Catholics were able to elect their people wherever they were in local majority. The British also sought to engage the main Catholic party, the SDLP, and because of the fairness that was brought into elections, the engagement became a successful one. The problems and successes that London has had in improving electoral fairness and administrative integrity have more than a little relevance to Delhi's similar but less successful efforts in J&K.

The big issue that police and judicial systems have always posed in Northern Ireland and continue to pose (it is today the principal hurdle in getting the IRA to disarm) also has great relevance. In an environment of counter-militancy warfare, it is very difficult to prevent the police and judicial systems from becoming unfairly oriented against the community from which militants rise. Catholics distrust the entire law enforcement system—the police and the judiciary—of the province. And there is no easy way to fix it. The failure of London to gain the confidence of most Catholics through reconstituting the RUC as PSNI, creating a police supervisory board and ombudsman, and repealing some of the harsh laws shows both how touchy the issue is and how difficult it is to deal with. In J&K the same issues are present and in an even more worrying manner.

London quickly recognised that while its vigorous and positive dealings with the SDLP—which had a good standing in the province unlike the post-1986 NC in J&K—were improving its credibility in the eyes of the Catholics, it had no choice but to deal with the Sinn Fein as well. London knew that the Sinn Fein was intertwined with the IRA—the enemy it was engaged in deadly military combat. Yet, the Sinn Fein was encouraged to take part in informal negotiations. While London tried hard to contain the IRA by putting pressure on the Sinn Fein, it did not put any obstacle in the way of the development of the Sinn Fein as a political party, and eventually a power sharing one at that. London was prepared to talk even with the IRA. Back channel talks with the IRA began as early as 1972. The IRA repeatedly broke its ceasefires (its violence continued till 1997), and there were frequent IRA attacks not only in Northern Ireland but also in Britain. But despite this, London maintained its contacts. Indian intelligence agencies have also engaged militant groups in talks. The difference is that London's engagement with the IRA has been aimed more at understanding their motivations and gauging their flexibility than at creating splits within their ranks.

If the Northern Ireland and J&K situations are juxtaposed, one can see some rough parallels between the Sinn Fein and Hurriyat at one level, and between the IRA and indigenous violent groups like the JKLF and the pre-1994 HM at another. If the Hurriyat has refused to accept the Indian constitution, the Sinn Fein has refused to declare allegiance to the British Crown. This is the reason why Sinn Fein MP-elects have still not been allowed to participate in the proceedings of parliament. The links that the Sinn Fein has with the IRA are comparable to, for example, what the JIJK has with the HM. Yet, the Sinn Fein has been facilitated to develop its electoral base and political legitimacy. This has helped to draw its moderates away from IRA hardliners. The evolution of Gerry Adams and Martin McGuinness, from IRA commanders to political leaders committed to peace, is illustrative.

There was always a huge difference in the final objectives of London (not to speak of the Unionists) and the Nationalists. They were seeking irreconcilable sovereign ends. As a result constructive ambiguity has been a key feature of Northern Ireland's formulations. The need to find wordings that would be acceptable to the main protagonists— London, Dublin, the Unionists and the SDLP–Sinn Fein—was never easy. Equivocal wordings were frequently used. But the effort was always to achieve convergence of positions by working towards progressively greater clarity. Progress in widening the content of agreement is very visible, if one looks at the Hillsborough Treaty of 1985, the Downing Street Declaration of 1993, the Frameworks Agreement of 1995, and the GFA of 1998. Between the Nationalist parties and the Unionists there was no common ground at all till the early 1990s, and disagreements between them used to be flat and unqualified. The SDLP's Nobel Prize winning leader John Hume once said during a break in negotiations, 'If you took the word "no" out of the English language, there'd be a lot of speechless people in there.'[4] Yet, it was those frustrating, seemingly dead-end negotiations that ultimately produced the GFA in 1998.

The development of innovative solutions to bridge seemingly unbridgeable differences has been a notable part of the Northern Ireland peace process. The grand bargain involving Nationalist acceptance that a majority within Northern Ireland shall determine the territory's status in return for power sharing and a possible future Nationalist majority being able to achieve union, is an excellent example of creating a compromise solution wherein both sides share success as well as disappointment. The complex arrangements arrived at to give

[4] Charles Hauss, *International Conflict Resolution: International Relations for the 21st Century,* London: Continuum, 2001, p. 105.

minority Nationalists an effective share in governing is another example of innovative solution-seeking, as is the decision to enlist Dublin's cooperation through the creation of some cross-border planning and overseeing structures.

A major point to learn from Northern Ireland is the importance of moulding public opinion in favour of peace. While peace undoubtedly needs to be built from the top, it needs to be built from below as well. Making opinion within any country more amenable to peace requires presenting the opponent's case in a fairer light. British governments have been making this effort since 1972. London has tried to promote a better understanding of the nationalist cause by presenting a more balanced and nuanced picture. It admittedly did not have much success because most of the British press, especially the Murdoch papers, have consistently played up the danger posed by the IRA and the Sinn Fein–IRA links. Public rituals that mark progress are important. The considerable publicity that the British government gave to the Hillsborough Treaty in 1985 is a good example. Visible signs of working together and positive public statements about one another are necessary. London, Dublin, the UUP, the SDLP and the Sinn Fein have tried to do this despite their many differences.

Till the agitations and violence of 1968–72 made it rethink its position. London was determined not to have any outside involvement in Northern Ireland. Bringing Dublin into the peace seeking effort led to the Sunningdale conference of 1973. Gradual and increasing cooperation eventually led to the Anglo–Irish Treaty of 1985. Letting Dublin play a role in the peace effort was not easy for Margaret Thatcher, but she was astute enough to see its advantage. It was Dublin's cooperation that made possible the move through the 1985 Hillsborough Treaty, the 1993 Downing Street declaration, the 1995 Frameworks Agreement and the 1998 Good Friday Agreement. Dublin, on its part, showed a very cooperative attitude to London. It understood the latter's needs as well as sensitivities, and sought to find solutions advantageous to both countries.

Northern Ireland provides an illuminating example of using an imaginative and well-crafted internal settlement to end an external, inter-state conflict. For nearly eighty years the positions of London and Dublin over Northern Ireland had brooked no compromise. It was the major political changes that Britain introduced within the territory, as well as the willingness it showed to establish some cross-border links, that made it possible for Eire to first soft-pedal and then relinquish a claim that went back to the island's partition in 1920. It is this inventive weaving of internal and external strands of peace effort that former US president Bill Clinton had in mind when he commended, in a March 2003 video talk to a Delhi audience, the Northern Ireland model for the solution to the Kashmir problem.[5] Clinton had played a big role in making the Good Friday Agreement possible. Therefore, his view that the Northern Ireland model has much to offer in seeking a solution in Kashmir was not an unreflected comment. It was a thoughtful suggestion made by a wise statesman and a good friend of India, and Pakistan's too.

---

[5] See *India Today*, 17 March 2003, p. 24.

CHAPTER 7

POINTERS FROM SRI LANKA

Unlike the Northern Ireland conflict, the Sri Lankan one is still a long way from reaching a confident peace path. Though a ceasefire has been in place for over two years, from December 2001 there has been little certainty that it will hold. Both Sinhalese–Tamil differences and intra-Sinhalese political competition continue to pose serious difficulty. Yet today, both among the Sinhalese and the Tamils, those who advocate a compromise peace outnumber those who see the tussle in Manichean terms. Majorities on both sides now think that peace is possible without compromising their core interests. One can see a reconceptualisation of core interests based on an examination of costs—both already incurred and those likely to be incurred in the future. The Sri Lankan conflict has been more damaging to the parties involved than the Kashmir one has been to India and Pakistan. The incentive to find a solution has therefore been greater. Despite this, and many other differences such as that the Sri Lankan conflict is wholly an internal one, a study of this conflict—its causes, its protraction and its peace efforts—can offer some useful pointers for Kashmir.

EVOLUTION OF THE CONFLICT

The first Sinhalese came to the island from India during the fifth and sixth centuries BCE. The first Tamils came no later than the third century BCE. As centuries went by a spatial separation between the two communities occurred, with the latter getting concentrated in the north and the east of the island. But there were never any hard boundaries. The ancient Sinhalese capital of Anuradhapura was frequently ruled by Tamil kings, and from 1739 to 1815 even the Kandyan kingdom, the heartland of Sinhalese–Buddhism, had Tamil kings. In 1815 the British completed their conquest of the island, taking the Kandyan kingdom. This posed a major threat to the traditional social order of the Sinhalese society. In the 1890s Anagarika Dharmapala created a Buddhist revival movement that captured the imagination of the Sinhalese intelligentsia. Dharmapala invoked the vision of a Golden Age when the entire island was supposed to be with the Sinhalese, and Buddhist precepts guided the country.[1] Despite this, the Sinhalese and the Tamils lived amicably. Sinhalese nationalism at that time was directed primarily against Western and Christian influence.

Sri Lankans did not have to fight for independence the way Indians had to. The step-by-step gains of the Indian struggle passed to them without much separate effort. The Ceylon National Congress (CNC) was formed in 1919, but it was not a mobilising movement. When universal suffrage was introduced in 1931 through the Donoughmore Constitution, the Sinhalese vote (nearly three-quarters of the total) became very important, and the competition to access it began. In 1934 Solomon Bandaranaike, who became Prime Minister later (as did his wife Srimavo and daughter Chandrika), formed the Sinhala Mahajana Sabha (SMS). Political divides among the three major communities—Sinhalese, Tamils and Moors—began to widen. But real political mobilisation only began when the United National Party (UNP) was set up in 1946 to fight the September 1947 elections, prior to independence in 1948. The UNP led by Don Stephen Senanayake, although a conglomeration of various organisations including the CNC and SMS, was a product of the country's anglicised elite which visualised a liberal, capitalist Ceylon. This created political space on

---

[1] A vivid example of this mix of history and myth is former President J.R. Jayawardene's book, *Golden Threads*, Colombo: Dept. of Government Printing, 1984.

the communal right and the economic left. To exploit both, Solomon Bandaranaike formed the Sri Lanka Freedom Party (SLFP) in 1951. Meanwhile, the gathering fears of the Tamils (the Soulbury Constitution of 1946 had reaffirmed the unitary nature of the state) led to a split in the Tamil Congress which had been formed in 1944. The Federal Party (FP), explicitly seeking a federal Sri Lanka, was set up in 1948 under S.J.V. Chelvanayakam who remained the undisputed leader of the Tamils till the late 1970s.

The UNP retained power in the March 1952 elections, but the SLFP was rapidly gaining strength among those Sinhalese who were inclined towards either communalism or socialism. The SLFP won the April 1956 elections in a surcharged ethno–religious atmosphere, for 1956 was also the year that Buddha's 2,500 years of enlightenment was celebrated. The SLFP immediately made Sinhala the sole official language. To the Sinhalese it was the overdue redemption of their Sinhalese–Buddhist nationhood. For the Tamils it was the capture of the state by the Sinhalese. Marxist leader Colin De Silva presciently remarked that year, 'Two languages, one nation; One language, two nations'. To mitigate Tamil fears, Prime Minister Bandaranaike and FP leader Chelvanayakam reached an agreement in July 1957 (known as the B–C Pact) that provided for benefits to the Tamils in the areas of language and devolution. Two days later, the FP passed resolutions calling for an autonomous Tamil linguistic state within a federal Ceylon, parity of status for Sinhala and Tamil, revision of the 1948–49 citizenship laws relating to Indian Tamils, and the cessation of state-aided Sinhalese settlement in the northern and eastern provinces. The Tamil Language (Special Provisions) Act to implement a part of the B–C Pact was introduced in early 1958, but was put aside when anti-Tamil riots rocked the island in May that year.

A Buddhist monk assassinated Solomon Bandaranaike in September 1959. The UNP won the March 1960 general election narrowly, but in another general election held four months later, the SLFP, now led by the assassinated leader's widow, Sirimavo Bandaranaike, came back to power. With no progress on the B–C Pact, the FP started a civil disobedience campaign in February 1961. The UNP came to power again in the March 1965 election. Shortly thereafter Chelvanayakam reached another agreement with the new Prime Minister, Dudley Senanayake, covering much the same ground as the 1957 B–C Pact. The Tamil Language Act was passed in January 1966, but the District Councils Bill (to provide a measure of devolution) faced opposition, and was abandoned in 1969. In May 1970 Sirimavo Bandaranaike came back to power heading an SLFP-led United Front. Meanwhile, social discontent was worsening and a major military effort was needed in April–May 1971 to subdue the JVP[2] uprising of disaffected rural Sinhalese youth. May 1972 saw the inauguration of the Republic of Sri Lanka with a new constitution that made the national state assembly (parliament) supreme and emphasised the unitary nature of the state. The constitution gave Buddhism the 'foremost' place, and reduced the status of Tamil relative to the 1966 Tamil Language Act. In 1973 the Bandaranaike government introduced a 'standardisation' scheme that effectively weighted higher education admissions in favour of Sinhalese candidates. This was taken further forward when 'district quotas' were introduced in 1974.

In response to the 1972 constitution, the three Tamil political parties of the island came together to form the Tamil United Front (TUF). Its constituents were the FP and the Tamil Congress representing 'Sri Lankan' Tamils, and the Ceylon Workers' Congress (CWC) representing 'Indian' Tamils. The Indian Tamils or Plantation Tamils had been brought to Sri Lanka in the 1830s, when the British introduced first coffee and later tea in the highlands of central Ceylon. The areas where they worked and lived were in the middle of Sinhalese territory, and they had little contact with native Tamils in the north and east of the island. The two groups remained spatially, socially and politically separate. In May 1972, the TUF issued a Six Point Plan. The plan reiterated long-pending demands regarding parity for Tamil language, equality of religions, fundamental rights and freedoms, citizenship for Indian Tamils, decentralisation of governance and abolition of untouchability.

By this time the moderate policies of the TUF were getting discredited in the eyes of Tamil youth who had seen their educational and employment opportunities steadily squeezed since 1956. Militant groups began to form. The first two, Tamil New Tigers (TNT), later to become the Liberation Tigers of Tamil Eelam (LTTE), and Tamil Eelam Liberation Organisation (TELO), were founded in 1972. The killing of nine Tamils by the police in Jaffna during an international Tamil conference in January 1974 fuelled unrest. In 1976 the TUF renamed itself TULF, adding the significant adjective 'Liberation'. On 14 May 1976 the TULF passed the Vaddukodai resolution, which

---

[2] JVP stands for Janatha Vimukthi Peramuna, or People's Liberation Front.

sought a 'free, sovereign, secular, socialist state of Tamil Eelam'. The same year saw the TNT become the LTTE, adding the crucial words Eelam and Liberation.[3] Fairly close ties developed between the TULF and the LTTE.

The leftist economic policies of the SLFP-led United Front government had in the meanwhile created serious socio-economic problems in the country. The regime, which had extended its tenure by two years through the 1972 constitution, became deeply unpopular and was decisively beaten by the UNP—now led by Jayawardene—in the July 1977 general election. Till this point the main adversary of the Tamils had been the SLFP. It was during the SLFP rule from 1956 to 1965 and again from 1970 to 1977 that the idea of Buddhist–Sinhalese hegemony gained legitimacy in the country, and much of the legislation detrimental to the Tamils was passed. The capitalist UNP had been seen as less chauvinist. The UNP's 1977 election manifesto had listed education, settlements, language, and public employment as areas of concern to the Tamils, and had promised to address them through an All Party Conference (APC). But the promise was not honoured in the face of the by-now-familiar Sinhalese backlash. The UNP, which ruled the country for the next seventeen years, soon alienated the Tamils no less than the SLFP had done.

Meanwhile, Sri Lanka was treading an authoritarian path. The 1972 constitution brought in by the SLFP had made the national assembly supreme, and in the process weakened the judiciary and made individual and group rights vulnerable. The UNP now moved further. The February 1978 constitution of the Second Republic created a powerful executive president—a post immediately filled by Jayawardene. Tamil violence in the Jaffna region, which had been increasing since 1977, now met with harsher response. The LTTE and similar organisations were proscribed in May 1978, and July 1979 saw a Prevention of Terrorism Act (PTA) being brought in. A state of emergency was declared in the north. By 1979 the Jaffna Peninsula had begun to resemble an occupied zone. In June 1981 the Municipal Library of Jaffna was burned down, destroying an irreplaceable collection of 95,000 Tamil classics. Government agencies were widely seen to have connived in this. Jayawardene was elected President for

---

[3] A good study of the rise of Tamil militant groups and the eventual monopolisation of militant power by the LTTE is M.R. Narayan Swamy, *Tigers of Lanka: From Boys to Guerrillas*, Delhi: Konarak, 1994.

a new term of six years in October 1982, and two months later a referendum extended the life of the UNP-dominated parliament by six years. In July 1983 an LTTE ambush killed thirteen soldiers in Jaffna. This led to a four-day orgy of violence, carried out with organised government support, that killed about 3,000 Tamils. More than half the Tamils in Colombo ended up in refugee camps. A large number of Tamil prisoners, mostly political, were killed in jails. Within two weeks of the Jaffna ambush, the Sixth Amendment to the constitution imposing a ban on political parties espousing separatism was passed. The eighteen TULF members of the national assembly refused to take an oath abjuring the advocacy of separatism and resigned en masse. Repression of Tamils, particularly in the Jaffna Peninsula, was stepped up. Eelam war I had begun. A serious refugee problem was created with large numbers going to India across the Palk Straits. In India there was resentment and anger at what was seen as terrorising the Tamils to submission. The later part of 1983 saw India providing military training and arms to Tamil militant groups.

President Jayawardene came to India in November 1983 when discussions were held on what came to be called the 'Annexure C proposals'. Jayawardene called an APC the next month to discuss the proposals, which included the formation of provincial councils and the merger of the eastern and northern provinces, a major Tamil demand. The SLFP withdrew from the APC soon after, and the consensus-development exercise was abandoned in December 1984. The APC discussions were largely intended to keep India at bay while the government forces crushed the militants. Relations with India had begun to worsen from August 1983 because of stepped up violence in Tamil areas, India's aid to Tamil militants, and Sri Lanka's efforts to seek military help from outside, avoiding India. Sri Lankan efforts to get military help from the US and the UK failed. But help in the form of intelligence and training came from Israel via an Israeli Interests section opened in the US embassy. Sri Lanka also hired a British mercenary firm.

In March 1984 Colombo constituted a National Security Ministry, with hardliner Lalith Athulathmudali as Minister, to oversee the destruction of militant groups. But Colombo also recognised that the groups were no pushover and that the country was not going to get useful external support by bypassing India. The need to talk to the militants, using India's good offices, became clear. Under Indian auspices, the Sri Lankan government held two rounds of talks with the TULF and major Tamil militant groups (LTTE, EROS, EPRLF, TELO and PLOTE) in the Bhutanese capital Thimpu, during July and August 1985.[4] The Tamil groups presented what later came to be known as the Thimpu Principles—recognition of the Tamils as a nation, recognition of the northern and eastern provinces as Tamil homeland, the Tamils' right to self-determination, and full rights to all Tamils who looked upon Sri Lanka as their country. Colombo did not offer anything beyond provincial councils. India sponsored another round of talks later the same month in Delhi, this time between the government and the TULF. But the latter pulled out within four months under militant pressure.

Discussions continued between India and Sri Lanka during 1986, and India also increased pressure on the LTTE, by now recognised as the dominant militant group. During the Sri Lanka–India discussions, a new set of proposals known as 'The 19 December 1986 Proposals' emerged. Following its rejection by the Tamil groups, Colombo began a determined military effort in January 1987 to take control of the Jaffna Peninsula, where the LTTE's writ had run since early 1985. By late May 1987 the government had made substantial military gains. But the campaign was brutal and this raised considerable concern in India, especially in Tamil Nadu. After failing to persuade Colombo to ease up, India made a military airdrop of relief supplies in Jaffna on 4 June 1987. The muted nature of international reaction to this forced Sri Lanka to change course and accept India as a mediator. This led to the 'India–Sri Lanka Agreement to Establish Peace in Sri Lanka', signed by the two heads of government on 29 July 1987. An exchange of letters between the two also took place that day, to take care of India's wider strategic interests in relation to Sri Lanka. The LTTE, with which India had been steadily getting disillusioned, especially after it had torpedoed the '19 December 1986 Proposals', was not consulted. India had already moved to the coercive mode with the LTTE.

In terms of benefit to the Tamils, the agreement provided for the return of refugees, provincial councils, immediate merger of northern and eastern provinces (to be ratified, however, by a referendum before

---

[4] See the list of abbreviations given in the book.

31 December 1988), equal official status for Tamil and English with Sinhala, and amnesty for all militants. The benefits to Sri Lanka were surrender of arms by militants within seventy-two hours of ceasefire, an Indian undertaking not to let Tamil militants use Indian territory, Indian military assistance to Sri Lankan armed forces, and the acceptance of Sri Lanka's unity, sovereignty and territorial integrity. For India, the exchange of letters that accompanied the agreement prescribed that there would be no employment of foreign military and intelligence personnel by Sri Lanka, that Trincomalee and other ports were not to be used by foreign military units, joint restoration of Trincomalee oil tanks by India and Sri Lanka, and the non-use of foreign broadcasting facilities for military and intelligence purposes.

The peace effort foundered on two grounds. One, the Tamils were not satisfied with the devolution package and were apprehensive that the North–East merger might get undone in a government-supervised referendum. Two, the LTTE was not prepared to see itself marginalised through surrender of arms. India had underestimated the dominance the LTTE had gained in the past few years. This proved a mistake, and in October 1987 the Indian Peace-Keeping Force (IPKF) had to launch operations against the LTTE, which had initiated hostilities with an ambush. The LTTE evacuated the Jaffna Peninsula and withdrew to the forested areas of the northern and eastern provinces. The IPKF's effort to defeat them there did not succeed.

In November 1987 Sri Lanka passed the Thirteenth Amendment to the constitution, creating nine provincial councils. The interim merger of the eastern and northern provinces was also made possible. Provincial council elections were held in these provinces in November 1988. Varadarajan Perumal of the EPRLF became the Chief Minister of the merged province with Trincomalee as the capital. In December 1988 Premadasa succeeded Jayawardene as President. With the IPKF fighting the LTTE, Premadasa was able to concentrate on the JVP in the south. The JVP was a violent, Maoist organisation of poor Sinhalese set up in 1964, and had become a serious problem in the deep south. By December 1989 the entire leadership of the JVP and large numbers of its cadres were killed, and the JVP ceased to be a threat. Meanwhile, beginning May 1989 Colombo began to talk with the LTTE and the following month Premadasa asked the IPKF to leave the country. In November, he dissolved the Northeast Provincial Council headed by Chief Minister Perumal. In January 1990 the Tamil

National Council comprising the EPRLF, ENDLF (Eelam National Democratic Liberation Front), TELO and PLOTE, set up under Indian auspices, collapsed. By then Colombo was supplying some arms to the LTTE. The IPKF, which had ceased operations in September 1989, finally pulled out of Sri Lanka in March 1990.

With the departure of the IPKF the common cause between Colombo and the LTTE vanished. The ceasefire between the two in force for thirteen months was broken in June 1990, when the LTTE attacked several police stations in the east. Within weeks, the LTTE had a stranglehold on the Jaffna Peninsula, although the Sri Lankan military continued to hold the Jaffna fort, the Palaly airbase and the Kankesuntarai naval base. Fighting during the next four years (Eelam War II) saw government forces making gains in the eastern province and the mainland areas of the northern province. But the Jaffna Peninsula remained under LTTE control. The period also saw several high profile assassinations by the LTTE. These included Deputy Defence Minister Ranjan Wijeratne in March 1991, Rajiv Gandhi in May 1991, President Premadasa and Lalith Athulathmudali in May 1993, and the UNP Presidential Candidate Gamini Dissanaike in October 1994. The assassination of Rajiv Gandhi (motivated by a combination of revenge and the fear of his returning to power) was a serious political blunder on the LTTE's part. Apart from generating anti-LTTE feelings throughout India, the act made it an 'international' terrorist organisation in the eyes of the world.

In August 1994 the SLFP-led People's Alliance (PA) under Chandrika Kumaratunga was elected to power in the national assembly. Kumaratunga had campaigned on a peace platform, and on becoming Prime Minister partially relaxed the economic embargo against Jaffna. This led to the peace negotiations that began in September 1994. In November Kumaratunga was elected President. The peace process broke down in April 1995, and a new round of high-intensity fighting (Eelam War III) began. Between October 1995 and December 1996 government forces captured most of Jaffna Peninsula, and the LTTE withdrew to Wanni and Mullaitivu areas. They soon began to be ousted from there as well. In July 1996 the government offensive received a setback when the LTTE overran the Mullaitivu army camp killing over 800 people. In September 1998 another big army camp was overrun in Killinochchi. In 1999 most of the Wanni area was captured by the LTTE. In April 2000 they captured the Elephant Pass, the main land approach to the Jaffna Peninsula. In tandem with these military successes in the north, the LTTE carried out a series of bomb attacks in the south. Colombo was hit hard with two devastating bombings in 1996 and 1997—of the Central Bank and the World Trade Centre. This led to the US banning the LTTE. In January 1998, the LTTE attacked the Dalada Maligawa, the country's holiest Buddhist temple, resulting in its being banned in Sri Lanka. In December 1999 the LTTE injured President Kumaratunga in a failed assassination effort.

After the failure of the 1994–95 peace process, Kumaratunga felt the need for a legal framework into which a possible settlement with the LTTE could be slatted. Her idea was to amend Sri Lanka's unitary constitution to make possible some devolution of power to provinces. In August 1995 Kumaratunga made public her proposals for devolution of power that were in advance of the offers made till then. This gave international credence to her claim that the military campaign she had launched against the LTTE three months earlier was a 'war for peace'. The PA did not have a two-thirds majority in parliament, and without the UNP's support no constitutional amendment could be enacted. Inter-party discussions therefore began in 1997. This led to the March 1997 accord between the PA and the UNP (called the Liam Fox Agreement after the British MP who brokered it) to pursue peace jointly. Although neither the PA nor the UNP had objections to making major concessions to the Tamils by then, the process got bogged down on the issue of Kumaratunga wanting to continue as Executive President. Kumaratunga won the presidential election held in December 1999, and in October 2000 the PA won the national assembly elections with a narrow majority.

The failure of the 1994–95 peace talks had made Kumaratunga recognise the need for a third party to facilitate future talks with the LTTE. Animus and distrust between the two sides were too deep for a bilateral process to work. This led the government to support a peace initiative by Norway that had its beginnings in mid-1998, and which formally got going in early 2000. Norway was one of the three countries that had briefly overseen the 1995 ceasefire. In early 2000 India offered its support for the Norwegian effort. On 25 December 2000 the LTTE declared a unilateral ceasefire, which it kept extending month by month. The government did not reciprocate (smarting as it was from the loss of Elephant Pass in April 2000), but it scaled down its military operations. In March 2001 Britain banned the LTTE which was a strong boost to the government's morale.

On the night of 24 May 2001, when the fourth extension of the LTTE's ceasefire was to expire, government forces launched a massive attack on LTTE positions on the northern approach to Elephant Pass. Colombo had interpreted their ceasefire offer of December 2000 as stemming from military and political weakness. Colombo had been engaged in a substantial military build-up since 1995—acquiring warplanes like Israeli Kfir and Russian Mig-27, and long-range weapon systems such as 155 mm guns, 120 mm mortars and multi-barrel rocket launchers. These acquisitions and the presence of foreign military advisors led to the decision to take the LTTE head-on. The political need for a battlefield victory (the government forces had been largely on the back foot for five years) was another consideration. As it turned out, the effort ended in disaster. Government forces had to withdraw after three days, suffering over 300 dead and about 2,000 injured.

July 2001 saw the PA coming under increasing parliamentary pressure and Kumaratunga prorogued the assembly and called for a referendum. The opposition introduced a no-confidence motion. Within two weeks of proroguing the Assembly came the devastating LTTE attack on the Katunayake airport—the country's only international airport. The attack, which destroyed half the country's airline fleet and several combat aircraft, was an economic catastrophe and a huge blow to the security forces. Even worse than the direct losses, estimated at $450 million, was the negative impact the attack had on tourist arrivals and business confidence. The attack directly led to Sri Lanka's economy shrinking by 1.4 per cent in 2001. Sri Lanka's average growth rate during 1994–2000 had been close to 5 per cent.

Meanwhile, the political current was running against Kumaratunga. In October, on the eve of the no-confidence vote, she lost her majority and called for fresh elections. In the December 2001 elections, the UNP-led United National Front (UNF) got a slim majority. The four-party Tamil National Alliance, which had declared before the elections that it considered the LTTE as the sole representative of Tamils, won 15 seats. The three anti-LTTE Tamil parties won 3 seats. Despite his victory, the new Prime Minister, Ranil Wickramasinghe was on a flaky wicket. Kumaratunga's tenure as President was till December 2005, and the constitution permitted her to dissolve the National Assembly any time after December 2002.

The LTTE declared another unilateral ceasefire within a fortnight of the UNF's victory. The government reciprocated, also unilaterally, within a week. Wickramasinghe followed up the ceasefire decision by relaxing the economic embargo in force against LTTE areas. He reduced checkpoints in Colombo and elsewhere in the country. He also asked Norway to resume its facilitator role, which had been effectively suspended by Kumaratunga the previous May. On 22 February 2002 the government and the LTTE signed an indefinite ceasefire agreement. Monitors from four Nordic countries soon arrived. On 22 March Wickramasinghe visited Jaffna—the first visit by a Sri Lankan head of government in twenty years. In the local government elections held the same month, Kumaratunga's PA was routed, winning only 4 out of 222 councils. This showed that, for the time being, Wickramasinghe had public support for his peace initiative.

On 4 September the government de-proscribed the LTTE, and on 16 September the first round of Colombo–LTTE peace talks began in Thailand. The first three rounds during September–December 2002 saw the two sides making unexpectedly impressive progress. Both sides accepted in principle a federal Sri Lanka and also showed a visible willingness to work together in a cooperative partnership. But the issue of what should be the nature of the interim administration and how the LTTE was to be fitted into it soon created tension. This led to the LTTE suspending the talks after six rounds on 21 April 2003. It also refused to attend the big, long-planned donor conference in Tokyo in June.

On 31 October the LTTE presented its proposals for an Interim Self-Governing Authority (ISGA). The proposals would not only have seriously weakened Colombo's control over the north-east province but would also have entrenched the LTTE's political dominance in the province. Four days later, President Kumaratunga struck out against Prime Minister Wickramasinghe by taking over the crucial portfolios of Defence, Interior and Mass Communications. Wickramasinghe responded by stating that unless the portfolios were restored his government would not be able to continue with the peace talks. On 14 November Norway announced that it was putting the peace process on hold. In January 2004 the SLFP-led PA and the chauvinistic JVP formed a formidable alliance to fight the next election scheduled for April 2004. If the PA–JVP alliance forms the next government—a strong possibility—the peace process could be in trouble. But it is unlikely to get wholly abandoned because Sri Lanka desperately needs that peace-contingent $4.5 billion pledged at the Tokyo donor conference in June 2003.

THE CONFLICT IN PERSPECTIVE

The conflict in Sri Lanka has two major dimensions. There is the political conflict between the Sinhalese and the Tamils that began in 1956, and the military one between the Sri Lankan state and the LTTE that began in 1983. Although it is the war with the LTTE that has been dominating the headlines, the broader Sinhalese–Tamil struggle at the socio-political level is of at least equal import.[5] The tussle between the Sinhalese and the Tamils is largely a post-independence product. Unlike in India, the British had not pursued a divide-and-rule policy (separate electorates for example) in Sri Lanka. The British period had seen the Tamils, who took to English education with alacrity, rising in disproportionate numbers in the professions and civil services, but their non-assertive conduct had helped to contain resentment. The elite of the two communities, both socially anglicised, also got on well. The situation changed with electoral competition. The size of the 'Sri Lankan' Tamil population was only a fifth of the Sinhalese. With such small numbers, they had much to lose in a unitary, post-colonial state. The split in the Tamil Congress at independence, and the creation of the Federal Party (explicitly standing for a Federal Ceylon) showed this fear.

The periodic ethnic riots which began in 1956, and worsened in the 1970s, fuelled Tamil disaffection. So did the increasing military presence in the north from the early 1970s. Many Tamils began to see the Sri Lankan state as a wholly Buddhist–Sinhalese construct with which they could not identify, nor feel much loyalty towards. If the 1956 Language Bill marked the beginning of Tamil alienation, the brutal violence unleashed against them in 1983 marked the onset of serious antagonism between the two communities. As the Tamil militants stepped up their attacks on the unprepared security forces in the north and the latter retaliated through indiscriminate violence

[5] For the origin of the Sinhalese–Tamil conflict, see Alfred Jeyaratnam Wilson, *Sri Lankan Tamil Nationalism: Its Origins and Development in the 19th and 20th Centuries*, London: C. Hurst and Co., 2000.

against the Tamils, the animus between the two communities rapidly rose.

Soon after independence the Sinhalese began to feel that the Sinhala language and the Buddhist religion had to reign supreme. The first was made possible with the 1956 Language Bill, and the second with the 1972 constitution. Sri Lanka did not learn from India, which had forestalled religious divides in 1950 through its secular constitution, and language divides in 1956 through the reorganisation of states on the basis of language and later in 1965 by extending the life of English as the official language at the national level. Instead, it chose the disastrous path of Pakistan. It took about a quarter century of post-independence communal hegemonism (1956–83) for separatism to gather strength in Sri Lanka—about the same time that it took in East Pakistan (1947–71).

The Sinhalese were seriously concerned at the vast extent of territory that the Tamils called their homeland. It accounted for a third of the country's land, although its population was only a sixth of the total. It had been a Sinhalese vision to improve the agricultural infrastructure in that area through irrigation and move the Sinhalese there from the crowded south. Any impediment to this was a major concern. The settlement of the Sinhalese in the eastern province had been going on from the late 1950s and gathered pace in the 1970s. The share of the Sinhalese population in the eastern province tripled between 1955 and 1985. The Sinhalese had reason to fear that an autonomous Tamil territory might turn out to be the prelude for an independent Eelam. The envisaged Tamil region, with a long coastline that included the Trincomalee harbour, was a viable independent country.

Not only did the language policy introduced in 1956 accord no status to Tamil at the national level (unlike the position of French in comparable Canada), it did not allow Tamil to be used officially even in the 97 per cent Tamil-speaking north and the then 85 per cent Tamil-speaking east. The 'Sinhala Only' policy in education brought down the university admission percentage of 'Sri Lankan' Tamils from 55 per cent in 1950 to 25 per cent in 1965, and to 10 per cent in 1975. In 1948 Tamils made up 30 per cent of the civil service, which dropped to 6 per cent in 1983. The problem was aggravated when the socialist policies of the SLFP vastly expanded the public sector. Between 1956 and 1970, out of the 200,000 people recruited into the newly-created state sector, 97 per cent were Sinhalese. During the two decades, 1956–76, Tamil recruitment to the expanding state sector came down from 15 to 2 per cent. By the early 1970s the Tamil youth in the country had become thoroughly disaffected.[6]

By the early 1970s, the vast majority of the Tamils were convinced that their economic difficulties could not be addressed without political power. They felt that the constitution of the country, which did not provide for decentralised governance or minority safeguards, as well as the country's socio-political ethos, made it impossible for them to influence policy. This transformed the Tamils' economic stake into a political one. They now wanted autonomy adequate to achieve effective economic control over the areas where their numbers predominated. They believed that such autonomy would also enable them to bargain with Colombo and improve their position in the country as a whole. Colombo's decision to strip the 'Indian' Tamils of their citizenship in 1948–49 and their resident status in 1964, which led to half of them being deported, did not affect the 'Sri Lankan' Tamils. Yet it caused considerable disquiet. As it happened, nearly a third of the 'Sri Lankan' Tamils too left the country through emigration. The explosions of violence against the Tamils that periodically rocked the country—in 1956, 1958, 1977, 1981 and 1983—and the brutal war in the north and east beginning 1983, were the major cause for this.

The Bandaranaike–Chelvanayakam Pact of 26 July 1957 had dealt with four issues—three concerning 'Sri Lankan' Tamils and one concerning 'Indian' Tamils. Those concerning the Sri Lankan Tamils were: that Tamil would be given official status for administration in the north and the east; that the number of Sinhalese peasants being settled in the newly irrigated areas of the north and east would be limited; and that a measure of autonomy would be given to the Tamils by raising the territorial unit of administration from the district to the province. The three issues of language, settlement and autonomy have dominated the grievances of the Tamils ever since. The fourth issue—no longer relevant—was about re-examining the disenfranchisement of Indian Tamils carried out during 1948–49.

---

[6] For the sharp swing that took place against the Tamils during the quarter century from 1956, in both economic and political terms, see Committee for Rational Development, *Sri Lanka, the Ethnic Conflict: Myths, Realities and Perspectives*, New Delhi: Navrang, 1984; Alfred Jeyaratnam Wilson, *Break-up of Sri Lanka: The Sinhalese–Tamil Conflict*, London: C. Hurst and Co., 1988; and William McGowan, *Only Man is Vile: The Tragedy of Sri Lanka*, London: Picador, 1993.

The Soulbury Constitution of 1946 enabled the Sinhalese leadership to wield unitary power throughout the country. The May 1972 constitution brought in by the SLFP made the national assembly supreme (strengthening majoritarianism) and emphasised the unitary nature of the state. The February 1978 constitution (currently in force) brought in by the UNP concentrated power in the hands of a directly elected president, and the ◆ scope for riding roughshod over minority concerns increased further. The domination of the political scene from 1951 by two powerful Sinhalese parties—the UNP and the SLFP— also made it difficult to accommodate minority concerns. The one-on-one adversarial culture operating between the two has made it impossible for either party to adopt a reasonable approach. The moment one explored accommodation the other would cry 'sell out'. The Sinhalese parties, on their own, can win over 85 per cent of national assembly seats. The Tamils, capable of winning about 8 per cent, and the Muslims half of that, have little relevance in national politics—the only politics that matter in Sri Lanka.

The class factor in Sinhalese society has also played a role in exacerbating the conflict. The small group of Sinhalese elite who know English took pride in Buddhism and Sinhala, but had little in common with the Sinhalese masses. Using the Tamils as an 'other' was politically useful to get the masses behind the elite. The SLFP pursued this strategy from the early 1950s, and when it reaped electoral success in 1956 the UNP too adopted it. Sinhalese chauvinism had become a major political force by then, and the SLFP never sought to weaken it during its sixteen years in power from 1956 to 1965 and from 1970 to 1977. The UNP, when it came to power in 1977 and wanted to shift from socialist to politically-risky capitalist economic policies, decided to persist with the hard line against the Tamils. This was to ensure that it had to fight only on the economic front in the intra-Sinhalese political struggle of the UNP vs. SLFP, with the Maoist-chauvinist JVP looming threateningly in the background.

During the first twenty-four years of independence, 1948–72, the mobilisation of Tamils was entirely political and almost wholly through the Federal Party led by Chelvanayakam. But by the 1970s it appeared to the Tamils that the peaceful path to autonomy was leading nowhere. During the next eleven years (1972–83), political and military mobilisation went parallel, with the TUF/TULF working the political line and about twenty groups of youth trying to develop an insurgent capability. In training some of them—EROS, EPRLF and PLOTE—the Palestine Liberation Organisation (PLO) in Lebanon played a significant role in 1975. The anti-Tamil frenzy of July 1983 opened the floodgates for Tamil youth wanting to join militant ranks. The shift of axis of the Tamil struggle from political to military in place since, 1972 now became complete. The parliamentary party of the TULF became discredited and began to wallow in the wake of militant groups.

The Tamil diaspora also played an important role in the mobilisation of Tamils which gathered pace during the 1970s. Proportionate to their native population, the Sri Lankan Tamils constitute one of the largest émigré groups in affluent countries. Their numbers have swollen since 1983 under family reunion and asylum schemes. Today, there are over a million Sri Lankan Tamils abroad, about three-quarters of them in the West, compared to the two-and-a-half million within Sri Lanka. About three-fourths of the Sri Lankan Tamils abroad are from the Jaffna area. In 1984, the majority of Sri Lankan Tamil diaspora came to recognise the LTTE as the group most likely to succeed in promoting the Tamil cause. They provided the LTTE with both money and international operations skills.

The mid-1970s saw the rise of an alphabet soup of Tamil militant groups—all sporting the word 'Eelam', and most 'liberation' as well. By the early 1980s five of them—LTTE, TELO, PLOTE, EPRLF and EROS—had become the major ones. There was little coordination among them and during 1973–85 they killed more of their own rather than of the enemy. Beginning mid-1983 India began to give covert training and logistic support to all the groups, yet their internecine war continued. In one week in April–May 1986, the LTTE virtually decimated the TELO, which together with the EPRLF was the group most under Indian influence. Later that year, in December, the EPRLF was also largely wiped out. PLOTE began to disintegrate and EROS became a satellite of the LTTE. By early 1987 the LTTE had become the only effective Tamil militant group. The others were being kept alive largely through Indian support.

The violent, Darwinian struggle through which the LTTE rose to the top has contributed a good deal to its characteristics. In the eyes of the LTTE it is their greater ruthlessness, absolutism and unwillingness to yield—qualities that others despise in them—that has helped them to first overcome other Tamil groups (which they considered weak and opportunistic) and then battle the Sri Lankan government to a stalemate. The LTTE knew that India would never support its goal of Eelam. It knew the limits of Sri Lankan Tamil influence upon Chennai, and of Chennai's upon Delhi. It knew that India would not encourage any rebel group to become dominant as it would reduce India's leverage. It therefore made a determined effort to break out of Indian control through the creation of an international support base using the Tamil diaspora. The conflict between India and the LTTE that erupted in warfare in October 1987 had been brewing for four years.

The links between the people of Tamil Nadu and the Sri Lankan Tamils have always been weak. The perceived lack of interest the Sri Lankan Tamils showed towards the plight of the 'Indian' Tamils when they were deported in the mid-1960s did not endear them to Tamils in India. Nor did the frequent clashes in the Palk Straits between the Tamil fishermen of the two countries. Notable support for Sri Lankan Tamils arose in Tamil Nadu only in 1977 when, as a result of anti-Tamil riots and the intensification of the military campaign in Jaffna, refugees poured into Tamil Nadu. That support reached a peak following the 'Black July' of 1983, but rapidly came down when the LTTE initiated hostilities against the IPKF in October 1987. India's primary concern in Sri Lanka during 1983–90 was its strategic interests. The concern for Sri Lankan Tamils was secondary. It was only in the early 1990s that Colombo recognised this reality.

When the war with the militants first gathered pace in 1983, the government believed that a determined military effort could overcome the splintered groups. In fact, the government and most Sinhalese were of the view that they were robbed of victory in 1984 because of Indian pressure and in 1987 because of Indian intervention. The LTTE's unexpectedly strong performance against the IPKF changed this thinking, but Colombo took heart from the fact that the LTTE now had a formidable foe in India. The 1990–94 war was less intense than the 1995–2001 one that followed. The latter saw nearly four times as many casualties. By 1995 the Sri Lankan military had grown to four times the size it was in 1983, and had inducted a good deal of modern equipment. It was therefore able to go on the offensive in 1995 and succeeded in capturing the Jaffna Peninsula. But it got bogged down thereafter.

Colombo has steadily gained in foreign support from 1987. In October of the same year India turned against the LTTE when it started fighting the IPKF, a turn that became decisive when it assassinated Rajiv Gandhi in May 1991. The LTTE's image in the West also began to change—from a group fighting oppression to a terrorist one—because of the large number of attacks against civilians and political assassinations it carried out in the early 1990s. By pursuing a well-crafted dual track of 'devolution promise' and 'war for peace' from 1994, Kumaratunga was able to gain considerable international goodwill. The dominant international perception of the Sri Lankan conflict became one of an accommodative government confronting a hardened terrorist group. This helped to have the LTTE banned in the US in 1997 and in Britain, Canada and Australia in 2001. These four countries together account for over three-quarters of well-to-do expatriate Tamils whose financial support is crucial to the LTTE. The bans have, therefore, greatly enhanced Colombo's negotiating leverage.

The costs that Sri Lanka as a state and the Tamils as a people have incurred during the twenty-year war have been enormous. The figures here have been taken from a publication by the National Peace Council of Sri Lanka.[7] The figures are for the period 1983–98 (fifteen years) and are in Sri Lankan rupees at 1998 prices. The direct military expenditure incurred by the government on the war is 213 billion. A further 40 billion has been spent on public order and safety. The LTTE is estimated to have spent 43 billion. The cost of repair and replacement of damaged infrastructure is 137 billion. The loss of potential earnings from tourism is estimated at 200 billion. The loss of foreign investment is reckoned at 75 billion. The total cost of war, including resources that would have been available for an alternative path of consumption, growth and investment (had they not been spent on the war or lost as a result of reduced output), is estimated at 1,443 billion. But for the war, the GDP of Sri Lanka in 1998 would have been 1,304 billion, compared to the realised 912 billion.

Sri Lanka's defence expenditure as a percentage of GDP went up from 1.1 per cent in 1983 to 3.5 per cent in 1985, and to 6.1 per cent in 2000. The Sri Lankan army lost 3,000 soldiers during 1990–94, and 11,000 during 1995–2000. The big losers, by far, have been the Tamils. The average net worth of a Tamil today, adjusted for inflation, is a quarter of what it was in 1983. Between 1983 and 2001, the per capita

[7] National Peace Council of Sri Lanka: *Cost of the War: The Economic, Socio-political and Human Cost of the War in Sri Lanka*, Colombo, 2001.

income in Tamil areas has dropped by about 40 per cent while in the rest of Sri Lanka it increased by approximately the same percentage. But for the war, the per capita income in both areas might have gone up by about 70 per cent. Of the nearly 70,000 killed, more than three-quarters have been Tamils. Of the close to a million displaced people, more than four-fifths are Tamils.

There has been some shift in Sinhalese public opinion in favour of devolving political power to the Tamils. War weariness is not an appropriate term to describe the Sinhalese mood for they have not really suffered. The desire for peace has come more from a feeling that while the LTTE can never win Eelam, it is capable of prolonging the war indefinitely. It is also being realised that the Tamils cannot be enticed or coerced into withdrawing support to the LTTE. There is also a better understanding that India cannot afford Eelam, and the realisation that there is very limited support in Tamil Nadu for Sri Lankan Tamils. These have helped build Sinhalese confidence that the Tamils will not be able to convert autonomy into freedom at a later stage. Yet, there are large swathes of continuing resistance against meaningful devolution. Two generations of politicians in both the UNP and SLFP have made their careers on the basis of being seen as protectors of Buddhist–Sinhalese hegemony. There is also the JVP that has shed its Maoism, but is clinging all the more tightly to its ethnocentric line to hold its support base. The Buddhist Maha Sangha is another centre of resistance.

The Tamils have paid a very high price for the war in terms of death, disablement, displacement, personal insecurity, loss of education, forced recruitment by the LTTE, loss of economic opportunity, and primitive living conditions. There is a felt desire to bring the war to an end and resume normal lives, which they have not known for a generation. There is serious concern at the LTTE's practices of taxation and recruitment of young children. Yet, the Tamils, especially those in the north, see the LTTE as their best guarantor. In all these decades, it is only the LTTE that has succeeded in narrowing the huge gap in bargaining strength between the Tamils and the Sinhalese. Almost all Tamils feel that no fair treatment can be expected from Colombo, except what can be extracted through resistance, and that the government has entered the peace process only because it could not defeat the LTTE. Most Tamils, therefore, think that the LTTE should be unconditionally supported till a just order gets embedded.

PEACE EFFORTS

The peace efforts in Sri Lanka can be divided into three phases. The first was the two decades of 1957–77, when Colombo and democratically elected Tamil representatives sought to find a solution. The second phase was 1983–89, when Colombo, Delhi and a variety of Tamil groups tried their hand. The third phase, beginning 1989, and which continues today, has seen Colombo negotiating with the LTTE between long spells of fighting.

The first round of negotiations during 1956–57 was a response to the heightened fear of the Tamils adopting the 'Sinhala Only' policy of April 1956 by the newly elected SLFP government. Prime Minister Solomon Bandaranaike and Federal Party leader Chelvanayakam then arrived at the 'B–C Pact' of July 1957. But the agreement lay in shambles following the anti-Tamil riots of May 1958, the biggest act of violence against the Tamils till then. When the UNP came back to power in March 1965, there was another attempt at peacemaking. An agreement was reached between the new Prime Minister Dudley Senanayake and Chelvanayakam. This led to the language issue being partly addressed through the January 1966 Tamil Language Act. In May 1970 the SLFP came back to power. The new constitution of May 1972 re-emphasised the primacy of Sinhala language, and the Tamils lost the minor gains that they had made in 1966 on the issue of language. Tamil militant violence began in Jaffna shortly thereafter. In July 1977 the UNP came back to power. In its election campaign the UNP had promised to address Tamil grievances through an APC. But in the face of huge anti-Tamil riots, the UNP resiled. This was the last opportunity to settle matters before violence gripped the country.

The commencement of the 'First Eelam War' in July 1983 saw India entering the peacemaking scene. The later part of 1983 saw the emergence of the 'Annexure C Proposals' negotiated between Colombo, Delhi and the TULF. The proposals included the formation of provincial councils, and the merger of the northern and eastern provinces. President Jayawardene called an APC to discuss the proposals but the APC was a charade, with neither the UNP nor the SLFP wanting any part of it. Delhi soon realised that the TULF had little clout to negotiate for the Tamils. It therefore got hold of the various militant groups and cobbled together a negotiating front. This paved the way for the July–August 1985 peace talks between Colombo and the Tamils in the Bhutanese capital Thimpu. With the Tamils asking for the acceptance of Tamils as a nation, the eastern and northern provinces as their homeland, and their right to self-determination, and Colombo unwilling to offer anything beyond separate provincial councils for the northern and eastern provinces, the talks broke down.

India continued with its efforts, and after fifteen months of talks between Colombo and Delhi the so-called '19 December 1986 proposals' emerged. The Tamil groups rejected this. The main objection came from the LTTE, which by then had emerged as the dominant Tamil group, with Delhi's influence on it notably diminished. Meanwhile, Colombo intensified military operations. Unable to restrain Colombo, Delhi went for a coercive airdrop of relief supplies in Jaffna on 4 June 1987. This forced Colombo to negotiate seriously with Delhi, and on 29 July the 'India–Sri Lanka Agreement to Establish Peace in Sri Lanka' was signed. It was a bilateral agreement between Delhi and Colombo, and the Tamil groups were not part of it.

The LTTE was resolutely opposed to the agreement as it required it to surrender all its arms 'within seventy-two hours', thereby losing the only leverage it felt it had against Colombo. It had no confidence that Delhi would be able to ensure Colombo's adherence to the terms of the agreement once the Tamils were disarmed. Moreover, the merger of the northern and eastern provinces, which was a vital issue for the Tamils, was not guaranteed. It was not surprising therefore that the LTTE started hostilities against the IPKF by October. In November Sri Lanka amended its constitution to create provincial councils and a year later, after elections, the northern and eastern provinces were merged pending ratification through a referendum. But the whole arrangement collapsed within a year, because neither could the IPKF defeat the LTTE nor would Colombo take the Delhi-sponsored Tamil government of the north-east province seriously.

The common need to get the IPKF out of the country brought Colombo and the LTTE together in 1989. Talks between the two began when the LTTE's London-based advisor Balasingham met President Premadasa in Colombo in April. The first round of talks in May went on for twenty-seven days, and a second round in June for seventeen days. Just before the second round Premadasa demanded publicly that the IPKF should leave the country. In September the IPKF ceased military operations preparatory to leaving the country. The purely tactical common purpose between Colombo and the LTTE now withered. The fourteen-month truce between the two sides collapsed in June 1990 when the LTTE attacked several police stations in the east. The 'Second Eelam War', which went on for the next fifty months, had begun.

In August 1994 the SLFP-led PA under Kumaratunga came to power, ending seventeen years of UNP rule. And in November Kumaratunga was elected President. During her parliamentary and presidential campaigns Kumaratunga had sensed a slight easing of hardline views in Sinhalese society. This enabled her to make an effort to shift public opinion in favour of seeking a negotiated peace. For the first time, a top Sinhalese leader had acknowledged that the Tamils had legitimate grievances which needed to be addressed in a substantive manner. This was not an easy message to convey given that competitive stoking of Sinhalese chauvinism had been the staple of Sri Lankan politics for four decades.

Immediately on becoming Prime Minister, Kumaratunga partially relaxed the economic embargo against Jaffna. Prabakaran responded with a letter to Kumaratunga on 2 September 1994. This led to the peace negotiations that went on till 19 April 1995. The real negotiations during those eight months were conducted through letters between the principals. Prabakaran wrote eleven letters to Kumaratunga and she in turn wrote twelve to Prabakaran. Face-to-face meetings between representatives, held in the then LTTE-controlled Jaffna between 13 October 1994 and 10 April 1995, totalled only five days.[8] Kumaratunga was negotiating in good faith, but the level of mistrust was such that she could not afford to lift the economic embargo that the LTTE had been insisting upon. The LTTE's effort was to improve its position on the ground to gain greater leverage before entering into discussions on the political settlement. Its refusal to continue with the talks, unless the economic embargo and the restrictions on fishing and movement of LTTE cadres in the eastern province was removed, led to the foundering of the talks.

The two sides had entered the peace process at the time without even a rough idea of the kind of political settlement that would be acceptable to the other side. Kumaratunga also did not know what she could sell to her own party and the opposition. She came from a

[8] For a detailed, though biased, insider account of this negotiation, see Anton Balasingham's *The Politics of Duplicity: Revisiting the Jaffna Talks,* Mitcham, England: Fairfax Publishing, 2000.

political and family background anchored in Sinhalese nationalism, and she had gone against her grain to campaign on a peace platform during the parliamentary and presidential elections of 1994. The LTTE was aware of this, and of the fact that the narrow victory of the PA in 1994 had more to do with the anti-incumbency feelings generated by seventeen years of UNP rule rather than with any support for the softer line towards the Tamils that Kumaratunga was advocating. The LTTE also distrusted Kumaratunga because of what it perceived as her attempt to undercut the LTTE politically by approaching the Tamil people directly.

The failure of the 1994–95 peace negotiations contributed a good deal to Kumaratunga's subsequent hardline attitude to the LTTE. The 'Third Eelam War' that began in April 1995 and continued for the next eighty months was the bloodiest of the three 'Eelam Wars'. In April 2000 Norway came into the peace effort as a facilitator. The LTTE declared a unilateral ceasefire on 24 December 2000, soon after Kumaratunga's re-election as President. But Kumaratunga did not respond. Instead, she initiated a big offensive on 25 April 2001, the day the ceasefire was to end. There were several reasons for her failure to respond to the LTTE's ceasefire. One was the hardened mind-set within the Sri Lankan government as a result of the brutal fighting that had been going on over the past sixty-eight months. Another reason was the fact that her constitutional bill to create a platform for negotiations with the LTTE was in limbo. Then there was the hope that through proscription in more foreign countries greater international pressure could be brought to bear on the LTTE. There was also some military confidence stemming from the acquisition of considerable new weaponry by the Sri Lankan forces since 1995.

The devastating attack on Colombo airport by the LTTE in July 2001, and the disastrous economic consequences it brought on, made a marked impact on Sri Lankan thinking. For the first time, the policy-influencing sections of the country began to have doubts about the wisdom of adopting an uncompromising attitude towards the LTTE. The UNP, under whose watch during 1977–94 the country had been continuously fighting the Tamils, sensed the shift in the public mood and decided to campaign on a peace platform in the December 2001 elections. Within a fortnight of the UNP/UNF's narrow election victory, the LTTE declared a unilateral ceasefire, as it had after

Kumaratunga's victory a year earlier. Prime Minister Wickramasinghe responded with an undeclared ceasefire, as well as a relaxation of the economic embargo in force against LTTE-controlled areas. He also rejuvenated the peace role of Norway, which had been in the doldrums since the previous May because of lack of support from Kumaratunga.

Both sides had stronger motivation to pursue peace than they had in 1994. The LTTE's territorial hold had become weaker; it was no longer in control of Jaffna Peninsula, and its position in the eastern province was less strong. Its branding as a terrorist organisation by the US, India, the UK, Canada and Australia, and the increasing difficulties experienced by the Tamil diaspora to help it financially were hurting. Colombo's position was also difficult. The Wanni area was under LTTE control, making the Jaffna Peninsula isolated by land. Colombo was also coming under mounting pressure from aid donors to reach a settlement. Sri Lanka's s defence budget was about the same as the $900 million aid it was getting annually. Besides, the confidence in Sri Lanka's economy, both within and outside the country, had suffered a body blow after the July 2001 airport attack. The GDP growth had turned negative for the first time in Sri Lankan history.

On 22 February 2002, the ceasefire that had been unofficially in force for the previous two months was converted into an official one, through the signing of an agreement at the level of the Prime Minister and Prabakaran, but without the two actually meeting. The agreement provided not only for an indefinite ceasefire, but also for its observance to be monitored by a fifty-five-member Sri Lanka Monitoring Mission from four Nordic countries. Soon after this landmark agreement, security restrictions were conspicuously reduced in Colombo as well as on the major highways to the north and east from Kandy—A-9 to Jaffna through the LTTE-controlled Wanni and A-5 to Trincomalee.

Several practical concessions came from the two sides before the first round of Colombo–LTTE talks began in Thailand on 16 September 2002. When they signed their agreement in February, Colombo effectively accepted the LTTE as the popular representative of the Tamils. The LTTE was given permission to enter government-controlled areas for political work. The LTTE's assurance on eschewing violence, in turn, enabled the government to lift security restrictions in Colombo and raise business confidence in the country. The deproscription of the LTTE on 16 September was a notable concession, as was the decision not to detain any LTTE cadre under PTA, although those already under detention were not to be freed.

At the very first round of talks, the LTTE indicated that it was willing to consider the option of autonomy instead of Eelam. This was confirmed on 5 December during the third round of talks in Oslo, when the two parties jointly and publicly agreed to 'explore a solution based on internal self-determination in areas of historical habitation of Tamils founded on a federal structure based on a united Sri Lanka.' Both sides had shifted position considerably to make this statement possible. The LTTE gave up its right to secede through exercising unrestricted self-determination rights. Colombo, on its part, agreed to a federal Sri Lanka—something it had determinedly resisted since independence—and also accepted the idea of an area of historical habitation by Tamils.

The fourth round of talks in Thailand in January 2002, the fifth in Germany in February, and the sixth in Japan in March did not produce much forward movement. In their second round of talks, the two sides had agreed to set up three joint sub-committees to deal with political, security and economic issues. Despite these, however, there was little 'joint' work done on the ground. The LTTE's dissatisfaction on this count was seen when it pulled out of the Sub-Committee for De-escalation and Normalisation in January after the fourth round of talks. On 10 March the Sri Lankan Navy sank an LTTE cargo ship. Meanwhile, the LTTE's complaints had been mounting about the lack of progress in resettling Tamil refugees. The army's security zones continued to occupy 190 sq. km of prime land in Jaffna Peninsula which has a total area of only 880 sq. km.

In mid-April the US refused to let the LTTE, which is banned in the US, to attend a donor conference in Washington to prepare for the big donor meet scheduled to be held two months later in Tokyo. The LTTE had attended the first donor conference in Oslo the previous November. Feeling that the peace process was working to its disadvantage, the LTTE announced on 21 April that it was suspending talks with the government till a satisfactory approach to creating an interim administration in the north and east was worked out. Despite considerable persuasion, the LTTE did not attend the donor's meet in Tokyo in June where as much as $4.5 billion was pledged. On 31 October, the LTTE came out with its proposals for the ISGA, which it wanted as the basis for restarting the negotiations stalled the previous April. But before the Wickramasinghe government could respond, Kumaratunga took over three key ministries, paralysing the government.

The six rounds of negotiations that went on from September 2002 to April 2003 have improved the abysmally low level of trust between the parties. They have also produced the important agreement to seek a solution based on a federal structure. But translating that in-principle agreement into practical steps is a massive and highly contentious task that has not even begun. The LTTE favours a two-stage approach, which the Wickramasinghe government was willing to go along with up to a point. The LTTE sees achieving normalcy of civilian life and building confidence between the two sides through an interim arrangement as the first stage. Final settlement issues should be addressed in the second stage, under the conducive conditions created by the first stage. Kumaratunga and the country's security establishment, on the other hand, want to first obtain agreement on core political issues and then, within the framework of that agreement, bring about conditions of normalcy. This approach will not allow the LTTE to wield any administrative power till the political issues concerning end-stage governance are settled.

A crucial issue is the LTTE's military capability. The Sinhalese feel that as long as that formidable capability is retained, the LTTE cannot be trusted not to go back to the fighting mode. The LTTE, in turn, is very wary of Colombo. Many past agreements between the Tamils and the government (beginning with the B–C Pact in 1957) that were reached after long negotiations were reneged on later by the government under Sinhalese pressure. The LTTE feels it would be foolhardy to give up its military capability—the only leverage it possesses—and rely on a paper agreement. It is for this very reason that it chose to fight the IPKF in 1987. Maintaining its military capability till autonomous governance is irreversibly established is crucial to the LTTE. It also does not want to enter into final-stage negotiations till it is able to acquire national and international legitimacy by becoming a legal governing party.

The core political issues to be incorporated in a final settlement are broadly four—the kind of autonomy the Tamils would enjoy under the new federal system of governance, the areas that would come under Tamil political primacy, the ensuring of democratic governance in those areas, and guaranteeing that the terms of settlement shall be adhered to by both sides. Constituent units of a federal system enjoy varying degrees of autonomy in different countries. The Canadian organisation, 'The Forum of Federations', had participated in discussions during the third round of Colombo–LTTE talks in Oslo, and both sides are studying the federal systems of Switzerland, Germany and Canada. All three countries give considerable freedom of governance to their units, and the LTTE and the Tamils ought to be happy with any of the three models.

The second core issue is whether the northern and eastern provinces should be combined. While the northern province is almost entirely Tamil, in the eastern province the Tamil strength is only about a third. A little more than a third are Muslims and the remainder Sinhalese—the majority of them post-1970 settlers. Colombo is keen to keep the two provinces separate, and so are the Muslims. The LTTE is unpopular among the Muslims, Tamil-speaking though they are. During their second spell of control in Jaffna beginning 1990, the LTTE had expelled about 90,000 Muslims. In the eastern province, there have been a number of LTTE–Muslim clashes. Without the two provinces merging, the Tamils cannot secure political power in the eastern province. And Sinhalese settlement there could well accelerate.

The third core issue is that of ensuring democracy and human rights in areas where the LTTE is likely to come to power. The LTTE has all along been a totalitarian organisation, and its strength has come from the fascist principles of one leader and iron discipline. The areas of the Jaffna Peninsula it governed during 1990–95 and of Wanni which it has governed since 1995 have experienced this. Ensuring full human rights and liberal democracy in LTTE-controlled areas is therefore a major concern for everyone. There is uncertainty about the proportion in which popularity and fear are mixed in the support that the LTTE enjoys among Tamils. This is particularly so in the case of the eastern province. The Batticalao Tamils there are culturally somewhat different from the Jaffna Tamils in the north, who constitute the core of the LTTE. Whether the LTTE will tolerate genuine political diversity, and whether it will accept the loss of power such diversity might lead to, are big questions. But there can surely be no autonomy for the areas of prospective governance by the LTTE without measures put in place to ensure full human and democratic rights.

The last issue is of ensuring that the provisions of the settlement arrived at are adhered to. For this, the ability of the LTTE to re-start military action has to be eliminated. At the same time, the ability of Colombo to go back on the provisions of the agreement has also to be guarded against. International interest in Sri Lankan affairs will rapidly dwindle once a settlement is in place. And so will outside ability to ensure adherence by both sides to the terms of settlement. Withholding financial aid, which Sri Lankans—both Sinhalese and Tamils—badly need, may be the only measure that can have a degree of outside influence over post-settlement events.

For the present, the LTTE has behind it the Tamil political parties that matter. This has in a way paved the way for the LTTE to enter the democratic process should a peace agreement come about. But there are problems. The LTTE has reason to worry that in a democratic arrangement, where Colombo is able to prop up parties opposed to it using governmental power and patronage, its grip over the Tamils might weaken, especially in the eastern province. The LTTE has lost close to 18,000 cadres, including nearly 4,000 women, in the last two decades of fighting. To its way of thinking, the gain from these huge sacrifices—forcing Colombo to negotiate seriously—should not be jeopardised by getting 'trapped' into democratic and human rights commitments that could create a new paradigm where the kind of power it has will matter less. The LTTE, unlike Sinn Fein/IRA in Northern Ireland, has not yet developed leaders with the political skills needed in a democratic set up.

The peace process is under threat, not only by the huge gap that still separates the Sinhalese and the Tamils on the contours of a final settlement, but equally by the ever present political struggle among the Sinhalese—between the SLFP and the UNP, currently represented by Kumaratunga and Wickramasinghe. The two parties know that while the Sinhalese masses are supportive of a compromise settlement, they are against conceding to the Tamils more than the absolute minimum required. Electoral fortunes thus depend on being seen as both flexible and tough. Each party is trying to show that it is both. Sri Lanka's executive presidency is almost guaranteed to bring about policy paralysis if the President and the Prime Minister are from rival parties. Progress in peace negotiations is unlikely unless elections produce a President and Prime Minister from the same party, or the executive presidency is abolished.

POINTERS FOR KASHMIR

The Sri Lankan problem, being an internal one, does not offer many insights with regard to the India–Pakistan dimension of the Kashmir conflict. The pointers it offers are primarily with regard to the handling of discontent in Kashmir. The conflict however holds one major lesson for Pakistan—secession is not a practical proposition in today's world. In 1994 and in 2001, the LTTE had fought Colombo to a military stalemate, a feat that the Pakistani-sponsored fighters in Kashmir have never even begun to approach. Similarly, the LTTE has controlled substantial areas of Sri Lankan territory since 1990—areas from where state authority has been excluded. Nothing like it has ever happened in Kashmir. Yet, in the end the LTTE has had to settle for a federal solution. Therefore, if Pakistani believes that any part of the areas currently with India can be separated from it is a delusion that can only serve to prolong the conflict without a strategic purpose.

There is some similarity between the problems that Delhi experienced in upholding its 1952 and 1975 agreements with Sheikh Abdullah, and those that Colombo experienced in staying true to its 1957 and 1965 agreements with Chelvanayakam. In both cases, these failures contributed to turning, over a period of time, political conflicts into military ones. The 1974 agreement that Indira Gandhi made and the 1957 one that Solomon Bandaranaike made were probably destined to be stillborn. But in the case of the 1952 and 1965 agreements, the national leaders involved—Nehru and Dudley Senanayake—were genuinely seeking solutions. Both were thwarted in their effort, in large measure, by the chauvinist resistance whipped up by their political opponents.

Sri Lanka offers a good example of the unlikelihood of hawkish strategies succeeding against one's own people when there is genuine cause for discontent. There can be little doubt that the Tamils suffered serious discrimination in Sri Lanka from 1956, and that Colombo never made an honest effort to deal with the problem. There was no violence at all on the Tamils' part till the early 1970s, and even when it began it was only sporadic. Colombo's response unfortunately was entirely military. This led to grievances mounting on both sides and violence climbing to a much higher level by 1977. Colombo continued to increase its repression in Jaffna, and that inevitably led to the explosive violence of 1983 and the commencement of the 'First Eelam War'. Thereafter, it has been a full-scale internal war with short breaks. Despite increasing the personnel strength of the military by a factor of six and the GDP share of the defence budget by a factor of four, the government has been unable to win. While continuously blaming the LTTE, Colombo never made a serious attempt to wean the larger Tamil population away from it. It could not do this because it was not prepared to make the kind of political concessions that such an effort would have called for.

Sri Lanka also demonstrates how important domestic politics is in prolonging or bringing a conflict to an end. The no-holds-barred tussle for political power that has gone on between the UNP and the SLFP from 1951, largely by pandering to the chauvinistic sections of the Sinhalese society, is now nearly as big an obstacle to peace as Sinhalese–Tamil differences. To promote its political fortune, the SLFP is perfectly willing today to align itself with the fanatical JVP and place in jeopardy a peace process that has brought to the country stability and business confidence unknown since 1983.

There are three aspects of the peace process in Sri Lanka that have particular relevance to Kashmir. The first is that peace cannot be achieved unless the leaders have popular winds behind them. In Sri Lanka, the Sinhalese willingness to explore a peaceful solution was not developed through an agreement between political parties, but rather by a change of thinking within the civil society. Kumaratunga's electorally-rewarding decision to campaign on a low-key peace plat-form in 1994 and Wickramasinghe's 2001 decision to do it more ex-plicitly were more a response to a shift in the public mood than that of seeking such a shift. Public opinion in Sri Lanka had begun to shift before leadership thinking had. This happened not only because people got tired of the war but also because they realised that, contrary to what hawkish moulders of opinion had been drilling into them, peace was possible without endangering vital interests. A new perspective at looking at war and peace rose in public discourse. Peacemaking gradually ceased to be a vote-loser.

The second pointer from Sri Lanka is that negotiations have to be well prepared and sustained. In 1994 Kumaratunga sought to en-gage the LTTE within days of a ceasefire. There was no preparation of the ground before the two sides started exchanging letters in secrecy. The effort that began in December 2001 was more measured. It was only after two months of unilateral ceasefire from both sides and a partial relaxation of economic embargo against rebel-controlled areas that the two sides signed a formal agreement. It was another seven months, by which time some peace dividend in terms of easing of conditions of life had reached both sides, before actual peace talks began. And because the ground had been well prepared earlier, the broad contours of the final solution—federally decentralised govern-ance for the Tamils within a united Sri Lanka—became clear at the very beginning of the talks. This greatly reduced the gap between the opening positions of the two sides. Good behind-the-scene cooperation also ensured that there was no public blame game, even when the LTTE suspended the talks on 21 April 2003. The negotiation styles adopted by the two sides since December 2001 also offer some lessons.

The third point of relevance is the way the concept of autonomy is being dealt with. At present all that has been agreed to is that there would be a 'federal' solution—an idea that would now have to be fleshed out. While models of other federations such as Canada (with its asymmetric devolution in respect of Quebec), Germany, Switzerland and Australia will no doubt be examined, eventually a model that meets the needs of both sides in Sri Lanka will have to be evolved. For the Sinhalese, such a model should never lead to the possibility of the Tamils being able to break away at a later stage. For the Tamils, the model should enable them to have control over their internal affairs without Colombo being in a position to intervene. In India, the term autonomy with respect to Kashmir is a red rag to many. This is largely because the term has never been explored with regard to the varied baskets of content it could have. Probable future discussions about the nuts and bolts of federal distribution of power in the Tamil areas of Sri Lanka should be educative to India and Pakistan as well as the discontented in J&K.

REFLECTIONS ON THE ISRAELI– PALESTINIAN CONFLICT

The primary value of studying the Israeli–Palestinian conflict in the context of the India–Pakistan tussle over Kashmir lies in what it might teach us about how very different are the structures of the two conflicts, and how much more potentially tractable the latter conflict is. Both Israelis and Palestinians lay claim to the whole of what was Mandated Palestine. For the extremists of the two sides, the other side must be displaced from the entire land that both nations claim as theirs. In Kashmir, the contested Valley holds less than half per cent of India's and Pakistan's combined population. Equally important, there is nothing in Kashmir to whip up passions the way the co-location of the Mount of Solomon's Temple and Haram al-Sharif does. Nor is there any resource stake comparable to that constituted in that parched land by the Jordan river system and the area's aquifers. India and Pakistan are both secure and comfortable in the territories they currently hold. This is distinctly not the case with Israel and the Palestinians.

The greatly increased interaction with Israel over the last decade has had an influence on Indian thinking with regard to the predicaments of the two countries. Israel has not only become India's second largest defence supplier but has also shown the ability to give India some very useful technologies that we could not have got from elsewhere. Some Indians are attracted by visions of US–India–Israel trilateral cooperation against a broad Islamic threat, with Israel paving the way for strong US–India strategic ties. While some of these notions are fanciful, there is no doubt that the benefits that can accrue to India from a good relationship with Israel are considerable. But it does not follow that the conflict structures confronting the two countries are similar or that both are comparably stymied in steering a way out.

There is anger towards India in Kashmir, but it is nothing like the visceral animus there is among Palestinians that has made matters so difficult for Israel. Also, a close study of the Israeli–Palestinian conflict will show that, contrary to popular perceptions, Israel's policy in Palestine after 1967 has not been a success in terms of its long-range interests. Israel has been unable to use its huge military and diplomatic superiority to achieve a durable peace—a victor's peace or a peace-maker's one. But it is not the lack of success attending Israeli policies that is of principal interest with regard to Kashmir. Instead, it is the fact that despite a superficially coaxing resemblance, Israel's problems with Palestinians (and Arabs in general) and India's difficulties in Kashmir are qualitatively different. And because of that, the peace-making potential in the two cases are very dissimilar.

Evolution of the Conflict

European Jewish leaders began to talk about a Jewish National Home in the latter half of the nineteenth century. About three-fifths of the world's Jews were then in Europe and the rest mostly in the Middle East. The obvious territorial choice for a Jewish state was Palestine, then under the control of the crumbling Ottoman Turks. Jews had been in that area in large numbers from the thirteenth century BCE, and Solomon's reign in the mid-tenth century BCE was the Jewish golden age. Assyrians overran them in eighth century BCE, and the Babylonians two centuries later. In early second century CE, Romans crushed the little political authority the Jews still had. They also destroyed the Second (or Solomon's) Temple, on the base of which the al-Aqsa Mosque now stands. The founding of Islam resulted in

Palestine coming under its sway in the seventh century. Palestine remained under Muslim control till 1917, except during the twelfth and thirteenth centuries when control of Jerusalem alternated between local Muslims and Christian crusaders. In 1517, Palestine came under the Ottoman Turks and remained with them till 1917, except for the period 1799 to 1840 when it fell under Egyptian control. The British captured the area from the Turks in 1917, and in 1920 it became a British-administered territory under a League of Nations mandate. For their support in the war against Kaiser's Germany, Britain made a pledge to Zionist Jews to create a Jewish National Home in Palestine through the Balfour Declaration of 1917.

The Jewish trek to Palestine began as a trickle in the 1880s. The flow accelerated when Palestine came under the British in 1917. At the end of the nineteenth century, about 25,000 Jews lived in Palestine. In 1922 the figure was 84,000, which was 11 per cent of the territory's population. The pace of migration quickened after 1933. In 1946 the number had risen to 608,000 or 33 per cent of the population. Hitler's persecution of Jews in Europe, Britain's permissive attitude in letting them enter Palestine, and the ease with which land could be bought contributed to this increase. As a reaction to this stepped-up inflow, a full-scale Arab revolt in which at least 5,000 died rocked the territory during 1936–38. In 1937 the London-appointed Peel Commission recommended that the territory be partitioned. To placate the Arabs, who were important in the Second World War, Britain severely curtailed Jewish immigration in 1939. It was now the turn of the Jews to revolt.

Beginning 1917, the Jews had a clear political purpose—the establishment of a Jewish state in as large a portion of Palestine as possible. In 1920 the military organisation of Haganah (Defence)—linked to Mapai (Land of Israel Worker's Party), the ruling party of Yishuv (Jewish community in Palestine)—was set up. In 1923 Ze'ev Jabotinsky, one of the founders of Haganah, initiated the Revisionist Movement demanding that Jews conquer Palestine by force. In 1931 the Revisionists established Irgun (National Military Organisation). In 1939 Avraham Stern broke with Irgun and set up Lehi or the Stern Group. Hagannah, Irgun and Lehi carried out a systematic ethnic clearing of Palestinians from strategic areas through the use of terror. Menachem Begin, Israel's first Likud Prime Minister, was the leader of Irgun, and Yitzhak Shamir, the second was one of the commanders of Lehi.

212 • Crafting Peace in Kashmir

The end of Hitler's war saw huge world-wide sympathy for the Jews. In November 1947 the UN General Assembly adopted a resolution calling for the establishment of a Jewish State in the undefined 'Land of Israel'. That paved the way for the UN-approved partition of Palestine whereby the Jews got 56 per cent of the territory, even though their population at that time was only a third of the total. The partition cut Palestine into seven pieces—three each for the Jews and Arabs, and Jerusalem under international control.

More than 200,000 Palestinians were dispossessed and dispersed between the adoption of the partition resolution and the declaration of the establishment of the State of Israel six months later on 14 May 1948. The Arab states bordering Palestine—Egypt, Jordan, Syria and Lebanon—attacked Israel the day it was established. By the time the war ended seven months later, Israel had captured a further 22 per cent of Palestine. About 800,000 Palestinians had become refugees, including the 200,000 before the war. The Palestinian population, once in the 78 per cent of the original Palestine territory that now came under Israel, shrank from 950,000 in 1946 to 150,000. About 65 per cent of all Palestinians and over 80 per cent of those whose homes had been within Israel were now refugees.[1]

The war left the Palestinians disoriented and rudderless, unable to chart a path for themselves. They were left with 22 per cent of Palestine, about 95 per cent of it in the West Bank (of Jordan river) under Jordanian control, and the remaining in the narrow Gaza Strip under Egyptian control. The attack on Israel by Egypt, Jordan, Syria and Lebanon, with no joint planning and coordination, resulted in the Palestinians losing 50 per cent of the territory given to them under the UN plan. Arab countries then (and later) had little interest in what would become of the Palestinians. Their interests were sacred Jerusalem and the amorphous notion of Arab pride. The 1948 war ended with Israel signing separate armistices with Egypt, Jordan, Syria and Lebanon.

The war humiliated all Arab countries, especially Egypt, the largest of them. King Farouk's overthrow in 1952 stemmed directly from the defeat. The new regime under Nasser took Egypt away from the West. This set the gradual trend dividing the Arab world into pro-West and anti-West groupings. In 1953 Egypt began to receive arms from the

[1] See Ghada Karmi and Eugene Cotran, eds., *The Palestinian Exodus 1948–1998*, Reading: Ithaca Press, 1999.

Soviet Union, and in 1955 it nationalised the Suez Canal, hitherto under Anglo–French control. This linked the Arab–Israeli conflict to the Cold War. Egypt breaking free from Western control was worrying to Israel. It joined Britain and France in their October 1956 attack on Egypt to wrest back the Suez Canal. Because of US opposition, the war enterprise did not succeed and Israel had to hand back the Sinai Peninsula it had captured. Meanwhile, Israel and Jordan were working together secretly: it was only the strong anti-Israeli public opinion in Jordan that prevented the two from signing a peace treaty. Lebanon, then dominated by Maronite Christians, was also cooperative. But Egypt and Syria stayed strongly anti-Israel, and also became increasingly unamenable to Western influence.

The inability of the Arab states to help them led the Palestinians to set up their own resistance groups. Fatah was founded in 1958 by Palestinians living in Kuwait. Other important groups like the Popular Democratic Front for the Liberation of Palestine (PDFLP) and the Popular Front for the Liberation of Palestine (PFLP) also came up about this time. In June 1964, at Egypt's initiative, the League of Arab States created the Palestine Liberation Organisation. This marked the beginning of the diffused Arab national movement for Palestine changing into a more self-reliant and focused Palestine national movement. Palestinian fighters were mostly located in the West Bank, Gaza Strip, Syria and Sinai in the mid-1960s. Armed attacks inside Israel increased from 1965, and this led to strong retaliatory and pre-emptive raids by Israel.

About this time Egypt and Syria, which had been receiving considerable quantities of Soviet weapons, were beginning to feel emboldened to challenge Israel. In June 1966 Egypt asked UN observers, positioned along its border with Israel after the 1956 war, to leave. Tensions increased and in 1967, following a major Israeli raid into Syria, Egypt closed the Sharam al Sheik straits thereby blockading Israel's Red Sea port of Eilat. This and war preparations on both sides led to Israel's pre-emptive attack on Egypt and Syria that started the six-day war of June 1967. The war was a rout of the Arabs. Israel captured the Gaza Strip and Sinai from Egypt, all of the remaining Palestine including the whole of Jerusalem from Jordan, and the Golan Heights from Syria. During the first four months after the war, some 250,000 Palestinians left the occupied territories, but this fell far short of the exodus precipitated in 1947–48.

The 1967 war shattered Arab morale and discredited Arab countries the world over. It also transformed the Palestine conflict. For Egypt and Syria, getting back their own territories became the greater concern. It became clear to the Palestinians, who had lost all their land to Israel, that they were now essentially on their own. Fatah joined the PLO in 1968, and Arafat became its head in February 1969. The PLO's 1969 charter called for the elimination of Israel and the restoration of pre-1948 Palestine as a secular country. By 1969 the PLO had developed substantial ability to hit Israeli targets inside and outside Israel. The decade and a half that followed saw a large number of plane hijackings and terrorist strikes by the constituents of the PLO, and vicious reprisals and pre-emptive strikes by Israel. In 1970 the PLO hijacked four airliners and forced three of them down in Jordan. Jordan, which was in the Western camp unlike Egypt and Syria, was uncomfortable with the PLO, which after the 1967 war had most of its guerrilla forces in that country. Jordan was fearful of both Israeli reprisals and the PLO's ability to destabilise the Hashemite monarchy. In September 1970, the Jordanian Army moved against the PLO and by early 1971 the latter was driven out of the country with most of its forces moving to Lebanon.

Meanwhile, a deflated Egypt was trying to salvage some pride. In September 1968 it began artillery attacks and raids across the Suez Canal whose Eastern Bank was with Israel after 1967. This 'war of attrition' went on till Nasser died in September 1970. His successor, Anwar Sadat, was a realist whose focus was Egyptian national interest and not the meta-nationalist Arab cause. Although the huge re-equipping of Egyptian forces after the 1967 war was done entirely with Soviet assistance, Sadat reasoned that to get back Sinai he would have to work through the US. He also knew that he had to improve his bargaining position with Israel. This led to Egypt's October 1973 surprise attack across the Suez Canal. Egypt gained nothing tangible from the war, but the war shook Israel. It was a touch-and-go situation in the beginning, and the US had to restrain the Soviet Union with a major nuclear alert. Israel too had placed nuclear weapons in aircraft. Israel lost over 3,000 men, four times the number in 1967. The war led to Arab countries tripling the price of oil. The confidence and sense of security that the 1967 war had generated in Israel was gone.

A major change in Israeli politics occurred in 1977. Labour, which had evolved from Mapai and had been in power since the founding of Israel, was replaced by Likud. Labour was by no means a soft party.

Its Prime Ministers—especially Ben Gurion, Golda Meir and Yishtak Rabin—were all tough. But compared to Labour, Likud was more hardline. After 1967 Labour had permitted Israeli settlements in the West Bank—mostly in the Jerusalem area for religious reasons and near the Jordan border for security reasons. But till 1977 the broad trend of public (not state level) thinking in Israel was to give up the captured territories of the 1967 war, except for Jerusalem, provided Egypt, Syria, Jordan and Lebanon signed peace treaties and accepted the demilitarisation of borders. But Menachem Begin, who took over as Likud Prime Minister in 1977, held radically different views and was determined to hold all of the West Bank and Golan Heights.

Many factors contributed to the rise of the Likud. There was the high-profile PLO terrorism of the 1970s instanced by the 1972 kidnapping of Israeli Olympic athletes in Munich, and the 1976 hijacking of an Air France airliner to Entebbe followed by a spectacular Israeli rescue. The Israelis were galled that while these terrorist acts were going on the Palestinian cause was prospering internationally. In 1974 Arafat addressed the United Nations General assembly (UNGA), and the next year the UNGA adopted a resolution equating Zionism with racism. (It was repealed in 1991 when the world order changed.) Meanwhile, the settlers in occupied territories had become a political force. Gush Emunim (Bloc of the Faithful) became a strong extra-parliamentary force supporting settlements. Then there were the Middle Eastern Jews (Sephardim), half of the Israeli population, who found themselves disadvantaged relative to the European Jews (Ashkemazim) who dominated the Labour Party. Labour was also out of step with Orthodox Jews, who disfavoured its liberal religious policies concerning Judaism. Finally, many Israelis saw the 'Hand of God' in the ease with which the West Bank, the Biblical lands of Judea and Samaria, was captured in 1967. Likud tapped into the veins of these diverse groups.

Likud was determined to keep the West Bank and Golan Heights for reasons of security, religious sentiment and water. There was little scope therefore for compromise with the PLO or Syria. Egypt's case was different. The Sinai desert did provide security depth, but it had much less significance in terms of sentiment, or even resources, although it had some oil. This made possible Sadat's historic trip to Jerusalem in November 1977, soon after hawkish Begin became Prime Minister. That visit led to the September 1978 Camp David meetings under the auspices of President Carter, and in turn to the March 1979

Israel–Egypt Peace Treaty and a shared Nobel Peace Prize for Begin and Sadat.

Israel's approach to the PLO had been hardening through the 1970s. The PLO's high-profile terrorism was one factor. Its growing international standing was another. In October 1974 the Arab League made the PLO the sole representative of the Palestinian people. In 1976 the PLO was made a member of the Arab League, and was also accorded permanent observer status in the UN. About eighty countries immediately recognised it. All this was difficult for Israel to digest, which was seeking to get the world to accept the dispersal of Palestinians (other than those living under Israeli control) outside Palestine. In 1978, while the Camp David negotiations were going on, Israel invaded Lebanon with a view to driving out the PLO but did not succeed. Israel's aim in trying to make the PLO inoperative was to reduce the status of the Palestinians from a national group to an ethnic minority.

Meanwhile, both Sunni and Shia Muslims in Lebanon were getting radicalised against the politically dominant Maronite Christians as well as Israel, seen as insensitive to Arab and Muslim concerns. Uncontrollable domestic violence forced Lebanon to seek help from Syria, its dominant neighbour, in August 1976. Hizbollah, a militant spin-off from Shiite Amal, had emerged in 1978 coinciding with Khomeini's rise to power in Iran. Syria, a friend of post-Shah Iran, supported Hizbollah. Attacks from Lebanon into Israel's northern border region had increased after the PLO's move into Lebanon in 1971. The rise of Amal and Hizbollah made the situation worse. In 1978 Israel captured a swathe of southern Lebanese territory up to the Litani River, and installed an Israeli-controlled 'South Lebanese Army' of Maronite Christians. Israel bombed Iraq's French-supplied nuclear reactor under erection in Osiraq in 1981. In April 1982, Israel completed its withdrawal from Sinai with Egypt agreeing to keep the peninsula demilitarised. Egypt's breaking ranks with militant Arab states not only made one of Israel's major borders secure, but also substantially strengthened the pro-West camp among the Arabs, which was a major objective of the US during negotiations.

Israel could now turn on the PLO. In June 1982 it invaded Lebanon. The twin objectives of the invasion were to expel the PLO forces there and to install a pro-Israeli government. Israel succeeded in its first aim, but failed in the second. The invasion was a brutal operation that led to heavy casualties, and there were cold-blooded massacres of Palestinians in camps.[2] The UNSC passed a resolution asking Israel to withdraw, but it ignored it as it had ignored similar resolutions after the 1948, 1967 and 1973 wars. The PLO shifted its headquarters to Tunis and continued to operate, but as a much-weakened organisation. Syria continued to be dominant in Lebanon. The invasion strengthened indigenous anti-Israeli forces in Lebanon, especially Hizbollah, and in 1985 Israel was forced to withdraw into the southern Lebanon security zone it had created in 1978. Meanwhile, the PLO was coming under pressure. The accelerated building of settlements in occupied territories after 1977 had shaken it. And its ejection from Lebanon in 1982 had sapped it much more than its 1970 expulsion from Jordan had. The PLO was also damaged by the Soviet decision in 1985 not to support radical Arab policies.

In December 1987, the intifada (uprising or shaking off), largely characterised by stone-throwing youth, erupted in the occupied territories. The intifada was not a sudden happening. Strikes and violent demonstrations had begun three years earlier. The PLO had little to do with the intifada. It was a popular uprising by a people who found their land taken over by Jewish settlers and their freedom of movement and work increasingly restricted. The beneficiary of this unrest was Hamas (Islamic Resistance Movement), which, unlike the PLO, was strongly Islamic. Israel found it difficult to subdue the intifada, and the brutal methods it used lost it a good deal of sympathy abroad. In July 1988 King Hussein of Jordan, prompted by the intifada, relinquished his claims to the West Bank in favour of the PLO. But internationally, the PLO's position was weakening. To improve its credentials, the PLO decided in November 1988 to accept Israel within its pre-1967 borders and to foreswear terrorism. This and the intifada induced the US to agree in December 1988 to begin a dialogue with the PLO.

Israel was still not prepared to recognise the PLO, or to deal with it. To overcome this, in early 1990, the US got the PLO to agree to let Egypt (the only Arab country with which Israel had a peace treaty) name the Palestinians who would take part in the proposed talks. But the whole process got derailed when Iraq invaded Kuwait in August that year. Iraq's subsequent linking of its withdrawal from Kuwait to

---

[2] Ariel Sharon, then Defence Minister, masterminded this operation, which led to the massacre by pro-Israeli Christian Lebanese of between 1,900 and 3,500 Palestinians in the camps at Sabra and Shatila, 16–18 September 1982.

Israel's withdrawal from the occupied territories made Palestinian opinion strongly pro-Iraq. This induced Arafat to side with Iraq. Inevitably, when the Gulf war ended the PLO and Arafat found themselves ostracised not only by the US but also by most Arab countries.

Although the Gulf war seriously weakened the PLO, it nevertheless gave the Palestine peace process a boost. The US had never had as much control over Arab countries as it did then. It wanted to seize the moment to settle the Palestinian problem and consolidate its hold. This led to the US (and nominally Soviet)-sponsored peace conference in Madrid in October 1991. Syria participated out of fear of being left out in the cold. The PLO was not invited, but some Palestinians from occupied territories participated in a joint delegation with Jordan. During the following twenty-one months (October 1991–July 1993) the US, Israel, Syria and Jordan–Palestine conducted ten rounds of talks but got nowhere.

In July 1992 Labour came to power in Israel, with Rabin as Prime Minister and Peres as Foreign Minister. Likud's tough approach under Shamir during 1986–92 had not brought peace in the occupied territories. Although the intifada had weakened after its peak in 1989 (and 1,200 Palestinian deaths), the occupied territories continued to simmer. With Hamas, potentially a much tougher proposition than the PLO from Israel's point of view, gaining strength at the expense of the PLO, there was a common Israeli–PLO interest to de-escalate. Israel figured that it was better to deal with the PLO (which had moderated its policy, especially after the Gulf war) than to have to deal with Hamas and Islamic Jihad. Meanwhile Hizbollah was harassing Israel in Lebanon. The displacement by 1992 of Maronite Christians from the political apex of Lebanon saw the end of Israel's search for a friendly government in that country. All this contributed to the secret Israel–PLO negotiations in Oslo that began in January 1993.

The Oslo talks made rapid progress, and on 9 September 1993 the two sides formally recognised each other. Four days later, the two signed a Declaration of Principles (DOP) agreement in Washington with the professed intent of achieving lasting peace within five years. A Palestinian Authority (PA) was to be created to administer the areas of occupied territories that were to be progressively handed over to it. On 29 April 1994 an agreement to implement the DOP was reached in Cairo. The Oslo and Cairo agreements made it possible for Jordan to move closer to Israel, and in October 1994 the two signed a peace treaty. Israel had now neutralised Egypt and Jordan, but Syria, the

PLO and Lebanon remained. Twenty-four months after Oslo and eighteen months after Cairo, the Interim Israeli–Palestinian Agreement on the West Bank and Gaza Strip (Oslo II) was signed in Washington on 28 September 1995.

Five weeks after the Oslo II agreement, Rabin was assassinated by a right-wing Israeli, with the declared objective of stopping the hand over of land. Peres, who succeeded Rabin, advanced the next Knesset election by six months to May 1996. Major violence erupted during February and March. Four suicide attacks killed nearly sixty Israelis. This enabled Binyamin Netanyahu, the new Likud leader, to squeak through with a 1 per cent margin of victory. In September Netanyahu opened a tunnel under Muslim holy places to help tighten Israeli military grip over East Jerusalem. The clashes that erupted two days later killed 86 Palestinians and 15 Israelis. There were gun battles between Israeli and PA troops. In March 1997 Israel approved the building of a huge apartment complex in Har Homa (Jebel Abu Ghneim) in East Jerusalem. Riots erupted and draconian measures were taken against the Palestinian population. In October 1998, Netanyahu and Arafat signed the Wye River Memorandum in the US that envisaged some pull-back by Israel. But this did not breathe life into the peace process. Netanyahu's support in Knesset dwindled and an early election was called.

In the May 1999 elections, the new Labour leader Ehud Barak (a former defence forces chief like Rabin) defeated Netanyahu decisively by a margin of 12 per cent in the prime ministerial election, although Labour's position in Knesset barely improved. Barak decided to push fast towards a final settlement as he felt that incremental progress was likely to lead to Palestinian violence and Israeli backlash. At a meeting in Sharam el Sheik in September 1999, Israel and the PLO agreed on further Israeli withdrawals and also agreed to speed up negotiations for a final settlement. Meanwhile, Israel was trying to reach agreements with Lebanon and Syria to improve its bargaining power with the PLO. Israel was losing twenty to thirty soldiers a year in southern Lebanon, and there was considerable popular demand for withdrawal. Barak's efforts to reach an agreement did not work because of Syrian pressure, and Israel was forced to make a unilateral withdrawal from Lebanon in July 1999. As for Syria, it continued to insist on a complete withdrawal from the 1,575 sq. km of land occupied by Israel in 1967.

The implementation of the Sharm el Sheik memorandum got bogged down. To speed up matters, a desperate Clinton (scheduled to leave office in six months) hosted Barak and Arafat at Camp David over 11–24 July 2000. Israel agreed to give the PA partial sovereignty over Jerusalem, and the PLO agreed to give up about 5 per cent of the West Bank in return for compensation elsewhere. In September Barak and Arafat met under Egyptian auspices to push matters further. But a deliberate, peace-sabotaging visit by Likud leader Ariel Sharon to Haram al-Sharif (Temple Mount) three days later led to widespread Palestinian protests. This was the beginning of the al-Aqsa intifada that in the next four months killed 302 Palestinians and seventy-eight Israelis. A meeting between Clinton, Barak, Arafat, President Mubarak of Egypt and King Abdullah of Jordan in Sharm el Sheik on 17 October 2000 could not bring down violence. On 10 December 2000, Barak resigned, paving the way for a prime ministerial election on 6 February 2001. In that election Sharon (who had set off the new intifada and now become its beneficiary) defeated Barak by a huge margin of 25 per cent. Sharon declared that he would not be bound by the offers Barak had made.

Under Sharon Israel substantially hardened its already tough policy under Barak, but there was no let up in violence. Efforts to restrain violence through former US Senator George Mitchell (who had earlier contributed to peace in Northern Ireland) in May 2001 and through CIA Chief George Tenet the following month got nowhere. The 11 September 2001 attacks in the US by the al-Qaeda gave the Sharon government an exceptional opportunity to try and decimate Palestinian resistance. Sharon's intensification of the assassination policy (there were about ninety targeted killings in 2001) led to Nationalist (Fatah and others in the PLO) and Islamic (Hamas and the Islamic Jihad) groups coming together at the grassroots to form mixed guerrilla groups. In December, Sharon declared that Arafat was irrelevant to the peace process, and confined him to his compound in Ramallah. Deliberate attacks were launched to destroy the PA's administrative infrastructure, including its law enforcement capability. Sharon clearly wanted not only Arafat's departure but also the collapse of the Palestinian Authority set up in 1994.

The Bush administration, which has been ideologically inclined to let Sharon have a free hand in bringing the Palestinians to heel, began to get worried when violence continued unabated even after a year of Sharon's rule. The US was also getting concerned that the anger in the Arab Street was making key allies like Egypt and Saudi Arabia non-cooperative to the US's plan to take out Saddam Hussain. The US therefore went along with the UNSC when, on 13 March 2002, it passed for the first time a resolution backing the idea of a Palestine State. This purely tactical move on the US's part hardly fazed Sharon. A massive Israeli operation in April eliminated an entire echelon of terrorist leaders and crippled the PA's financial and operational infrastructure.

On 24 June 2002, Bush made a policy speech, largely incorporating Sharon's thinking, and calling for the reform of the Palestinian Authority (to sideline Arafat), a new constitution, elections, and externally supervised restructuring of security institutions as preconditions for the resumption of peace talks. By August Israel had reoccupied virtually all the areas it had handed over to the PA. In October Israel started building a 650-kilometre security barrier to pen in Palestinians in the West Bank. The barrier would put 14.5 per cent of the most fertile West Bank land in the hands of Israel. In March 2003 the quartet of the US, UN, EU and Russia released their long-delayed road map for peace, which, through a set of reciprocal steps, was to lead to the creation of a Palestine State by end 2005. A new post of PA Prime Minister, PA, was created in April under US pressure, and was filled by Mahmoud Abbas. But Arafat continued to call the shots in the PA and Abbas could not survive. Ahmed Qurei replaced him in September. By December 2003, over 2,250 Palestinians and over 800 Israelis had been killed in relentless violence since the al-Aqsa intifada erupted in September 2000.

THE CONFLICT IN PERSPECTIVE

When World War II ended, the creation of Israel was seen as a necessary atonement for the holocaust. It was the moral need to compensate the wronged European Jews that became the defining issue; dispossessing the Palestinians became peripheral. The Jews with good reason believed that they were reclaiming their ancient land. But to the Palestinians they were colonising settlers. Moreover, although the ratio of European and Middle Eastern Jews in Israel is about even now, there was never any doubt that Israel was a project of European Jews.

For the Arabs, the Israelis were not just outsiders but people of a race that had once colonised them.[3] The Arabs felt that the Israel of the UN plan was only a beginning— a bridgehead that would inexorably expand. Under the Zionist dream all Jews were to return from their 'exile', and in 1948 only 10 per cent of the world's Jews were in Palestine (today there are 40 per cent). The Arabs wanted to destroy the European bridgehead before it could expand. Their defeated attempt to do that in 1948, and the superiority that Israel showed during its 1956 offensive, tempered their hopes. The spectacular Israeli victory of 1967 then put a seal on all thoughts of defeating Israel militarily. No Arab country thereafter was willing to use military power on behalf of the Palestinians. The initiation of the 1973 war by Egypt had nothing to do with the Palestinians. It was solely intended to de-freeze the Sinai occupation. Neither the 1987–92 intifada nor the al-Aqsa intifada beginning September 2000 saw any tangible, state-level support from Arab countries for the Palestinians, although moral support among the Arab masses has remained strong.

It is the 1967 war, largely precipitated by Egypt and Syria, that has made the conflict so difficult to deal with. Till then the Israelis were ready to settle for the 78 per cent of the Palestine that they had, and the Palestinians could have been persuaded to settle for the balance area if generous funding to resettle them there and elsewhere were provided. But the obtuseness and the obstinacy of the Arab states made such a deal impossible. The Cold War too played a part in making a deal difficult. If Arab countries, especially Egypt and Syria, were the main problem till 1967, Israel became the prime obstacle to peace thereafter. The 1967 war gave Israel land that it could have traded for a comprehensive peace agreement. But militarised thinking that could not envisage durable, cooperative peace made that trade impossible.

The war improved Israel's military position considerably. With Israeli forces on the Eastern Bank of the Suez Canal, it became impossible for Egypt to mount an attack into Israel's heartland. Similarly, the Golan Heights gave the Israelis not only valuable high ground

---

[3] For a broad understanding of the conflict, see Ahron Bregman and Jihan el-Tahri, *The Fifty Years War: Israel and Arabs,* London: Penguin, 1998; James Climent, *Palestine/Israel: The Long Conflict,* New York: Facts on File, 1997; Dilip Hiro, *Sharing the Promised Land: A Tale of Israelis and Palestinians,* New York: Olive Branch Books, 1999; Kenneth Cragg, *Palestine: The Prize and Price of Zion,* London: Cassel, 1997; and Deborah Gerner, *One Land, Two Peoples,* Boulder: Westview, 1994.

against Syrian forces, but also put them just 60 kilometres from Damascus, thereby constituting a huge deterrent. From a military point of view, the most important capture of 1967 was the West Bank including Jerusalem. The West Bank bulges into central Israel from the east. A hostile state there, using Jordan as hinterland, can pose a serious threat. Conversely, a West Bank under Israel poses a sharp threat to Jordan with Amman just 65 kilometres away. Within the West Bank, Jerusalem has great strategic value. Jerusalem and the surrounding new townships enable Israel to divide the West Bank into two parts and dominate it militarily.

The 1967 war not only tripled Israel's territory and gave it Jerusalem, but it also unleashed nationalistic and extremist forces. There was what veteran Israeli diplomat Abba Eban called the 'intoxication of the 1967 victory'. This strengthened the maximalists and made the perspective of the opponent seem irrelevant. The 1973 war came as a stunning shock. But far from making Israel re-think the strategy of freezing the new status quo, it made it more determined to maintain it. After the war, the distrust of the Arabs redoubled. The anger against Arabs, and particularly Palestinians, was also fanned by the frequent acts of terrorism committed from the late 1960s. This distrust and anger contributed to the election of Likud in 1977. Gradually that party's hardline views became the mainstream of Israeli thinking.

Till 1987 the Palestinians in the occupied territories were a subdued lot. It was the groups outside that were carrying out terrorist acts against Israel. The occupied territories were controlled by just a thousand Israeli troops. The intifada that began in December 1987 came as a big surprise. The Israeli public was unaware of the radicalisation of minds in the occupied territories during the previous two decades, which led to this explosion of popular rage. The PLO, languishing in Tunis since 1982, had little to do with it. Even Hamas was formed only after the intifada began. Although it could not break Israel's grip on the territory, the intifada destroyed the low-cost system that had controlled the Palestinians for twenty years. Worse for Israel, the Palestine problem metamorphosed from an international one where Israel's deterrent and diplomatic weight mattered, to an internal one where neither was of much help. Israel's problem with the intifada was that it had to use brutal methods to quell it, and that provided fresh recruits into the militant ranks. It also damaged moderate Palestinians whose numbers were then sizeable, especially in the West Bank.

If the Palestinians were pushed to the 1993 Oslo talks by the collapse of the Soviet Union and the Gulf War, the Israelis were pushed by the intifada. The Oslo Process moved well during 1993–95, but went rapidly downhill thereafter. There was violence during 1996–2000 and even earlier, but violence truly exploded only in September 2000 when the al-Aqsa intifada began. The new violence engulfed both the occupied territories and Israel. It was fuelled by a broad Palestinian perception that the seven years of the Oslo Process had only deepened their dispossession and deprivation. Unlike the 1987–92 intifada, during which almost all the dead were Palestinians, this time about a fourth of those killed were Israelis. Normal life in Israel was destroyed, and the Israeli public felt more vulnerable than ever before. Initial Palestinian tactics—shooting attacks on Israeli vehicles, attacks on Israeli Defence Force (IDF) outposts, and rocket attacks on Jewish settlements—achieved little. Using good intelligence, the IDF was able to destroy much of the Palestinian military capability. This led to suicide bombings becoming the basic mode of Palestinian operations.

There is no military in the world that has the technical and operational capabilities that Israel possesses in the field of counter-guerrilla and counter-terrorism warfare. Israel is using extremely sophisticated means to monitor Palestinian communications and movements to carry out targeted attacks. The Palestinians are pinned down in very small areas (most smaller than 2 square kilometres) with very little ability to take coordinated action. There are no porous borders through which they can get military aid, nor do they have any sanctuaries. Yet, it has not been possible for Israel to stop Palestinian attacks. The key change that has made the Israeli position difficult is the support the Palestinian community as a whole is extending to those using violence. Suicide bombing has got legitimated within their community. At the ground level, there has been a strengthening of links between Hamas, al-Aqsa brigades of Fatah, and Islamic Jihad.

Israel has treated the PLO as its chief enemy from the time Arafat galvanised it in 1969. The neutralisation of Egypt and Syria through the 1967 war, the upswing of Palestine terrorism from 1969, and the legitimacy that the PLO began to acquire internationally all contributed to this. Arafat became a hate figure partly because he was seen as the head of an organisation spreading terror. But a more important reason is that Arafat was largely responsible for keeping the Palestinian cause alive after it was abandoned in military terms by Arab states in 1967. Through constant manoeuvring and balancing of factions, he has kept the PLO and the Palestinians—half in the occupied territories, half elsewhere—together and focused. This has been difficult for the Israelis to take, as they want the Palestinians to fade away like so many other displaced and dispersed nations in the past.

Till the intifada exploded in 1987, the general Israeli thinking had been that they had the people of the occupied territories under control (as they had the Arab Israelis earlier), and that the main problem was the Palestinian diaspora that took its cue from the PLO's leadership in Tunis. This assessment proved wrong. After the Palestinian Authority was established in 1994, it was the PLO's 'Tunisians' (about 100,000 of whom had been allowed to come to the occupied territories) who have been more amenable to Israeli directions than the homegrown veterans of the 1987–92 intifada. The main reason why Israel is set against free elections in the occupied territories is that it would lead to many office-happy 'Tunisians' being replaced by less malleable homebred leaders.

Hamas was founded in December 1987. Lebanon's Hizbollah had provided example and inspiration. A feature of Hamas, apart from its Islamic orientation, is that it represented the worst-off sections of Palestinians who are largely concentrated in the Gaza Strip. In 2001 the per capita income in the Gaza Strip was $400 against $900 in the West Bank—and $17,400 in Israel. Hamas was weakened during the 1993–2000 Oslo process, but when the al-Aqsa intifada began its popularity rebounded. It was Hamas that made suicide attacks a standard operating procedure and which made Fatah resort to it later. Hamas is now an institutionalised part of the Palestinian political landscape. It has created a steady stream of young people willing to use their lives as weapons. In the last five years, suicide attacks have accounted for over 80 per cent of Israeli deaths. And many of these attacks are now taking place within Israel.

The condition of Palestinians inside the occupied territories has always been bad. For twenty-five years the territories have seen a disenfranchised Palestinian majority and a privileged Jewish minority living side by side with different legal, administrative, and security systems, and lopsidedly dissimilar access to land, water and the outside world. In the Gaza Strip, a million Palestinians are squeezed into as little as 240 sq. km. There is more space in the West Bank, but Palestinian movements are restricted to cater to settler security. Measures such as collective punishment, internal exile from one village to another, and expulsions across the border are common. So are non-justiciable detention, confiscation of assets, house demolitions, and security measures such as prolonged closures and curfews.

One reason that has made the Palestine conflict so difficult to deal with is the consolidation of right-wing thinking in Israel. The military orientation of the broader society as well as religious zeal has contributed to this. From the founding of Israel, military security has dominated state thinking. There is an ingrained preference to seek military solutions for security problems.[4] Coercion is privileged over conciliation, and unilateralism over negotiations. As years went by, this approach got intertwined with religious fervour, which was not surprising in a country which seeks to synthesise religion, nation and state. There are parties within the government that want Israel to become a Halachic state, much like a Muslim Sharia state. The convergence of religious zeal and militarised thinking has strengthened hardline views.

An integral part of the Israeli right-wing is the settlers in the occupied territories. A major strategic objective of settlements is to fragment territory, thereby making a viable Palestine State impossible. The settlement drive continued with no deceleration during the Oslo Process. The settlements, which involve a clear violation of international law that forbids colonisation of territories seized by military force, are highly subsidised, and many settlers have been attracted by cheap housing and tax breaks. But there are also large numbers of ideological colonists, most with military training and a high propensity for vigilante violence. Israel cannot protect these 390,000 settlers living amidst 3.5 million Palestinians without imposing draconian restrictions on the latter.

The unrelenting violence that has been going on for over three years has shattered Israel's small peace camp, and for that matter moderate Jewish opinion in the US. The ordinary Israeli, with good reason, blames Arafat and the PLO for attacks inside Israel that became serious only after the PLO-controlled Palestine Authority was set up in 1994. The violence has spread antagonism towards Palestinians even among liberal sections of Israeli society. There is a sizeable section of moderate post-Zionist Jews in Israel, but in conditions of raging violence they are unable to offer a feasible peace path. A feeling that true peace can never be realised, and that the Palestinians can only be controlled

[4] See Uri Ben-Eliezer, *The Making of Israeli Militarism*, Bloomington: Indiana University Press, 1998.

by force has grown. Most moderates are exasperated that the Palestinians refused in July 2000 a deal that Israel would not have offered them even a year earlier. They hold the Palestinians responsible for denying Israel peace options.

The hardliners in Israel have nothing to offer the Palestinians except stopping punishment and life in a truncated, cantonised 'Palestine State' dotted with Israeli settlements. For them the deal with the Palestinians must be 'peace for peace' and not 'land for peace'. They feel that the PA will slowly come round because even limited administrative power is better than nothing. The problem is that the more they squeeze the PA, the more they strengthen extremist groups within the PLO as well as the Islamic groups outside it. The new hardline policy of confining the Palestinians behind tight security barriers is also unlikely to work in the long term, although it will certainly cut down suicide attacks in the short term. As years pass, the 'wall' would lead to intense frustration among boxed-in people with little economic opportunity and outside access. Impoverishment and anger levels will scale new heights.

The policies of Sharon are now coming under criticism even within the Israeli security establishment. In a joint statement to the daily *Yediot Ahronot* on 14 November 2003, four former heads of Shin Bet (Israel's internal security agency) said that as a result of Sharon's policies 'we are going downhill towards near catastrophe'. Together, these four—Yaakov Perry, Avrahom Shalom, Ami Ayalon and Carmi Gilon—have headed Shin Beth for eighteen years. Ayalon added that Israeli policy was 'taking sure steady steps to a place where the state of Israel will no longer be a democracy and a home for Jewish people'. Gilon said that the Sharon government was 'only dealing with the question of how to prevent the next attack and so ignores the question of how we get out of the mess we find ourselves in today'. Even more noteworthy was the statement of the serving IDF Chief of Staff, Lt. Gen. Moshe Yaalon towards end October 2003. He said that unrelenting pressure on the Palestinians was playing into the hands of those who recruit suicide bombers and that 'in our tactical decisions we are acting contrary to our strategic interests'.[5]

From the beginning, Israel has been exceptionally reliant on external support. The emotions of the holocaust resonate strongly in the West. In the 1950s Israel got as much support from Western Europe as it

---

[5] *International Herald Tribune*, 19 November 2003.

did from the US. During that decade France was Israel's biggest military supplier, and it was French assistance that made Israel's nuclear bomb possible. American support for Israel shot up in the late 1950s when Soviet weapons began to pour into Egypt and Syria. Israel came to be seen as a bastion in the Middle East—a useful hedge against the fall of pro-Western Arab states. At the popular level the Jewish community in the US has made a big difference. Of the 13 million Jews in the world, 6 million are in the US. They make up only 2 per cent of the population but are uniquely cohesive and organised. A combination of admiration for and empathy with Israel is widespread in the US. The Old Testament's portrayal of the Jews as God's chosen people, and ancient Israel as their rightful homeland, has a strong appeal among Christians, especially the evangelicals in the US. The desire to further strengthen Israel's position vis-à-vis the Arabs was at least a major contributory reason for the US invasion of Iraq.

Israel now faces a major demographic problem. Within Israel, there are 1.2 million Palestinians living with 5.4 million Jews. In addition, there are 3.5 million Palestinians in the occupied territories. There are thus 5.4 million Jews and 4.7 million Palestinians in the area controlled by Israel. Now that most former communist-bloc Jews have come in (a million came during 1985–95), significant new Jewish immigration is unlikely. With the Palestinians having a higher birth rate, the demographic advantage enjoyed by the Jews (currently 54 to 46), is likely to erode. Many consider a Palestinian majority within Israel and the occupied territories likely before 2020, even without Palestinian refugees from outside coming in.

Another problem is the surge of anti-Jewish, not just anti-Israeli feelings in the Arab and Islamic worlds. There had been no antagonism between Muslims and Jews in the past. But this has changed. The Organisation of Islamic Countries came into existence directly as a consequence of the al-Aqsa Mosque being set on fire in August 1969 by a Jewish fanatic. Over the years, marked anti-Jewish sentiments have crept into Arab media and textbooks. The holocaust and the Jews' historical links to Palestine are untruthfully downplayed. The al-Aqsa uprising of September 2000 had a strong Islamic dimension, unlike the December 1987 eruption. There are widely differing views (as may be seen from the writings of scholars like Samuel Huntington and Bernard Lewis on the one side and John Esposito and Edward Said on the other) about the causes of Muslim anger. But there is little doubt that Israel has now become its main focus. The al-Aqsa uprising led to the first instance of agitating Arabs being shot and killed inside Israel. November 2002 saw the first attempt at aircraft hijacking by an Arab Israeli. The month also saw a Bedouin Arab lieutenant colonel of the IDF arrested for links with Hizbollah.

The conflict has resulted in huge costs on both sides. Israel's GDP growth rate during the past fifty-four years has averaged only 3.5 per cent despite the fact that throughout this period it has received more per capita financial aid than any other country in the world. Including half a billion in private donations, Israel gets $3.7 billion a year (completely untied money) from the US alone. It also gets huge loan guarantees. Israel's economy grew at an average of 6.5 per cent during 1990–95, when the country was seen to be moving towards peace. After Netanyahu's 1996 election, the growth rate came down to an average of 2.5 per cent, till it picked up again in 1999 when Barak came. In 2001, after Sharon's arrival, the economy actually shrank by 1 per cent. And in 2003 there has been no growth. This, despite the fact that because of reduced conventional threat Israel's defence budget since 1990, as a percentage of its GDP, has averaged less than half of what it was during 1965–85.

Israel has also paid penalties in social and psychological terms. It is a liberal democracy for the Jews, but an illiberal one even for those Arabs (18 per cent of the population) who live within Israel. For two decades after 1948, Arab Israelis had to endure military rule. Even today their civil rights are constantly violated. The Jews whose social philosophy is strongly laced with liberalism and humanism have ended up creating one of the most minority-repressing states in the world. Many thoughtful Israelis are concerned about this. On 29 January 2002, Knesset Speaker Avraham Burg said, amidst howls from most of those present in the house: 'The occupation corrupts, or more accurately the occupation has already corrupted .... The unending cycle of terror attacks and retaliation, deaths and vengeance, funerals and anger, has made us hard and cruel.'[6]

The Palestinians have suffered far more. From being one of the more prosperous Arab societies in the late 1940s, they have now become one of the poorest. Thirty-six years of military occupation has destroyed their economy. The average income of a Palestinian in the occupied territories is one-twentieth that of a Jewish Israeli. A third of the working population has become a cheap labour pool for Israel,

---

[6] *Economic and Political Weekly*, 9 February 2002, p. 511.

one that can be easily squeezed by closing the border. There has been a dramatic upsurge in unemployment and poverty levels since the current uprising began. In December 2003, unemployment was 46 per cent. People below the poverty line ($2 a day) were 57 per cent in the West Bank and 84 per cent in the Gaza Strip. Most people are packed into overcrowded shantytowns where health and environmental conditions are primitive. Few children receive a decent education. Adding to the economic misery is the fear factor, the constant fear of being questioned, arrested and shot at.

What one sees in Israel/Palestine today is a competition between two valid national movements—a competition that has grown steadily bitter since the 1930s. For most Israelis their prior claim to the land is all-important. They feel that the Palestinians who are a part of the larger Arab world should accept resettlement elsewhere. On the other side, even those Palestinians who understand the Jewish roots in the land wonder why Israel is not satisfied with the 78 per cent of Palestine it had before 1967. They fail to see the Jewish insecurity generated by decades of Arab hostility, and centuries of oppression in Europe earlier. Personal security has replaced national security as the dominant concern in Israel. There is no fear for the nation any more. The fear is for the lives of people. Many Israelis see a Palestine State as incompatible with their personal security. The Palestinians, on the other hand, believe that the only bargaining leverage they have is their new-found ability to threaten Israeli lives. They know that it is the Palestinian violence that strengthens Israeli hawks, but they also believe that if the violence stops even the Israeli doves would not offer them a fair deal.

Israel–Egypt Peace

From an India–Pakistan peacemaking perspective the aspect of the Arab–Israeli conflict that offers most food for thought is how Israel and Egypt made peace and have sustained it for a quarter century without running serious risks of it unravelling.[7] The Israel–Egypt

---

[7] For a range of insights into the Egypt–Israel peace process, see William Quandt, *Camp David: Peacemaking and Politics*, Washington, DC: Brookings, 1986; Moshe Dayan, *Breakthrough: A Personal Account of the Egypt–Israel Peace Negotiations*, New

peace project got its start from the 1973 war initiated by Egypt. That war created a sense of crisis, putting political pressure on Israel to withdraw from Egypt's Sinai Peninsula it had captured six years earlier. The US got deeply concerned when immediately after the 1973 war the price of oil nearly tripled—from $1.83 to $4.89 a barrel—and Saudi Arabia, Iran, Iraq, Kuwait and Abu Dhabi stopped supply to the US. Under US auspices, Israel and Egypt signed a disengagement of forces agreement in January 1974 that required Israel to withdraw its troops to a line 10 to 14 km east of the Suez Canal. With continuing US prodding, an interim agreement was signed in March 1975. It restored the control of both banks of the canal to Egypt and paved the way for its re-opening.

The US knew that Egypt was susceptible to Arab radicalism and that renewed Soviet influence was a real possibility. After becoming President in January 1977, Carter indicated that the Geneva Framework, involving among others the USSR, might have to be revived to push the Arab–Israel peace effort forward. This posed a danger to Israel. When Begin succeeded Rabin in May 1977, he rejected the possibility of a comprehensive settlement involving all Arab parties. Sadat too did not want to risk the chances of an agreement on Sinai at a multilateral forum. Bilateral discussions under US auspices suited both. This led to the secret talks between Egypt and Israel in September 1977, and Sadat's trip to Jerusalem two months later. Begin knew that withdrawing from the barren Sinai that Israel did not really need would help resist pressures to withdraw from the valuable captures of 1967—the West Bank and the Golan Heights. Moreover, Egypt, Israel's strongest foe, would be made to leave the hitherto unbroken Arab coalition. Sadat understood this. He also knew that hardliner Begin would be able to sell the Sinai withdrawal to the Israelis.

Before they met at Camp David in September 1978, Begin and Sadat broke major psychological barriers by visiting each other's capitals. Israel's willingness to return Sinai and Egypt's willingness to recognise Israel were also indicated. Both were radical pre-Summit concessions. There was hard bargaining at Camp David, centred on the completeness and the timeframe of Israel's withdrawal. Eventually, Israel agreed to withdraw completely from the Sinai over three years,

York: Alfred Knopf, 1981; Ismael Fahmy, *Negotiating for Peace in the Middle East*, Baltimore, MD: The Johns Hopkins University Press, 1983; and Major General Avraham Tamir, *A Soldier in Search of Peace: An Inside Look at Israel's Strategy*, London: Weidenfeld and Nicholson, 1988.

in return for a large, limited-force zone there, and Egypt establishing diplomatic and economic relations with Israel. Israel extracted a memorandum of understanding from the US guaranteeing the treaty. As for gains, Israel succeeded in splitting the Arab coalition and putting the Palestinian issue on the backburner. Egypt got back the entire territory it had lost in 1967. Both got huge, long-term aid commitments from the US. The US on its part strengthened its position in the Middle East, undercut the Soviet Union and consolidated its grip on oil supplies.

Israel completed its withdrawal by April 1982. Fourteen Israeli settlements including the town-size Yamit were dismantled. Israeli airbases in the Sinai were shifted to the Negev with the US footing the bill of $2.5 billion. The US has continued to pump money into Egypt. Egypt has been getting an average of 28 per cent of all US foreign aid. (Israel gets 40 per cent.) The US has also used its power in the IMF and the World Bank, and its leverage with other rich countries, to keep Egypt stable, pro-West and reasonably Israel-friendly. Although Sadat was assassinated in October 1981 for breaking the Arab ranks and making peace with Egypt, his successor Mubarak has kept anti-Israel and anti-American feelings under control. Mubarak, ruling for twenty-three years, is no democrat but he has delivered.

The Israeli–Palestinian Peace Effort

Israel's strategy towards the Palestinian territories it captured in 1967 was first outlined in a plan formulated by Deputy Prime Minister Yigal Allon. The plan was to divide the West Bank between Israel and Jordan, with an Israeli security border along the Jordan river and Israeli control of important localities. The bulk of the population was to be taken by Jordan so that there would be only a small increase of Arab population within Israel. A variant of the plan suggested joint Israel–Jordan rule over some areas. There was hope that the Palestinians in the areas absorbed by Israel could be made to emigrate by the difficult conditions within and generous financial incentives. But the plan did not work because Jordan could not afford to play along.

At the Begin–Sadat–Carter summit at Camp David in 1978, Palestine had formed a subsidiary track to the principal track of Sinai.

Begin would not go beyond autonomy. Even the autonomy discussions soon foundered, because Begin would not agree to elections in the occupied territories despite being pressed by Carter. While Peres was Prime Minister over 1984–86 and Foreign Minister over 1986–88, there was an effort to find a way forward. As a first step, a system of shared Israel–Jordan–Palestinian administration over most of the territory was thought of. Israel's strategy continued to be to reach a settlement that would box in the Palestinians using Jordan.

It slowly became clear that this approach, despite the further weakening of the Palestinians following the 1990–91 Gulf War, was not working. The Madrid Conference came and went without making an impact. When he became Prime Minister in July 1992, Rabin gave the go-ahead to Foreign Minister Peres to take up the 'land for peace' formula. The spadework for the talks had started the previous month by a Norwegian social scientist Teje Larsen, and Shimon Peres's protégé Yossi Beilin. On 19 January 1993 Israel repealed the law banning meetings between Israelis and PLO representatives. The Oslo track began the next day.[8]

The Oslo agreement arrived at in September 1993 was only a Declaration of Principles that visualised a five-year process. It was felt that a complex and gradual approach was needed because of the large number of difficult issues involved and the deep mistrust that prevailed. The interim and final status issues were de-linked with the latter to be taken up when the negotiating climate improved. The immediate step was the mutual recognition by Israel and the PLO. In April 1994 talks took place in Cairo to implement DOP. After another eighteen months and more negotiations, another agreement (Oslo II) was signed in Washington in September 1995. This agreed on the concept of the West Bank being divided into three categories of area—Zone A where PA was to assume authority for order and internal security, Zone B where PA was to be responsible for order and Israel for security, and Zone C under full Israeli control. The areas handed over to the PA (Zones A and B) were to progressively enlarge.

---

[8] For a good account of the Oslo talks of 1993, see Jane Corbin, *The Norway Channel*, New York: Atlantic Monthly Press, 1994. For good analyses of the long road that led to Oslo, see David Makovsky, *Making Peace with PLO: The Rabin Government's Road to the Oslo Accord,* Boulder: Westview Press, 1996; and Sela Avraham and Moshe Ma'oz, eds., *The PLO and Israel: From Armed Revolution to Political Solution 1964–1994,* New York: St. Martin's, 1997.

But two months after this agreement, the Oslo Process suffered what was to prove a mortal blow when Rabin was assassinated.[9] Netanyahu, who became Prime Minister in May 1996 refused to hand over Hebron as Israel had agreed to at Oslo II. In the Hebron Protocol signed in January 1997, the PA effectively conceded Israel's right, overriding Oslo II, to determine from where and when it would withdraw. Under US pressure Netanyahu negotiated the Wye River agreement in October 1998 but that did not take matters forward.

After Barak came to power in May 1999, there was a spate of Israel–PA meetings at the US's initiative. It culminated in the long Camp David conference hosted by Clinton in July 2000. It was at Camp David that the central issues of Jerusalem, the right of refugees to return, the Israeli settlements, the borders of the Palestine State and the status of the Palestine State were first discussed. Reports on what Israel offered at Camp David vary a good deal, because no offer was presented clearly or unconditionally. But it is apparent that both sides offered significant concessions. Israel agreed to withdraw from about 88 per cent of the West Bank. Arafat agreed to Israel's retention of major settlement blocks if compensated with equivalent area elsewhere. In East Jerusalem, he offered to give up the Jewish quarter, the Western Wall and the Jewish settlements. But on Haram al-Sharif, where Arab and Muslim opinion drew a clear red line, he refused to compromise sovereignty.

Arafat was under serious pressure from the Palestinians. The idea that much of East Jerusalem would stay under Israel, and that Israel would retain complete control over the borders of the Palestine State and its water resources, was unacceptable to them. They felt that Israel was exerting coercive pressure by forcing them to negotiate final status issues when the PA controlled only 17.2 per cent of the West Bank and 66 per cent of the Gaza Strip in isolated, encircled enclaves. Besides, the Palestinians had little confidence that Barak, who was then heading a minority government, would have been able to get an

---

[9] For accounts of the problems encountered after Oslo, see Geoffrey Kemp and Jeremy Pressman, *Point of No Return: The Deadly Struggle for Middle East Peace,* Washington, DC: Brookings Institution Press, 1997; George Giacaman and Dag Jorund Lonning, *After Oslo: New Realities, Old Problems,* London: Pluto Press, 1998; Neill Lochery, *The Difficult Road to Peace: Netanyahu, Israel and the Middle East,* Reading: Ithaca Press, 1999; Efraim Karsh, ed., *From Rabin to Netanyahu: Israel's Troubled Agenda,* Ilford, Essex: Frank Cass, 1997.

agreement ratified in Knesset. For the first time since Oslo began the Palestinians refused to be pressured.

On 23 December 2000 (when violence was raging with the al-Aqsa intifada having erupted in September) Clinton defined the parameters of a possible agreement. According to US diplomat Dennis Ross, closely associated with the discussions, Clinton offered the Palestinians 97 per cent of the total territory, all of East Jerusalem except the Jewish neighbourhoods, sovereignty over Haram al-Sharif, an international force instead of the IDF in the Jordan valley, and the unlimited right of refugees to return to the Palestine State. There would be no cantons and there would be independent borders for the West Bank with Jordan and the Gaza Strip with Egypt. Since the offer was never written down, it is difficult to categorically say whether it actually existed. Besides, with Clinton due to shed office within four weeks and Barak facing elections within six weeks, it was not an offer that could be seriously considered.

The final round of Barak–Arafat discussions took place in Taba in Egypt over 20–21 January 2001. At Taba the Israelis offered an additional 6.5 per cent of territory over and above the 88 per cent they had offered at Camp David. With Clinton gone and Barak facing a certain-to-lose election in two weeks, the Taba discussions were not serious. The common view is that the Palestinians, by their intransigence, prevented a good, mutually advantageous settlement at Camp David and Taba. The reality is that while from an Israeli point of view Barak had shown enormous flexibility, the settlement terms that were on offer (even if Knesset were to ratify them) would not have created a viable Palestinian State.[10]

The Oslo Process faced rejections from the beginning. Netanyahu said of Rabin, 'You are worse than Chamberlain. He imperilled another people, but you are doing it to your own people.'[11] The Israeli Right felt that the concessions offered at Camp David were unwarranted, given the circumstances of power. They constituted not only a betrayal of Israeli rights but would be taken as a sign of weakening

---

[10] See Robert Malley and Hussain Agha, 'Camp David: The Tragedy of Errors', *New York Review of Books*, 9 August 2001; Ron Pundak, 'From Oslo to Taba: What went Wrong?', *Survival*, Vol. 43, No. 3 (Autumn 2001), pp. 31–45; Jerome Slater, 'What Went Wrong? The Collapse of the Israeli–Palestinian Peace Process', *Political Science Quarterly*, Vol. 116, No. 2 (Summer 2001), pp. 171–99.

[11] Avi Shlaim, *The Iron Wall: Israel and the Arab World*, New York: W.W. Norton, 2000, p. 521.

Israeli will. A permanent solution must await the creation of a sub-missive mindset among the Palestinians, and the Arabs in general. Even among ordinary Israelis who did not want to hold on to the conquests for religious or nationalist reasons, there was fear that a Palestine State could become a base for terror attacks. On the Pales-tinian side, apart from radical groups like Hamas, there were those who objected to Oslo on grounds of principle. Intellectuals like Edward Said, Haider Abdel-Shafi and Clovis Maksoud felt that Oslo formal-ised Israel's rejection of five decades of UN resolutions and removed the Israel–Palestine conflict from the realm of international law to the realm of bilateral negotiations where the far stronger Israel could impose its will.[12]

When Sharon became Prime Minister in February 2001, the Oslo track ground to a dead stop. Sharon took the position that Arafat, who had been a hate figure to most Israelis from 1969, either did not want peace or was using violence as a tool in negotiations. Israeli hardliners believe that if Arafat were removed and the internal dy-namics of the PA were altered, the Palestinians would become easier to deal with. The reality is that the 74-year-old Arafat has huge legit-imacy and leverage within the Palestinian movement. Most outsiders and thoughtful Israelis feel that sidelining or eliminating him would deprive Israel of a valid negotiating partner. They believe that Arafat had become more pragmatic from the late 1980s. Abba Eban has written that 'Rabin ended his life believing that Arafat was a viable partner for implementing Oslo accords'.[13] But Sharon was determined to see that the offers that Barak made at Camp David in July 2000 and in Taba in January 2001 did not constitute baselines for future negotiations. The best way to achieve this would be to freeze out Arafat.

The basic reason why the Oslo track got dead-ended is that the two sides have incompatible needs that are almost existential in nature. In an arguably ascending order of difficulty, these differences concern refugees, territory, Jerusalem, Israel's security and the viability of a future Palestine State. There are 3.8 million registered Palestinian refugees. Of these, over three-quarters trace their ancestral origin to Israel. Before the intifada erupted in 1987 the flame of Palestinian

---

[12] See Edward Said, *Peace and its Discontents*, New York: Vintage, 1996.

[13] Abba Eban, *Diplomacy for the Next Century*, New Haven: Yale University Press, 1998, p. 96.

nationalism was kept alive largely in crowded refugee camps seething with anger at dispossession. Israel will not accept more than a token number of these refugees, and in any case many of them may not want to return to Israel. But Israel does not want large numbers to move into the occupied territories either.

During the 2000–2001 negotiations, the principle that the Palestinians should be given territory fully equal to the area that was captured in 1967 emerged.[14] However, the problem is not just with the extent of the area to be transferred, but also with its shape. Today Jewish settlements, military bases and bypass roads occupy a third of the West Bank. Israel wants to annex at least three large settlement blocks (80 per cent of settlers) occupying about 10 per cent of the total area, and to compensate Palestinians with less attractive land from Israel. This annexation would effectively split the remaining West Bank into four cantons—northern, central, southern and East Jerusalem. There is also the issue of how much of the water resources of the territory would be appropriated by Israel.

On Jerusalem there are religious, political and military issues involved. At the religious level there is the basic Temple Mount/al-Aqsa Mosque clash. For all Arabs and Muslims, the need for Muslim sovereignty over Haram al-Sharif where the al-Aqsa Mosque stands is a non-negotiable matter. For many Jews on the other hand, the very existence of a mosque over the Temple Mount is an affront. Then there is the matter of ensuring unimpeded access to the holy sites of Jews, Muslims and Christians that lie intermingled in the area. At the political level most Jews do not want to share Jerusalem as a capital with a Palestine State. And militarily, Israel's control of Greater Jerusalem, which is the centre of life in the West Bank, would enable it to dominate the entire transportation system of a Palestine State.

Many Israelis are now prepared give back to Palestinians over 90 per cent of the territory captured in 1967, but they cannot find a way to make the deal without, as they see it, endangering their security. There is the fear that a Palestine State could become a sanctuary for terrorists, willingly or unwillingly. The Sharon coastal plain where most Israelis live is only 15 to 25 kilometres wide, and there is no buffer between it and the central hilly region, much of which would

[14] For the logic of a Palestine State, see Samih K. Farson and Christina E. Zacharia, *Palestine and the Palestinians*, Boulder, CO: Westview Press, 1997; and Barry Rubin, *The Transformation of Palestinian Politics*, Cambridge, MA: Harvard University Press, 1999.

go to a Palestine State. It is likely that if a Palestine State were formed, the West Bank's present population of 2.5 million would swell to 4 million or more with influx from the Gaza Strip and refugee camps abroad. There is also the danger of these people mixing with the 3 million Palestinians in Jordan. Tight border control and an effective interposed military capability between the new State and Jordan is seen as vital for Israel.

Israel also has a more fundamental security fear. If Israel achieves peace with the Palestinians (and Syrians), it might cease to be a martial state. Many in Israel do not want this to happen. While there are those who believe that peace treaties with the Palestinians and Syria would provide the country with a safe neighbourhood, there are many who consider that state-level agreements cannot overcome popular Arab hostility and that non-state groups would still cause trouble. They are worried that a 'false peace' might make Israelis complacent and erode their willingness to fight instantly and unflinchingly. There is also the concern that a Palestine State and a 'normal' Israel might hearten Arabs inside Israel, and lead to demands for autonomy in parts of Galilee and the Negev where they are inching towards a majority. Many Israelis feel that they can never hope for cooperative security with the Arabs, and that one-sided deterrence alone can keep them safe.

These security fears make a viable and fulfilling Palestine State impossible. Israel would want a security zone all along the Jordanian border with necessary military infrastructure. And inside the Palestine State, it would want surveillance stations and airspace control. It would want naval control in the territorial waters abutting the Gaza Strip as well as in the Palestinian waters of the Dead Sea. It would need to control the passage of goods and people to and from the Palestine State. Control would also have to be exercised between the two parts the state—the West Bank and Gaza Strip. It is obvious that such a State, subservient to Israel, would make it impossible for its people to live in freedom, dignity and security.

There are also economic implications. Border, airspace and territorial water control exercised by Israel will inevitably impede the new state's economic integration with neighbouring Arab countries—something that is vital for its prosperity. A forced economic association with Israel would inevitably result in the new state being exploited, considering that even before the outbreak of major violence in 1996 the per capita income in the occupied territories was only one-twelfth that in Israel. There is also the matter of water. Today, Israel takes 80 per cent of its water from the West Bank's aquifers and the Jordan river tributaries that flow through it. With the West Bank and Golan Heights providing Israel with 70 per cent of its drinking water and 45 per cent of its agricultural water, arriving at an equitable sharing of water with the new state will be very difficult.

In 1978, even before Begin and Sadat started talking at Camp David, the basic principle of their agreement had been set out clearly—full Israeli withdrawal from Sinai in return for full recognition and acceptance of Israel by Egypt. Matters like demilitarised zones were relatively minor. But in 1993, neither a core principle nor a joint vision of destination was enunciated. There was neither a road map nor a schedule. The ambiguity of the DOP allowed both sides to ignore the implicit deal and, as years went by, made it captive to the hawks on both sides. Israel continued with settlement building and the Palestinians with violence. The idea of 'sliding into peace' and the hope that the fruits of the agreement would make both sides more flexible did not work.[15] For Israelis the post-Oslo years saw their lives being disrupted through violence in an unprecedented manner. Nearly as many Israeli civilians have been killed post-1996 than in all the years before.

The Palestinians are even more disenchanted with Oslo. After Oslo, 130,000 more settlers have moved in and 40,000 more acres of Palestinian land have been confiscated. By January 2000, nine months before the al-Aqsa intifada began, the Palestinian areas of the West Bank had been cut into 227 parts and of the Gaza Strip into three parts, with access controlled by Israelis. By then, Palestinians living below the $2-a-day poverty line had nearly tripled compared to 1990. Since Oslo, three times as many Palestinians as Israelis have been killed.

During the Oslo process the Palestinians were looking for their rights, while the Israelis were focused on their security. Israelis wanted well-defined 'peace' while Palestinians wanted well-defined 'justice'. Both sides could not see that it was impossible to achieve one without the other. Israel was looking at peacemaking as though the conflict had begun in 1967, while for the Palestinians it had begun in 1948, if not earlier. Israelis think that a compromise peace must allow them to exercise the victor's right and to retain some of the gains they had made in 1967. Moderate Palestinians think that a fair compromise is

---

[15] For a good exposition of why Oslo failed, see Sara Roy, 'Why Oslo Failed: An Oslo Autopsy', *Current History*, Vol. 101, No. 651, January 2002, pp. 8–16.

for Israel to retain the 22 per cent of Palestine that it captured in 1948, plus the Jewish areas of Jerusalem, and return to Palestinians the additional 22 per cent it captured in 1967.

After the PA was set up in 1994, Israel's attempt has been to control the Palestinians. It seemed that Israel's plan was not to end the occupation but to 'normalise' it by changing Israeli control from direct to indirect. The PA had to meet its commitments to Israel, but it also had to maintain popular support, which called for steady progress towards independence. With Israel unwilling to halt settlement construction, and returning bits of territory only grudgingly, the PA could not generate the popular support needed to clamp down on radical groups and confiscate weapons. With dissent against the PA snowballing (polls showed that Arafat's popularity had sunk from 82 to 31 per cent during 1994–2000), the PA's ability to meet the Israeli demands for ending incitement, disarming radicals and handing over terrorists diminished.

Yet, back in 1993 Oslo had begun with great promise.[16] Israel and the PLO recognising each other was a huge step, as was the creation of the PA. While the Palestinians constituted a weak entity militarily, they had legitimacy. During the three years after Oslo, forty-one countries including the Arab countries of Oman, Tunisia and Morocco recognised Israel. Not a single Arab country and very few others had done this when Israel and Egypt made peace in 1979. The post-Oslo Middle East economic conference in Casablanca in 1994 brought together a thousand businessmen from sixty countries.[17] But as the peace process waned so did Israeli influence in shaping an economically-linked Middle East. This was shown by attendance tapering off in later conferences in Amman (1995), Cairo (1996) and Doha (1997).

Israel is caught in a peculiar situation: while it can keep the Palestinians under control, it cannot ensure that Israelis—within Israel and the occupied territories—live normal, secure lives. Unless the Palestinians are given a State (constrained though it might have to be in terms of sovereign freedom of action) where they are able to live with dignity and economic opportunity, violence is unlikely to end. But neither

---

[16] In fact, some believed that the Oslo Process held lessons for India and Pakistan. See Moonis Ahmar, *The Road to Peace in South Asia: Lessons for India and Pakistan from the Arab–Israeli Peace Process*, ACDIS Occasional Paper, AHM: R2, University of Illinois at Urbana Champaign, 1996.

[17] For the euphoric thinking of that time see Shimon Peres with Arye Naor, *The New Middle East*, New York: Henry Holt, 1993.

the Israeli state nor the country's articulate public opinion thinks this is possible given Israel's security and ideological needs. There is little that ties the Israelis and the Palestinians across the racial, cultural, religious and linguistic divides that separate them. There is virtually no social interaction between them, even within Israel where they have lived together for over half a century. Both sides see peace as being possible only through separation, and not by forging bonds. In the final analysis, the Oslo Process failed less because of missed opportunities than because of what the parties saw as genuinely irreconcilable needs.

THOUGHTS FOR KASHMIR

If one looks at the Israeli–Palestinian/Arab conflict closely in relation to the Kashmir conflict, one is struck most by the fact that the structure of the latter is so much simpler. In the India–Pakistan conflict there is no claim for each other's total land, no Jerusalem, no Temple Mount/ Haram al-Sharif co-location, no racial or cultural gap, no refugees, no fight over resources, no difficulty in giving equal rights to all groups, and no demographic threat. These fundamental differences in the structures of the two conflicts are not recognised by most. It is not seen that unlike in the Israeli–Palestinian case, the 'structure' of the conflict is not a serious problem in the India–Pakistan context. The real problem is with the other two key dimensions of the persistent conflict—attitude and behaviour.

The conduct of Egypt in this conflict ought to make Pakistan introspect. Egypt had conceived itself as the leader of the Arab family of nations. It had triggered three of the four Arab–Israeli wars—1948, 1967 and 1973. (The 1956 war was an Anglo–French–Israeli enterprise.) Yet, in 1977 Egypt decided to pull out of the conflict. It was not an easy decision to make. It led to Egypt being ostracised by almost all Arab countries, and also created deep popular anger within the country. Nevertheless, looked at from Egypt's national interests and the welfare of its people, it was an eminently rational thing to do. Since the 1979 peace treaty, Egypt's economy has grown at an average rate of 4.8 per cent when other Arab countries as a group could average only 2.9 per cent. And Egypt is arguably once more the most influential of all Arab countries.

There is some resemblance between the ways in which the conflicts over Palestine and Kashmir have got transformed over the decades. Initially both conflicts had manifested themselves in the form of inter-state wars—1948, 1956, 1967 and 1973 in the former case and 1947–48, 1965 and 1971 in the latter case. As the intifada changed the Palestinian struggle into an internal one in 1987, militant actions converted the Kashmir conflict in 1989 from an inter-state one to an internally located one—no doubt with extensive external support. It is an interesting coincidence that the current phases of conflict in both Palestine and Kashmir began during 1987–89, after a nearly equal gestation period of four decades. It is also worth noting that both Israel and India have had much more difficulty in handling the new internally-located fighting than the earlier, well-defined external wars. Also noteworthy is the fact that in both Palestine and Kashmir, what started as territorial contests got infused more and more with religion as years passed. Not only has the salience of religion increased in both conflicts, but nationalist and religious zeal have got intertwined—first on one side, then on both sides.

The Israeli–Palestine conflict also illustrates the importance of individuals in a peace process. The Oslo Process became possible primarily because of Prime Minister Yitzhak Rabin. Rabin, a military hero whose reputation grew through every war that Israel had fought, had a unique political credibility to pursue peace. The majority of his people had confidence that in seeking peace he would never put Israel's security at risk. Rabin was as hard-headed as they come. But his experience as defence minister, coping with the intifada during 1987–90, had convinced him that a negotiated peace, bringing Israel's vast superiority to bear on its outcome, was the only realistic way forward. His assassination in 1995 was a blow from which the peace process could not recover.

An interesting insight from Israel is how public opinion can harden and soften. The Lebanon debacle of 1982 shifted Israeli opinion towards the centre, making Peres Prime Minister in 1984. The unexpected intifada violence that began in December 1987 shifted it to the right, bringing in Shamir in 1988. The failure of his hardline approach (Israel remained bogged down in Lebanon, and the occupied territories remained restive) led to a shift back to the centre in 1992, leading to the election of Rabin. The eruption of violence inside Israel in 1996 brought another rightward shift in the election of Netanyahu. The inability of Netanyahu to curb violence brought a reverse shift towards the centre in the election of Barak in 1999. Worsening violence prompted another shift to the right in 2001, bringing in Sharon. This plastic, reactive nature of public opinion is a feature everywhere—including in India and Pakistan.

Finally, neither the Israelis nor the Palestinians have been able to convert violence into political achievement. Suicide bombings by Palestinians have only made the Israelis more uncompromising and strengthened the hardline political forces in the country. On its part, Israel has been unable to use its huge military superiority and draconian approach to cow down the Palestinians. What is more, the Israeli approach has led to extremist Islam, in the form of Hamas and Islamic Jihad, gaining ground among the Palestinians.

MOVING FROM
CONFLICT TO PEACE

This chapter discusses some general issues involved in moving from conflict to peace and is a prelude to the final chapter on 'Creating a Peace Path in Kashmir'.[1] Resolving a long-running conflict poses very different challenges from crisis management which is largely confined to diplomatic, military and intelligence institutions. These institutions work somewhat alike in most countries and, therefore, crisis management literature can provide insights across situations. Long-running conflicts, which go deep into the political and societal hearts of nations, are different. Attempts to deal with them bring into play a variety of forces, many of which are not only unamenable to state

---

[1] There is a large body of conflict resolution literature. For examples see Charles Hauss, *International Conflict Resolution: International Relations for the 21st Century*, London: Continuum, 2001; Michael Banks and Christopher Mitchell, *Handbook of Conflict Resolution*, London: Pinter, 1996; John Burton and Frank Drakes, *Conflict: Practices in Management, Settlement and Resolution*, New York: St. Martin's Press, 1990; and John Darby and Roger MacGinty, *Contemporary Peacemaking: Conflict, Violence and Peace Processes*, London: Palgrave Macmillan, 2002.

direction but also show little similarity across sets of parties. It is difficult therefore to link protracted conflicts and their resolution potential through theory.

Yet, there are some factors that have relevance to the efforts to shift any conflict to a peace-seeking path. One of them is the kind of peace that should be aimed at. There are different types of freedom from conflict, ranging from wary agreement to reconciled peace. What is appropriate and practicable in each case has much to do with the circumstances surrounding it. Then there is what might be called strategic re-thinking. To recognise the need for peace and to see it as a practical project, adversaries need to go through a process of re-examining the conflict in light of current and prospective circumstances, and review the courses of action currently open to them. Unless such a reappraisal, conducted not only in offices of power but also in the public domain, brings out both the desirability and feasibility of peace, it is difficult to create a workable peace path. Related to this is public opinion that has a bearing on policy. It is essential that such opinion should support peace building.

Peacemaking calls for strategy. Not only must a peace strategy be well-crafted, it has to be developed and implemented in a more inclusive fashion than a war strategy. The broad contours of the approach have to be widely debated in public in each country and a rough consensus needs to emerge. Also, the approaches developed by both sides should move towards a common, broadly defined solution zone. The matter of negotiations is also relevant. There are many channels and many levels that can be used in negotiations. There are also many negotiating approaches that fall within the two main subsets of bargaining and problem-solving. Finally, there is the role that external parties might play in easing a conflict and nudging it towards peace.

CONCEPTS OF PEACE

Peace covers a wide spectrum. At one end is confrontational peace as seen in Korea since 1953. At the other end is reconciled peace such as that achieved between France and Germany after Saarland was returned in 1957. In between, there are many shades of peace that can be tagged with a variety of adjectives such as fragile peace (China and Taiwan), cold peace (Israel and Egypt), constrained peace (Israel and Jordan), suspicious peace (Japan and Russia), wary peace (Thailand and Vietnam) and unreconciled peace (Japan and South Korea). The nature of peace achieved is important for it determines the benefits that can be derived from peace. Post-peace economic bene-fits can, depending on the kind of peace achieved, range from reduced military expenditure to a greatly improved economic environment. External diplomatic advantage and internal societal benefit can similarly vary.

Other than ultimate victory, there are four basic approaches in deal-ing with conflicts—Management, Settlement, Resolution and Recon-ciliation. Managing a conflict is often the easiest approach for a state party. In a protracted international conflict it is generally in the interest of both parties to keep conflict dynamics under control—except for periodic testing of strength and will through crisis-creation. In the case of internal conflicts too the management approach is generally preferred because state parties are convinced that they can eventually wear down the non-state party. Settlement of disputes—which general-ly involves partial satisfaction of incompatible goals—is also frequently attempted. Its success depends largely on the stakes involved—real or perceived. If stakes are low, thoughtful parties often prefer settlement to management because it frees resources. But when stakes are high, settlement is generally very difficult to achieve within the paradigm that has been sustaining the conflict. If a change of paradigm becomes possible, the objective normally shifts to the realm of resolution.

For a settlement that does not lead to resolution to endure, it is ne-cessary that its terms are unambiguous and the power relations that underpinned it at the time stay unaltered. A settlement often deals only with the behaviour of parties, and not with the causes that had given rise to the conflict. A settlement can be arrived at even if the positions of the parties and their feelings of dissatisfaction remain unchanged. Resolution, on the other hand, is a process that addresses underlying causes and attempts to remove or substantially ameliorate dissatisfaction. Unlike in the case of settlement, in the case of reso-lution both parties see the post-conflict situation as more satisfactory than the previous one. Resolving conflicts—inter-state or intra-state— is much harder than arriving at settlements, especially where conflict dynamics are entrenched or the values being contested are high.

Conflict resolution is a more stable and durable achievement than dispute settlement, but it is nevertheless a political process.

Reconciliation in contrast is a sociological process. It involves societies as much as states. Reconciliation is a need that is generally felt more at the end of an intra-state conflict than an inter-state one. But reconciliation can be very useful even in inter-state conflicts if societies are significantly involved. A conflict is often fuelled at the political level. In such cases, if resolution is achieved reconciliation becomes easy. Management, settlement, resolution and reconciliation are not discrete processes. There are overlaps. If, for example, a conflict is managed by reducing tension over a period, it can often lead to settlement. Similarly, a good settlement that is not wholly power-determined can chart a path to resolution. And reconciliation is often a ready sequel to resolution.

The Cold War experience has made 'management' the dominant contemporary approach to dealing with conflicts. The US and the USSR could never hope to resolve the disagreements between them. Theirs was a huge contest for power that manifested itself in direct and proxy conflicts throughout the world. It was impossible to resolve all, or even most of them. The only practical approach was to control the intensity of the contest. This they did by developing certain norms of conduct that kept their struggle within a wide, but manageable band. The conditions undergirding their contest also made such an approach feasible. They had no common borders and had no claims on each other's territory. Neither was using emotive factors like religion in pursuing its goals. The contest did not reach the domestic structure of either country's state or society. It did not vitiate domestic politics or create internal tensions. And despite the ideological baggage they carried both parties were shrewd practitioners of realpolitik.

But a management approach is difficult to make a success of in conflicts where high levels of emotion are in play. Or, in cases where armies are in confrontation mode, guarding or threatening contested territories. Many Third World countries, trying to follow a management approach, have been unable to control either the dynamics or the costs of their conflicts. Management is also not a comfortable process to sustain indefinitely, nor is it an approach that can lead to peace dividends for the contestants. When Willy Brandt became German Chancellor, after a quarter century of the Christian Democratic Party's confrontational posture towards the East, he decided to open the alternative path of Ostpolitik. Brandt believed that something better than controlled hostility was possible with East Germany and the Warsaw Pact countries. His approach contributed substantially to the Helsinki Accords and the OSCE, as well as making Gorbachev possible in the Soviet Union.

STRATEGIC RE-THINKING

All protracted conflicts have real clashes of interest that revolve round security, political, economic and emotional needs. Some differences can be bridged through attitudinal changes and creative solutions, but some necessarily call for material concessions by the opposing sides. Neither party to a conflict will be in a position to make such concessions unless, through strategic re-thinking, it has concluded that such sacrifice will result in a compensating advantage of a higher order. When a conflict is underway, each party believes that it has a politico-military strategy geared to achieve success. It is only when realisation dawns that the sought-for combination of military and political success is unattainable through persistent conflict that parties decide to seek peace.

In almost all cases it is the costs incurred that lead to strategic re-thinking. The costs of conflict must get factored into the thinking of both state authorities and the public at large. This often does not happen till costs become very high. Even when it does, there is no certainty of any reconsideration. After starting from equal positions in 1950, in the next fifty years North Korea's per capita GDP became one-twentieth ($1,000 and $19,400) of South Korea's, and its defence expenditure as a percentage of GDP eleven times as much (31.3 and 2.8). Yet, North Korea wants to continue confronting.

The direct costs of a conflict include military and civilian casualties, as well as military and civil spending related to war. Indirect costs include deterioration of the general economic environment, fracturing and coarsening of society, a diminished external image, and leadership distraction. Indirect costs are difficult to calculate, and there are always differing estimates. There are also opportunity costs—the gains foregone by not employing the resources spent in conflict pursuit. Opportunity costs are more difficult to estimate than even indirect costs. But that they can be very substantial is proved by the experience of every country that has been involved in a prolonged, active conflict.

Low-intensity warfare is generally not very demanding in terms of casualties and direct economic costs, although there can be exceptions such as Sri Lanka. In most cases it does not add significantly to the defence budget. Moreover, if the affected area is small and can be sequestered effectively, even the indirect economic impact can be low. But there are other adverse impacts such as the conflict distracting the national leadership from social and economic development. Reaction to conflict costs vary across countries. Casualty tolerance tends to be high where soldiering is in demand for economic reasons and where socio-economic conditions make people less sensitive to deaths. In protracted conflicts, reaction to costs can also be dampened by the perception that having incurred so much already it would be unwise to fret about additional costs. The focus turns to sunk costs, and current and future costs become marginal issues.

Even when the reality of costs are factored in, it is not easy to reconsider the basic assumptions that have kept a conflict going. In a protracted conflict, views of what the conflict is about and what the possibilities of its resolution are get firmly cast. Analyses tend to become superficial and confined to tactical issues. Arguments and stances developed to serve domestic political purpose and bolster international support get accepted as truths and go unchallenged. Moreover, the changing fortunes of fighting, inevitable in any prolonged conflict, make the assessment of costs and its correlation to political objectives difficult.

In a conflict, parties have both interests and positions. Interests are essentially situation-determined, while positions are what parties calculate they need to take to protect their interests. While interests are rooted more in the structure of conflict than positions are, they too are not unchangeable. Nor for that matter are they necessarily objective. In the case of the Sri Lankan conflict it is a moot point whether Colombo's true interest lies in an island enjoying harmony or in one that maintains Sinhalese–Buddhist hegemony. Similarly, although the original interest was Sinhalese–Buddhist hegemony, should it continue to be so in light of the problems that the pursuit of that interest has created? In the case of Israel, should its interest lie in appropriating more of the Biblical Land or in developing amicable relations with the Palestinians it cannot get rid of? There are no easy answers to such questions, but it is important that they be raised.

There is the serious problem of looking at one's own motives and actions and those of the adversary's through different lenses. One's own hostile actions are rationalised as reactions that are forced upon one, while those of the opponent are regarded as wilful. One's own freedom of action is seen as less than the adversary's, and the very real constraints that could be operating on him are discounted. This helps to justify policy and shift blame. It is also common to view the adversary's conduct as unrelated to one's own behaviour and attitudes. The interacting linkages that exist between the patterns of perception and the conduct of one side with those of the other are ignored. This leads to the commonly held view that an end to the conflict depends entirely on how the opponent changes. Coercing or stonewalling him into a reasonable frame of mind is often seen as the only contribution to peace that one's own side needs to make.

Hawks and doves are present within any party engaged in conflict, but as long as there is no serious prospect of peace it is the influence of hawks that stays dominant. The need to prosecute a conflict effectively—in political, military and diplomatic domains—makes it necessary to bring a war perspective to bear on it. A neutral perspective that looks at peace possibilities objectively is seen, with good reason, as distracting from the task at hand, which is the single-minded pursuit of the conflict. Institutions of state get set in a war mould, and the prosecution of conflict gets privileged over exploring opportunities for settlement. This is an attitudinal reality present in conflicts the world over, and it erects as big a barrier on the path to peace as does the structure of the conflict in terms of objective clash of interest.

Though a protracted conflict may impose serious long-term costs, it does not generally cause political difficulty for the leadership. Except in a crisis, it does not therefore attract top-level attention. Its normal prosecution is left to security institutions. When a militarised conflict has been running for some time, and a zero-sum, win-lose perspective freezes organisational thinking in a confrontational mode, the voices of moderation within these institutions get silenced. Actions become routinised, and responses reflexive. Prosecution of conflict becomes more a matter of administration than a conclusion-seeking exercise. Institutions rarely have a clear idea of how the results of their actions will turn out, but they develop a confidence that they can handle whatever might happen. Their action-focus therefore is invariably on short-term political, diplomatic and military management. As a result, strategic re-thinking in favour of peace is very difficult to emanate from within these institutions.

Perhaps the most noteworthy example of strategic re-thinking in recent times is the Nixon–Kissinger initiative that led to the US–China rapprochement of 1971–72. There were strong anti-China feelings in the US then that went back to the communist ouster of the US-supported Kuomintang government in 1949, the bloody US–China fighting in the Korean war of 1950–53, and China's support to North Vietnam that was to bleed the US for a decade. Yet the US decided to ignore the past and made a deal with China because of the advantages they saw in this—splitting the communist world, ending the Vietnam war and opening economic cooperation. Though it was overwhelmingly superior to China on every count in 1971, the US decided to offer major concessions—effective recognition of China's claim over Taiwan and ending China's political and economic isolation. Both were huge departures from US policy over the past twenty-two years, and constituted a remarkable display of rational cost-benefit calculation winning over emotion and inertia.

INFLUENTIAL PUBLIC OPINION

Public opinion plays a large role, both in prolonging a conflict and in bringing it to an end. In security matters, it is the opinion of what is called the 'security attentive public'—the people who contribute to security policy discussions in public—that gets construed as public opinion, although they form only a small segment even within the elite and the middle class. The views expressed in the media and the findings of polls tend to be heavily skewed in favour of this small group. In countries like Israel and Northern Ireland, where the elite and the middle class constitute about 80 per cent of the population, the articulated public opinion tends to be fairly representative of the society as a whole. But in countries like India and Pakistan, where literacy and the percentage of the middle class are far lower, there is much greater variance between the views of the vocal 'security attentive public' and that of the less involved masses.

In security matters, governments have much greater influence on the public than in other areas. There is generally a parallelism in the views of a country's government and its security intelligentsia. The primary customers of security think tanks are those who are involved in prosecuting conflicts. As a result, what comes to dominate their research is the means of achieving greater effectiveness in waging war, politically and militarily, and not in bringing it to a conclusion. Their research stresses the justness of one's cause, the treacherousness of the opponent, the seriousness of stakes, the disadvantages in seeking a compromise, and the virtues of hanging tough. The broader intelligentsia take their cue from the security intelligentsia.

The media follow the line of the security establishment for they have few independent sources of information and analysis. Media comment on security matters that has its origin in the security establishment, gets fed back to the latter, producing a closed and self-reinforcing loop of hardline thinking. In all the four conflicts considered in this book, the media have played a consistent role in inflaming passions. Conflict news is 'framed' in black and white terms, and through 'cues' the public is primed to view developments in a certain way. People respond to their information environment, which can become very unbalanced on conflict matters. It is not that the media want to promote aggressive thinking; but they need stirring content, and conflict-related 'patriotic' commentary provides just that.

Peace, or its palpable prospect, can change both media attitude and public perception. It is common to see opinion change rapidly and substantially after the conclusion of a durable peace, but rare to see it change earlier, unless the prospect of the peace effort succeeding appears bright. Till peace is assured and assured durably, many see it as a political and military necessity to keep the flame of enmity burning. Also, there is invariably a war constituency to which the very idea of negotiated peace is repugnant. The central problem that public opinion poses to a leadership keen to negotiate peace is that, while the views of the public will change in favour of peace after it is secured, negotiations have to be carried out while public perceptions are still set in a mould of enmity.

During a long struggle, each side would have internalised strongly biased perceptions about the virtue of one's own side and the evil of the other. Reservoirs of hatred and negative stereotypes would have been built up. In such a situation, any attempt at peace will invite accusations of weakness, gullibility and sell-out. The power of hawks, cynics and pessimists can be considerable at the beginning of a peace process. Images of the enemy can be overcome, but when they exist they make it hard for adversaries to deal with each other in a constructive way. In reality, most people do not hold strong, stable attitudes on security matters. Hostility levels vary considerably with events.

Public support in the UK for the Iraq war went up from 30 to 70 per cent in one month—in March 2003. It came down to 40 per cent four months later. Public opinion is not erratic, but it responds to events. It is much more fluid, conditional and nuanced than popular poll findings indicate.

Very often peace efforts are viewed as a vote-loser and an electoral liability. In reality, in most countries—rich and poor—foreign policy and security issues rarely play a role in the way masses vote. There have been many instances of parties advocating tougher stances come a-cropper during elections held in times of tension and when the media is filled with conflict commentary. It is only small sections of the elite and the middle class that hold hardline and set-in-groove views. Other sections among them and the masses, constituting preponderant numbers, generally do not. As a result, the electoral risk in pursuing peace is in most instances much less than is portrayed.

PEACE STRATEGY

No major conflict can be brought to a peaceful conclusion without a peace strategy. Crafting such a strategy is not easy, given the major revisions it would call for in institutional thinking and public opinion. A peace strategy cannot succeed with tactical bargains. There must be a commitment to strategic cooperation, and to a resolution that safeguards the vital needs of both parties. The strategy must lead the parties away from backward-looking justification of positions to forward-looking attempts at problem-solving. It must provide incentives to both sides. The timeframe cannot be short. It is only when medium- and long-term calculations are made that shared interests emerge. The war perspective that parties bring to bear on each other is a major problem. Mindsets have to gradually shift from confrontational to cooperative, and from military–strategic to political–strategic. The conceptualisation of the problem must shift from coercing the opponent to providing him inducement.

For a workable peace strategy, both sides must be clear about the kind of peace they want. There are agreements that alter the attitudes of parties to one another and thereby lead to improved relations. There are others that are considered by one or both parties as merely a breather. Demands raised to revise what are called unequal agreements stem from the feeling on the part of one party that the agreement was extracted from it under pressure. For a peace agreement to continue in good health both parties should feel that they have made gains. What one side promises can be reneged upon, but that is less likely if the basic conditions that had been supporting the conflict are altered. A good peace should interlock relationships in such a way that hostile attitudes cannot be reintroduced without both sides paying high costs. This is what has happened increasingly in the case of US–China rapprochement.

To develop a good peace strategy, both parties need to examine the structural position of the conflict and the attitudinal and behaviour patterns of the two sides in as objective a manner as possible, and with the minimum number of elements taken as fixed. How the interests and objectives of each side may have mutated over the years needs to be analysed closely. This could lead to new understandings about one's own and the opponent's current bottomlines on issues, as well as each side's evaluations of risks and costs. The extent to which positions taken by one side are responses to the other side's positions, and how it may be possible to move them closer through simultaneous movement can also be better understood. Similarly, a better grasp of the cognitive processes of both sides can help with the very important separation of true goal incompatibilities from psychological barriers.

A peace process involves a large number of variables that can interact in many different ways, depending on the initiatives taken and the responses made. There are many possibilities at every turn, and both sides need to know them well. Without proper analysis to support their decision-making, neither party can have the confidence to move from established paths. Strategic gaming is increasingly recognised as a very useful tool to arrive at this understanding. By testing assumptions and stretching imagination, games can focus on creative problem-solving in a way 'discussions' never can. Gaming provides a framework where key issues can be concentrated upon and different ideas tried out. It can separate fact and opinion better, and enable a less subjective examination of where different paths could lead in the medium- and long-term. It can better explore the options open to both sides and the likely dynamics of moves and responses. The area of the unknown gets reduced. Options that were either not thought of or were summarily dismissed get appraised.

To move towards peace, both sides need to agree on a 'solution zone'. If that zone is not too large, there can be a better appreciation of the compromises and innovations needed to move further. If negotiations begin without an agreed idea of where they need to go, the parties will find themselves travelling along paths that cannot converge. Both sides would have to shift positions to get to the solution zone. The extent and nature of concessions by each side would depend on power relativity. Where there is large power disparity, it can lead to an outcome close to the original position of the stronger side. Even if it is not very large, the stronger side can still use it to achieve a settlement closer to its own position than the adversary's. But the stronger side must know how to use its power advantage and, equally important, must know its limitations. An attempt to over-leverage power difference could lead to a dead end. The weaker side will lose incentive. The weaker side, and not the stronger one, always sees power difference as less serious and more open to circumvention.

Making a peace process internally sustainable is a formidable challenge. The creation of an internal consensus on the need, as well as the approach, to be adopted to make peace is as demanding and problematic an effort as that of dealing productively with the opponent.[2] When a conflict gets protracted, a large number of institutions of the state get involved in it. And each of them develops an institutional perspective that is appropriate from its point of view to carry on with the business of prosecuting the conflict. The foreign ministry, the military, the intelligence agencies and others all get set into moulds that are largely determined by the needs of each institution. Ways of thinking that do not conform to these moulds become effectively illegitimate. This is the first of the two big domestic barriers to peace.

The other barrier is the influential public opinion in the country, which would also have got set in a cast of enmity during a protracted conflict. Governments find it difficult to abandon popularly accepted goals for which they or their predecessors have repeatedly expressed commitment. Being accused of betrayal is a strong deterrent to replacing the original conflict goal with a more attainable one. A government seeking peace has to generate a climate of calm and optimism. It has

---

[2] See Peter B. Evans, Harold K. Jacobson and Robert D. Putnam, eds., *Double-edged Diplomacy: International Bargaining and Domestic Politics*, Berkeley: California University Press, 1993.

to make the enemy image less salient, and improve political atmospherics. Inevitably, governments have to present the peace calculus in a manner that leads to electoral gains. Political benefit to the party or group in power is always as big a consideration as national advantage. While there is political profit to be gained when a peace effort succeeds, there is always political risk in the run up to agreement. For a good peace strategy it is essential for each side to understand the domestic political difficulties faced by the other side.

Ultimately, reciprocal self-interest is the only workable logic in peace strategies. A pragmatic peace process has to be based, at least partly, on an exchange of concessions. Each side must feel that the other is also giving up important goals and is taking risks. Sacrifice of goals is very difficult for both sides. To minimise that, a good peace strategy must also develop positive-sum solutions. It is often not difficult to craft solutions that are objectively win-win, but it is not easy to package them positively and find the political will to attempt them. When attitudes have hardened over years, it is difficult to accept that what you give to your adversary is not necessarily a loss to yourself. The Siachen issue is a classic example where concessions can be useful to both sides, yet where circumstances have made them hard to make.

There are different views on the best way to create a peace path. Some advocate a step-by-step approach, dealing with issues in their ascending order of contention. This is premised on the belief that agreements that are easy to arrive at can help generate the trust and goodwill needed to tackle more serious issues of dispute. Some commend packaging several issues so that opportunities for multi-stranded trade-off can be created. Some counsel that in the initial stages only a rough road map should be agreed upon, as attempts to produce a clear delineation of the final outcome will create deadlocks. Others consider that an initial agreement couched in too general terms will make progress hostage to extremists on both sides, as has happened with the Oslo Process. Peace approaches have succeeded and foundered following all these approaches. Historical records show that the choice of approach is much less significant than the strength of mutual commitment to seek peace.

Coercion and resistance are as much a part of peace making as co-operation is, because parties are seeking advantage as well as peace. The coercion–resistance model will always be in operation at the pre-negotiation stage because each party would want to negotiate from a position of strength or one of minimal weakness. Even when a peace process is moving, coercion and resistance will continue to play a role because the parties involved would want to improve their leverage. Starting a track of cooperation in such circumstances is a major challenge. But unless a cooperative track is created and steadily strengthened, and the coercion–resistance track weakened, there can be no serious forward movement. A cooperative track is essential to generate trust, which is the most important constituent of a successful peace process. Calibrating cooperation and coercion within a peace engagement poses a daunting challenge, and diplomatic history is full of examples of getting the wrong mix.

Where a conflict is characterised by continuous or recurrent violence, some de-escalation of military activity is necessary before a peace process can make headway. A problem with de-escalation is that the capabilities of the two sides are often asymmetric, and specific de-escalatory measures can have a different impact on the two sides with regard to current and future fighting capabilities. De-escalatory measures that result in one side's position eroding disproportionately are difficult to agree upon, and if agreed upon, to sustain. Insurgencies, given their ideological needs and fragile logistics, cannot be switched on and off. Most insurgent groups, therefore, see a long ceasefire as constituting a serious loss of leverage. More fundamentally, de-escalatory measures such as ceasefire can serve little purpose unless they are made part of a process that is actually moving towards settlement.

NEGOTIATIONS

Unless they stem from genuine strategic re-thinking, negotiations between parties to a long-running conflict are rarely conducted with a serious intent to seek peace. Instead, the objective is often to gain a respite from fighting, probe for changes in the opponent's thinking and placate third parties. Negotiations are often focused on international opinion and domestic public opinion—wanting to appear peace-seeking to the former and a vigilant guardian of national interest to the latter. This leads to posturing more than discussions. Negotiating exchanges get limited to show of resolve, reiteration of old positions and new packaging of unacceptable proposals. With an attitude that 'peace talks are fine, but my positions are firm' it is little surprise that new talks end up as another go at the familiar treadmill.

If fortunes have not turned irresistibly in one party's favour, serious negotiations cannot take place without both accepting the need to make concessions that could be painful—material or psychological or both. What those concessions shall be are going to be determined less by what happens when negotiations begin than by the tacit bargaining that would have taken place earlier. Tacit bargaining—largely through pressure and resistance—would have updated both parties' strategic perceptions about the current structural circumstances of the conflict, including the corelationship of (generally asymmetric) power. Unless tacit bargaining has narrowed the gap in understanding on this account, negotiations may not only stall but could end up worsening relations. The disastrous India–Pakistan summit of July 2001 in Agra is a good example.

Even when both parties are embarked on a genuine search for settlement, the process of negotiations is not easy. There are always pre-negotiation skirmishes and manoeuvres for the best possible position from which to negotiate. The terms on which substantive issues should be discussed is crucial, for they determine the range of potential outcomes. There is also the delicate matter of communicating the desire to compromise without giving an impression of weakness. And the reverse one of signalling resolve without vitiating the atmosphere. Negotiating preliminaries—done through public statements and working-level meetings—are carried out to determine the dimensions of the bargaining space. In the India–Pakistan context, the manner in which the Kashmir issue should be discussed is a perennial and fiercely contested preliminary. The sequencing of issues within an agreed agenda is also a matter for contesting, as items taken up first can have an influence on those taken up later. During the Vietnam peace talks in Paris in 1972, the US wanted to discuss military aspects first while North Vietnam wanted to address political issues first. Eventually it was decided to discuss both in parallel, just as in 1997 India and Pakistan agreed to discuss 'Kashmir' and 'Peace and Security' together.

Purposeful negotiations for peace are geared to achieve two kinds of solutions—compromise and creative. Compromise solutions require parties to make concessions with reference to their positions.

The search for compromise solutions is inevitably underpinned by bargaining. But bargaining has to be tempered by the need for constructive political and psychological processes. In most negotiations there exists a bargaining disparity between the sides. This disparity would depend largely on the quality of alternatives each side has if a settlement does not materialise. Opening bids or maximalist positions are of little consequence. The effective bargaining range and the eventual agreement point is determined by the true bottom lines of the parties, which in turn are determined by the character of each side's no-agreement alternative. On each side there will be groups with different bottom lines. In objective terms it should be the effort of each side to strengthen the accommodative groups on the other side. By hard bargaining, the two sides often accomplish precisely the opposite.

A well-intentioned and well-structured search for compromise solutions can gradually raise trust levels to the point where creative solutions become possible. Creative outcomes that bridge interests are not possible in an atmosphere of distrust and animus. In such a climate, neither side wants mutual gain. Each wants gain at the expense of the other. Reducing hostility and augmenting trust are, therefore, essential prerequisites to embark on a positive-sum path. Creative solutions are geared to protect the interests of both parties by changing the structure of the conflict. It calls for the understanding—very difficult to promote—that advantage need not always be gained at the other's expense. For both compromise and creative solutions, a milieu has to be found where parties can shift position without being seen as climbing down. A good settlement must avoid loss of face to both sides, even if the losses cannot be. A win-win formulation must look at sentiment as much as substance.

Negotiations between two state parties and that between a state party and a dissident group have different dynamics. State parties are always reluctant to accord negotiating partner status to dissidents, and even when they do, it is always heavily conditional. There is also the problem of finding a reliable negotiating partner among dissidents. They are often badly split among themselves, with none of the groups having the needed representative value. On the other hand, where dissidents are unified—such as Sinn Fein/IRA and the LTTE—governments tend to feel insecure. In most cases, governments are also on the lookout to create splits in dissident ranks. But negotiating with split groups often does not help. Frequently, after an agreement is signed with one group, others continue with the fight. India has experienced this with the Nagas and the Philippines with the Moros.

Experience world-wide has shown that settlements of protracted conflicts are very difficult to achieve if negotiations are limited to formal channels. Broadly, the channels of negotiations available to states attempting to end a conflict are formal official channels, informal official channels known as back channels, and Track II channels. Accredited representatives operate formal official channels. Special representatives, occasionally from intelligence agencies, operate back channels. And non-officials, sometimes with a lacing of officials participating in a non-official capacity, take part in Track II meetings.

Formal official channels, while essential in developing purpose and communicating commitment, have the handicap of being burdened by public positions and public expectations. Tight negotiating briefs hem in officials, even when negotiations are conducted in secrecy. The very fact that meetings are taking place is enough to set off speculative comment. There is also the well founded fear of leaks, from one's own side as much as from the other's. Exploring options is also a problem for formal channel participants because of considerations such as disclosing one's hand or being seen as succumbing to pressure. It is difficult for them to take initiatives without some idea of the likely response. This is where back channels can make a contribution. The main advantage of back channels is that they operate without publicity, and therefore are less vulnerable to sabotage and counter-mobilisation by anti-peace constituencies. The disadvantage is that packaging understandings arrived at through back channels in a manner that will not create problems when they are eventually made public, can often pose major difficulty.

Track II discussions differ from the first two in that they have no official standing, and most of what passes through them ends up in the public domain. Their main strength is that they are able to discuss a conflict in an analytical as opposed to a bargaining framework. Trial balloons can be floated without constituting offers. But unless its usefulness is recognised and appropriate methods and structures are created to take advantage of the ideas it develops, this track can do little good. Also, if this track is to throw up fresh ideas, it must have participation from a wide circle of expertise including politicians and businessmen. In Southeast Asia, Track II channels have played a useful role for decades. A new development in informal meetings is people-to-people group meetings. Here large groups of people from the two sides get together to create a climate of goodwill. Their target is atmosphere, not issues. These groups have done good work in many places including Northern Ireland. Several such groups have come up in India and Pakistan too.

Creating public support for negotiating flexibility has become critical. With the media debating every move, diplomacy is now a public spectacle. States find themselves transacting business simultaneously with their opponents as well as with their own publics. Sheltering negotiations from hardline domestic constituencies has become impossible because of intense and persistent media attention. State parties invariably spin the media to help their hand in negotiations. At the same time they are confronted with the problem of multiple signalling—to the opponent, to domestic opinion and to international watchers.

External Role

The stronger party to a conflict is always averse to involve a third party in peacemaking. Where the conflict is intra-state, the demands of sovereignty make such involvement awkward. Where it is inter-state, the stronger party would like to make its strength felt in a bilateral setting. But there are times when a third party can be of advantage even from the stronger party's point of view. When animus and distrust dominate, a productive dialogue may simply not be possible in a bilateral setting, even with the help of back and Track II channels. In such situations third parties can often provide some useful emollient. They can also help create a setting for free-ranging analyses, exchange of ideas and exploration of options without commitments. They can help alter the understanding of a conflict by exploring and analysing beliefs, the way values operate, and how costs are calculated.

Third parties may have an interest in negotiations for several reasons. These could include their preference for a particular type of outcome, their greater support for one of the sides, and their interest in enhancing their leverage with one or both parties through their very participation. An interested third party can often be dangerous, because its own interests will be its prime concern. There are third parties, however, which may have little or no interest in the outcome of a peace process, except with regard to its success. These are normally small countries that do not have the ability to play a major role globally, and more so in the region concerned.

Third parties can play another role when negotiations reach their final stage. There might be a need for an outside monitoring group to observe compliance with the terms of agreement. High distrust levels might also call for an endorsement by others on an agreement reached, as in the case of Israel and Egypt. For it to serve a useful purpose, endorsement must be by powers that can inflict penalty on the party that might break the terms of agreement. Major powers can also play a role by providing incentives and rewards for reaching a settlement, or even for emarking on a path to settlement, as has happened in Sri Lanka.

THE INDIA–PAKISTAN CONTEXT

If apposite experiences from elsewhere are related to the India–Pakistan context, a few inferences become apparent. Perhaps the most important is that, given the highly active interface that exists between the conflict and the domestic politics of the two countries, 'managing' the conflict is extremely difficult. Even a 'settlement' that does not have popular support in both countries will be of little avail. Only a 'resolution' at the political level, paving the way for 'reconciliation' at the societal level, can work. A sustainable peace in the subcontinent must give a measure of remedy to all parties, even if varying substantially in proportion. If peace is to endure benefits from it must be shared.

The kind of strategic re-thinking needed to move from a conflict path to a peace path had a very tentative start in both countries in 2003. Costs of conflict are beginning to get recognised, but are far from being seriously factored into policy. Tactical considerations more than strategic ones lie behind the recent keenness to explore peace. In neither country is there adequate recognition yet that the circumstances surrounding the conflict have changed considerably over the past fifty-six years, and that the true clash of stakes has substantially reduced as a consequence. While there is a desire for peace, there has been no examination of what a peace effort might entail. Both countries are far from developing internal consensus on the kind of shifts that they are prepared to make from existing positions.

Both compromise and creative solutions are needed to bridge the wide gaps existing today on positions and perceptions. Possibilities for achieving positional compromises, which do not translate into compromising stakes and interests, are present in the India–Pakistan conflict. But to recognise them, stakes and interests need to be re-examined through a realist lens and the relationship between them and diplomatic positions has to be seriously re-looked at again. There is large scope for creative solutions too, but this has not been examined at all so far.

There has been no public identification of the solution zone. Thoughtful people in both countries understand that a solution can be built only around the twin concepts of the LoC becoming the final border, and adequate and parallel autonomy being provided on both sides of the LoC. But this idea has yet to be accepted, or even explored, in both countries. In neither country is the public being prepared for a feasible, mutually acceptable destination zone.

Given the public rigidity of existing positions on both sides, it is very difficult for a solution zone to be agreed upon through public diplomacy. Back-channel discussions, or at least of the semi-secret type that are currently going on between India and China, are needed to agree upon the kind of solution that India and Pakistan could both live with. It is only when such an acceptance of the solution zone has been arrived at without destructive public arguments that formal negotiations can have a chance to succeed.

Global experience shows that third parties can have only a very limited role in a peace effort, except in cases where the contestants are weak or outsiders have a powerful interest in achieving peace. The first condition does not apply in the India–Pakistan context, and the second only to a limited degree. In the subcontinent, a third party role can only be a very peripheral one.

No non-capitulatory peace process has succeeded without the parties going through an exercise in strategic re-thinking, and coming to the mutual conclusion that achieving a settlement is both desirable and feasible. Peacemaking requires rational, unemotional calculation of costs, and working for medium- and long-term benefit. A shared understanding of the true bottom lines and no-agreement alternatives of both sides is essential. A peace process needs perseverance; it cannot be an on-off process. Protracted conflicts have rarely been settled with a few rounds of negotiations. Nor have they been settled with negotiations stretching interminably. Finally, without a solution zone being jointly identified before public talks begin, success is very unlikely.

CREATING A PEACE PATH
IN KASHMIR

T he India–Pakistan conflict had started with a fair degree of genuine clash of interest. But now it is increasingly driven by factors that have little to do with the preservation or promotion of national interest. Slanted understandings about the past, kept going by partisan reportage and commentary, have made emotion the biggest factor in the conflict. Three big wars and two small ones, spread over half a century, and constant violence in the last fifteen years have created deeply pessimistic mindsets. True national interests are being pushed back in the febrile context of battle. Pakistan's deeply afflicted political system and an army that is prisoner to an increasingly unworkable offensive-defence strategy have made the country incapable of showing flexibility. India, on its part, is in an assertive, power-oriented mood. It does not want to appear irresolute or swayable. This prevents it from seeing the opportunity it has to make a peace good for both countries— largely on India's terms.

Objectively viewed, the half-decade that has passed since mid-1998 should constitute a major learning period for India and Pakistan. Never have so many bilateral ups and downs been packed into so short a period. First, there were the nuclear tests of May 1998 that have given a dangerous new edge to the India–Pakistan conflict. Five months later came the foreign secretary-level talks when, for the first time since the Simla Agreement, India and Pakistan discussed Kashmir on a structured basis, and as part of what was to be a purposeful, multi-stranded dialogue. This was followed within three months by the India–Pakistan Summit of January 1999 in Lahore. Four months later, relations plummeted following the discovery of Pakistan's winter encroachment across the LoC and the three-month Kargil War that resulted. Within a year there was another brief thaw that ended all-too-predictably with the acrimonious Agra Summit of July 2001. Pakistan-sponsored terrorist attacks that had mounted in intensity from 1998 led, five months after Agra, to the biggest military confrontation the two countries have ever had—India's ten-month Operation Parakram that lasted till October 2002. Relations once again began to thaw in April 2003, and in January 2004 the parties agreed to resume their composite dialogue.

All this has taken place against a global backdrop of military-led unipolarity, and since late 2001 that of the war against terrorism as well. Adjusting nimbly to changing conditions, both countries have vied to get close to the US. In India a BJP-led government came to power in 1998, ushering in a mood of paradigm shift, ambition and pragmatism. A year later, the Army returned to centrestage in Pakistan, after eleven years of directing from the wings. Military power-play—terrorism with nuclear deterrence in the background by Pakistan, and conventional threat by India—did not do much to change ground positions. But Pakistan's decision, under duress, to turn against anti-US Islamists in the country has had a major fall-out. It has driven a wedge between the top leadership of the Army and the more extremist Islamists, and has made instrumental use of the latter against India a trickier proposition.

There is little to show yet that there will be a productive dialogue when talks resume. Positions continue to be too hardened and too far apart for negotiations to make headway. Many in India believe that Pakistan now has no choice but to break with Islamist radicals, and thereby lose its leverage in Kashmir. Pakistani policy-makers think that the US's need to ensure an effective, pro-US regime in the country will make America lean on India to make concessions. The friendly signals that began flashing between the two countries in late 2003 are thus based on expectations that major concessions are likely to be forthcoming from the other side, without reciprocal ones from one's own side. There is also the cynical expectation that this thaw too will pass, and a new phase of hostilities will soon begin.

This kind of wishful and tactical thinking is unlikely to hew a sustainable peace path. For such a path to become possible, there has to be a genuine change in the way both parties look at the conflict, and the demands of peace-making. The two governments cannot, and would not, want to do this unless the public mood in the two countries changes. There are some optimistic signs today that such a change in outlook is possible. Both Pakistan and its Army are under serious and sustained pressure, and are looking for a way to conclude the conflict with their honour intact. In India, there is a growing groundswell of opinion that wants to put this distracting tussle behind, so that the tempo of economic growth can be stepped up further. And finally, not only has the US unprecedented, substantial and concurrent influence over both countries, there is also a growing understanding in the US that an India–Pakistan rapprochement can make a major contribution to the goal of curbing Islamic extremism, suppressing terrorism and reducing nuclear risks.

THROUGH A REALIST LENS

The view through a realist lens must focus on the realities as they exist today, and as they are likely to get shaped tomorrow. Ideological and legal arguments are no longer of consequence in Kashmir. Nor is the over chronicled 'burden of history'. What matters today are the applicable politico-military power of India and Pakistan, and the quality of the two sides' no-agreement alternatives in the medium term. When contesting with asymmetric power, it is easy and seductive for each side to define the conflict in terms that suit it, and to exaggerate the value of its resources and strategies. Such wishful thinking is often a major reason for missing or ignoring settlement possibilities.

There are two parallel conflicts in Kashmir, with only a permeable membrane separating the two. The visions of Pakistan and the Kashmiri discontented are divergent, but each is using the other against India. This has become possible because the two positions that India is defending in Kashmir—a territorial one against Pakistan and a relationship one with the discontented in the state—have got linked over the years. India has to defend the first resolutely, for otherwise religious tensions in the subcontinent will greatly worsen. But clinging to the relationship status quo is not to India's advantage. India can defend the territorial position with far less trouble if it can handle the relationship position better.

India's current strategy in Kashmir is shaped by the view that, with India steadily increasing its already big lead over Pakistan in the global power league, a delayed settlement shall be to India's advantage. The costs that India is bearing are seen as endurable and worthwhile. It is reasoned that, just as India is not actively contesting Aksai Chin on account of China's possession and strength, Pakistan too will be forced to give up in Kashmir. There are hardliners in India, small in number, who want to use Pakistan's entrapment in the struggle to bring about its collapse. They believe that only a 'defeat' will make Pakistan accept an India-led regional order. Such views do not reflect the thinking of the overwhelming majority of Indians. What most Indians want is that the part of J&K it currently has should stay with India, and Pakistan should cease to promote violence there.

Pakistan knows that under no circumstances will India let go of any part of the state with it, and that while Pakistan can create problems it cannot gain territory. Pakistan's objective has become increasingly negative. It wants to prevent India from gaining the allegiance of the Kashmiris and, in the larger context, consolidating a tolerant society within India. It feels that by promoting terrorism and violence it can force India to maintain a pervasive and stifling military presence in J&K, which will worsen disaffection in the state and, in the long run, harm communal harmony in India as a whole. There is also the military calculation that by keeping a large portion of the Indian Army tied down in J&K in difficult and irregular warfare conditions, the threat to Pakistan can be reduced. Furthermore, by being stuck in this unhappy contest with Pakistan, India will not be able to exploit its superior growth potential as well as it otherwise could.

The military hawks in Pakistan think that conventional capability is not relevant within Kashmir, and that a conventional attack outside Kashmir can be deterred with nuclear weapons. More important, they see India as incapable of addressing the political challenge it faces in the state. Continuing military pressure in Kashmir, through low-cost asymmetric warfare, is seen as possible because the longer the conflict goes on the more Islamised the Kashmiris will become. It is argued that the West cannot afford a collapsed Pakistan, and that nuclear weapons have revived international interest in Kashmir. Pakistani hawks have always had difficulty establishing a realistic link between goals and capabilities. It was bad enough competing with India in the years before 1980 when Pakistan had a 1.5 per cent economic growth rate advantage. But to do that with an India, whose economy is not only seven times larger but is also growing at a 2.5 per cent higher average rate since 1992, has become suicidal. Increasing numbers of Pakistanis are aware of this, and their views are now rapidly diverging from those of the hawks.

Nuclear weapons, covertly acquired by Pakistan around 1990 and overtly wielded by the two countries since 1998, have had a big impact on India–Pakistan relations, but not in the simplistic 'equaliser' fashion that the hawks in Pakistan imagine it to be. Nuclear weapons have reduced the chances of war, but have not eliminated them. In fact, maladroit risk-taking by Pakistan can now precipitate a nuclear instead of a conventional war. The risks and consequences of nuclear escalation have yet to sink into the collective minds of the two societies. Nuclear devastation still remains an abstract concept. In a nuclear exchange more Pakistanis and, therefore, a much higher percentage of its smaller population, will perish. But Pakistan will be able to cause substantial casualties in India too—dead and radiation-sick in millions.

Nuclear weapons now pose a big challenge to Pakistan. While its arsenal can provide security against an unprovoked attack from India, it cannot underpin the promotion of violence in Kashmir beyond a steadily falling point. As a nuclear power, Pakistan has to develop a far more responsible image than it currently has. The recently confirmed transfer of nuclear technology from Pakistan to North Korea, Iran and Libya has been soft-pedalled by the US administration because of tactical compulsions, but there can be little doubt that Pakistan's image has been badly tarnished the world over. Nuclear weapons do not mix well with religious extremism or trans-border military activity. Sooner or later India is going to get accepted as a recognised nuclear power. Pakistan has to decide whether it wants to be a responsible nuclear power like India, or degenerate into an unacceptable one imprisoned by sanctions and threats. Pakistan's current Kashmir policy is a massive impediment to gaining nuclear legitimacy.

Pakistan has evolved over the years. The separation of Bangladesh in 1971 changed the country fundamentally. It no longer carried the significance, or the burden, of being the 'homeland' of subcontinental

Muslims. It also ceased to be an unnatural construct in political atlases. The forced shedding of internal colonialism in the east has made it a more viable socio-economic entity. Yet, Pakistan's fortunes have not improved. Three decades after 1971, it is in grievous trouble and most people in the country, including in the military, know it. If the 1980s turned out to be disastrous for Pakistan in social terms, the 1990s proved to be so in economic terms as well. More and more Pakistanis are becoming aware that the country is facing slow enervation from which there is no easy escape.

The compelled U-turn of Pakistan's policy in Afghanistan in September 2001 has shaken the establishment and the society to the core. Within the establishment there is a growing acceptance that the use of extremist Islam for domestic political and foreign policy purposes have now run aground, and that without shedding it Pakistan cannot become stable or prosperous. Thoughtful Pakistanis have long understood this. The comprehension has now spread wider. The link between Muslim extremism and the country's Kashmir strategy is also getting better recognised. Pakistanis have become less aggressive towards India, and this change in attitude is discernible across classes. There is grudging, but growing, appreciation that Pakistan has no way of balancing India and that India's broad dominance in South Asia cannot be undone.

This does not mean that there is any momentum in support of 'giving up' Kashmir. What there is instead is a weariness with the costs involved, and a desire to shift the struggle to a less active plane. Some sections among the upper- and middle-classes are ready today to settle Kashmir on the basis of status quo, but the vast majority, including two crucial groups—the Army and the clergy-influenced lower classes—are not. There is the realisation that the extremist groups, which have torn Pakistan's society and economy apart for a long time, and post-2001, have brought on international opprobrium and even danger, need to be reined in. But Pakistan finds itself unable to do this without weakening its leverage in Kashmir.

India has changed a good deal too. The major political change during the 1990s, in the eyes of many observers, has been the rise of the BJP and the Hindutwa ideology. In terms of India–Pakistan relations, this is seen by many as a new and major barrier to peace.[1] But

---

[1] The BJP is actually quite well-positioned to deliver peace. It is less vulnerable to the charge of 'sell out' than the Congress is. Also, the party's modernist wing has

the political ascent of the BJP is not the only big Indian story of the last decade. An even bigger one is the way economic thinking has changed. In the economic field, India is an altogether different country from what it was a decade go. In recent years, its growth rate has been second only to China's. Elite and middle-class Indians are against any course that would hurt economic growth. The BJP's decision to shift focus from identity to development politics in its 2004 general election campaign shows the changed mood in the country. Disproving predictions, the Gujarat riots of 2002 were not replicated elsewhere in the country.

At elite- and middle-class levels, India has become very outward looking in recent years. There are nearly 6 million Indians in the West and the Middle East. The advanced West is being brought to India in many ways—the latest being business process outsourcing that not only pulls in money but also an understanding of how systems operate and lives are lived in rich countries. There is a new concern about how the world sees India. India wants to look good so that investment, trade and overseas work opportunities expand. Indians want the country to shed its image of being strife-ridden. They want the $3 billion annual foreign direct investment flow to multiply ten times and get closer to China's. Increasing numbers of Indians now realise that the magnetism China exerts on FDI has much to do with the peaceful conditions in that country. If peace with Pakistan becomes possible on terms that safeguard India's broad interests, the bulk of the Indian elite and middle-class will happily opt for it.

The outside world's interest in Kashmir and India–Pakistan relations has largely been confined to avoiding war and nuclear proliferation. The 1998 nuclear tests, the 1999 Kargil War and the 2002 Parakram confrontation have served to conflate these areas and create a new, much-gazed-through prism of nuclear war risk. Within a year of the 1998 tests, the US and others recognised that there was no chance of containing the nuclear capability of the two sides through the NPT–CTBT–FMCT path. A few now think that the problem may be better handled through dispute-settlement in Kashmir, but those who are familiar with South Asia know how difficult it is for outsiders to play a serious role.

recently been gaining policy ascendancy, and coalition compulsions have been curbing its extremist instincts.

Major powers know that there is little they can do to move India or Pakistan against their judgement. India has always been too big and independent, and Pakistan has been adept at exerting counter-pressure in a variety of ways. India's strengthening relations with the US has made sure that no pressure will be exerted against its core interests in Kashmir. The concern against Islamic terrorism is certain to constrain Pakistan's ability to promote violence in Kashmir, but it is unlikely to eliminate it entirely. Pakistan is now painfully caught between the US and the jihadis, but the US is unable to exert pressure that is strong enough to make Pakistan do a U-turn in a matter as important as Kashmir is to it. The country's nuclear capability and the fear of Islamists gaining strength act as limiting factors.

For both countries, giving up territory already with them—fought for in four wars—is an absolute political no-no. No peace can therefore be built except upon the existing division. Aside from the fact that there is no political alternative to it, the existing LoC has a fair degree of security and cultural logic as well. The divide reflects the two countries' power-reach at partition. It was arrived at after fifteen months of fighting, in which the political hold of the two sides on different sections of the state's people as well as their military reach played roles. It is a defendable divide too for both sides. Very little territory could be captured across it during the 1965 and 1971 wars. The LoC is also a broad cultural divide. The Kashmiri-speakers are mostly on the Indian side, while the Punjabi dialect speakers are mostly on the Pakistani side.

Since India—in implicit bottom line terms—has always been willing to accept the LoC as a permanent division, the obstacle is Pakistan. How can Pakistan be made to accept a solution that has been effectively on offer for half a century, and which Pakistan has consistently spurned? How can that country, which has used grievance against India on account of Kashmir as glue for national unity, maintain its cohesion after rescinding its claim? How can the Pakistan Army, which stands to lose a great deal as a result, accept such a deal? How can Muslim radicals, who have built themselves up largely on the basis of fighting for Kashmir, accept it? Finding practical answers to these questions constitutes the heart of a peace strategy in Kashmir. But before getting there, it is necessary to be clear about who the key players are on the two sides—the players who have the ability to move the conflict to a peace path should they want to.

THE KEY PLAYERS

The key players in this conflict, whether in the default mode of shuffling between tension and crisis or in the occasional mode of working towards peace, are not the governments of the day in Delhi and Islamabad, much less the heads of governments on whose pronouncements so much media attention is showered. Even powerful heads of government like Nehru, Indira Gandhi, Rajiv Gandhi and Vajpayee on the Indian side, and Ayub Khan, Zulfiqar Bhutto, Zia-ul-Haq, Nawaz Sharif and Musharraf on the Pakistan side have enjoyed little freedom of action with regard to India–Pakistan relations. In India, prime ministers have always been captive to the country's influential public opinion. In Pakistan, leaders have had to defer to the Pakistan Army as an institution. No peace effort has a chance of success unless the peace process and the end it could lead to are recognised by these principal players—India's influential public and Pakistan's Army—as serving their national as well as group interests. The emphasis on these two players must not, however, allow one to overlook the presence of a key third player in the field, and whose importance has grown over the years—the people of the Kashmir Valley who seek autonomy within India.

Unless a desire for peace underpinned by realpolitik develops within the wider Indian elite, there can be little hope in Kashmir. The elite in Pakistan, outside the Army, does not have anything close to the influence in security matters that the elite in India has. The term elite is used here in a specific sense to include all those who can influence policy, even from the periphery in India. In national security and foreign policy matters, the remainder of the Indian population, over 95 per cent, takes its cue from this group. Security and foreign policies have never been an electoral issue of consequence in the country. The politico-bureaucratic establishment and the media, both of which represent the elite, shape them. The Indian elite is far from uniform in its views, but in security matters the spread of opinion is relatively less. It is capable of considerable flexibility. The last decade has seen big shifts in elite views on issues like central planning, global engagement, and the role of the US in the world.

On Pakistan and Kashmir, the elite has long-held views which it has not felt necessary to re-think. Not much economic or strategic advantage is seen in seeking better relations with Pakistan, or in improving governance within Kashmir. The economic and strategic arena of relevance to India is the wider world, not the subcontinent. Moreover, Pakistan with its Islamic zealotry, military dominance and feudal politics is not seen as a viable peace partner. The prescription of security experts—'wait for Pakistan to change and ignore it in the meanwhile'—is considered sensible. The question whether India was not aiding regressive Islam and the Army's grip in Pakistan by its policy of hostile non-engagement is not asked. Or, related questions such as, can the Pakistani masses be expected to shake off the Army when they feel plausibly threatened by India, and can the Army be made to break with fundamentalist Islam when it finds the jihadis its best weapon against India.

After the brief Jinnah–Liaquat period, the only powerful civilian leaders that Pakistan has had are Zulfiquar Bhutto and Nawaz Sharif. Both, especially Sharif in his second innings, had strong electoral mandates. Yet, neither could stand up to the Army when it came to the crunch. Is there reason to expect that another democratic leader—friendly to India and capable of keeping the Army in its place—has a chance to come up? On a different plane, is India's opposition to the Pakistan Army based on democratic principle or on the Army's structural opposition to India? It cannot be the former, for India has excellent relations with Iran, Saudi Arabia, Bhutan and Myanmar. The real problem India has with the Pakistan Army is its interest in perpetuating hostility towards India. Can this vested interest be altered by applying an incentive-based strategy? The widely-shared perception in India is that it cannot be. The Pakistan Army is seen as privileging institutional interests over national interests, inextricably linked to fanatical Islamists, incapable of thinking in the long term and unamenable to incentives. These are perceptions that deserve a closer look.

The political centrality of the Army in Pakistan rests a great deal on its role as the nation's guardian against India. But the unstable base of Pakistan's democracy has also contributed. Ayub's military take over in 1958 and Zia's in 1977 had nothing to do with India; they were wholly centred on Pakistan's domestic politics. Policy towards India was a factor in Musharraf's 1999 coup, but domestic factors—especially Sharif's attempt to split and weaken the Army—were also important. Anti-Indianism is not an Army monopoly. The Pakistani leader most hostile to India so far has been Zulfiqar Bhutto. He was primarily responsible for the failure of the 1962–63 talks on Kashmir and played a major role in Pakistan's attack on India in 1965, and in precipitating the 1971 war. He was, as he claimed, the father of Pakistan's nuclear bomb. Later, Benazir Bhutto and Nawaz Sharif alternated as heads of government from before militancy began in Kashmir in 1989 till Sharif was toppled after Kargil. Out of office, each castigated the other for being weak towards India. Sharif was Prime Minister during the Kargil War, and he had approved the operation. The Pakistan Army was certainly the greater villain in all these, but the fact remains that neither Bhutto nor Sharif could muster public support to rein in the Army.

The degree to which the rise of fundamentalist Islam should be attributed to the Army is also worth thinking about. Extremism-promoting Saudi money that poured into Pakistan from 1974, and the post-1979 US-supported use of the mujahideen against the Soviets in Afghanistan, were the major factors that promoted fundamentalism. There are Islamists, and in sizeable number, in the Army. But they are also part of all sections of Pakistani society. There are more officers with Islamic fervour today than before Zia came along. But it is worth noting that, after Aslam Beg who succeeded Zia, Pakistan has not had an Army Chief who could be called an Islamist. The Army has used Islamic extremists against India with zeal. But while some officers—like ISI chiefs Hamid Gul and Javed Nasir—were ideologically aligned with them, the Army as an institution has largely looked upon them as instruments. The Army and the Islamists are not natural bedfellows anywhere. Turkey, Algeria, Indonesia and Egypt are examples. Islamists are difficult to control and control is a basic requirement for any Army.

The Army has pulled the strings in Pakistan since 1958, regardless of whether the country has a democratic or a military façade at a given time. Possession of nuclear weapons has enhanced its status. Wielding direct or indirect power for forty-five years, it has both experience and confidence. It now dominates political institutions and processes even when exercising indirect control. It has an institutional ally in the civil bureaucracy, and as a result it is more resourceful than political parties and Islamic groups. Yet, while the Army can outmanoeuvre political parties much of the time, it has serious weaknesses. It cannot provide a clean government or overcome the massive structural impediments to economic growth. Ayub Khan, Yahya Khan and Zia-ul-Haq all ended up deeply unpopular.

Rabid anti-India feelings in Pakistan are now confined to Islamic extremists who form only a small minority. Basing the Army's political fortunes on such a group is dangerous—domestically because of the small size of the group, and internationally because of the group's anti-US instincts. It is difficult to juggle military dictatorship, militant Islam and nuclear weapons. The Army is also confronted with the rapid widening of the India–Pakistan military gap. The enlarging differential in the size of the economies, and the determination of an enraged India to bleed Pakistan through arms competition, are making the Pakistan Army's position steadily more difficult. Russian and Israeli military technologies are playing a usefully complementing role, and the excellent access India has to both is making Pakistan's military hardware rapidly obsolescent.

Thoughtful elements within the Pakistan Army understand that the present confrontational policy towards India is pushing the country along a path of socio-economic decline, and that in turn would strengthen domestic opposition to the Army. The people of Pakistan are now more aware that it is utterly beyond the country's capability to alter the territorial status quo in Kashmir. Trying to keep alive the contrary hope, in conditions of serious economic malaise and political unrest, is risky. The damage done to the Army's image by the self-inflicted Kargil wound was a sobering lesson. Objectively viewed, the time has come for the Army to seriously reconsider its policy towards India. But it is difficult for it to do that without India's help. The army cannot—without suffering a decisive military defeat—accept the LoC as the permanent border unless the deal is dressed up to look like an honourable one.

India's distaste for the Pakistan Army combines realpolitik with ideology. Military rule stigmatises Pakistan and gives India a plausible reason not to engage it. But India needs to ask whether it is possible for a democratic dispensation in Pakistan, guarding its flanks against both the military and the Islamists, to settle with India. Can a peace agreement that is not in the Army's interest be made? The reality is that if a deal were to be made, the Army would want to take the credit. It will not let a political leader take it. The continuing acceptance at the mass level of the Army as the ultimate guarantor of Pakistan— seen as a vulnerable Muslim state next to a big, hostile neighbour—is a fact of life. It is only the Army that can make an accommodation with India politically acceptable.

But would the Army want to do it? The Army has an anti-Indian attitude that is more organic than among political parties. The threat seen from India is more sharply defined in its worldview than that of others. The Army knows that it is to this threat that it primarily owes its dominant domestic position. Normalisation of relations with India will not only force upon the Army a difficult recasting of its strategic rationale, but also a disagreeable acceptance of reduced political power and its attendant advantages. But on the other hand, the choices available to the Army are diminishing. Pakistan's financial and political constraints are rapidly widening the conventional military gap. This in turn is worsening the country's dangerous dependence on the two extremes of the military spectrum—terrorism and nuclear weapons. If India creates cross-border incidents and carries out sharp, punishing strikes that the Pakistan military is unable to handle, the Army's standing within the country could badly suffer.

Although the Indian elite and the Pakistan Army make the most important parties in a peace process, the people of J&K are important too. No doubt, the people of the state have no option but to go along with whatever agreement India and Pakistan might arrive at. But the constraints in the situation make it impossible for India and Pakistan to strike a deal without involving the Kashmiris. Both sides need them to bargain better, and to make the post-settlement path smoother. It is fortunate for India that it does not have to talk to any militant group. The ones it would have to talk to and find common ground with are the groups demanding autonomy in a peaceful fashion. Some of them may now be mouthing *azadi*, but their bottom line is autonomy, and the discussions with them would only entail its extent.

A Peace Strategy

As in many conflict-resolution cases, the big difficulty in Kashmir is not the end solution, but the creation of a path towards the solution zone. This is often not seen to be the case because the current official position of Pakistan— 'the LoC cannot be the solution because it is the problem'—is considered inflexible, and therefore not compatible with a realistic resolution. But, as has been brought out earlier, Pakistan can be made to accept the 'LoC as final border' idea, provided it is made part of a broader deal. Today, both sides do not want to explore that approach. Diplomatic positions, military measures and internal political stances on each side are intricately inter-connected, and there is fear that a shift in one would have a weakening fall-out on the others. Both sides have a problem analysing the impact of possible changes because neither is adequately unified nor purposive in policy-making. Actions are contingent and improvised. And vested interests and prejudiced mindsets dominate.

India and Pakistan have always shared one strategy towards each other: a war strategy, whether there has been actual fighting underway or not. A war or coercive strategy is conceived in terms of how one actor can force the other to do things it does not want to do. A peace strategy, on the other hand, must be ideated in terms of encouraging the opponent to respond positively. It must create a path that would lead to both sides finding it advantageous to change and cooperate. Such a strategy calls for more hard-headed, realist thinking than a war strategy, because it needs suppressing emotions a good deal. There is a need to shift from tactical to strategic thinking too. Today, both countries are focusing on tactics—in foreign policy, in war-fighting and in internal political policy. Both have been fairly good at it, but neither has been able to consolidate tactical gains into strategic success. It is important that a peace strategy must leave the weaker opponent a bearable way out. An Indian peace strategy should threaten neither Pakistan nor its power structure.

Considering that there are two parties that India has to deal with in Kashmir—Pakistan and the discontented in the state—there are theoretically two extreme approaches from India's point of view. One is to arrive at a territorial division that satisfies Pakistan, and thereafter treat J&K like any other state in India. The other is to satisfy the autonomy aspirations in J&K and make Pakistan irrelevant. There is no possibility of a territorial adjustment that can assuage Pakistan. The option of placating the state's Muslims through greater autonomy and ignoring Pakistan is also unlikely to work, because Pakistan now has the ability to dissuade a significant part of the state's Muslims from accepting a deal that Pakistan cannot live with. A workable deal has to bring on board both Pakistan and the moderate Muslims in J&K. Since the wishes of the two parties are very different from one another's, and India is the party both have to deal with, India has considerable clout to make the two compete when serious negotiations begin.

The key Indian requirement is that India should be able to work out an arrangement with the Kashmiri discontented, without Pakistan intervening negatively. The key requirement for Pakistan is to be able to withdraw from the tactically-offensive strategy it has adopted, without its security being jeopardised, or its political self-respect compromised. The Pakistan Army's play in Kashmir is one of offensive–defence. It is not aimed at gaining territory. The aim is to keep India distracted and on the defensive so that neither Pakistan nor the Army's grip on power is threatened. India has to help Pakistan and its Army feel secure without having to play this game.

A realistic peace strategy has to be built around two key principles—one, the grievances of the Kashmiris' need to be addressed through political restructuring, and two, the solution has to be built around the LoC. The challenge is to bring these ideas together and weave them synergistically. Pakistanis, including the military, know that there is no prospect of gaining any territory with India through any means—military force, irregular warfare, terrorism, international pressure or bilateral negotiations. The only way Pakistan can gain and project any satisfaction is by being able to claim that it has been successful in securing a degree of autonomy for the people of J&K. Fortunately, unlike in the case of ceding territory, most Indians do not have a non-negotiable position on autonomy.

Linking the concepts of LoC-into-border and autonomy poses major political challenges. For Pakistan, it will be tough to sell to its public the idea that autonomy for J&K within India is a partial recompense for giving up its fifty-six-year old claim for the state. One way a Pakistan government can sell it is by claiming that India has ceased 'repressing' the Muslims of Kashmir. In recent years Pakistan has been stressing 'repression' more than the right of self-determination. This gives a Pakistani leader some manoeuvrability to present an autonomy deal as a partial success for Pakistan. But to make such a dangerous effort at political marketing, a Pakistani leader would need both incentive and help—in large quantities. Cranking down institutional hostility is as much a problem in Pakistan as it is in India. And in dealing with religion-driven movements, Pakistan's problem is greater.

For India too there is a big political challenge. To link negotiations with Pakistan and autonomy arrangements in J&K is to accept an indirect role for Pakistan in Kashmir—something India has strenuously denied all along. Selling this shift to the Indian public will not be easy, although it would be less difficult than what the Pakistani government would have to do. For India, there is also the practical problem of coordinating the Pakistani and Kashmiri tracks of the talks, maintaining a tricky mix of linkage and distance. Only the tangible prospect of an entirely new relationship with Pakistan, closing the Kashmir chapter permanently, can induce India to attempt these challenges.

The other big 'linking challenge' in a Kashmir peace strategy is connecting the process of negotiations with a broadly agreed end result. In most peace-making efforts, the matter of 'process' is looked at differently by the two parties. The stronger and more status quo-oriented party will project an ample, evolving process as necessary to soften mindsets, and build cooperative attitudes. The weaker and change-seeking party sees a long-drawn-out process as designed to weaken it further. The idea, popular in India, of a slow accretion of small measures—political, military, economic and cultural—that can gradually transform the conflict is unacceptable to Pakistan, because it sees a 'normal' relationship increasing India's negotiating weight. Pakistan is convinced that a slow, fuzzy track will work markedly to its disadvantage and, therefore, its insistence that peace negotiations must be front-loaded.

Any peace process must involve a series of steps. It is impossible to agree on a quick package-deal that takes care of all differences at one go. The issue therefore is not of choosing between an instant agreement and a stretched out negotiating process. It is instead about the speed of negotiations and the presence of a joint vision of the destination zone. A leisurely approach to peace, spread over several years and with no clear idea of where the process might lead to, is possible if the atmosphere is not vitiated by violence. But such a path is difficult when fighting makes the negotiating climate stressful and strengthens the hawks on both sides. In such a situation a road map-approach, with reciprocal commitments and a joint understanding of the end game, has a much higher chance of success.

The ambient conditions necessary for productive peace talks in Kashmir, created through reduction in violence, cannot hold long unless tangible progress is made in addressing substantive issues. The Oslo Agreement between Israel and the PLO—two parties that had never talked to each other earlier—was hammered out in eight months. The decisive part of the negotiations that preceded the 1972 US–China Shanghai Communiqué had lasted only a year. Realistically, about a year is the maximum time that it should take to reach an agreement on principles on Kashmir. If it is not achieved within this timeframe, negotiations are likely to dribble off the field again. It is also important that, when the principles of settlement are agreed upon, there is a major event like the 1972 Shanghai Communiqué that decisively modifies the optics through which the two sides look at the conflict and at each other.

Large segments of influential public on both sides have flexible views. Intellectually convinced or viscerally rigid hardliners form only small percentages. In both countries, it is the pessimism about the success of peace-making, more than anything else, that contributes to the hang-in-there approach. People who understand the link between economic development and a stable socio-political environment is growing in number in India and Pakistan. With the growth of private enterprise, the numbers who can relate the advantages of peaceful conditions to their own well being are also growing. Animosity in India towards Pakistan, in a widespread sense, is largely the product of post-1989 Pakistan-promoted violence. A softening of Indian mood is very likely if a successful peace process becomes a palpable prospect.

Many fail to note the light and shadow quality of feelings between Indians and Pakistanis. A clear indicator that people-level anger is largely a reflection of state-to-state hostility is that when Indians and Pakistanis meet as individuals or families there is rarely any tension. It is only when they meet in groups that political differences and postures come up, pushing aside cultural commonality. Those who travel across the border the first time are always surprised at the warmth and grace they encounter. Opinion surveys, reaching out to true cross-sections of society, will bring out the vast reservoirs of the corked goodwill and desire for peace that are present in both countries. Such surveys are likely to show several things. One, views are plastic and respond significantly to events, especially violence. Two, among the less well-off people, constituting a huge majority in both countries, there are no hardened feelings. Their feelings are roused in times of tension, but they do not stay roused. Three, the dominant emotion in the two countries is anger towards the other side's government, not dislike towards each other as people. This is an important fact that has a great bearing on how the opinion on options can change when peace becomes a genuine prospect.

The media in both countries have a big role to play in any peace process. Today, people are conditioned by the sameness of negative headlines and comment. In both countries people talk of the other side's media as extensions of its foreign ministry. There are several mainstream TV producers and editors in both countries who support peace. Yet, their channels and papers always give prominence to hardline views. In commentaries, extreme statements are mined and quoted. 'Facts' about Kashmir are liberally shaped by emotion, and the past distorted by selective historical presentations. In recent years, the Indian media has become a little more aggressive towards Pakistan. Pakistan-sponsored violence in Kashmir has been the main cause. On the other side, the Pakistani media has toned down a fraction the high levels of bellicosity that was on display earlier—reflecting perhaps a better understanding of current realities.

The case that Kashmir rightly belongs to it has been strongly built in both countries. Pakistan's 'Kashmir runs in our veins' and India's 'Kashmir is the core of our nationhood' are examples of the rhetoric in vogue. This makes it difficult to move towards peace without mutual help. To pursue peace, the leaders of India and Pakistan need each other much more than they are prepared to admit. It is the signals from the other side, even more than from one's own side, that impact on the public. Pakistan's leadership needs India's help for it to want to, and to be able to, sell the reality of a permanent LoC to its people. India needs Pakistan's help to achieve normalcy in Kashmir, and to convince Indians that autonomy, on both sides of the new border, can help with both security and peace.

An India–Pakistan agreement on Kashmir, if it is to lead to long-term amity, may have to be built along the following lines. The LoC should become a mutually accepted international border. Jammu & Kashmir, or at least the Muslim majority areas of the state should be given substantial autonomy. There must be corresponding autonomy in POK. Equal and substantial autonomy to both parts, accompanied by low levels of military presence is likely to best succeed, not only in arriving at a mutually acceptable agreement but also in sustaining it without tension. For its psychological and associational value, some inter-governmental organisations at the levels of Srinagar–Muzaffarabad and Delhi–Islamabad should be created to oversee subjects such as environment and tourism in the two parts of the state.

India and Pakistan should have adequate military presence in their respective parts of the state to assure external and internal security. But this should be kept to the lowest possible level. An India–Pakistan treaty should be concluded to seal the agreement. The UNSC resolutions on plebiscite should be rescinded. This approach has one major difference from the position agreed upon in Northern Ireland, as well as from the solutions suggested by many with regard to Kashmir. It is that the agreement arrived at should be final and there should be no provision for ascertaining the views of the people of the state at a later stage.[2] Any provision for a future reference will keep the two parts of the state unsettled and place India and Pakistan in a competitive framework, something that must be determinedly avoided.

There are several reasons why cross-border links would be desirable in J&K. One, they will act as a check on military activity on both sides. Two, they will provide forums for regular India–Pakistan cooperation and to deal with problems in their embryonic stage. Three, since the original state shall now be permanently divided in terms of sovereignty, there should be some means to ensure that ethnic and cultural bonds are not severed. In addition to cross-border links, it would be desirable to have a somewhat softened border between the divided parts. This will help the people in each part to get a good idea of what is going on in the other part. It will help promote democracy in Pakistan's part of the state, and eventually in Pakistan as a whole. A soft border does not mean an open border; it only means that there should be several crossover points for people to move freely using identity cards, or even passports, but without pre-issued visas.

Economic dynamism between India and Pakistan, and within South Asia as a whole, should be a crucial component of a peace strategy. Mutual grant of MFA status, adhering to WTO commitments, and opening multiple transport corridors in J&K (such as Jammu–Sialkot, Srinagar–Uri–Muzzafarbad and Kargil–Skardu) as well as outside could be the first steps. The already agreed upon South Asia Free Trade Area should be seriously promoted. The best start in economic relations can perhaps be made through gas pipelines to India from West and Central Asia across Pakistan. Gas pipelines will not only be of substantial economic benefit to both countries, but will have a big impact on popular thinking because of the implied long-range commitment to cooperation. An Iran–Pakistan–India pipeline has been estimated at $3.1 billion at 2001 prices, and a Turkmenistan–Afghanistan–Pakistan–India pipeline at $4.8 billion. Suitable penalty

---

[2] For a recent example of wanting to push the final decision into the future, see Kashmir Study Group, *Kashmir: A Way Forward*, Larchmont, NY, February 2000.

clauses triggering sanctions should be able to guard against disruption of flow.

A good place to make a positive start in Kashmir is the Siachen glacier area, which is geographically a part of J&K. There is no population in this disputed area other than soldiers risking pulmonary oedema. The soldiers too have been there only since 1984—thirty-seven years after the Kashmir problem erupted. The area has no resources and no strategic value. No military thrust in any direction can be mounted from or through it. The absence of people, resources and a strategic angle make it possible to demilitarise the Siachen area quite easily. A 'neutral zone', between the two alignments claimed by India and Pakistan from Point NJ9842 to the China border, should suit both countries. Today, India employs some 10,000 men and Pakistan about 4,000 to maintain and support their precarious, hugely expensive perches above the glacier.

It has been suggested that both sides should withdraw their forces and treat the area as a jointly-managed Wilderness Reserve. This proposal, if implemented, would create a healthy track of cooperation. A Siachen agreement also has the advantage in that Pakistan can project the area's demilitarisation as a 'gain' to partially offset its acceptance of the LoC as permanent. On Siachen, popular opinion in India is primarily concerned with not letting go an area that India took possession of in a daring operation, and has held for two decades facing huge difficulties. There is also an erroneous belief in the area's strategic value, because of the spin given to it at the time of the operation and frequently thereafter. These perceptions will alter when the realities are presented in conditions leading to peace.

The two remaining disputes concern Sir Creek and Wullar/Tulbul. Sir Creek forms the mouth through which the waters of the Rann of Kutch and the Arabian Sea link. The India–Pakistan boundary runs through the Sir Creek for 64 kilometres. Including this, the last 104 kilometres of the boundary is disputed. Since the meeting point of the boundary with the sea is questioned, there is also a dispute about the dividing line between the EEZs. The resolution of this dispute is desirable (fishing boats are frequently impounded for EEZ violation), but it is not critical. Arbitration, as in the case of Rann of Kutch in 1966–68, is a possibility.

The Wullar/Tulbul dispute concerns a barrage built by India across the Jhelum river, whose waters have been assigned to Pakistan under the Indus River Treaty. Pakistan disputes the Indian view that the barrage is only to facilitate navigation, and that it cannot impact on the flow of water. This too is not a major issue, although unless it is settled there is scope for more such disputes to arise. India is the upper riparian country for the Indus, Jhelum and Chenab—the rivers that flow through J&K with waters allotted to Pakistan. There is already a burgeoning dispute about the Baglihar dam on the Chenab.

Finally, there is the issue of military confidence building measures, including with respect to nuclear weapons. To avoid tension there should be fairly large zones on both sides of the permanent border in J&K that are either demilitarised or subject to restricted military presence. There should be provision for cooperative surveillance to a certain depth on either side, assisted perhaps in the initial years by an international force. There is some asymmetry in the way the LoC relates militarily to the border security of the two sides. Pakistan has shorter supply lines to the LoC but also has more vulnerable points, including cities, close to the LoC. This difference would have to be addressed when working out demilitarisation arrangements. But the bigger problem is to make sure that there is no infiltration across the new permanent border.

Some understanding with regard to the broader military capabilities of the two sides outside J&K—both conventional and nuclear—would be desirable, but might be difficult to arrive at. Discussions on conventional force-level relativity between the two countries cannot be fruitful, not only because of India's concerns about China but also because of India's need to build up its forces in a manner appropriate for a country of its size. The disparity between the two countries' conventional forces will continue to grow, propelled by India's economy which is seven times bigger. What could be attempted realistically is to evolve some restrictive regimes with regard to exercises and deployments close to the border.

Nuclear weapons pose a problem too. If a peace treaty is signed, the current momentum to increase the readiness levels of weapons can certainly be checked. Both countries could also perhaps be persuaded to sign the CTBT and the FMCT, though not the NPT. Achieving greater transparency of arsenals with regard to numbers and deployment may not be possible for a long time because of fears of preventive and pre-emptive attacks. There is also the matter of both countries getting fitted into the international nuclear weapons regime. It would not be an easy matter. But something that can certainly be done is to improve the security of weapons and fissile material with the two sides, especially Pakistan's. There are ways of addressing this without the two countries having to reveal their weapon locations.

The Autonomy Issue

The matter of providing adequate and parallel autonomy on both sides will be a major political challenge for India and Pakistan. The bulk of India's public understands that J&K is different from other states, and needs to be treated differently. But as matters have taken shape on the ground, the state's once-considerable autonomy has been greatly reduced. Reversing this will not be easy. In Pakistan, the challenge might be even greater because the demand for autonomy has been voiced only feebly there, and the government and the public have not had to think about it.

In India there is little understanding of the long process that led to discontent in the state getting first politicised and later militarised. Nor of the sustained project pursued to destroy the autonomy once enjoyed by the state, and still aspired to by its people. The fact that the administration of the state cannot be improved without political loosening and that Kashmiri politicians trying to stay in power squeezed between Delhi and the Kashmiris can achieve little is not recognised. There is a lack of realisation that the money that Delhi has poured into the state all these decades has not helped and that pouring more in the future is unlikely to help—unless the politically-imposed constraints on governance are removed. It is also not seen that while India as a whole is an admirable liberal democracy, the state of J&K has not been one because of political and security demands. And there is little introspection about the causes that have stood in the way of India winning over the Kashmiris during 1947–87, and especially during 1972–87 when cross border interference by Pakistan—military or political—was very little.

Many in India do not see that autonomous governance is needed to relieve India of delegitimising unrest in J&K. And that autonomy offers the best means to segregate the political and territorial dimensions of the call for *azadi*. Pakistan's entire leverage against India rests on the discontent in Kashmir. It is not and cannot be sustained only through foreign militants. Moreover, the critical issue in J&K is not administrative efficiency, but democratic justness. It is a reality that, in the eyes of most J&K Muslims, Delhi has substantially altered, without the consent of the people of the state, the conditions under which the state acceded to India. This perception needs to be addressed. The control of the Kashmiri life has long been with a combination of Delhi-beholden politicians, senior officers from the All India Services (administration and police) and senior officers of the Army, para-military forces and intelligence agencies. The Delhi-appointed governor has always been more powerful than the chief minister. This setting must be changed.

The integrity of elections in the state has always been an issue. The 2002 election that unseated the NC has been deservedly hailed as cleaner than most previous elections, but it is obvious that a genuine determination of popular will is hard to carry out in the face of widespread military presence. While the probity of elections can be monitored in Srinagar and major towns, it is difficult to do the same in the six-and-a-half thousand agricultural and pastoral habitations covered by military and para-military presence through the 'grid system', and where the media is largely absent. It is noteworthy that in Srinagar, which is well exposed to media scrutiny, the turnout in elections is invariably far lower than in the countryside. It is a reality that both militants and security forces have been curtailing the electoral freedom of the state's people.

The civil and economic rights of J&K Muslims have never been threatened in a direct manner. There has never been discrimination as in Palestine, Sri Lanka and Northern Ireland. But the territorial challenge posed by Pakistan has forced India to curtail political rights (through the misuse of Article 370 and unfree elections), which gradually led to civil rights and economic opportunities getting squeezed as well. Yet, despite these, the Kashmiris realise the benefits of staying in democratic India. What most of them want is an acceptance of the fact that J&K joined India under special circumstances, and that the state must be given greater freedom of governance than other states in India. In specific terms, they want a substantial reduction in the presence of security forces, to make the bureaucracy and the police at senior levels conform to the state's demographic profile, to make elections genuinely fair, and to make sure that elected governments are not at the mercy of Delhi. None of this poses serious difficulty to India provided India's requirements to ensure external and internal security are taken care of.

In terms of particular measures, an Indian security expert and Kashmir specialist has recently called for the restoration of the titles of Sadar-i-Riyasat and Wazir-e-Azam, giving the state a role in the selection of governor, provisions to prevent the misuse of Article 356, giving the state services more authority and increasing its quota (to 75 per cent for twenty years) in senior appointments, appointing a regional election commissioner for the state, and providing guarantees against future reneging by the provision that any constitutional change must be approved by a referendum within the state.[3] The State Autonomy Commission Report, passed by the state assembly in June 2000 but rejected by Delhi without discussion, had proposed, among other suggestions, that Article 370 should be made permanent, India's constitutional authority in the state should be limited to the three areas specified in the 1950 constitutional order, the emergency powers with Delhi should be removed, All India Services should be withdrawn, and the titles of Sadar-i-Riyasat and Wazir-e-Azam should be restored.[4]

There has been no serious discussion yet in India about how J&K might be given more powers. There is a need to encourage an active debate on meeting the political demands of the state's people. This must be done with the government making it clear that while the contours of autonomy can be discussed, there can be no discussion on two matters—the sovereignty position, and India's security requirements in the state. A freewheeling discussion will bring to the fore the divisions, at present under wraps, between the moderates who make up the vast majority of the discontented, and the extremists. Today the talk about additional powers—whatever little there is—is being conducted at the theoretical level, bandying un-fleshed-out terms like autonomy, devolution and decentralisation. To be useful, discussions need to focus on specific demands and their rationale, and not degenerate into a conceptual debate on autonomy, where meeting points are difficult to find.

Providing additional powers to the state does not call for any amendment to the Indian constitution. Existing constitutional provisions

[3] Amitabh Mattoo, 'Next Steps in Kashmir', in Karan R. Sawhny, ed., *Kashmir: How Far Can Vajpayee and Musharraf Go?* New Delhi: Peace Foundation, 2001, pp. 27–44.
[4] *The Report of the State Autonomy Committee*, Srinagar: Government of Jammu and Kashmir Press, 1999.

are flexible enough to explore a wide range of arrangements, both with respect to J&K as a whole and to the relationship between its parts. By changing some central and state laws it is possible to steer the legal base of autonomy in any politically-desired direction. There is no need to go back to the Instrument of Accession of 1947, the constitutional order of 1950, or the 1952 agreement between Nehru and Sheikh Abdullah. The 1974 agreement, arrived at between Indira Gandhi and Sheikh Abdullah (which provides for a review of most post-1953 changes), has in it an adequate political basis for restructuring autonomy.

India has to find the means to talk to the sections of the discontented that are linked to the Hurriyat leaders. Two aspects in this regard are widely ignored in India. One, the bottom line for the vast bulk of the leaders of the Hurriyat is autonomy within India, not secession. Two, there is considerable support for increased autonomy even within parties which have governed the state with Delhi's approval—the PDP which is a partner in the current government and the NC that had monopolised power earlier. By insisting that everyone in the Hurriyat is a creature of Pakistan, India has made it difficult to negotiate with the discontented who matter. This approach, if persisted with, could cut the ground from under more moderates. The PDP could end up losing credibility the way the NC has. To say that India will not talk to unelected leaders does not conform to what India has been doing elsewhere. The 1975 Accord with the Naga National Council, founded by A.Z. Phizo, was signed with unelected leaders living abroad. And for the past six years India has been negotiating with the Isaac–Muivah group of Nagas that has never fought elections and whose leaders too had been living abroad.

A major source of objection to autonomy lies within J&K. Hindus of Jammu and Buddhists of Ladakh feel that any increase in Srinagar's powers would hurt them. Greater powers to the state would, therefore, have to be tied to decentralisation within J&K. The State Autonomy Committee had recommended that the state should be divided into eight sub units, with decentralised power. Others have suggested that the present division into Kashmir, Jammu, and Ladakh should remain, although Jammu would be nearly one-third Muslim and Ladakh nearly one-half Muslim. There is also the issue of the non-Muslims of the Valley (Pandits) feeling secure, and once again becoming equal political participants there. An alternative to regionalising is the concept of power sharing in vogue in Northern Ireland. The idea of power sharing in the Kashmir context could be that on key issues a simple majority in the state assembly would not be enough. There would also have to be majority approval within the caucus from each region. This approach may or may not be accompanied by proportional representation. There are problems with power sharing such as greater likelihood of legislative deadlocks, but it has advantages such as softening regional and religious identities.

An essential requirement for autonomous governance in J&K is parallel autonomy in POK. It will not be easy for Pakistan to match the 'democratic autonomy' that India might extend to its side of the LoC. The military-dominated, authoritative form of governance within Pakistan as a whole will pose difficulty. Azad Jammu and Kashmir (AJK) got adult franchise only in 1970. The people there are unhappy with the control exercised from Islamabad through the MKA. The majority of the people there, while wanting to stay with Pakistan, would like greater control over their affairs. There is also a desire for the northern areas to be re-connected to it. In the Shia-majority northern areas there is considerable ethnic (eight major groups) as well as sectarian (four Muslim sects) diversity. Despite the 1979 establishment of the elected Northern Areas Council, this vast, sparsely-populated territory is still essentially army-administered. Full adult franchise was introduced as recently as 1994. Both AJK and northern areas would need to be substantially liberalised politically for the concept of parallel and equal autonomy to work on the ground.

NEGOTIATIONS

Heavy historical baggage accumulated over many decades has made it difficult for India and Pakistan to engage in productive discussions. The hardened framework of conflict in which they interact makes negotiations an exercise in warfare by other means. Both foreign ministries have a globally-noted negotiating reputation for obduracy. Since both sides feel that any concession might start them down a slippery slope, talks invariably degenerate into exercises in posturing. Today, both sides look at talks primarily as forums to gain propaganda advantage. It is also a pertinently noted fact that India–Pakistan negotiating sessions never last long enough to discuss matters systematically and in depth. Meetings consist largely of re-stating earlier positions in new language and talking past each other. There are four basic reasons for the persistent failure of India–Pakistan negotiations. The first is that the parties go into talks with positions so far apart that there is no chance of gaps being narrowed during discussions. On Kashmir, India is not only unwilling to make any territorial compromise but is also unable to offer anything else. The second problem is that the public on both sides are not sensitised to the need to move from previously-held positions. Both governments, understandably, do not want to mould public opinion positively when there is no prospect of agreement. The third obstacle is the high level of distrust between the two sides. Neither considers the other a trustworthy negotiating partner. There are strong suspicions of thin-end wedges, traps and backtracking. The fourth difficulty is that neither side is unified with regard to negotiating flexibility. In Lahore in January 1999, Nawaz Sharif was prepared to be a good deal more flexible than the Army was. And in Agra in July 2001, Vajpayee was willing to go further than his powerful deputy, Advani.

For negotiations to have a chance of success all four difficulties need to be addressed. It has long been clear that foreign ministry-level talks can and have narrowed the gaps between the positions on Siachin and Wullar/Tulbul, and can even do so on Sir Geek, but it is not possible with Kashmir. If either side shows flexibility on Kashmir during formal negotiations, the hawks of that side will take wing. Back channels, perhaps involving a discreet third party in whom both sides have confidence, can be useful. Such channels will enable options to be examined without committing the parties publicly in any manner. Only when mutually acceptable concepts emerge need they be brought up formally. During 1998–2001, there was a back channel in operation but it had little feed into decisive discussions.

The second problem—preparing the influential public for a shift in stances—also needs forthright addressing. The atmosphere outside negotiating rooms is as important as what goes on inside them. As matters stand, the public mood in both countries needs to be thawed before governments can act. This requires confidence building steps such as curbs on propaganda, the re-opening of Mumbai and Karachi consulates, overland cross-border travel, easier grant of visas, and more freedom of travel within each other's country. Some hard rhetoric might be necessary to convey 'strength' to the other side and to keep the hawks on one's own side grounded, but it must not get out of hand. Given the past record of India–Pakistan negotiations, it is dangerous to allow momentum to be lost. With strong and entrenched anti-peace constituencies on both sides, loss of momentum (as in Agra) can prove very damaging. It is useful to stage well-publicised, cooperative 'events' with significant symbolic value. Track II meetings, with their exploratory and analytical discussion content released to the media, can also play a useful role.

Reducing distrust is the third big difficulty. Distrust arises largely from negative expectations about the willingness of the other side to change. Back channels can play a useful role in drawing out and recognising the other side's flexibility. Flexibility is reciprocal and conditional. Unless it is sought through a cooperative effort, it will not be found. There is a big difference between goodwill gestures and signalling flexibility. The former can help thaw frozen positions, but cannot underpin useful negotiations. For that, each side's willingness to re-examine positions has to be conveyed. In India–Pakistan negotiations, the broad contours of a possible agreement (LoC into border, substantial and parallel autonomy, cross-border links, and cooperative security arrangements) must be accepted by both sides early enough so that discussions can move on to the many variants possible within that framework. Discussions would call for careful analysis of mutual misgivings and anxieties. The steps needed to address these in a progressive manner must be identified. Tacit bargaining involving some coercive effort is an inevitable parallel to negotiations, but it should be calibrated. Great care is needed not to get into a mutually reinforcing negative cycle, typical of India–Pakistan interactions.

The last major difficulty lies in getting each side to develop a unified negotiating stance in favour of peace. In policy-making circles in both countries there are fairly integrated views about their respective national interests with regard to the Kashmir issue, but there is a fair spread of opinion about how best they should be promoted. Some are more aware of how ground realities have altered over the years and how the global environment has changed, while others are still stuck in old grooves. As a result, while negotiations might start because some sections within both establishments are willing to explore peace, sooner or later those who oppose the process are able to sabotage it. Lahore 1999 and Agra 2001 are warning examples. It is vital therefore that there is effective internal agreement on each side, not just about starting negotiations, but also about the changes from previous stances that it is prepared to make.

A major negotiating challenge for India is the need to carry out in parallel a strategic dialogue with Pakistan and a political dialogue with the Kashmiris. India's insistence that the Pakistani and Kashmiri tracks should remain entirely unconnected has led to a situation where no effective dialogue is possible with either party. Considering that the eventual solution would have to interface the conversion of the LoC into a permanent border with the provision of autonomy to both parts of J&K, there is an inevitable complementarity between the internal and external tracks of negotiations. To carry both through, yet prevent them from developing interactive dynamics, is not easy but it is a challenge that cannot be side-stepped. Track II discussions, where all three parties can be represented, might have a role to play.

THE OUTSIDER'S ROLE

The only outsider who has the potential to play a useful role in India–Pakistan peace-making is the US. There is an unprecedented situation today where the key players in the conflict—the Indian elite and the Pakistan Army—are both looking to the US for help in pursuing their divergent objectives. Neither trusts the US completely. Neither knows how the size and potential of India on the one side, and the strategic geography and the Islamic context of Pakistan on the other, will play out in US calculations over a period of time. Both are conscious that the non-proliferation concerns of the US could play a major role in its approach.

The basic US approach to Kashmir has been to keep the situation under control. The US wants leverage with both countries. An unsettled Kashmir or a settlement that both sides are happy with can provide this, but not a settlement that makes one side seriously aggrieved. At present, the US thinks that India wants to let Kashmir drift. It sees little point in investing effort in a no-hope endeavour. This will change if it assesses that India is interested in a settlement that Pakistan can live with. If that happens, it will put pressure on Pakistan to reach a settlement that takes into substantial account the facts of possession and power relativity.

Today, there is potential for a properly structured, low-key US initiative to make headway, as it has to some extent already. The major difficulties facing such a venture—moving beyond easing of tensions to resolution of differences—are: the US's disappointing level of interest in South Asia, the continuing misgivings within sections of India's security community about a US role, and the considerable popular hostility that exists towards the US in Pakistan. A US role cannot be an overt one. There will be protests in both India and Pakistan, spearheaded by hard-set nationalists and Islamists respectively. But there is scope for a discreet role, because at the governmental level there are large sections in both countries that are not opposed to it. These sections recognise that, with distrust levels as high as they are, it is very difficult for India and Pakistan to embark on a serious peace process entirely by themselves.

From the US's point of view, it is much easier to contribute to bringing to an end the India–Pakistan conflict than the Israeli–Palestinian one. Although many in the US do not appreciate it, the structural position in Kashmir is much less problematic than that in Palestine. In Kashmir, a US President will also not be domestically constrained as he is in Palestine. The question of course is what is in it for the US to make a serious peace-making (not just crisis containment) effort in Kashmir. There are, in fact, two big incentives. One, it is considerably in the US's interest to eliminate Kashmir as a potential nuclear flashpoint. In a post-conflict situation it would also be a little easier to interface the nuclear capabilities of the two countries with the global non-proliferation regime. Two, it is in the US's interest to break the nexus between the Army and the Islamists in Pakistan. It is Kashmir, even more than Afghanistan, that ties the two together. The US can and should seek to make the Pakistan Army more like its Turkish counterpart—determinedly against extremist Islam and more acquiescent to democracy.

The US and others can also play a useful role in a post-agreement situation. A Simla Agreement-type compact may not tie either country fully to its commitments, but an internationally underwritten one is likely to be more effective. Moreover, in the beginning there might be a need for neutral surveillance capability along the new border to handle complaints. The US can also lead the international community to contribute to the economic development of the two parts of Kashmir, which is the best way to make peace grow roots there. The population is only 10 million on the Indian side and 4 million on the Pakistani side—small enough for aid money to make a big impact. Both parts of Kashmir have considerable tourist, horticultural and hydroelectric potential. If the necessary infrastructure is developed in an integrated manner, both can become prosperous with big stakes in maintaining peace.

THE CENTRAL REALITIES

The structure of the India–Pakistan conflict, particularly with regard to the stakes, is much less difficult to deal with than is generally perceived. India's composite nationalism and Pakistan's Islamic nationalism no longer threaten one another. Neither country has a real need—in security, resource and internal coherence terms—for the part of J&K that is with the other country. The Kashmiris are happy to stay with India as long as their autonomy aspirations are met. And Indians in general have no serious objection to increasing the state's autonomy provided Pakistan does not exploit it to promote trouble. These positive, helpful realities are currently ignored.

There is a new and growing understanding in Pakistan that the LoC will have to become a permanent border some time. But it is not possible for a Pakistani government to concede this without some creative political cover. The most practical way in which India can help is by agreeing to substantially restore J&K's autonomy. India's fundamental problem with autonomy is the fear of its impact on the security of the state. If Pakistan can allay this fear, many in India who oppose the idea today will change their minds. Autonomy for the part of J&K that is with India must necessarily be accompanied by parallel autonomy for the part of the state with Pakistan. There must also be some cross-border links between the separated parts. Within the part of the state with India there should be either decentralisation or power sharing so that the Valley does not dominate the rest of the state.

While the basic agreement on J&K has to be between India and Pakistan, it is necessary that the aspirations of the people of the state are also taken into account. This is not only a matter of justice; it is also a structural need. The structure of the conflict, as it has evolved, makes it impossible to arrive at sustainable peace without the support of key sections of the people of J&K, especially the Valley Muslims and the Jammu Hindus. India needs to recognise that the political system in J&K is broken and calls for a major overhaul. Persisting with measures that have not worked in the past is unlikely to help.

The Pakistan Army has long been the biggest, though by no means the only, hurdle to India and Pakistan improving relations. Fortunately, the Army now knows that its position is deteriorating inexorably, both domestically and internationally. The only way it can arrest the slide is by making peace with India. India, on its part, needs to recognise that the Army is the only power structure in Pakistan that is capable of making peace in a foreseeable timeframe. Trying to achieve peace by marginalising the Army can only make its prospects more distant. Genuine democracy in Pakistan is much more likely to follow peace than the other way round.

Islamists are a fact of life in Pakistan. Their core is small, but large segments of Pakistani society support them. Today, they are also the country's primary means of exerting pressure in Kashmir. The Army, therefore, will not want to de-claw them despite the serious threat that they now pose to the Pakistani state, and indeed to the Army's own long-term interests. This position will only change when they are no longer seen as vital for 'national security'. The India–Pakistan conflict is also the key factor that sustains support for Islamic radicals in Pakistani Punjab, just as the Afghan conflict props them up in Pashtun areas. A J&K settlement will cut the ground under extremist Islam in much of Pakistan, especially Punjab.

Today, unlike earlier, the US has the ability to play a useful role in the India–Pakistan context. At governing levels in both countries, there is no serious objection to a discreet US part although there certainly is at other levels. To be productive, a US role would have to be very low-profile. The US will have to restrain the urge to bring into the process its own agenda items, such as the nuclear arsenals of the two countries. Like democracy in Pakistan, nuclear risk-reduction in the subcontinent is a more realistic proposition post-peace than ante-peace.

While the objective conditions in the subcontinent today do give rise to mild optimism, it is necessary to recognise that the thaw that began in India–Pakistan relations in late 2003 does not yet mark a decisive change. There is reason to believe that the parties are still thinking tactically, not strategically. It is the lure of possible inter-national pickings from a peace process, rather than any desire to secure the large and lasting gains from peace itself, that seems to be driving the process at this stage.

A Pakistani perception that India is desperate to get rid of a Kashmir millstone is as misplaced as an Indian belief that the Pakistan Army can be compelled to eliminate the jihadis root and branch through international pressure. It is unrealistic for India to think that an LoC-solution can be achieved without a fair degree of autonomy accorded in Kashmir. It is as unrealistic for Pakistan to think that autonomy can be confined to the Indian side. More fundamentally, India is not prepared for a peace that puts the security of J&K in even distant jeopardy. Nor is Pakistan in favour of a peace that can destabilise it internally. Without the two governments preparing themselves, and their publics, for psychologically painful shifts away from long-held positions (Pakistan's on the LoC and India's on autonomy), a realistic peace path cannot be created.

SELECT BIBLIOGRAPHY

INDIA–PAKISTAN

Ahmed, Feroz, *Ethnicity and Politics in Pakistan,* Karachi: Oxford University Press, 1998.

Allen, Douglas, ed., *Religion and Political Conflict in South Asia: India, Pakistan and Sri Lanka*, Delhi: Oxford University Press, 1993.

Arif, General Khalid Mahmud, *Working With Zia: Pakistan's Power Politics 1977–88,* Karachi: Oxford University Press, 1995.

———, *Khaki Shadows: Pakistan Army 1947–97,* Karachi: Oxford University Press, 2001.

Aziz, Khursheed Kamal, *The Murder of History: A Critique of History Textbooks in Pakistan,* Lahore: Vanguard, 1993.

Bajpai, Kanti P. et al., 'Brasstacks and Beyond: Perception and Management of Crisis in South Asia', ACDIS Research Paper, Urbana–Champaign, 1995.

Bokhari, Imitiaz H. and Thomas Perry Thornton, *The 1972 Simla Agreement: An Asymmetrical Negotiation,* Washington, DC: Foreign Policy Institute, Johns Hopkins School of International Studies, 1988.

Brines, Russell, *The Indo–Pak Conflict,* London: Pall Mall Press, 1968.

Burki, Shahid Javed, *Pakistan: Fifty Years of Nationhood,* Boulder, CO: Westview Press, 1999.

Chari, P.R. and Pervaiz Iqbal Cheema, *The Simla Agreement 1972: Its Wasted Promise,* Delhi: Manohar, 2000.

Cloughley, Brian, *A History of the Pakistan Army,* Karachi: Oxford University Press, 1998.

Cohen, Stephen Philip, *The Pakistan Army,* revised edn., Karachi: Oxford University Press, 1998.

———, 'Causes of Conflict and Conditions of Peace in South Asia', in Roger E. Kanet, ed., *Resolving Regional Conflict,* Urbana: University of Illinois Press, 1998.

———, *India: Emerging Power,* Delhi: Oxford University Press, 2001.

Cohen, Stephen P., P.R.Chari and Pervaiz Iqbal Cheema, 'The Compound Crisis of 1990: Perceptions, Politics and Insecurity', ACDIS Research Report, Urbana–Champaign, IL: University of Illinois at Urbana-Champaign, 1995.

Dixit, J.N., *Anatomy of a Flawed Inheritance: Indo–Pak Relations, 1970–94,* Delhi: Konarak, 1995.

———, *Across Borders: Fifty Years of Indian Foreign Policy,* New Delhi: Picus, 1998.

Durrani, Major General Mahmud Ali, *India and Pakistan: The Cost of Conflict and the Benefits of Peace,* Karachi: Oxford University Press, 2001.

From Surprise to Reckoning: The Kargil Review Committee Report, New Delhi: Sage, 2000.

Ganguly, Sumit, *Conflict Unending: India–Pakistan Tensions Since 1947,* New York: Columbia University Press, 2001.

———, ed., *India as Emerging Power,* London: Frank Cass, 2002.

Gauhar, Altaf, *Ayub: Pakistan's First Military Ruler,* Karachi: Oxford University Press, 1994.

Gundevia, Y.D., *Outside the Archives,* Hyderabad: Sangam, 1984.

Habib, Ifran, Suvira Jaiswal and Aditya Mukherjee, *History in the New NCERT Textbooks: A Report and an Index of Errors,* Kolkata: Indian History Congress, 2003.

Harrison, Selig S., Paul H. Kriesberg and Dennis Kux, eds., *India and Pakistan: The First Fifty Years,* Cambridge: Cambridge University Press, 1999.

Hasan Askari Rizvi, *Military, State and Society in Pakistan,* London: Macmillan, 2000.

Hassan Gardezi and Jamil Rashid, eds., *Pakistan: The Roots of Dictatorship,* Delhi: Oxford University Press, 1983.

Hassan, Lieutenant Colonel Javed, *India: A Study in Profile,* Rawalpindi: Army Press, 1990.

Hussain, Asaf, *Elite Politics in an Ideological State,* Folkestone, Kent: Dawson, 1979.

Hussain, Ishrat, *Pakistan, The Economy of an Elitist State,* Karachi: Oxford University Press, 1992.

Jackson, Robert, *South Asian Crisis: India–Pakistan–Bangladesh,* London: Chatto and Windus for IISS, 1975.

Jaffrelot, Christophe, ed., *Pakistan: Nationalism Without a Nation,* New York: Zed Books, 2001.

Jalal, Ayesha, *Democracy and Authoritarianism in South Asia: A Comparative and Historical Perspective,* Cambridge: Cambridge University Press, 1995.

Khan, Maj. Gen. Akbar, *Raiders in Kashmir,* Karachi: Pak Publishers, 1970.

Khan, Lt. Gen. Gul Hassan, *Memoirs of Lt. Gen. Gul Hassan Khan,* Karachi: Oxford University Press, 1993.

Khan, Roedad, *Pakistan—A Dream Gone Sour,* Karachi: Oxford University Press, 1997.

Krepon, Michael and Mishi Faruqee, eds., 'Conflict Prevention and Confidence Building Measures in South Asia: The 1990 Crisis', Occasional Paper 17, Washington, DC: Stimson Center, April 1994.

Kukreja, Veena, *Contemporary Pakistan*, New Delhi: Sage, 2003.

Kumar, Krishna, *Prejudice and Pride: School Histories of the Freedom Struggle in India and Pakistan*, New Delhi: Viking, 2002.

Mahmood, Safdar, *Pakistan, Political Roots and Development 1947–1999*, Karachi: Oxford University Press, 2000.

Malik, Hafeez, ed., *Dilemmas of National Security and Cooperation in India and Pakistan*, Basingstoke: Macmillan, 1993.

Malik, Ifthikar H., *State and Civil Society in Pakistan: Politics of Authority, Ideology and Ethnicity*, New York: St. Martin's Press, 1997.

Nadeem, Azhar Hassan, *Pakistan: The Political Economy of Lawlessness*, Karachi: Oxford University Press, 2002.

Noman, Omar, *Economic and Social Progress in Asia: Why Pakistan Did Not Become a Tiger*. Karachi: Oxford University Press, 1997.

Philips, C.H. and Mary D. Wainwright, *The Partition of India: Policies and Perspectives, 1935–47*, London: Allen & Unwin, 1970.

Raghavan, V.R., *Siachen: Conflict Without End*, New Delhi: Viking, 2002.

Rizvi, Hasan-Askari, *Military, State and Society in Pakistan*, London: Macmillan, 2000.

Rose, Leo and Richard Sisson, *War and Secession: Pakistan, India and the Creation of Bangladesh*, Berkeley: University of California Press, 1990.

Schofield, Victoria, ed., *Old Roads, New Highways: Fifty Years of Pakistan*, Karachi: Oxford University Press, 1997.

Sen, Lt. Gen. (Rtd.) L.P., *Slender Was the Thread: Kashmir Confrontation, 1947–48*, New Delhi: Orient Longman, 1969.

Shafqat, Saeed, *Civil–Military Relations in Pakistan: From Zulfiqar Ali Bhutto to Benazir Bhutto*, Boulder: Westview, 1997.

Siddiqui, A.R. *The Military in Pakistan: Image and Reality*, Lahore: Vanguard, 1996.

Singh, Jasjit, ed., *Kargil 1999: Pakistan's Fourth War for Kashmir*, Delhi: Knowledge World, 1999.

Sinha, Maj. Gen. S.K., *Operation Rescue: Military Operations in Jammu and Kashmir 1947–49*, New Delhi: Vision Books, 1977.

Sood, Lt. Gen. V.K. and Pravin Sawhney, *Operation Parakram: The War Unfinished*, New Delhi: Sage, 2003.

Talbot, Ian, *India and Pakistan: Inventing the Nation*, New York: Oxford University Press, 2000.

Tellis, Ashley J., C. Christine Fair and Jamison Jo Medby, *Limited Conflicts Under the Nuclear Umbrella: Indian and Pakistani Lessons from the Kargil Crisis*, Santa Monica, CA: RAND, 2001.

Veer, Van der, *Religious Nationalism: Hindus and Muslims in India*, Berkeley: University of California Press, 1994.

Weiss, Anita M. and Zulfiqar Gilani, *Power and Civil Society in Pakistan*, Karachi: Oxford University Press, 2001.

Ziring, Lawrence, *Pakistan in the Twentieth Century: A Political History*, Karachi: Oxford University Press, 1999.

KASHMIR

Abdullah, Sheikh Mohammed, *Flames of the Chinar: An Autobiography,* New Delhi: Viking, 1993.

Akbar, M.J., *Kashmir: Behind the Vale,* New Delhi: Viking, 1991.

Bhattacharjea, Ajit, *Kashmir: The Wounded Valley,* New Delhi: UBSPD, 1994.

Blinkenberg, Lars, *India–Pakistan: The History of Unsolved Conflicts,* Vol. II, Odense: Odense University Press, 1998.

Bose, Sumantra, *The Challenge in Kashmir: Democracy, Self-determination and a Just Peace,* New Delhi: Sage, 1997.

———, *Kashmir: Roots of Conflict: Paths to Peace,* New Delhi: Vistaar, 2003.

Chopra, Pran, *India, Pakistan and the Kashmir Tangle,* Delhi: HarperCollins, 1994.

Dasgupta, C., *War and Diplomacy in Kashmir, 1947–48,* New Delhi: Sage, 2002.

Ganguly, Sumit, *The Crisis in Kashmir: Portents of War, Hopes of Peace,* Cambridge: Cambridge University Press, 1997.

Gupta, Sisir, *Kashmir: A Study in India–Pakistan Relations,* Bombay: Asia Publishing House, 1966.

Hewitt, Vernon, *Reclaiming the Past? The Search for Political and Cultural Unity in Contemporary Jammu and Kashmir,* London: Portland Books, 1995.

———, *Towards the Future? Jammu and Kashmir in the 21st Century,* Cambridge: Granta, 2001.

Jha, Prem Shankar, *Kashmir 1947: Rival Versions of History,* Delhi: Oxford University Press, 1996.

Joshi, Manoj, *The Lost Rebellion: Kashmir in the Nineties,* New Delhi: Penguin, 1999.

Kadian, Rajesh, *The Kashmir Tangle: Issues and Options,* Boulder, CO: Westview, 1993.

Kashmir Study Group, *Kashmir: A Way Forward,* Larchmont, NY, February 2000.

Lamb, Alastair, *Kashmir: A Disputed Legacy, 1846–1990.* Lahore: Oxford University Press, 1990.

———, *Incomplete Partition: The Genesis of the Kashmir Dispute, 1947–1948,* Karachi: Oxford University Press, 2001.

Madan, T.N., *Modern Myths, Locked Minds,* Delhi: Oxford University Press, 1997.

Mattoo, Amitabh, 'Next Steps in Kashmir', in Karan R. Sawhny, ed., *Kashmir: How Far Can Vajpayee and Musharraf Go?* New Delhi: Peace Foundation, 2001, pp. 27–44.

Newberg, Paula R., *Double Betrayal: Repression and Insurgency in Kashmir,* Washington, DC: Carnegie Institute for International Peace, 1995.

Puri, Balraj, *Simmering Volcano: Study of Jammu's Relations with Kashmir,* New Delhi: Sterling, 1983.

Rahman, Mushtaque, *Divided Kashmir: Old Problems for India, Pakistan and the Kashmiri People,* Boulder, CO: Lynne Rienner, 1996.

Razdan, Omkar, *The Trauma of Kashmir: The Untold Reality,* Karachi: Oxford University Press, 2001.

Sawhny, Karan R., ed., *Kashmir: How Far Can Vajpayee and Musharraf Go?* New Delhi: Peace Foundation, 2001.

Schofield, Victoria, *Kashmir in Conflict*, London: I.B. Tauris, 2000.

Singh, Jasjit, ed., *Pakistan Occupied Kashmir Under the Jackboot*, New Delhi: Siddhi Books, 1995.

Thomas, Raju G.C., ed., *Perspectives on Kashmir: The Roots of Conflict in South Asia*, Boulder, CO: Westview, 1992.

The Report of the State Autonomy Committee, Srinagar: Government of Jammu and Kashmir Press, 1999.

Wani, Gul Mohd. (compiler), *Kashmir: From Autonomy to Azadi*, Srinagar: Valley Book House, 1996.

Wirsing, Robert G., *India, Pakistan and the Kashmir Dispute: On Regional Conflict and its Resolution*, London: Macmillan, 1994.

NUCLEAR WEAPONS

Betts, Richard K., *Nuclear Blackmail and Nuclear Balance*, Washington, DC: Brookings, 1987.

Bidwai, Praful, *South Asia on a Short Fuse: Nuclear Politics and the Future of Global Disarmament*, Delhi: Oxford University Press, 2000.

Carter, Ashton B., John D. Steinbruner and Charles A. Zracket, *Managing Nuclear Operations,* Washington, DC: Brookings, 1987.

Chengappa, Raj, *Weapons of Peace: The Secret Story of India's Quest to be a Nuclear Power*, New Delhi: HarperCollins, 2000.

Joeck, Neil, 'Maintaining Nuclear Stability in South Asia', Adelphi Paper 312, Oxford: Oxford University Press, for IISS, 1997.

Karnad, Bharat, *Nuclear Weapons and Indian Security: The Realist Foundations of Strategy*, New Delhi: Macmillan, 2002.

Krepon, Michael and Chris Gagne, eds., 'The Stability–Instability Paradox: Nuclear Weapons and Brinkmanship in South Asia', Report 38, Washington, DC: Stimson Center, June 2001.

Lavoy, Peter R., Scott D. Sagan and James J. Wirtz, eds., *Planning the Unthinkable: How the New Powers will Use Nuclear, Biological and Chemical Weapons,* Ithaca: Cornell University Press, 2000.

Mazarr, Michael J., ed., *Nuclear Weapons in a Transformed World*, London: Macmillan, 1997.

Menon, Rear Admiral Raja, *A Nuclear Strategy for India*, New Delhi: Sage, 2000.

Perkovich, George, *India's Nuclear Bomb: The Impact on Global Proliferation*, Berkeley: The University of California Press, 1999.

Posen, Barry P., *Inadvertent Escalation: Conventional War and Nuclear Risks*, Ithaca, NY: Cornell University Press, 1999.

Raju, A. Subramanyam, *Nuclear India: Problems and Perspectives*, Denver: Academic Books, 2000.

Ramana, M.V. and C. Rammanohar Reddy, eds., *Prisoners of the Nuclear Dream*, New Delhi: Orient Longman, 2003.

Ramana, M.V. and Zia Mian, 'The Nuclear Confrontation in South Asia', *SIPRI Year Book 2003*, New York: Oxford University Press, 2003.

Sagan, Scott Douglas, *The Limits of Safety; Organisations, Accidents and Nuclear Weapons*, Princeton: Princeton University Press, 1993.

Sagan, Scott D. and Kenneth N. Waltz, *The Spread of Nuclear Weapons: A Debate Renewed*, New York: W.W. Norton, 2002.

Schelling, T.C., *The Use of Force in the Nuclear Age*, London: IISS, 1968.

Shahid-ur-Rehman, *The Long Road to Chagai*, Islamabad: Print Wise Publications, 1999.

Sundarji, General K., 'India's Nuclear Weapons Policy' in Jorn Gjelstad and Olav Njolstad, eds., *Nuclear Rivalry and International Order*, London: Sage, 1996.

Tellis, Ashley J., *India's Emerging Nuclear Posture: Between Recessed Deterrent and Ready Arsenal*, Oxford: Oxford University Press, 2001.

GLOBAL SETTING

Bobbitt, Philip, *The Shield of Achilles: War, Peace and the Course of History*, London: Allen Lane, 2002.

Brzezinski, Zbignew, *The Grand Chessboard: American Primacy and its Geostrategic Imperative*, New York: Basic Books, 1997.

Cohen, Stephen P., 'The United States, India and Pakistan: Retrospect and Prospect', in Selig S. Harrison et al., eds., *India and Pakistan: The First Fifty Years,* Cambridge: Cambridge University Press, 1999.

Datta-Ray, Sunanda K., *Waiting for America: India and the US in the New Millennium*, New Delhi: HarperCollins, 2002.

Garver, John H., *Protracted Contest: Sino-Indian Rivalry in the Twentieth Century*, University of Washington Press, 2001.

Gould, Harold A. and S. Ganguly, *The Hope and the Reality: US–India Relations from Roosevelt to Reagan*, Boulder: Westview Press, 1992.

Kapur, Ashok, Y.K. Malik, Harold A. Gould and Arthur G. Rubinoff, eds., *India and the United States in a Changing World*, New Delhi: Sage, 2002.

Kux, Dennis, *Estranged Democracies: India and the United States*, New Delhi: Vistaar, 1993.

———, *The United States and Pakistan, 1947–2000: Disenchanted Allies,* Karachi: Oxford University Press, 2001.

McMahon, Robert S., *The Cold War on the Periphery: The United States, India and Pakistan*, New York: Columbia University Press, 1994.

Mohan, C. Raja, *Crossing the Rubicon: The Shaping of India's New Foreign Policy*, New Delhi: Viking, 2003.

Nye, Joseph S., *The Paradox of American Power: Why the World's Only Superpower Can't Go it Alone*, Oxford: Oxford University Press, 2002.

Sidhu, Waheguru Pal Singh, 'Enhancing Indo–US Strategic Co-operation', Adelphi Paper 313, New York: Oxford University Press, 1997.

Tahir-Kheli, Shirin, *The United States and Pakistan, The Evolution of an Influence Relationship*, New York: Praeger, 1982.

Tahir-Kheli, Shirin, *India, Pakistan and the United States: Breaking with the Past*, New York: Council on Foreign Relations, 1997.

Northern Ireland

Arthur, Paul and Keith Jeffrey, *Northern Ireland Since 1968*, London: Blackwell, 1996.

Cox, Michael, Adrian Guelke and Fiona Stephen, eds., *A Farewell to Arms? From 'Long Peace' to Long War in Northern Ireland*, Manchester: Manchester University Press, 2000.

English, Richard, *Armed Struggle: The History of the IRA*, New York: Oxford University Press, 2002.

Holland, Jack, *Hope Against History: The Course of Conflict in Northern Ireland*, New York: Henry Holt, 1999.

McCall, Cathall, *Identity in Northern Ireland: Communities, Politics and Change*, Basingstoke: Macmillan, 1999.

Mitchell, George, *Making Peace*, New York: Knopf, 1999.

O'Toole, Fintan, *The Life of the Land: Irish Identities*, London: Verso, 1997.

Patterson, Henry, *The Politics of Illusion: A Political History of the IRA*, London: Serif, 1997.

Ruane, Joseph and Jennifer Todd, *The Dynamics of Conflict in Northern Ireland*, Cambridge: Cambridge University Press, 1996.

Stevenson, Jonathan, *We Wrecked the Peace: Contemplating an End to Northern Irish Troubles*, London: Simon and Schuster, 1997.

Tannam, Etain, *Cross-border Co-operation in the Republic of Ireland and Northern Ireland*, Basingstoke: Macmillan, 1999.

Sri Lanka

Arunatilake, N., S. Jayasuriya and S. Kelagama, 'The Economic Costs of War in Sri Lanka', *World Development*, vol. 29, no. 9, 2001.

Balasingham, Anton, *The Politics of Duplicity: Re-visiting the Jaffna Talks,* Mitcham, England: Fairfax Publishing, 2000.

Chelvadurai, Manoharan and Bryan Pffaffenberger, eds., *Sri Lankan Tamils: Ethnicity and Identity*, Boulder, CO: Westview Press, 1998.

Committee for Rational Development, Sri Lanka, *The Ethnic Conflict: Myths, Realities and Perspectives*. New Delhi: Navrang, 1984.

Jayawardene, J.R., *Golden Threads*, Colombo: Dept. of Government Printing, 1984.

McGowan, William, *Only Man is Vile: The Tragedy of Sri Lanka*, London: Picador, 1993.

Muni, S.D., *Pangs of Proximity: India and Sri Lanka's Ethnic Crisis*, New Delhi: Sage, 1993.

National Peace Council of Sri Lanka, *The Cost of the War: The Economic, Socio-Political and Human Cost of the War in Sri Lanka*, Colombo, 2001.

Rotberg, Robert I., ed., *Creating Peace in Sri Lanka: Civil War and Reconciliation*, Washington, DC: Brookings, 1999.

Rupasinghe, Kumar, ed., *Negotiating Peace in Sri Lanka: Efforts, Failures and Lessons*, London: International Alert, 1998.

Swamy, Narayan M.R., *Tigers of Lanka: From Boys to Guerrillas*, Delhi: Konarak, 1994.

Wilson, Alfred Jeyaratnam, *Break-up of Sri Lanka: The Sinhalese–Tamil Conflict*, London: C. Hurst and Co., 1988.

———, *Sri Lankan Tamil Nationalism: Its Origins and Development in the 19th and 20th Centuries*, London: C. Hurst and Co., 2000.

ISRAEL–PALESTINE

Abu-Nimer, Mohamed, *Dialogue, Conflict Resolution and Change: Arab–Jewish Encounters in Israel*, Albany: SUNY Press, 1999.

Ahmar, Moonis, 'The Road to Peace in South Asia: Lessons for India and Pakistan from the Arab–Israeli Peace Process', ACDIS Occasional Paper, AHM: R2, University of Illinois at Urbana-Champaign, 1996.

Arhari, M.E., *Change and Continuity in the Middle East: Conflict Resolution and Prospect for Peace*, New York: St. Martin's, 1996.

Avraham, Sela and Moshe Ma'oz, eds., *The PLO and Israel: From Armed Revolution to Political Solution 1964–1994*, New York: St. Martin's, 1997.

Ben-Eliezer, Uri, *The Making of Israeli Militarism*, Bloomington: Indiana University Press, 1998.

Bregman, Ahron and Jihan el-Tahri, *The Fifty Years War: Israel and Arabs*, London: Penguin, 1998.

Carey, Roane, ed., *The New Intifada: Resisting Israel's Apartheid*, London: Verso, 2001.

Climent, James, *Palestine/Israel: The Long Conflict*, New York: Facts on File, 1997.

Corbin, Jane, *The Norway Channel*, New York: Atlantic Monthly Press, 1994.

Cragg, Kenneth, *Palestine: The Prize and Price of Zion*, London: Cassel, 1997.

Dayan, Moshe, *Breakthrough: A Personal Account of the Egypt–Israel Peace Negotiations*, New York: Alfred A. Knopf, 1981.

Dowty, Alan, *The Jewish State: A Century Later*, Berkeley: University of California Press, 1998.

Fahmy, Ismael, *Negotiating for Peace in the Middle East*, Baltimore, MD: The Johns Hopkins University Press, 1983.

Farson, Samih K. and Christina E. Zacharia, *Palestine and the Palestinians*, Boulder, CO: Westview Press, 1997.

Frankel, Glenn, *Beyond the Promised Land: Jews and Arabs on the Hard Road to a New Israel*, New York: Simon and Schuster, 1994.

Gerner, Deborah, *One Land, Two People*, Boulder: Westview, 1994.

Ghanem, As'ad. *The Palestinian–Arab Minority in Israel*, Albany: State University of New York Press, 2001.

Giacaman, George and Dag Jorund Lonning, *After Oslo: New Realities, Old Problems*, London: Pluto Press, 1998.

Hiro, Dilip, *Sharing the Promised Land: A Tale of Israelis and Palestinians*, New York: Olive Branch Books, 1999.

Inbar, Efraim, *Rabin and Israel's National Security*, Baltimore, MD: Johns Hopkins University Press, 1999.

Karmi, Ghada and Eugene Cotran, eds., *The Palestinian Exodus 1948–1998*, Reading: Ithaca Press, 1999.

Karsh, Efraim, ed., *From Rabin to Netanyahu: Israel's Troubled Agenda*, Ilford, Essex: Frank Cass, 1997.

Kemp, Geoffrey and Jeremy Pressman, *Point of No Return: The Deadly Struggle for Middle East Peace*, Washington, DC: Brookings Institution Press, 1997.

La Guardia, Anton, *Holy Land, Unholy War*, London: John Murray, 2001.

Lochery, Neill, *The Difficult Road to Peace: Netanyahu, Israel and the Middle East*, Reading: Ithaca Press, 1999.

Makovsky, David, *Making Peace With PLO: The Rabin Government's Road to the Oslo Accord*, Boulder: Westview Press, 1996.

Pappe, Ilan, *The Israel/Palestine Question*, London: Routledge, 1999.

Quandt, William B., *Peace Process: American Diplomacy and the Arab–Israeli Conflict Since 1967*, Washington, DC: The Brookings Institute, 1993.

Quandt, William, *Camp David: Peacemaking and Politics*, Washington, DC: Brookings, 1986.

Rabinovich, Itamar, *Waging Peace: Israel and the Arabs at the End of the Century*, New York: Farrar, Strauss and Giroux, 1999.

Roy, Sara, 'Why Oslo Failed: An Oslo Autopsy', *Current History*, Vol. 101, No. 651, January 2002, pp. 8–16.

Rubin, Barry, *The Transformation of Palestinian Politics*, Cambridge, MA: Harvard University Press, 1999.

Said, Edward, *Peace and its Discontents*, New York: Vintage, 1996.

Sayigh, Yezid, *Armed Struggle and the Search for a State: The Palestinian National Movement, 1949–1993*, Oxford: Clarendon Press, 1997

Segev, Samuel, *Crossing the Jordan: Israel's Hard Road to Peace*, New York: St. Martin's, 1998.

Sherman, Martin, *The Politics of War in the Middle East: An Israeli Perspective on the Hydro-Political Aspects of the Conflict*, Basingstoke: Macmillan, 1998.

Shlaim, Avi, *The Iron Wall: Israel and the Arab World*, New York: W.W. Norton, 2000.

Sternhill, Zeev, *The Founding Myths of Israel: Nationalism, Socialism and the Making of the Jewish State*, Princeton, NJ: Princeton University Press, 1998.

Tamir, Major General Avraham, *A Soldier in Search of Peace: An Inside Look at Israel's Strategy*, London: Weidenfeld and Nicholson, 1988.

Peace and Conflict

Banks, Michael and Christopher Mitchell, *Handbook of Conflict Resolution*, London: Pinter, 1996.

Brown, Michael E., ed., *The International Dimensions of Internal Conflict*, Cambridge, MA: MIT Press, 1996.

Bull, Hedley, *The Anarchical Society: A Study on the Order of World Politics*, London: Macmillan, 1977.

Burton, John and Frank Drakes, *Conflict: Practices in Management: Settlement and Resolution*, New York: St. Martin's Press, 1990.

Cousens, Elizabeth M. and Chetan Kumar, *Peacebuilding as Politics: Cultivating Peace in Fragile Societies*, Boulder, CO: Lynne Rienner, 2001.

Darby, John and Roger MacGinty, *Contemporary Peacemaking: Conflict, Violence and Peace Processes*, London: Palgrave Macmillan, 2002.

Darby, John and Roger MacGinty, eds., *The Management of Peace Processes*, Basingstoke: Macmillan, 2000.

de Mesquita, Bruce Bruno and David Lalman, *War and Reason: Domestic and International Imperatives*, New Haven: Yale University Press, 1992.

Eban, Abba, *Diplomacy for the Next Century*, New Haven: Yale University Press, 1998.

Evans, Peter B., Harold K. Jacobson and Robert D. Putnam, eds., *Double-edged Diplomacy: International Bargaining and Domestic Politics*, Berkeley: California University Press, 1993.

Galtung, Johan and Carl Jacobsen, *Searching for Peace*, London: Transcend, 2000.

George, Alexander L. and William E. Simons, eds., *The Limits of Coercive Diplomacy*, second revised edn., Boulder, CO: Westview, 1994.

Hampson, Fen Osler, *Nurturing Peace: Why Peace Settlements Succeed or Fail*, Washington, DC: United States Institute of Peace, 1996.

Hauss, Charles, *International Conflict Resolution: International Relations for the 21st Century*, London: Continuum, 2001.

Hopmann, P. Terrence, *The Negotiation Process and the Resolution of International Conflicts*, Columbia, SC: University of South Carolina Press, 1996.

Jabri, Vivienne, *Discourses on Violence: Conflict Analysis Reconsidered*, Manchester: Manchester University Press, 1996.

Jervis, Robert, *Perception and Misperception in International Politics*, Princeton: Princeton University Press, 1976.

Keen, Sam, *Faces of the Enemy: Reflections on the Hostile Imagination*, New York: Harper and Row, 1986.

Kriesberg, Louis, *International Conflict Resolution: The US–USSR and the Middle East Cases*, Ann Arbor: Edward Brothers, 1992.

———, *Constructive Conflicts: From Escalation to Resolution*, Lanham, MD: Rowman and Littlefield, 1998.

Lederach, John Paul, *Building Peace: Sustainable Reconciliation in Divided Societies*, Washington, DC: United States Institute of Peace Press, 1997.

Lewis, Justin, *Constructing Public Opinion: How Political Elites Do What They Like and Why We Seem to Go Along with It*, New York: Colombia University Press, 2001.

Licklider, Roy, *Stopping the Killing: How Civil Wars End*, New York: New York University Press, 1993.

Liska, George, *Expanding Realism: The Historical Dimension of World Politics*, Oxford: Rowman and Littlefield, 1998.

Miall, Hugh, *The Peacemakers: Peaceful Settlement of Disputes Since 1945*, London: Macmillan, 1992.

Mitchell, C.R., *The Structure of International Conflict*, London: Macmillan, 1981.

Ottunu, Olara A. and Michael W. Doyle, eds., *Peacemaking and Peacekeeping for the New Century*, Lanham, MD: Rowman and Littlefield, 1998.

Rupasinghe, Kumar, *Civil Wars, Civil Peace: An Introduction to Conflict Resolution*, London: Pluto Press, 1998.

Sammadar, Ranabir and Helmut Reifeld, eds., *Peace as Process. Reconciliation and Conflict Resolution in South Asia*, Delhi: Manohar, 2001.

Snyder, Jack, *Myths of Empire: Domestic and International Ambition*, Ithaca: Cornell University Press, 1991.

Stagner, R., *Psychological Aspects of International Conflict*, Belmont, CA: Brooks, 1967.

Van Evera, Stephen, *The Causes of War: Power and the Roots of Conflict*, Ithaca, NY: Cornell University Press, 1999.

INDEX

About the Author

V ice Admiral Verghese Koithara PVSM, AVSM, VSM (Rtd.) is an independent strategic analyst. His primary research focus is on peace processes, nuclear issues and maritime developments. He retired from the Indian Navy in 1998. He has a Ph.D. degree in political science. His first book *Society, State and Security—The Indian Experience* was published in 1999. He carried out a study on Kashmir for the Ministry of External Affairs, Government of India in 2001. He was a visiting fellow at the Centre for International Security and Co-operation, Stanford University in 2002, where he published a paper on 'Coercion and Risk-Taking in Nuclear South Asia'. He lives in the Nilgiris.